# *Bob Flowerdew's*
# COMPLETE
# FRUIT BOOK

# Bob Flowerdew's
# COMPLETE
# FRUIT
# BOOK

## A DEFINITIVE SOURCE BOOK TO GROWING, HARVESTING AND COOKING FRUIT

KYLE CATHIE LIMITED

First published in Great Britain in 1995 by
Kyle Cathie Limited
20 Vauxhall Bridge Road, London SW1V 2SA

This edition published 1995

ISBN 1 85626 185 9

Photographs © Christine Topping 1995 © Sally Maltby 1995
© Michelle Garrett 1995. For additional photographic
acknowlegdements see page 256.

Artwork © Sally Maltby 1995

Design by Geoff Hayes

Colour separations by Colour Symphony Pte. Ltd. Singapore

Printed and bound in Great Britain by
Butler & Tanner Ltd, Frome and London

Bob Flowerdew is hereby identified as the author of this work in
accordance with Section 77 of the Copyright, Designs and Patents
Act, 1988.

A Cataloguing in Publication record for this title is available from
the British Library.

I dedicate this book to my fiancée and best friend Christine Topping, without whose patience and care I would never have had time to write this book.

# CONTENTS

# INTRODUCTION

Fruits are fantastic. There are few other foods that have the same range of colour, texture and flavour, and there are few other plants that can give one the satisfaction offered by the sight of a fruit tree or bush laden down with a ripe crop.

As a form of gardening, fruit culture is not only rewarding but also rather easy, especially compared to vegetables. It is the nature of fruiting plants to fruit, if we just give them the right conditions. They are less demanding than other crops such as carrots or cauliflowers, which are being asked to perform almost unnaturally well. Most fruiting plants are perennials and thus they need no regular digging, sowing, planting out, hoeing or annual purchase of seeds.

Thus growing fruit is eminently suited to the busy or lazy gardener and even neglect is less detrimental. Many fruits, such as apple and plum trees, will even crop for years with no care or attention whatsoever. The work is done at the beginning, and then one reaps the harvest for many years; only a few fruits take more than a couple of years to come into production and rarely is much attention required. Pruning is light work compared to digging!

The birds are rightful heirs to the fruits, and much of the fruit gardener's work is to prevent them and other pests making off with our harvest. However, they are also valuable allies in our war on smaller pests, so with cunning and nets we prevent them stealing more than their fair share. Nature intends them to eat her fruits so we should not take their depredations too personally.

After all, with fruit, we, or other animals and birds, are induced by the plants to eat some of the proffered flesh in order to distribute the plants' seeds. (We can include the closely allied group of nuts, where we eat the seeds, as presumably the plants are satisfied if a small percentage of the nut seeds are distributed to grow elsewhere.)

Thus we can consume our fruits with a clear conscience. The plants give them freely for us to eat, providing us with food so we may wax strong, travel far and spread their seed as we go. How different from growing flowers for cutting, which we take to a sterile death indoors, and our vegetables which we so thoughtlessly hack to pieces, possibly even while feeling virtuous for spurning meat!

Balanced nutrition is important, and I do not advocate any fruitarian diet, no matter how squeamish we might become about slaughtering cabbages. However, although many fruits may contain fewer vitamins and minerals than some vegetables, it is also much more pleasant and far easier to consume much more fruit.

There is almost the same value in drinking a glass of mixed fruit juice as munching your way through a whole plateful of salad. Which would you rather eat – 500g/1lb of iceberg lettuce, or three peaches, or four apples, or four pears, or 50g/2oz strawberries, all of which each have more vitamin C than the lettuce? So if you want strawberries don't plant turnips, as the Chinese saying goes.

Of course we may choose to grow fruit plants just because we are curious, even though we know full well they are rarely likely to fruit. Countless avocado stones, date stones and lemon pips are grown and loved on windowsills the world over. What delightful, satisfying and educational houseplants they make. With a heated greenhouse or conservatory, it is even possible to win a crop with many of them.

The ecology around us is of vital importance to us all. The permanent nature of most common fruiting plants means their cultivation makes less demand on peat, heat and consumables than other types of gardening such as the vegetable patch or ornamental bedding schemes. Their permanence makes it easier to build up a beneficial ecosystem around them. Fruiting plants have flowers in quantity and variety which are especially valuable to our pollinating, parasitising and predatory insect friends.

The greatest benefit fruit gardeners can offer to the ecology and wildlife is that if we do not use and protect our crops, the wildlife can, and will, take advantage of it, which is more than can be said for bad rows of surplus vegetables.

We can therefore choose to make a fruit garden with wildlife in mind. We can add the shelter, water and other conditions needed to establish a thriving ecology in our backyard. If we are cunning, we can have sufficient fruit ourselves and enough to spare to share around for all our other garden inhabitants and friends.

# Fruits and Gardens : Their History is as One

Our earliest diet as hunter-gatherers, millions of years ago, must have included a wide range of seeds, fruits, nuts, roots, leaves and any moving things we could catch. As we lived for the great bulk of that time, according to theory, in warm areas, we would almost certainly have eaten much fruit in our diet. A warmer climate means more fruit in variety all year round.

Nomadic peoples learned to follow circuits to coincide with flushes of food. And of course, seemingly by magic, when they returned to a previous campsite they would find their favourite fruit trees and bushes waiting for them. Moreover, these trees and bushes would be more prolific than 'wild' ones, as the 'magic' trees would be growing on the immensely fertile site of the tribe's midden or waste heap.

Thus, as early populations perambulated, they spread the very plants that sustained them. In those early days the pickings must have been glorious, with vast areas swathed in ripening fruits. But as populations grew, the consequent demand for land caused them to spread to colder and drier regions.

The hunter-gatherer lifestyle became difficult in temperate zones as there is little plant food naturally available for half the year. We developed livestock as a means of storing the food, the summer's harvest becoming winter meat and cheese. Animal culture had other advantages; it was a more readily exchangeable form of wealth, mobile and 'in season' all year round. If enemies threatened, you could head for the safety of the hills with your flocks.

It is no good planting an orchard if you are unsure of next month, let alone next year. As annual crops were more sure than perennial, farming for cereals and quick-return crops predominated and gardens were rare except where civilisation was long established, such as the Hanging Gardens of Babylon. Thus the development of gardening and fruit culture serves to characterise times and places of peace and stability.

The Classical Greek period was a time of wars and there was little chance for gardening. The Roman Empire was the longest time of (relative) peace known. The Romans enjoyed most of our everyday fruits in abundance. They had the apple, pear and quince, the peach, plum, cherry and almond, the mulberry and the grape on sale in their streets and markets along with figs, dates, olives and exotic fruits from around the Mediterranean and North Africa.

One of the earliest places in which gardens developed was the Arab courtyard. Centred about water, representing an oasis, and protected by shading walls, their gardens were planted with the fruit trees, flowers and plants they adored. Their influence extended

**A mosaic of fruit and leaves, Pompeii, first century BC**

throughout the Middle East and into the Mediterranean region and trade with Rome. Their fruit gardens were emulated by the Romans, but in more extravagant style.

Roman gardens were built around water, fruit trees, bushes and especially vines, and they introduced the idea of organising a garden into areas, 'inventing' the herb garden and the orchard. After the Roman civilisation crumbled, northern Europe entered the Dark Ages. The violence of the period worked against the cultivation of fruit, and almost all the knowledge of the Romans was lost, along with most of their varieties. The little that was preserved was due to the monasteries and royal gardens.

Rich and powerful individuals have always had their own, usually well protected, private gardens. These were often viewed very pragmatically, being usefully filled with fruiting plants and herbs. Many a tyrant preferred to eat fruits he could watch daily, and thus ensure their freedom from poison, and if the oppressed did revolt there was a ready food supply till help arrived.

The monasteries similarly guarded fruits and herbs for their own use and also for their medicinal value. In a time of frequent famine and annual winter dearth, the commonplace scurvy and vitamin deficiencies would have seemed to many people almost miraculously cured by monks' potions containing little more than preserved fruits full of nutrients and vitamin C.

By the time of the Norman invasion, England had become a farming and herding society. The civilising influence returned and brought back gardens and orchards, mostly to provide the cider which necessarily replaced wine. Most great houses and manors had gardens for fruit, herbs and vegetables.

The Crusades re-introduced Mediterranean fruits which had been forgotten since the Romans and interest in gardening was rekindled. The Low Countries specialised in fruit and market gardening and developed many new varieties during the next centuries. Henry VIII actively encouraged the planting of orchards and fruit gardens to try and break the Dutch monopoly, but they have reigned on and still are the centre of world horticultural trade.

The 'discovery' of the New World by Europeans in the fifteenth century was an enormous upheaval. It brought in so many new and exotic plants that gardening became a respectable hobby for the rich. It could even be a profitable business as people clamoured for these exciting new tastes. The development of the orangery was a breakthrough, as it allowed the over-wintering of tender plants. In response to this, market gardeners started growing many of these new exotic fruits for the home market.

Private gardeners with rich patrons wanted such choice fruits for their masters. Early doctors followed on in the traditions of the monasteries and had physic gardens of medicinal herbs, and of course wanted to include all these new fruits with so much potential value. Thus was born the botanic garden with its hothouses and stovehouses.

As industrialisation proceeded, glass and materials became widely and cheaply available and glasshouses or greenhouses became common. Although many ornamental plants were grown, most effort went into securing crops of very different fruits, both exotic varieties and also common ones grown out of season. It is said that Queen Victoria's gardens had to be able to provide her with four pounds of strawberries any day of the year!

By the end of the Victorian period the humble villager still had a small cottage garden, with fruit trees and bushes underplanted with herbs and simples, and maybe a share in an orchard if he was lucky. Almost every house, from the nobleman's down to the vicarage, had its walled gardens lined with fruit trees and a hothouse producing out-of-season and tropical fruits. Of course labour and coal were cheap and families and staff were huge. The First World War saw the end of the large garden, as labour and fuel became expensive.

Between the world wars was a time of depression. Prices were cheap, so there was less incentive to grow your own fruit. Moreover, most people had no garden and what gardening was done was by a leisured class who dabbled in rock gardens and alpines – while a man 'did' for them in the fruit garden and vegetable bed.

The Second World War caused tremendous changes in gardening and horticulture, especially in Great Britain, which was threatened with starvation by blockade. The enforced uprooting of vast acreages of commercial fruit trees and bushes to grow more cereals and vegetables meant little fruit was available in the shops. Much was grown at home and in the public parks and gardens, which were dug up for allotments. Fruit was discouraged in favour of supposedly more worthy vegetables, but a considerable amount was nevertheless planted – mostly soft fruit such as blackcurrants.

The necessity for home food production, both during the war years and throughout a decade of rationing afterwards, meant an inevitable reaction later. People enjoying improving wealth chose once more not to grow and preserve themselves, but to buy ready made. 'Home made' even became snobbishly regarded as poor or shoddy in comparison with the 'luxury' of imported and commercial products.

Clever and expensive advertising ensured we bought our fruit, not for flavour but on appearance and other features easier to manipulate. One apple variety dominated the market, marketed on its supposed texture, despite its tasting only marginally better than a turnip! Amazingly, even canned fruits were sometimes seen as more acceptable than the fresh, home-grown item.

**An Ecuador Indian displaying New World fruits, 1783**

Then there was a sea change in the public's perception of food in general. Some had already rebelled against the blandness and cost of mass-produced foods. However, the realisation that we had polluted our environment and destroyed much of the ecology of our farms, countryside and gardens was to bring about a real revolution. A mass revulsion against chemical-based methods was mirrored in the rise of organic production and the slowly improving availability of better foods. Vegetarianism also increased as many people turned away from meat, in part because of the barbaric treatment of animals in factory farms. As we became more aware of the true costs of meat production, the health implications of modern farming methods and the need for a balanced diet, many people started eating much less meat. More and more consumers are choosing to buy it from better sources, such as direct sale organic producers.

These trends mean that there is now a much increased demand for fruits and vegetables as their wider use replaces meat. The simultaneous demands for organic production, fuller flavour, and a wider range has led the supermarkets to reassess their position and mean that many of us can now enjoy a very wide choice of fruits on sale throughout most of the year. But there is also a move by people towards growing their own.

The hippie movement back to the land in the 1960s and '70s had shown the way, but few fancied the rigours of life actually tilling the soil. Now, however, there is a new movement back to gardening and home production. The health benefits, ecology and economy of gardening, especially the permaculture aspect of growing fruit, appeal to a greener generation. And of course it is all so much easier to use and store for ourselves nowadays, with food processors,

**A fruit market in nineteenth-century Vienna**

juicers and deep freezers.

With dwarfing rootstocks, earlier and later seasons and better storing varieties, and automatic irrigation, glass or plastic cover, micro-processor controlled heating, shading, cooling and artificial sunlight, it is now possible to grow almost any fruit at home. However, in our rush to make full use of the excitingly exotic, the everyday fruits should not be overlooked just because of their availability. A well stocked garden, brim full of strawberries, raspberries, currants, apples, pears and plums, is still a most satisfying feast for the eye, the soul and the stomach.

# FRUITS A-Z

I have defined a fruit as plant flesh which we are induced by the plant to eat, in order to distribute its seeds. I've included the closely allied group of nuts, which are in fact the seeds themselves. Presumably the plants are satisfied if a small percentage of the nut seeds are distributed to grow elsewhere. I have not included many seed crops such as some spices and the pulses, even if we do eat their flesh or pod, as, for example, green beans.

The fruits have been divided into the groups according to the manner in which we most usually grow them in temperate gardens. Those that require some protection or cover, such as the annual, perennial and tender fruits, are mostly fruits that are not hardy enough outdoors for the UK and northern European gardener, but are achievable in southern Europe, Australia and much of the USA. Of course we commonly grow many of these, such as tomatoes and melons, grapes and even lemons, quite easily with the aid of a greenhouse, in cooler regions.

I've also included many exotic tropical and sub-tropical fruits on sale in supermarkets and abroad which may be grown (or eaten!) out of curiosity and interest. Most of these were once grown and fruited in Victorian stovehouses, and can often be fruited at home with a modest heated glasshouse or conservatory. Failing that, most of these make spectacular, educational and decorative houseplants. (Please bear in mind, however, the potential final height and size of your humble date palm seedling before you start dreaming of ever ripening a crop!)

The shrub and flower garden fruits are those forgotten and unsung heroes which are only called upon in times of shortage and famine, and by those country folk who appreciate the sharp, strong flavours these piquant fruits offer. The potential of these fruits has often been overlooked; many of them are worthy of deliberate cultivation, and with only a little breeding and selection they could become sweet and tender attractions for our delectation. The strawberry today is gigantic and succulent compared to those of two centuries ago; we can only imagine what new fruits we may conjure from nature's raw materials in the future.

# ORCHARD FRUITS

When fruits are mentioned these are probably the first that come to mind: apples, pears, plums and cherries – the tree-hard or top fruits as they are known. They consist of two main groups: the pome fruits, which are the apple- and pear-like members, and the stone fruits, which are the plums, cherries, peaches and apricots. The pomes have small seeds in a core around which the 'stalk' from immediately behind swells, enclosing them with flesh. The stone fruits have a single seed in a hard shell around which the flesh forms. Both of these groups are related as they are both members of the *Rosaceae* family. Mulberries and figs come from different families. None the less all are similar in hardiness, size and manner of cultivation to orchard trees.

Most of these fruits have been cultivated since ancient times. They were nearly all known to the Romans, who spread them throughout their empire. However, much knowledge of their cultivation was then lost during the Dark Ages. The monasteries, and a few noblemen, maintained fruit gardens and orchards, but the common people reverted to farming and cropping from the wild with little interest in fruit cultivation.

Indeed fruits were often seen as poor fare compared to meat, and more suited for animal feed. If it was not for the ease with which many of these fruits could be fermented to make intoxicating beverages, they would probably have been even more neglected. After the Norman Conquest of England the new lords proved to be more interested in fruit than the Saxons they had defeated, bringing many of their own improved varieties with them from France. Orchards became more widely planted, and the wealthy vied with

each other in collecting the greatest number and variety and in having the earliest and longest lasting fruits.

In the sixteenth century, Henry VIII brought many new fruit varieties from the Netherlands and France, and the streets of London became full of home-grown and imported favourites. The impetus of completely different and new fruits from the New World caused more interest in horticulture, reviving interest in the old fruits as well as the new discoveries. As old trusted varieties were exported to the colonies, new species and varieties were imported. These produced new varieties which followed the old abroad at the same time as descendants of the first wave were already returning.

By the Victorian era the number of varieties in cultivation had escalated from a few hundred to many tens of thousands, if you counted local varieties worldwide. The great cities were served by the immense orchards and market gardens that surrounded them. Every gentleman aspired to a house with grounds that would include an orchard at least, if not a grouse moor.

In this century, since the two World Wars, the labour to maintain great gardens and orchards has not been available and the land was needed for more basic crops. Orchards were grubbed up for cereals and more exciting fruits became available from abroad. The British orchard all but disappeared from many counties. Houses with grounds and orchards were demolished to make way for executive hutches at ten to the acre.

However, the green movement combined with people's increasing awareness of the utility of trees, the value of fruit, and the ecological advantages of permanent culture as opposed to annual crops, have all caused a reawakening of interest in orchard fruits. More are now being planted than for nearly a century.

*Malus domestica* from the order *Rosaceae*

# CULINARY AND DESSERT APPLES

*Tree up to 10m/33ft. Life span: medium to long.  Deciduous, hardy, sometimes self-fertile.*
*Fruits: up to 15cm/6in, spherical, green to yellow or red. Vitamin value: vitamin C.*

Malus domestica apples are complex selections and hybrids of *M. pumila* with *M. sylvestris* and *M. mitis*. Thus the shape of the fruit varies from the spheres of **Gladstone** and **Granny Smith** to the flattened buns of **Bramley** and **Mère de Ménage,** or the almost conical **Spartan**, **Golden Delicious** and **Worcester**

**Granny Smith**

**Pearmain**. The colour can be green, yellow, scarlet orange or dark red to almost purple. The texture can vary from crisp to pappy and they may be juicy or dry, acid or insipid, bitter, bland or aromatic. All apples have a dent in the stalk end, the remains of the flower at the other and a central tough core with several brown seeds. These are edible in small amounts, though there is a recorded death from eating a quantity as they contain small amounts of cyanide.

The trees will often become picturesque landscape features, particularly when seen in an orchard. They frequently become twisted or distorted when left to themselves. They have soft downy or smooth leaves, never as glossy as pear leaves. The flowers are often pink- or red-tinged as well as snow white.

Apples are native to temperate Europe and Asia. They have been harvested from the wild since prehistory and were well known to the ancient Phoenicians. When Varro led his army as far as the Rhine in the first century BC, every region had its apples. The Romans encouraged their cultivation, so, although Cato had only noted a half dozen varieties in the second century BC, Pliny knew of three dozen by the first century AD. The Dark Ages caused a decline in apple growing in Britain and only one pomerium (orchard), at Nottingham, is mentioned in the Domesday Book. However, interest increased after the Norman invasion. Costard and Pearmain varieties are first noted in the twelfth and thirteenth centuries, and by the year 1640 there are nearly five dozen varieties recorded by Parkinson. By 1669, Worlidge has the number up to 92, mostly cider apples. *Downing's Fruits*, printed in 1866, has 643 varieties listed. Now we have over five thousand named apple varieties, representing about two thousand actually distinguishable clones. Several hundred are easily obtainable from specialist nurserymen, though only a half dozen are grown on a commercial scale.

This sudden explosion in numbers was most probably due to the expansion of the colonies. The best varieties of apple trees from Europe mutated and crossed as they were propagated across North America, and then later Australia, and these then returned to be crossed again.

**Orleans Reinette**

Apples are now grown extensively in every temperate region around the world. The first apples in North America supposedly were planted on the Governor's Island in Boston Harbour, but the Massachusetts Company had requested seeds in 1629, and in 1635 a Mr Wolcott of Connecticut wrote he had made five hundred hogsheads of cider from his new apple orchard.

**Golden Delicious**

## VARIETIES

The oldest variety known and easily available is **Court Pendu Plat** (mid-winter, dessert) which may go back to Roman times and is recorded from the sixteenth century. It is still grown because it flowers late, missing frosts. **Nonpareil** and **Golden Pippin** also come from the sixteenth century and keep till mid-spring. However, they are rarely available, though there are a dozen and a half part-descendants all called **Golden Pippin**. **Golden Reinette** (mid-winter, dessert) is still popular in Europe and dates from before 1650. The large green **Flower of Kent** (1660) has nearly disappeared. This was the apple that prompted Sir Isaac Newton in his discoveries of the laws of motion and gravity. **Ribston Pippin** (mid-winter, dessert) has one of the highest vitamin C contents and superb flavour. It was bred in 1707 and is not happy on wet heavy soils. From 1720 comes **Ashmead's Kernel**, one of the best-tasting, late-keeping dessert apples, but it is a light cropper. **Orleans Reinette** (mid-winter, dessert) is known from 1776. It is juicy, very tasty with a

rough skin and is not very good on wet cold sites. 1785 saw the birth of the rare but choice **Pitmaston Pine Apple** (mid-winter, dessert). This has small fruits with a rich, honey-like flavour. **Wagener** is a mid to late winter, hard-fleshed keeper, which was raised in New York State in 1791.

**Bramley's Seedling** (mid-winter, culinary) raised in 1809, has one of the highest vitamin C contents of cooking varieties. It grows large, so have it on a more dwarfing stock than others. The **Cornish Gillyflower** is a very tasty, late-keeping dessert raised in 1813.

**Cox's Orange Pippin**

Unlike many other apples, it will flourish in a mild wet climate; It is unsuited to training or cordon culture. One of the best dual purpose apples is **Blenheim Orange** (mid-winter), a wide, flat, golden russeted fruit and a large tree. Raised in 1850, **Cox's Orange**

**Spartan**

**Pippin** (late autumn) is reckoned the best dessert apple. However, it is not easy to grow as it is disease-prone, hates wet clays and does best on a warm wall. **Sunset**, raised in 1918, and **Suntan**, in 1955, are more reliable offspring. **Beauty of Bath** is one of the best known earlies, fruiting in late summer with small, sharp, sweet and juicy, yellow fruits stained scarlet and orange. It was introduced in 1864. It is a tip bearer and not suitable for training. **Egremont Russet** (late autumn), bred in 1872, is one of the best russets, a group of apples with scentless, roughened skin and crisp, firm flesh, which is sweet and tasty but never over-juicy or acid. Just a century old is **James Grieve** (mid-autumn, dessert). It is prone to canker, but makes a good pollinator for **Cox** and is a good cropper of refreshingly acid, perfumed fruits. The ubiquitous **Golden Delicious**, so much grown commercially in Europe, is a conical yellow. It actually tastes pretty good when grown at home, but

must be waxed for keeping as otherwise it wilts. It was found in West Virginia in 1916. **George Cave** is a modern (in horticultural terms), early dessert variety from 1945. It crops in late summer. Better flavoured than **Beauty of Bath**, it can be pruned normally, though it is inclined to tip bearing. **Discovery** was introduced in 1962. It is an early scarlet fruit with creamy white flesh that comes in late summer to early autumn. The flowers are fairly frost tolerant and it is scab resistant. It is rapidly dominating the early apple market because it will keep better and longer than most other early varieties.

It is interesting to note some varieties have much more vitamin C than others which grow in the same conditions. **Ribston Pippin** typically has 31mg/100g, **Orlean's Reinette** 22.4mg, **Bramley's Seedling** 16mg, **Cox's Orange Pippin** 10.5mg, **Golden Delicious** 8mg and **Rome Beauty** 3.6mg. Maybe the famous saying should go 'A Ribston Pippin a day keeps the doctor away'.

**Egremont Russet**

## CULTIVATION

Apples are much abused trees. They prefer a rich, moist, well-drained loam, but are planted almost anywhere and yet often still do fairly well. What they will not stand is being water-logged, or growing on the site of an old apple tree or near to others that have been long established, and they do not thrive in dank frost pockets. Pollination is best served by planting more than three varieties, as many apples are mutually in-compatible, having diploid or triploid varieties with irreconcilable differences in their chromosomes. A Cox and a Bramley will not fruit on their own, but if you add a James Grieve all three bear fruit. Crab apples usually prove good pollinators for unnamed trees.

### Growing under Glass
Apples do not like being under glass all the time as they need a winter chill, and they are more susceptible to pests and diseases, especially if hot and dry, but the usual remedies apply. Some French varieties, such as the classic Calville Blanche d'Hiver, can only be grown to perfection under cover in Britain.

### Growing in Containers
On very dwarfing stocks apples are easily grown in large pots. They need hard pruning in winter and in summer the lengthening shoots should be nipped out, thus tip bearing varieties are not really suitable. Special varieties have been developed for containers which supposedly require little pruning.

### Ornamental and Wildlife Value
The pink and white blossom is wonderful in late spring. The flowers are valuable to insects and the fruits are important to birds.

### Maintenance Calendar
*Spring* Weed, mulch, spray seaweed solution monthly.
*Summer* Thin fruits, summer prune, spray with seaweed solution, apply greasebands.
*Autumn* Use poor fruits first, pick best for storage.
*Winter* Hard prune, add copious compost, remove mummified fruits.

### Propagation
Apple pips rarely make fruiting trees of value; however many of our best varieties were chance seedlings. Apples are grafted or budded on to different rootstocks depending on site and size of tree required. Few grow them from cuttings on their own roots or as standards on seedling stocks as these make very large trees only suitable for planting in grazed meadows. Half standards are more convenient for the home orchard and these get big enough on M25 stock at about 5.2m/17ft high and 6m/21ft apart. At the other extreme, the most dwarfing stock is M27, useful for pot culture, but these midgets need staking all their lives and the branches start so low you cannot mow or grow underneath them. M9 produces a 2m/7ft tree, still needing staking but good for cordons. On such very dwarfing stocks the trees do badly in poor soil and during droughts. M26 is bigger, growing to 2.8m/9ft and still needs a stake but is probably the best for small gardens. It needs 3m/10ft on each side. MM106 is better on poor soils, and on good soils is still compact at about 4m/13ft, needing 4.5m/15ft between trees.

### Pruning and Training
Apple trees are often left to grow and produce for years with no pruning other than remedial work once the head has formed. They may be trained and hard pruned summer and winter, back to spur systems, on almost any shaped framework, though rarely as fans. For beauty and productivity apples are best as espaliers; to achieve the maximum number of varieties as cordons; for ease and quality as open goblet-pruned small trees. Some varieties, especially many of the earliest fruiters, are tip bearers. These are best only pruned remedially as hard pruning will remove the fruiting wood. They can be grown on a replacement system as for peaches (see page 43) but it is work. As important as the pruning is

**This distinctive Ballerina 'Waltz' apple tree dominates its container**

**Golden Delicious**

the thinning. Removing crowded and congested, damaged and diseased apples improves the size and quality of those remaining and prevents biennial bearing. Thin after the June drop occurs and again twice after, disposing of the rejects to destroy any pests.

### Weed, Pest and Disease Control

Apples are the most commonly grown fruit tree in much of the temperate zone. They have thus built up a whole ecosystem of pests and diseases around themselves. Although they have many problems they

**Trained apples underplanted with herbs**

still manage to produce enormous quantities of fruit for many years, in often quite poor conditions. Vigorous growth is essential as this reduces many problems, especially canker. The commonplace pests require the usual remedies (see page 228), but apples suffer from some annoying specialities. Holes in the fruits are usually caused by one of two pests. Codling moth generally makes holes in the core of the fruit, pushing frass out at the flower end. They are controlled by corrugated cardboard band traps, pheromone traps, permitted sprays as the blossom sets, and hygiene. The other hole-maker is apple sawfly which bores narrow tunnels, emerging anywhere. They may then eat into another or even a third. They are best controlled by hygiene,

removing and destroying affected apples during thinning. Permitted sprays may be used after flower set, and running poultry underneath an orchard is effective. Many varieties are scab-resistant. If it occurs, it affects first the leaves then the fruits and, like brown rot and canker, is spread by mummified apples and dead wood. It is worst in wet areas. All of these problems, and mildews, are best controlled by hygiene, keeping the trees vigorous, well watered and mulched, and open pruned. Woolly aphis can be sprayed or dabbed with soft soap or derris. Sticky non-setting tree bands control many pests all year round, especially in late summer and autumn. Apples also get damaged by birds, wasps and occasionally earwigs, so for perfect fruits, protect them with paper bags.

**Winston apples forming a decorative arch**

**A handy apple store**

### Harvesting and Storing

Early apples are best eaten off the tree. They rarely keep for long, going pappy in days. Most mid-season apples are also best eaten off the tree as they ripen, but many will keep for weeks if picked just under-ripe and stored in the cool. Late keepers must hang on the trees till hard frosts are imminent, or bird damage is getting too severe, then if they are delicately picked and kept cool in the dark they may keep for six months or longer. Thus apples can be had most months of the year, providing early- and late-keeping varieties and a rodent-proof store are available. They are best picked with a cupped hand and gently laid in a tray, traditionally padded with dry straw. (This may taint if damped so better use shredded newspaper.) Do not store early varieties with lates nor near either pears, onions, garlic or potatoes. The fruits must be free of bruises, rot and holes and the stalk must remain attached for them to store well. If apples are individually wrapped in paper they keep longer. Apples can be puréed and frozen, or juiced and frozen, or dried in thin rings, or made into cider.

## COMPANION PLANTING

Apples are bad for potatoes, making them blight-prone. They are benefited by *alliums*, especially chives, and penstemons and nasturtiums nearby are thought to prevent sawfly and woolly aphis. Stinging nettles close by benefit the trees and, dried, they help stored fruits keep.

## OTHER USES

Apple wood is used for mallet heads, golf clubs and in engraving. It is delicately scented when burnt, and is useful for smoking foods and as fire logs.

**Egremont Russet apple blossom**

## CULINARY USES

Apples are excellent raw, stewed and made into tarts, pies and jellies, especially with other fruits which they help set. The juice is delicious fresh and can be frozen for out-of-season use, and made into cider or vinegar. Cooking apples are different from desserts, much larger, more acid and less sweet raw. Most break down to a frothy purée when heated and few retain their texture, unlike most of the desserts. Bramleys, Norfolk Beauty and Revd Wilkes are typical, turning to sweet froths when cooked. Lane's Prince Albert, Lord Derby and Encore stay firm and are the sorts to use for pies rather than sauces.

*Flying Saucers*
per person

*1 large cooking apple*
*approx. 3 dessertspoons*
  *mincemeat*
*knob of butter*
*7g/¼ oz sesame seeds*
*cream or custard to serve*

Wash, dry and cut each apple in half horizontally. Remove the tough part of the core but leave the outside intact. Stuff the hollow with mincemeat, then pin the two halves back together with wooden cocktail sticks. Rub the outside with butter and roll in sesame seeds, then bake in a preheated oven at 190°C/375°F/gas mark 5 for half an hour or until they 'lift off' nicely. Serve the saucers immediately with cream or custard.

*Malus pumila* from the order *Rosaceae*

# CRAB AND CIDER APPLES

*Tree up to 10m/33ft. Life span: long. Deciduous, often self-fertile.*
*Fruits: 1–7cm/½ –3in, spherical, yellow, green or red. Value: make tonic alcoholic beverages.*

Crab apples grow wild in hedgerows and have smaller, more brightly coloured fruits than cultivated varieties. The fruits vary from being unpalatable to completely inedible raw though they make delicious jellies. Cider apples are more like eating and cooking apples, with fruits in-between in size but similarly bitter and astringent. Selected crab apples are grown ornamentally and are useful pollinators for other apples, so they may be found on semi-dwarfing stocks as small trees. Cider apples were always grown on strong or seedling stock, gaining immense vigour which they needed to tower above animals grazing underneath.

Crabs have been used since prehistory and doubtless cider has been made for as long. It was probably brought to Cornwall initially by Phoenician tin traders.

Old varieties of cider apples from Sarah Bowen's orchard

Immature crab apples

## VARIETIES

Many crabs are well known ornamentals, such as **John Downie**, which has long golden orange fruits, and **Golden Hornet**, with bright yellow. Most are mixed hybrids of *Malus pumila* with the native *M. sylvestris* which has sour, hard, green fruits and is sometimes thorny, and *M. mitis*, from the Mediterranean region, which has softer leaves and sweeter, more coloured fruits. *M. baccata*, the **Siberian crab**, and *M. manchurica*, from China, are widely planted for their bright red fruits. Cider apples are more improved and closer to *M. domestica* hybrids. Every local variety is rated the best. In trials, **Yarlington Mill** was thought outstanding. **Sweet Coppin, Kingston Black, Tremlett's Bitter** and **Crimson King** are also excellent.

## CULTIVATION

Tougher than the finer apples, these may be grown almost anywhere not waterlogged or parched.

**Growing under Glass**
Neither crab nor cider apples are happy permanently under glass and do better in the open. They need a winter chill otherwise they crop badly. They are hardy enough for most places.

**Growing in Containers**
Crab apples can be fruited in pots; indeed they often do even in the small pots in which garden centres sell them. Cider apples are shy and less likely to produce heavy crops.

**Ornamental and Wildlife Value**
The crabs are very attractive in flower and many also in fruit, Cider apples are bigger and less pretty. Both are valuable to insects when in flower and to birds, rodents and insects with their fruit.

**Maintenance Calendar**
*Spring* Weed, mulch and spray seaweed solution.
*Summer*
*Autumn* Pick fruit.
*Winter* Prune, and spread the compost.

**Dabinett**

### Propagation

Although some crabs can be grown from seed they are not reliable. Named varieties are grafted on to rootstocks suitable for the size and site intended. Neither crab nor cider apple varieties are usually available on the most dwarfing rootstocks, but on more vigorous stock they make large trees.

### Pruning and Training

Crab apples are usually worked as half standards on semi-dwarfing stock and are only pruned remedially in winter. Cider apples are worked as standards on strong growing stocks and make big trees. Likewise, cider apples should only be pruned remedially after forming a head.

### Weed, Pest and Disease Control

Although these can suffer from the same problems as dessert and culinary apples, the crops are rarely badly affected. Crab apples are usually remarkably productive whatever care they get. For cider apples many problems such as scab are also mostly irrelevant.

### Harvesting and Storing

Crabs can be picked under-ripe for jellying, but you can hang on, as the birds do not go for them as fast as softer fruits. Cider apples are left as long as possible to get maximum sugar and to soften. If they are shaken down they bruise, so the apples are then best pressed immediately, not stored in heaps to soften further before pressing.

## COMPANION PLANTING

The plants that benefit dessert and culinary apples (see page 22) also associate well with these varieties. Both crab and cider apples are often grown in hedgerows and grazed meadow orchards. They seem content with grass underneath and old trees often have mistletoe growing in their boughs, to no obvious detriment.

**Michellin**

## OTHER USES

Pressed apple pulp can be dried and stored till late winter for wild bird and livestock food.

**Apple cider**

## CULINARY USES

Crab apples make delicious tart jellies by themselves, or mixed with other fruits which have less pectin and so do not set so easily. Cider apples are used solely to make cider. They are cleaned, crushed and pressed and the juice is fermented, often with the addition of wine yeast and sugar. After fermentation, cider may be flat, cloudy, sweet, or sparkling, green or yellow, depending on local taste. Ciders are made from several varieties of apple, to give a blend of acidity, sweetness and tannin. (Palatable cider can be made from a mixture of dessert and cooking apples.) Some cider is made into vinegar, deliberately.

### Crab Apple Jelly
Makes approx 3.5kg/7lb

*2kg/4lb crab apples*
*approx.1.5kg/3lb sugar*

Chop the apples, then simmer them in water to cover until soft. Sieve or strain through a jelly bag and weigh the juice. Add three-quarters of its weight in sugar. Return to the heat and bring to boil, stirring to dissolve the sugar. Boil until setting point is reached, then skim and pour into warm, sterilised jars. Cover while still hot.

*Pyrus communis* from the order *Rosaceae*

# CULINARY AND DESSERT PEARS

*Tree up to 20m/65ft. Life span: very long. Deciduous, hardy, rarely self-fertile.*
*Fruits: up to 8x18cm/3x7in. Value: potassium and riboflavin.*

**Conference**

Pears very closely resemble, and are related to, apples, but there are no known natural hybrids between them. Pears have a fruit which elongates at the stalk end, which stands proud, whereas an apple's stalk is inset in a dent in the top of the fruit. Some pears such as **Conference** and **Bartlett** will set fruit parthenocarpically (i.e. they fruit freely without pollination). However, these fruits are usually not as good as fertilised ones, being misshapen and of course lacking seeds. Pear trees resemble apples but have shiny leaves, more upright growth and the fat stems usually have a glossier brown hue and more angled buds than apple. Pears on their own roots make very big trees, too big to prune, spray or pick, and the fruit is damaged when it drops. Pears are thus usually worked on quince roots, which makes them smaller, more compact trees.

**Doyenne du Comice**

Pears are native to Europe and Asia. The first cultivated varieties were selected from the wild in prehistory. The ancient Phoenicians, Jews and pre-Christian Romans grew several improved sorts; by the time of Cato there were at least a half dozen distinct fruits, Pliny records forty-one and Palladius fifty-six. A list of fruits for the Grand Duke Cosmo III, in late medieval Italy, raises the number to 209, and another manuscript lists 232. In Britain in 1640 only five dozen were known. This rose to more than 700 by 1842. In 1866 the American author T.W. Field catalogued 850 varieties. The rapid increase in numbers and quality, from poor culinary pears to fine desserts, was mainly the work of a few dedicated breeders in France and Belgium at the end of the eighteenth century, who selected and bred most modern varieties.

**Durondeau**

## VARIETIES

As pears are used more for eating raw than in cooking, and dessert pears can be cooked, but not vice versa, it is not worthwhile growing purely culinary pears. **Doyenne du Comice** (late season) is by far the best dessert pear. None other approaches it for sweet, aromatic succulence, and the fruits can reach a magnificent weight. These are very choice and deserve to be espaliered on the best warm wall. **Bartlett/ Williams' Bon Chretien** (early/mid-season) is widely grown for canning, but is an excellent table fruit – if a bit prone to scab. It is also parthenocarpic, as is **Conference** (early/mid-season). This latter is a reliable cropper on its own and is scab resistant. Raised in1770 in Berkshire, it is now very widely grown. **Jargonelle** is an old variety first recorded in 1600. It crops for me in early August in East Anglia, about the same time as **Souvenir de Congress**. These are the earliest with good flavour. **Improved Fertility** (mid) is very hardy and crops heavily and regularly. Other superb pears are **Clapp's Favourite, Dr Jules Guyot** (both early/ mid season); **Glou Morceau**

and **Durondeau** (both late) keep into the New Year. There are hundreds of other pear varieties, many of which are cooking not dessert, and several species which have more ornamental than edible value. The **Birch-leaved Pear**, *P. betulifolia*, comes from fourteenth-century China. Almost all parts were eaten, flowers and leaves as well as the small fruits. The **Kumoi** is the most apple-like pear, brown green, russeted and crunchy, juicy, but a bit insipid, easy to grow, partly self-fertile and productive. Similar is the **Chinese Sand Pear**, *P. sinensis*. In Syria the **Three-lobed-leaved Pear**, *P. trilobata*, is popular. This may be the same as the native Turkish *Malus trilobata*.

**Buerre Hardy**

**Lattilac**

## CULTIVATION

Dessert pears need a rich, well-drained, moist soil, preferably light and loamy. They can be cropped in the open in southern England, but need a wall further north. The blossom and fruitlets need protection from frosts as they flower early in spring. Pollination is best ensured by planting a mixture of varieties. Do not plant deep as pears are prone to scion rooting, which allows them to make big, less fruitful trees.

**Growing under Glass**
Pears appreciate a warm wall, but are not easy under glass as they do not like to get too hot and humid; they are thus difficult to grow in the tropics. Ideally plant in containers, keep indoors for flowering and fruiting, and put outdoors for summer and most of winter as they need some chill. They are hardy and can stand light frost, but the roots are most susceptible in pots.

### Growing in Containers

Pears have often been fruited in tubs. They are amenable to hard pruning, and so respond better than most other fruits to this and to the cramped conditions of a pot.

### Ornamental and Wildlife Value

Why plant an ornamental flowering tree when you can plant a pear? They are just smothered with blossom and buzzing with bees in early spring. The fruits are splendid, but soon eaten in autumn by insects and birds.

### Maintenance Calendar

*Spring* Weed, mulch, spray with seaweed solution monthly, protect flowers against frosts.
*Summer* Thin fruits.
*Autumn* Pick fruit.
*Winter* Prune hard or not at all, compost heavily.

### Propagation

Pears do not come true from seed, reverting to their unproductive forms. They may root from cuttings and can occasionally be layered, but get too big on their own roots. Normally they are grafted on to quince rootstocks which are generally best. For heavy, damp soils and for big trees, pear seedling stock was always used, but there is little demand for this nowadays. Pears have been grafted on to apple stocks and even onto hawthorn. As some varieties do not bond readily with quince stock they are 'double-worked', or grafted on to a mutually compatible inter-graft on the quince. This takes more work and an extra year in the nursery.

**A pear espalier**

**Josephine Malines**

### Pruning and Training

Grown as trees or bushes, pears can be left to themselves except for remedial pruning. They tend to throw twin leaders which need rationalising. Alternatively they respond better than most fruits to hard winter pruning and are almost as amenable to summer pruning, thus they can be trained to an endless variety of forms. As they benefit from the shelter of a wall, they are commonly espaliered, and are more rewarding for less work than a peach in the same position. There are many specialised training forms for pears in addition to the cordon, espalier and fan, and equally intricate and specialised pruning methods. These include Pitchforks and Toasting Forks, with two or three vertical stems on short arms, the Palmette Verriers, with long horizontals that turn vertical at the ends, and the multi-curved L'Arcure. Pears will take almost any shape you choose, and you will not go far wrong if you then shear almost all long growths off by three-quarters in summer and then again by a bit more in winter. Take care not to let them root from or above the graft, which destroys the benefit of the rootstock!

### Weed, Pest and Disease Control

Pears suffer fewer problems than apples. Providing the flowers miss the frosts and have a warm summer they usually produce a good crop of fruits despite any attacks. However, ripening is poor in very cool or hot weather and results in hard or mealy fruits. Leaving the fruit too long on the tree or in storage causes them to rot from the inside out. Pear midge causes the fruitlets to blacken and drop off; inspection reveals maggots within. These are remedied by the hygienic removal and disposal of affected fruits; running poultry underneath in orchards is as effective. Fireblight causes damage resembling scorching. It usually starts from the blossoms. Prune and burn damaged parts immediately, cutting back to clean wood. Scab is a problem in stagnant sites. It affects the fruits before the leaves, which is the opposite from apples. Sprays are usually unnecessary with the more resistant varieties such as Conference. Good open pruning and healthy growth, not overfed with nitrogen, reduce attacks. Always remove all mummified fruits and dead wood immediately. Leaf blistering is usually caused by minute mites. These used to be controlled with lime and sulphur sprays before bud burst. Modern soft soap sprays have also proved to be effective.

**Harvesting and Storing**
Early pears are best picked almost, but never fully, ripe. They should come off when lifted to the horizontal. Left on the tree they go woolly. Watch them carefully while they finish ripening. They will slowly ripen if kept cool, faster if warm. Late pears should be left until bird damage is too great, and picked with a stalk. Kept in a cool, dark place, late varieties last for months, ripening up rapidly if brought into the warm. Do not wrap them with paper as one does with apples, and take care not to store the two fruits near each other as they will cross-taint.

## CULINARY USES

Pears are exquisite as dessert fruits and may be used in much the same way as apples, sliced and used in tarts, baked, stewed or puréed. They are delicious pickled with onions and spices in vinegar.

### *Pear Islands*
Serves 4

*4 large pears*
*90g/3oz caster sugar*
*half bottle sweet Muscat wine*
*2 level tablespoons cornflour*
*splash of milk*
*dark chocolate to taste*

Peel, core and halve the pears. Dissolve two-thirds of the sugar in the wine over a gentle heat and poach the pears in this syrup. Place the pear halves on an oiled baking tray, dredge with the rest of sugar, pop under a hot grill for a minute or two until the tops caramelise. In the meantime, blend the cornflour with a little milk and stir it into the syrup. Return to the heat and cook gently, stirring, until thick. Pour the sauce into a serving bowl, grate on some dark chocolate and set the pear halves into this. Serve piping hot or chilled.

Durondeau

## OTHER USES

The bark contains a yellow dye and arbutin, an antibiotic. The leaves have been used medicinally for renal and urinary infections. The wood is hard and uniform so loved by carvers. It is beautifully scented and good for smoking foods.

## COMPANION PLANTING

Pears are hindered by grass, so this should not be allowed near them in their early years. However, the pears may be grassed down later, especially if they are situated in rather too heavy and/or damp conditions.

**Pear dye**

*Pyrus* from the order *Rosaceae*

# PERRY PEARS

*Tree up to 20m/65ft. Life span: very long. Deciduous, rarely self-fertile. Fruits: up to 10x7cm/4x3in, variable, pear-shaped, yellow, brown or red. Value: make a healthy tonic beverage.*

Perry pear fruits are smaller and hardier than their culinary and dessert cousins, while the trees are generally enormous. As these fruits were wanted in quantity for pressing, they were selected for large trees that would stand well above grass and the depredations of stock. The fruits are bitter and astringent, containing a lot of tannin even though they may often look very appealing. They are pressed for the juice, which ferments to an alcoholic beverage.

Perry pears may have been brought to Britain by the Romans, but they were introduced in force by the Normans. Normandy was by then well established as a perry-growing region and the Normans found parts of the West and Midlands of England equally suitable. Many of the original pear orchards would probably still have been planted for perry without the Norman influence, as early pears tended to be unpalatable raw anyway. The colonists of North America certainly did not start off without perry pears. By 1648 a booklet entitled *A Perfect Description of Virginia* describes a Mr Kinsman regularly making forty or fifty butts of perry from his orchard. Whereas cider has remained a popular drink, perry consumption waned in the nineteenth century. It is now made rarely, except for one or two specialist brands and for local consumption.

A mature perry pear tree with a heavy crop of fruit

## VARIETIES

There are some two to three hundred perry pear varieties known, though these are called by twice as many names, each district having its own local variation. The **Thorn Pear** is recorded from 1676 and grows on a very upright tree. Other early varieties such as **Hastings** and **Brown Bess** could be eaten or made into perry. Later varieties such as **Holmer** are more single purpose and almost uneatable. In the nineteenth century, breeders thought dual-purpose pears would be useful and produced **Blakeney Red** and **Cannock**. The Huffcap group all make very big trees with fruits of a high specific gravity; Rock varieties make even stronger perry, but are still often called Huffcaps.

## CULTIVATION

Perry pears are less demanding than culinary or dessert pears and will do quite well in fairly poor soils. They do not like shallow or badly drained sites.

### Growing under Glass
These are fairly hardy and will make big trees, so are generally not likely to thrive under glass.

### Growing in Containers
Although they would resent it by being short-lived and light-cropping, it should be possible to grow these in large tubs.

### Ornamental and Wildlife Value
Perry pears make a mass of flowers and are tall attractive trees that live for several hundred years, making them very suitable as estate and orchard trees, but too big for most gardens except on modern dwarfing stock. The flowers are good for insects and the fruits are eaten by birds in winter.

### Maintenance Calendar
*Spring* Cut grass, spray with seaweed solution.
*Summer*
*Autumn* Cut grass, collect fruits.
*Winter* Prune and spread compost.

### Propagation
Perry pears were often grown from seed or grafted on to stocks grown from pips in order to get large trees. Now they can be had on dwarfing stocks, such as quince, and are more manageable.

### Pruning and Training
Once the initial shape is formed these are only pruned remedially, though care should always be taken to ensure that such large trees are sound.

### Weed, Pest and Disease Control
These suffer the same few problems as dessert and culinary pears which make little impression on the immense crops. Fireblight is a risk, but there is little one can do with such large trees.

### Harvesting and Storing
Immense crops are produced; a ton or even two per tree is possible, after a wait of several decades. One tree in 1790 covered three-quarters of an acre and produced six tons per year. Perry pears do not keep and rot very quickly. Perry is usually pressed from one variety only, with sugar and yeast added. Dessert and culinary pears do not make a perry of any value, but can be made into a pear wine.

## COMPANION PLANTING

Young trees were usually cropped between with cereals or hops and then grassed down as they matured, often grazed by geese.

## OTHER USES

The wood is useful for carving and, as firewood, scents the room.

**A standing cup made of pearwood, dating from the early seventeenth century**

## CULINARY USES

Perry pears are not normally very good for eating even when they are cooked, though Blakeney Red was once considered a good baker.

*Pressless Perry Wine*

3kg/6lb pears
1.5kg/3lb sugar
4.5litre/1 gallon water
approx. 1 teaspoon wine yeast

Chop the pears, peel and all, into the boiling water. Stir in half the sugar, and bring back to the boil, then allow to cool to 22°C/7°F before adding the yeast. Seal with a fermentation lock and keep warm for one week, then strain and add the remaining sugar to the liquor. Reseal with the lock and ferment in a warm place till all action has stopped. Siphon off the lees and store in a cool place for 3 months, then bottle and store for a year before drinking.

*Cydonia vulgaris /C. oblonga* from the order *Rosaceae*

# QUINCES

*Tree up to 6m/20ft. Self-fertile, deciduous, hardy, long-lived.*
*Fruits: 7x12cm/2x5in, yellow and fragrant.*

Portuguese
Quince
blossom

These are small, bushy trees, often twisted and contorted. There are two forms: a lower mounded one with lax branches, more suited to ornamental and wildlife use, and a stiffer, erect type, which bears larger fruits and is better for orchards. The leaves are downy underneath, resembling apple leaves more than pear. They turn a gorgeous yellow in autumn. The decorative pink and white flowers resemble apple blossom, but appear singly on short shoots, 12–15cm/6–8in long, that grow before the flower opens, so they are rarely bothered by late frost. In some varieties the unfurled flower bud looks like an ice-cream cone with strawberry stripes, or a traditional barber's pole. The quinces are hard fruits somewhat resembling pears in shape and colour, often covered with a soft down when young, inedible when raw, but delicious and aromatic when cooked. Because they have long been used as rootstocks for pears and other fruits, they are sometimes found as suckers, surviving long after the scion has passed away.

Quinces are old fruits, still much grown in many parts of Europe though originally from Persia and Turkestan. Dedicated by the ancients to the Goddess of Love, they were promulgated by the Roman Empire as one of their favoured crops and were well known to Pliny and Columella. In 812 AD Charlemagne encouraged the French to grow more and Chaucer refers to them by the French name as coines. Their pulp makes *Dulce de Membrillo* or *Marmelo*, still popular in Portugal and Spain, and the origin of the marmalade we now make from citrus fruit.

## VARIETIES

The **Portuguese** is pear-shaped, vigorous, but slow to crop. **Vranja** (Bereczki) is from Serbia, large-fruited, pear-shaped and with erect growth. **Meech's Prolific** is also pear-shaped, early to bear and late keeping. **Champion** is rounder and mild-flavoured. Also available are **Ispahan** from Persia and **Maliformis** (apple-shaped). Also in the USA: **Orange, Pineapple** and **Smyrna**.

## CULTIVATION

Quinces need a moist soil and flourish as waterside specimens. They prefer a warm site, doing rather badly in cold or exposed places. Plant them at least 3m/10ft apart. Normally they will only need staking in their first years of life. They are self-fertile.

### Growing under Glass and in Containers
There is little to be gained by growing quinces under glass. They can be grown against a wall with some success and could be grown in pots and taken indoors by those living in harsh climates, but the fruit hardly merits such efforts.

Quince fruits and flowers

### Ornamental and Wildlife Value

Quinces will make excellent small specimen trees as the flowers, fruits, autumn colours and then the knotted branches give year-round interest. The flowers feed beneficial insects, while the fruits are relished by birds and other wildlife after all the apples and pears have long gone.

### Maintenance Calendar

*Spring* Spray monthly with seaweed solution, weed and mulch well.
*Summer* Spray monthly with seaweed solution and weed.
*Autumn* Remove rotten fruit and pick best for storing.
*Winter* Prune out dead and diseased wood, add plenty of compost.

### Propagation

Quinces can be had from seed or by suckers removed from pear trees as these are usually grafted on to quince stocks. Better fruits will always result from buying a ready-formed tree of an already named variety.

### Pruning and Training

Quinces can be trained but the twisted, contorted growth makes this difficult. They are best grown as bushes or standards, with pruning restricted to removing dead, diseased and crossing wood.

### Weed, Pest and Disease Control

There are no widespread problems for quinces. Even the birds and wasps will ignore the fruits for most of the autumn.

### Harvesting and Storing

Pick the fruits in autumn before they drop and keep them in a cool, airy place. Do not store with apples or pears or vegetables as they may taint.

**Quince fruits**

## COMPANION PLANTING

Like pears and apples, quinces may be expected to benefit from underplantings of chives, garlic and the pungent herbs.

## OTHER USES

The wood is hard and prunings make good kindling. The fruits are excellent room perfumers and can be used as bases for pomanders.

## CULINARY USES

Quinces can be made into aromatic clear jelly, jam or a pulpy cheese that goes well with both sweet and savoury dishes. Pieces of quince (if you can hack them off) keep their shape when cooked, adding both texture and aroma to apple and pear dishes.

### *Quince Cheese*
Makes approx 2kg/4lb

*1kg/2lb ripe quinces*
*1 unwaxed small orange*
*a little water*
*approx.1kg/2 lb sugar*
*1 or 2 drops orange flower or rose petal water (optional)*

Roughly hack the quinces into pieces. Finely chop the orange and simmer both, with just enough water to cover them, until they are a pulp. Strain the pulp and add its own weight in sugar. Bring to boil and cook gently for approximately 1½ hours. Add the orange flower or rose petal water if liked. Then pot into oiled, warmed bowls, seal and store for three months or more before using.
Turn the cheese out of the bowl and slice for serving with cooked meats or savoury dishes.

**Reine Claude blossom**

*Prunus domestica* from the order *Rosaceae*

# PLUMS

*Tree 6m/20ft. Long-lived, deciduous, hardy, slender, thorny, not usually self-fertile. Fruits: ovoid, usually 3–6cm/1–2in in any colour. Value: rich in magnesium, iron and vitamin A.*

Plums come in more variation than most other fruits. They differ in season, size, shape, colour and taste. We have mixed hybrids, descendants of plums originally selected from fifteen or more different wild species. The European plum, *Prunus domestica*, is thought to be predominantly a hybrid between *P. cerasifera,* the cherry plum or **Myrobalan**, and *P. spinosa,* the **sloe**. It is a small to medium, slender, deciduous tree with small white blossoms.

The European plum came from Western Asia and the Caucasus. It naturalised in Greece first and then throughout most of the temperate zone. Pliny describes cultivated varieties from Syria coming to Italy via Greece, and it is likely they were spread by the Roman Empire to Britain and northern Europe. They were reintroduced in the Crusades. Henry VII is recorded as importing a 'Perdrigon' plum and Brogdale Fruit Research Station have a plum grown from a stone salvaged from the wreck of the *Mary Rose*, Henry VIII's splendid warship. Plum stones were ordered in 1629 for planting in Massachusetts, and plums became widely cultivated in the temperate parts of North America. In 1864 over 150 varieties were offered in nurserymen's catalogues. Some American plums returned to Europe; California, for example, became famous for exporting prunes – late, dark-skinned plums which are dried on the tree. Although unsuccessful in cool, damp climates, they can be dried with machinery. **Fellemberg** and **Prune d'Agen** are from Europe, but are more widely grown in California.

**Coe's Golden Drop**

## VARIETIES

There are hundreds of good varieties which ripen through the season. **Victoria** is fully self-fertile, pollinates many others and is always worth having. It has golden-yellow-fleshed, large, yellow, ovoid fruits, flushed with scarlet. **Victoria** ripens middle to late August in Sussex, where it was found around 1840. **Coe's Golden Drop** is a shy cropper, but superb. It needs a warm spot or a wall and closely resembles an apricot. **Severn Cross** is a delicious golden seedling from **Coe's** and self-fertile. **Oullin's Gage** is self-fertile. A plum with a richer, sweeter flavour, it flowers late, missing frosts. **Czar** has frost-resistant flowers and is self-fertile; it is for culinary rather than dessert use. **Marjorie's Seedling** is dual purpose, late cropping and self-fertile.

## CULTIVATION

Plums like a heavier, moister soil than many other fruits. This means they often may be relegated to cold, damp sites and heavy soils, which they really do not like. Even on a shady wall some, such as **Victoria** or **Czar**, do well.

**Growing under Glass and in Containers**
Because of their susceptibility to spring frost, brown rot and wasps, plums are worth growing under glass. However, they would be best confined to large pots so they can spend sometime outdoors, as they do not relish hot conditions.

**Victoria**

### Ornamental and Wildlife Value

Plums are wonderful during their short blossoming. The flowers are loved by early insects and the fruits by birds, insects and rodents, who also chew the bark.

### Maintenance Calendar

*Spring* Protect blossom from frost, weed, mulch, spray with seaweed solution, prune.
*Summer* Put out wasp traps.
*Autumn* Remove mummified plums.
*Winter* Protect buds from birds with cotton or nets.

### Propagation

Graft on **Pixy** and other new dwarfing stocks, unless you have a big orchard and want immense quantities. Plums can be grown from stones, but take years to fruit and do not come true.

### Pruning and Training

Plums make good high standards because, eventually, heavy fruiting branches weep, bringing the fruit down to a skirt. Overladen branches will need propping. Plums are usually grown as a short standard or bush. Leave them alone once a head is formed, except to cut out dead and diseased wood. Any work is best done in the growing season. They can be usefully trained on walls if on dwarfing stock, for example **Pixy**. Plums prefer herringbone not fan shapes.

### Weed, Pest and Disease Control

Plums get a host of the usual pests and a few more besides, but when they avoid the frost and crop at all they are so prolific there is usually a surplus for private gardeners. They are susceptible to silver leaf disease, so should not be pruned in autumn, winter or early spring – only in late spring and summer and during dry weather.

### Harvesting and Storing

Plums picked under-ripe for cooking will keep for days, but often have poor flavour compared to plums picked ripe off the tree. Many varieties can be quite easily peeled, and this avoids some of the unfortunate side effects of too many plums.

**Marjorie's Seedling**

## COMPANION PLANTING

Avoid anemones which harbour plum rust. In the USA curculios are reportedly kept off by surrounding plum trees with garlic.

## OTHER USES

Potent brandy is made from plums in Hungary and in central Europe.

## CULINARY USES

They can be turned into jam, juice or cheese, or frozen if stoned first, and are Epicurean preserved in plum brandy syrup.

### Prunes in Semolina
Serves 4

250g/8oz dried prunes
100ml/4fl oz plum brandy
100 ml/4fl oz water
900ml/1½ pts milk
twist of lemon rind
½ teaspoon salt
7 dessertspoons semolina
2 dessertspoons honey
2 small eggs, separated
grated nutmeg to taste

Soak the prunes in the brandy and water overnight. Strain off the juice and simmer it down to syrup. Put the fruits and syrup into the base of a pudding basin. Boil the milk, lemon rind, salt and semolina for 10 minutes, stirring continuously. Cool a little, remove the lemon rind and stir in the honey and egg yolks. Whisk the egg whites and fork them in. Immediately pour the mixture over the back of a spoon on to the fruit and syrup. Grate nutmeg over the surface and bake in a preheated oven at 200°C/400°F/gas mark 6 for 20 minutes, or until the top is browning.
As delicious cold for breakfast as it is hot for dinner.

### Double Victoria
Serves 6–8

500g/1lb Victoria plums
50g/2oz honey
25g/1oz flaked blanched almonds

for the sponge:
100g/4oz sifted self-raising flour
100g/4oz vanilla-flavoured caster sugar
100g/4oz softened butter
2 eggs, pinch salt

Wash, halve and stone the plums. Place in a buttered pudding dish and dribble the honey over them. Beat together the ingredients for the sponge in a mixer until creamy and light in colour. Dollop the sponge mixture over the fruit, smooth and garnish with almonds. Bake in a preheated oven at 190°C/375°F/gas mark 5 for 35 minutes or until golden brown and firm to the touch.

**Prunes**

*Prunus italica* from the order *Rosaceae*

# GREENGAGES

*Tree/bush 4–5m/13–16ft. Hardy, long-lived. Fruits: 2–4cm/1–1½in, green to red.*

Greengages are like plums, fruiting in mid-season with sweet, greeny yellow or golden, lightly scented flesh. The fruits are smaller, firmer, more rounded and less bloomed than plums. They have a deep crease down one side and frequently russet spotting. The trees are sturdy, not often thorny, and bushier than most plums though not quite as hardy.

Wild greengages are found in Asia Minor. Possibly introduced to Britain and northern Europe by the Romans, they disappeared from cultivation during the Saxon period or Middle Ages and were not reintroduced until 1725. Originally known in France as the **Reine Claude**, the first greengage was brought to Britain by, and named after, Sir Thomas Gage, who lived in Bury St Edmunds, Suffolk – under 20 miles from where I now write. He was fortunate to live in East Anglia as the conditions suit greengages, which need a drier, warmer summer than plums. The original greengage almost always came true from seed, but there are some larger-fruited selections, and also some good crosses between gages and plums.

## VARIETIES

The **Old Greengage** is original, but can be unreliable; an improved seedling is **Cambridge Gage**. The **Transparent Gage** is another old variety from France and is honeyed in its sweetness. It has almost transparent, golden-yellow

**Early Transparent Gage**

flesh and is heavily spotted with red. It fruits in late summer. The true **Mirabelle** is very similar, smaller fruited and of dwarf growth, but is rarely found except in southern France. (Sometimes the yellow Myrobalan plums may erroneously be called Mirabelles to make a sale!) **Denniston's Superb** comes

from the USA and is close to the original in flavour, but is larger fruited, hardier, regular cropping and, most valuable of all, self-fertile. **Jefferson** is similar, later, but not self-fertile. **Reine Claude de Bavay** possibly has a plum as one parent. It fruits a fortnight or so after the previous varieties, in early autumn.

It makes a most delicious jam, a touch more acid and tasty if the fruit is picked a week or so early. **Golden Transparent**, another hybrid, is a large, round, transparent yellow. It ripens late and needs a wall in most cool areas, but is self-fertile.

# CULTIVATION

Greengages need a lighter soil than plums but still need it to be rich, moist and well aerated. They are easiest to tend as standards at least 6m/20 ft apart. In colder areas they need a wall. Some, such as Denniston's Superb, Early Transparent Gage, Jefferson's Gage or Oullins Golden Gage, will fruit on a shady wall.

### Growing under Glass and in Containers

Greengages, especially the choicer Mirabelle or Transparent varieties, are worth growing in pots as this is the only way to restrict their growth. They can then be taken under cover for the flowering and ripening periods. Greengages will need a rest in winter.

### Ornamental and Wildlife Value

As for plums (page 35).

### Harvesting and Storing

Greengages are loved by the supermarkets green and hard, as in that condition they keep for weeks. Picked fully ripe off the tree they are delectable, but do not last, especially if wet. They can be jammed, turned into cheeses, juiced or frozen if stoned first.

### Pruning and Training

They are usually grown as low standards or bushes with remedial pruning in late spring once the shape has formed. Overladen branches need propping, but not as much as for plums. As they also tend to irregular bearing, thinning of heavy crops is sensible, but not as effective as for most fruits. Gages are best worked like plums in a herring-bone pattern on a wall, and summer pruned.

### Maintenance Calendar

*Spring* Protect blossom from frost, weed, mulch, spray with seaweed solution, then prune.
*Summer* Put out wasp traps.
*Autumn* Remove mummified fruits.
*Winter* Protect buds from birds with cotton or nets.

### Weed, Pest and Disease Control

As greengages are so sweet they suffer particularly from bird damage, and the buds are attacked as well as the fruits! The damage caused also allows dieback to get a foothold, so trees need netting or cottoning over the winter in bird-infested areas. Wasps also make a mess of the crop, so be prepared to be ruthless!

### Propagation

Gages are usually grafted on to Myrobalan stocks, but newer dwarfing stocks mean that it is easier to fit them on to walls. Cuttings can be taken in late autumn with some success and the oldest varieties come nearly true from stones.

# COMPANION PLANTING

Greengages benefit from being positioned on the sheltered, sunny side of the larger plums.

# OTHER USES

Prunelle (left) is a liqueur from Alsace and Angers, made from Mirabelles. Slivovitsa, an *eau-de-vie*, comes from the Balkans.

# CULINARY USES

They make the best plum jams. True Mirabelle jam is almost apricot flavoured, but even better.

### Greengage Jam
Makes 2kg/4lb

*1kg/2lb greengages*
*1kg/2lb sugar*
*a little water*

Wash, halve and stone the gages. Crack a few stones, extract the kernels and add these to the fruit. Pour in enough water to cover the bottom of the pan and simmer until the fruit has softened. Add the sugar and bring rapidly to the boil, then carefully skim, jar and seal.

*Prunus* species from the order *Rosaceae*

# DAMSONS

## BULLACES AND JAPANESE PLUMS

*Tree/bush up to 5m/16ft. Long-lived, some self-fertile.*
*Fruits: 2cm/1in. Some vitamin value.*

Bullaces (*P. insititia*) have globular, bluey-black or greeny-yellow fruits which ripen in late autumn, at least a month later than most other plums. The fruits are small and generally too acid to eat raw, but make good preserves. The trees are sometimes thorny. Damsons (*P. damascena*) are closely related to bullaces, with larger, blue-black fruit which more closely resemble plums. However, they are more oval, with less bloom, and have a sweet, spicy flavour once cooked. Damson trees are compact and are reasonably self-fertile. The **cherry plum** or **Myrobalan** (*P. cerasifera*) is less brittle and can be woven into hedges; it is often used as a windbreak. The white flowers open at the same time as the leaves, which are glossier than those of other plums. They are self-fertile. The fruits are yellow, red or purple, spherical and a little pointed at the bottom. They have a sweet, juicy, if somewhat insipid, flesh and make good jam.

Japanese plums (*P. salicina* and *P. triflora*) are large, conical, orangey-red or golden fruits without much flavour. They blossom early and are vulnerable to cold, but they are also more productive and tolerant of a wider range of warm conditions than ordinary plums, so are extensively grown in Australia, South Africa and the USA. They have shiny, dark twigs, white flowers on bold spurs and leaves which turn a glorious red in autumn.

Bullaces are native to Europe and Asia Minor, but the current apparently wild stock has probably been inadvertently selected over the centuries. Damsons come from Damascus, or certainly that region, and were brought to Europe during the Crusades in the twelfth century, supposedly by the Duke of Anjou, after a pilgrimage to Jerusalem. Cherry plums come from the Balkans, Caucasus and Western Asia and were introduced to Britain in the sixteenth century. Some of these went to the New World and were interbred with American native species to cope with the harsher climatic conditions. Japanese plums, originally natives of China, were introduced to Japan about 1500 and only to the USA in 1870. Being rather tender they have never really expanded into Europe.

## VARIETIES

The choice of Bullaces is down to the purpley-blue **Black Bullace** or the greeny-yellow **Shepherd's Bullace**. Though now difficult to find, the common wild plum of central Europe, **Zwetsche** or **Quetsche**, the source of many good liqueurs, has blue-black berries with golden-yellow flesh on a compact but twiggy tree. Damsons are now found in only three varieties: **Farleigh**, from Kent, is a heavy cropper if well pollinated and a sturdy bush often used as a windbreak; **Merryweather** has slightly larger fruits with greenish-yellow flesh, earlier in autumn; the **Shropshire**, or **Prune damson**, which ripens last, has the better flavour, but is a light cropper. **Cherry plums** are most often called **Red** or **Yellow Myrobalans**. There are several ornamental forms that may fruit; some have pink flowers, many are purple-leaved. Japanese plums, such as **Burbank**, may be available. Similar is **Beauty**, which is red with sweet, juicy, yellow flesh that clings to the stone.

**Immature fruits and leaves of Merryweather**

## CULTIVATION

A Merryweather damson tree with tansy in foreground

Most of these are more tolerant of soil and site conditions than true plums, except for the Japanese, which require warmer conditions.

### Growing under Glass and in Containers

As most of these plum types are hardy and culinary, it seems unprofitable to fruit them under cover. If only small quantities are required then these plums could be tried in pots.

### Ornamental and Wildlife Value

The trees are not imposing until they flower, then they froth and foam. Later their displays of fruiting profligacy are quite stupendous. Great masses of fruits continue to feed the wildlife through many months.

### Maintenance Calendar

As for plums (see page 35).

### Propagation

Most types do well on Myrobalan stocks and many on their own roots. Japanese plums can bear in three years or so, the others maybe in five. Those on their own roots can be grown from suckers, and seedlings of most will come nearly true.

### Pruning and Training

As for plums, these are best left alone except for remedial work.

### Weed, Pest and Disease Control

These varieties of plums are generally not as susceptible to brown rot as true plums.

### Harvesting and Storing

Bullaces and damsons are supposedly mellowed and taste better raw after frosts, but the birds will have eaten them by then.

## CULINARY USES

### Damson Cheese
Makes 2.5kg/5lb

*1.5kg/3lb damsons about1kg/2lb light brown sugar*

Almost all of these fruits are now used only culinarily for jamming, jellying, fruit cheeses, winemaking and liqueurs.

Wash the fruit and then simmer till soft with just enough water to prevent burning. Sieve and boil the pulp with three-quarters its own weight of sugar. Cook until the scum has finished rising and the jam is clear. Pot the pulp in warmed oiled bowls and seal.

## COMPANION PLANTING

Avoid anemones which harbour plum rust.

## OTHER USES

As hedges and windbreaks the bullaces and cherry plums are excellent. Damsons can be planted in sheltered sections.

Merryweather damsons with fruit

*Prunus armeniaca* from the order *Rosaceae*

# APRICOTS

*Tree up to 6m/20ft. Hardy, deciduous, self-fertile. Fruits: 3x5 cm/1½ x2in. yellow/orange. Value: rich in vitamin A and potassium.*

This small tree has white flowers (occasionally tinged with pink) very early in spring, well before the leaves emerge. These are spade-shaped and often glossy. The young shoots can also appear glossy as if varnished in red or brown. The leaves are more similar to those of a plum than those of a cherry or peach and apricot fruits closely resemble some plums but the stone is more spherical and the flavour distinct. Some think that **Moorpark**, one of the commonest varieties, is a plumcot (a plum-apricot hybrid).

The first apricots came from China or Siberia, not Armenia where Alexander the Great found them. The fruits became loved by the Romans, but they never succeeded in transplanting any to northern Europe. Apricots reached Britain in the thirteenth century and were introduced again, more successfully, in the sixteenth. **Bredase** may be the oldest variety in cultivation. It closely resembles descriptions of Roman apricots.

**Moorpark in flower**

## VARIETIES

**New Large Early** is the first, **Alfred** and **Farmingdale** ripen next and the latter has some dieback resistance. **Moorpark** is exquisite; the traditional variety, it ripens a little later. **Hemskerke** is early and worth trying on walls in cold areas. Also available are **Breda**, **Bredase**, **Goldcot**, **Hongaarse**, **Shipley's Blenheim** and **Tross Orange**. **Hunza** wild apricots of northern India can be grown from the stones of dried fruits bought in natural food shops. They make large bushes with more ornamental than cropping potential. The **Japanese Apricot**, *Prunus mume*, has scented flowers and sour fruit, usually eaten salted or pickled.

## CULTIVATION

Like most stone fruits, apricots need a cold winter period to rest and warm summers to ripen the fruit. The plants themselves are tough, but the flowers are so early that they are always in danger from frost. The soil should not be heavy nor the site wet. In most cool areas they will only crop reliably against a wall.

### Ornamental and Wildlife Value

Apricots are not noticeable trees, though the flowers are pretty enough. Ornamental varieties and **Hunzas** are attractive but unfruitful. Their earliness makes the flowers useful to bees and beneficial insects.

### Growing under Glass and in Containers

Grown under glass, apricots are more sure to crop if allowed a cold resting period, so do not plant in continuously heated greenhouses. A better plan may be to confine them in large pots. Keep these outside unless very cold, bring them under glass for flowering and take them back outside again once the weather is warm.

**Moorpark fruits well on a warm wall**

### Pruning and Training

The least work is to grow apricots as trees, only removing dead and diseased wood as necessary. Cut out all the dieback until no discoloration is seen. The wood is brittle, so watch for overladen branches and prop or prune early. On walls, build a fan of old wood with fruiting spurs. Prune the frame and any dieback in late winter, then prune again in summer to restrict the growth.

### Weed, Pest and Disease Control

Apricots are not particularly bothered by pests. Ants may introduce and farm scale insects and occasionally caterpillars and aphids may be seen. Apricots do suffer from dieback and gummosis, however, the twigs dying back and resiny gum oozing out of the branches or, worse, the trunk. Both these conditions are symptomatic of poor growth and every effort should be made to improve the conditions; fewer weeds, more compost, more mulches, more water or better aerated roots, seaweed sprays and hard pruning should do it.

### Propagation

Apricot trees are obtained budded on to suitable rootstocks, such as St Julien A in the UK. This is better for wetter, heavier soils; seedling peach or apricot rootstocks suit lighter, drier ones. Successful trees have been raised from stones.

### Maintenance Calendar

*Spring* Cover flowers on frosty nights, weed, mulch and spray with seaweed solution monthly.
*Summer* Thin the fruits early, summer prune, bag fruits against wasps and birds.
*Autumn* Keep weeded, tie in new shoots.
*Winter* Protect from really hard frosts, prune out dieback.

### Harvesting and Storing

Apricots ripened on the tree are heavenly, but soon go over. Picked young enough to travel, they never develop full flavour. Thus they are best eaten straight away, or jammed or frozen.

**Alfred trees espalier-trained after fruiting**

## CULINARY USES

Apricots make scrumptious jam and can be preserved in brandy and syrup. Unlike the majority of Prunus fruits most apricot kernels are sweet and edible and can be used to make ratafia biscuits.

### Apricot Sponge
Serves 6–8

*500g/1lb apricots*
*knob butter*
*coarse, light brown sugar*

For the sponge:
*55g/2oz each of butter, fine, light brown sugar, white self-raising flour*
*1 large egg ,a splash of milk real vanilla extract*

Halve and stone the apricots (score or remove the skin if you prefer) and place in a buttered flan dish, cut side up. Sprinkle with coarse sugar. Cream together the butter and sugar, stir in the egg, then fold in the flour, together with the milk if the mixture is stiff, and the vanilla extract. Spoon the sponge mixture over the apricots and cook in a preheated oven at 190°C/375°F/gas mark 5 for about half an hour. When cold, turn out and serve with whipped cream.

## COMPANION PLANTING

Do not grow tomatoes, potatoes or oats near apricots, but they benefit from *alliums* nearby, especially garlic and chives.

## OTHER USES

The wood is brittle, but of use as kindling.

*Prunus persica* from the order *Rosaceae*

# PEACHES

*Tree/bush up to 5x5m/16x16ft. Generally short-lived. Self-fertile, deciduous.*
*Fruits: 6–8cm 2½–3½in, yellow, orange, red. Value: rich in vitamin A, potassium and niacin.*

Peach trees are small and resemble willows, with long, lightly serrated leaves. They bloom before the leaves appear. The smaller the flowers, the darker rose coloured they are, with the largest being lightest pink. Flowering a fortnight later than almonds, they are closely related, the almond having a tough, inedible, leathery skin over a smooth stone. Peach skin has a partition line along which it easily splits. Most peach stones are ribbed or perforated with small holes in the shell. In varieties known as clingstones the flesh clings to this shell; in others, the freestones, the fruit is free and easier to enjoy without having to tease it off the stone. The flesh may vary from white to yellow; there are even blood peaches with red staining. The texture varies with cultivar, soil and climate. The skin colour can be from dull green through yellows and orange to dark red. The most distinctive feature of peaches is the soft downy fluff on the skin.

The peach was known three hundred years BC to the Greek philosopher Theophrastus, who thought it came from Persia, and so it became named. Early Hebrew writings make no reference to it, neither is there a Sanskrit name, so it seems likely peaches did not reach Europe to any extent until shortly before the Christian period. Dioscorides mentions the peach during the first century, as does Pliny, who states that the Romans had only recently imported it from Persia.

Peaches are, in fact, of Chinese origin. They are mentioned in the books of Confucius from the first century BC, and can be traced back to the tenth century BC in artistic representations. The Chinese still have an immense number of varieties and these were initially spread by seed. The stones produce trees with ease, but of course do not come true. The variability may have accounted for the slow spread to Europe. However, this was more likely to have been because peaches were initially tried in hot countries at too low altitudes. Thus the trees did not get their winter dormancy and would have fruited badly, effectively discouraging further experiments. Pliny indeed mentions that peach trees were taken from Egypt to the island of Rhodes, but this transplantation did not succeed; they were then brought on to Italy.

It took till the middle of the sixteenth century for peaches to reach England and in 1629 a quantity of peach stones was ordered by the Governor of the Massachusetts Bay Colony of New England. The peach found its new home in North America highly suitable and spread abundantly. In fact it spread so rapidly through the wild that it was thought to be a native fruit. Peaches spread so widely that they had conquered much of South America by Darwin's time. He spotted them on islands in the mouth of the Parana, along with thickets of similarly fugitive orange trees.

**Rochester is a prolific fruiter**

## VARIETIES

**Amsden June** is early with greenish-white flesh, semi-freestone and a month behind its name. **Duke of York** has better flavoured, creamy white flesh and is also semi-freestone. **Hale's Early** has pale yellow flesh and is freestone. **Peregrine** is the best choice for a bush tree in the UK and has yellowish-white flesh of excellent flavour. It is freestone and comes mid-season. **Rochester** is my second favourite for a bush; it is not quite so well flavoured and yellow fleshed. **Royal George** comes late, has tasty, big, yellow fruits, flushed dark red with pale, yellowish-white flesh and a small free stone, but is prone to mildew. **Bellegarde** is a heavy freestone cropper of beautiful red fruits, produced so late that in cooler areas the fruits will often not ripen. But with a wall, under glass, or in a warmer climate Bellegarde can be excellent. Varieties also now available include: **Alexandra Noblesse, Barrington, Dymond.**

## CULTIVATION

Peaches ideally need a well enriched, well aerated, but moist piece of soil. They prefer open gravelly soils to heavy, and need to be planted at least 6m/20ft apart. If they take (peaches do not always), they establish quickly and need no staking after the first year. They need copious quantities of compost annually and mulches are obligatory to ensure the constant moisture they demand. Where they are planted against walls, great care must be taken to ensure adequate water constantly throughout the season or the fruits will split. However, they are most intolerant of any waterlogging. Peaches also should not be planted near to almonds, as the two fruits may hybridise, resulting in bitter nuts.

### Growing under Glass and in Containers
Peaches are often grown under glass, where the extra efforts of replenishment pruning and tying in are repaid by gorgeous, succulent, early fruits free from the depredations of birds. The greenhouse must be unheated in winter to give peaches a dormant rest period. More problems occur under cover – the red spider mite can be especially troublesome unless a high humidity is maintained. Peaches are good subjects for large pots as they can take heavy pruning if well fed and watered. Pots enable them to be kept under cover during the winter and through flowering and then brought out all summer, thus avoiding peach leaf curl and frost damage. The flowers must be protected from frosts and so must the young fruitlets. The flowers are more susceptible to frost damage after pollination and the fruitlets likewise for a further fortnight.

### Ornamental and Wildlife Value
The peach is a pleasure to have. The willowy leaves are held well into autumn and the sight of a good crop of fruits is magnificent. The blossom is wonderful too; peaches in bloom are a joy. The wildlife value of the tree is rather low in wet areas as the trees succumb to leaf curl, but in some drier areas peaches become weeds and are appreciated by birds, insects and rodents.

### Pruning and Training
Peaches fruit on young shoots, thus it is essential to have plenty of these growths. They are best obtained by a partial pollarding operation late each winter. This makes the pruning more akin to that of blackcurrants than to that of most other tree fruits. Basically the top ends of the higher branches are removed to encourage prolific growth from the lower branches and stubs. This also serves to keep the peach bushes lower and more manageable.

On walls and under cover, peaches are usually fan trained. Selected young shoots are allowed to spring from a main frame and then tied in to replace the previous growths once those have fruited.

Fortunately, if the pruning of peaches is temporarily neglected, healthy bushes respond to being cut back hard by throwing plentiful young growths. More important than pruning is thinning. Peaches are prone to overcropping, breaking branches and exhausting themselves. Thin the fruits hard, removing those touching or anywhere near each other. Do this very early and then again later.

**Duke of York in a greenhouse**

## Maintenance Calendar

*Spring* Protect tree from leaf disease with Bordeaux sprays before buds open and blossom. Protect blossoms from frost. Hand pollinate. Weed, mulch and spray with seaweed solution monthly.
*Summer* Thin the fruits early, and often. Protect fruits from birds and wasps.
*Autumn* Remove mummified fruits from the trees.
*Winter* Prune hard. Spray with Bordeaux mixture.

## Propagation

Peaches can be raised from stones, but the results are haphazard and take years to fruit. Budded on to suitable stocks, St Julien A in the UK, for example, peaches will normally fruit in their third year. Plum stocks are more resistant to wet, but for warmer, drier conditions seedling apricot or peach rootstocks are better.

## Weed, Pest and Disease Control

Peaches suffer most losses from birds and wasps. Small net or muslin bags will protect the crop. Earwigs can get inside the fruits and eat the kernel out, but are readily trapped in rolls of corrugated paper around each branch. Protect the bark from animals such as rabbits and deer. Peaches get minor diseases such as peach scab, but their main problem is peach leaf curl. This puckers and turns the leaves red and yellow and they cease to function properly. Severe attacks cripple the tree and can even kill it. Keeping the plant dry under cover or under a plastic sheet prevents the disease almost completely. Spraying with Bordeaux mixture prevents the disease if done several times as the buds are opening in late winter. Dieback and gummosis are symptomatic of poor growth and are best treated by heavy mulching and hard pruning in very late winter.

**Peach jam**

## Harvesting and Storing

A truly ripe peach is a bag of syrup waiting to burst. If picked under-ripe the flesh never develops the full gamut of flavour, or the liquidity. A good peach is a feast, drink and all. As with so many fruits, they are best eaten straight off the tree. They can be picked a few days early if handled with absolute care. Kept cool, they may last. The slightest bruising, however, and they decompose.

## COMPANION PLANTING

Peaches are benefited by *alliums*, especially garlic and chives. Clover or alfalfa leguminous green manures give the richness they need. Nettles nearby are reputedly helpful in preventing the fruit from moulding.

## OTHER USES

Peach stones are used for making activated charcoal for filters. The wood is brittle, but the prunings make good kindling. In some countries, gluts of peaches are used for feeding the local livestock.

**Peregrine blossom**

## CULINARY USES

Peach jam is more aromatic than plum and a glorious use for the many fruits that never look like ripening intact or early enough. Fruits can be frozen for winter use and retain some texture afterwards. The juice is the nectar of the gods, and peaches will also make excellent chutneys.

### Peach Macaroon Cheesecake
Serves 4–6

*125g/4oz macaroons*
*125g/4oz digestive biscuits*
*100g/3oz butter, melted*
*1kg/2lb peaches*
*15g/½ oz gelatine*
*250g/8oz cottage cheese*
*125g/4oz natural yoghurt*
*100g/3oz honey or peach jam*
*few drops vanilla essence*
*125g/4oz alpine strawberries*

Crush the macaroons and biscuits and mix with the butter. Press into a flan dish. Peel, slice and chill the peaches. Simmer the skins and stones in minimal hot water, sieve and dissolve the gelatine in the warm liquid. Beat the cottage cheese, yoghurt, honey or jam and vanilla, then stir in the gelatine. Immediately pour over the biscuit base, chill and leave to set. Top with peach slices and alpine strawberries.

*Prunus persica* from the order *Rosaceae*

# NECTARINES

**Tree up to 5m/16ft. Generally short-lived, self-fertile, deciduous.**
**Fruits: up to 8cm/3in, greenish yellow, orange and red.**
**Value: rich in vitamin A, potassium and niacin, as well as riboflavin and vitamin C.**

**Elruge**

In almost every way nectarines are just varieties of peach. However, there are several subtle and fascinating differences. Nectarines are more difficult to grow and are less hardy. The fruits are smaller, on average, than peaches. The flesh is firmer and less melting than a peach and more plum-like, less prone to falling apart while you eat it. Nectarines have a definite, almost peculiar, rich, vinous flavour quite distinct and in addition to that of a well ripened peach. The colour of some nectarines also makes them distinguishable from peaches, as many of the older varieties have a greenish or sometimes even a purplish hue over a quite yellowish or greenish  ground. Most noticeably, nectarines do not have that downy fuzz on the skin so typical of peaches, but instead are smooth and shiny; indeed they closely resemble a very large plump plum.

Darwin noted how peach trees occasionally spontaneously produced nectarines, and also the converse; he even noted the case of a nectarine tree that produced a fruit that was half peach, half nectarine and then reverted to peaches. Despite the peach's long history of cultivation, however, rather strangely no mention is made of nectarines by pre-Christian authors. Pliny mentions an unknown fruit, a duracina, but the first, if indirect, reference is by Cieza de Leon, who lived in the early sixteenth century and described a Caymito of Peru as being 'large as a nectarine'. They were seen growing amongst peaches in Virginia in 1720 and A.J. Downing listed 19 varieties in the USA by 1857. Many dozens of peach varieties are now in cultivation, and travellers also report local varieties of nectarine in most of the world's peach growing areas, so that their spontaneous emergence is not really a rare phenomenon.

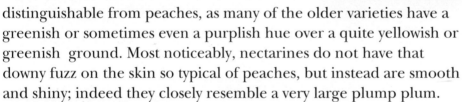

**Early Rivers**

## VARIETIES

**Early Rivers**, white-fleshed and the earliest, comes just before **John Rivers**. It is followed by **Lord Napier**, a tasty, white-fleshed mid-season, succeeded in turn by **Elruge**. **Pineapple** is late and may fail to ripen in many cooler areas.

## CULTIVATION

Nectarines need even better conditions than peaches do. Good water control is critical to prevent the fruit splitting, so thick mulches are obligatory. They are less likely to set crops as bushes than peaches, so in any cool region they must be given a wall or extra shelter.

**Lord Napier**

### Growing under Glass and in Containers

Nectarines are more suited than many plants to culture under glass, preferring warmer conditions than are found in most temperate areas. However, they must be given a cool period of rest each winter or they will be unfruitful, so they can only really be grown in greenhouses unheated through winter. They can be grown in large pots and can fruit successfully, but only if religious attention is given to watering. Hand pollination is desirable.

### Pruning and Training

Also exactly as for the peach.

### Propagation

Nectarines sometimes come from peach stones and vice versa. More often they occur when a peach bud produces a sport. Most varieties are budded on suitable stocks as for peaches.

### Weed, Pest and Disease Control

In the USA nectarines are not much grown away from the Pacific coast as a common pest, plum curculios, can easily do much damage to their smooth skins. Spray against peach leaf curl.

### Ornamental and Wildlife Value

Nectarines are almost exactly the same as peaches and are attractive, with the long, glossy leaves being held late into the season. The pink flowers are beautiful and appreciated by early insects; the lack of fruits reduces their wildlife interest. Nectarines require spraying to prevent peach leaf curl in many areas, so cannot be left to themselves.

### Maintenance Calendar

Exactly as for the peach.

### Harvesting and Storage

Also as for the peach.

Nectarines can be used in similar ways to peaches, but as their skin is not fuzzy it is less of a barrier and makes them more toothsome to eat fresh. The firm flesh is also less melting and reduces one's need for a bib to catch half the juice as with a ripe peach. This makes the nectarine a civilised fruit for eating at the dinner table, and this is only enhanced by the succulent vinous flavour.

### *Nectarine Melba*
(all quantities according to taste)

*nectarines, honey, vanilla pod
vanilla ice-cream (the real sort!)
frozen raspberries,
bitter chocolate, nutmeg*

Halve, peel and stone, say one ripe nectarine per person. Poach half of them, those that are the least decomposingly ripe, in a syrup made by gently warming the vanilla pod in the honey. Poach the nectarines very gently until they are tender but not breaking down, then drain and chill well. Create a bed of vanilla ice-cream, interspersed with the chilled ripest halves. Lay the poached halves on this base. Crush the frozen raspberries in the drained honey syrup. Chill, then pour over the nectarines followed by a generous grating of bitter chocolate and a hint of nutmeg.

# COMPANION PLANTING

Again as for the peach.

# OTHER USES

As for peaches.

*Prunus avium* from the order *Rosaceae*

# SWEET CHERRIES

*Tree up to 10m/33ft.  Long lived, deciduous, not self-fertile.*
*Fruits: 2cm/1in, yellow, red, black, rich in ribflavin.*

Although described as sweet cherries some varieties, and particularly wild ones, are not actually sweet. Tall trees, often reaching over 9m/30ft, with white blossoms, occasionally pink, which are a massive display at about the same time as the peach. The leaves are plum-like with a lengthening and thinning at the tip. Dangling in pairs on long pedicels, the near spherical fruits hang in groups along the fruiting branches. The flesh is cream or yellow, sweet or bitter, but once ripe is rarely acid.

**Morello blossom**

The wild form native to Europe, known as the bird cherry, gean or mazzard, is of little value as fruit except in Central Europe, where it is used for liqueurs. Mazzards, little improved from the wild version, still survive and have richly flavoured black fruits only slightly larger than the wild. They make good seedling stocks for better varieties, though if left to themselves they can grow to 20m/70ft or more high. Gean fruits were thought to have softer more melting flesh and varieties called **Bigarreau** had a crisp texture. Years of continuous selection and cross breeding have given us sweet cherries of mixed parentage. One group, the Duke or Royal cherries, have some Morello blood which serves to make them tasty and lightly acid as well as generally more hardy.

## CULTIVATION

Sweet cherries are very particular to soil and site. They need plentiful moisture at the roots but loathe waterlogging and need a very rich but well aerated soil. Poor soil conditions can be helped by growing through grass and was the traditional manner.

### Growing under Glass and in Containers

As the trees get so big and are particular to site and weather, pot cultivation is the most effective way to get cherries. In this way you avoid damage to the flowers from frost or rain and likewise protect the fruits. Do let the trees have a cool dormant period in winter.

## VARIETIES

There are countless varieties, but finding combinations compatible for pollination is difficult so most useful cherries for private orchards are partly self-fertile. One is **May Duke** which is very early, often ripening before the longest day, and will even fruit on a north wall. **Stella** is fully self-fertile, a vigorous and upright tree with sweet, dark red fruits a month later. **Sunburst** is another new self-fertile cherry. **Governor Wood** and **Napoleon Bigarreau** are my favourite mutually compatible pair. The former has red fruits a week or so before the yellow of the latter, which makes the bigger tree. One useful alternative is any late flowering cherries you want (there are many **Merton** varieties worth considering) and also a **Morello** to pollinate them successfully.

**Stella**

### Ornamental and Wildlife Value

Sweet cherries are quite staggering to behold in blossom, as if festooned with snow. The fruits are one of the most addictive to birds, and they will come despite all discouragement. The number of pests suggests that cherries must benefit some wildlife immensely.

### Propagation

Normally budded on to strong growing rootstocks which make for big trees, they are now offered on dwarfing stocks such as **Colt**. This makes them smaller and easier to constrain. Stones grow, but take years to fruit and get tall by then.

### Pruning and Training

Prune as little as possible after the initial head formation. Any pruning must be done early during the growing season and then only to remove any dead and diseased growth.

### Weed, Pest and Disease Control

Cherries really suffer from bird damage, but at least escape the wasps by fruiting early in summer. Bacterial canker can kill the tree, and there are several virus diseases, but these are only treatable by improving the conditions. Warm drizzle during flowering can cause the flowers to mould and a sudden heavy rain during ripening invariably succeds in splitting the fruits.

### Maintenance Calendar

*Spring* Protect the flowers, weed, mulch and spray seaweed solution monthly. Prune if necessary.
*Summer* Protect the fruits from birds with netting or muslin sleeves.

### Harvesting and Storing

Cherries can be picked and kept for several days if absolutely dry. Leave them on the sprigs and do not pack them deep. They can be frozen, but are fiddly as they are better stoned first.

## COMPANION PLANTING

They are normally grown in grass sward, include clover and alfalfa, to give more fertility. Cherries supposedly suppress wheat and make potatoes prone to blight.

## OTHER USES

Cherry wood is much loved by turners and makes a sweet firewood.

**Governor Wood**

**Traditional cherrywood and kingwood secretaire**

## CULINARY USES

Sweet cherries often do not make as good culinary dishes as sour cherries because many lack acidity. Their jams and jellies are better combined with redcurrant or whitecurrant juice for this reason.

### Pickled Cherries
Makes about 3½lb/1.5kg

*1kg/2lb cherries*
*300ml/½pt vinegar*
*500g/1lb sugar*
*6 cloves*
*15g/½oz fresh ginger, peeled*
*    and chopped*
*hint of cinnamon*

Wash and stone (if desired) the cherries. Dissolve the sugar in the heated vinegar and add the spices. Simmer the cherries in the spiced vinegar for a few minutes, then pack them into warmed jars, and cover with the vinegar. Seal and store.
    Eat with pâtés, cold meats and especially quiches.

### Cherry Jam

*2.25kg/5lb cherries*
*3 lemons, squeezed*
*1.25kg/3½lb sugar*

Wash the fruit thoroughly, remove stalks and stones. Put the fruit into a pan with the lemon juice and simmer gently for 30–35 minutes. Warm the sugar and add it to the cherries over a gentle heat and allow the sugar to dissolve. Then bring the jam to a rapid boil and continue boiling until setting point is reached; this will take about 15 minutes. Test for setting point, remove from the heat and leave for 5 minutes. Pot and cover. Store in a dry place.

*Prunus cerasus* from the order *Rosaceae*

# MORELLO CHERRIES

## SOUR CHERRIES AND OTHERS

*Tree up to 8m/27ft.    Long-lived, deciduous, self-fertile.*
*Fruits:    2cm/¾ in, crimson to black. Value: rich in vitamin A.*

Morello cherries are similar to sweet cherries, except they are not sweet, so are only useful for culinary purposes. The trees are smaller than sweet varieties, with slightly lax, more twiggy branches and greener foliage that does not have such a red tinge when young. The fruits have shorter stalks, tend to have darker colours and are more acid.

Sour cherries were selected from *Prunus cerasus* (also known as *P. acida*) which grew wild around the Caspian and Black Seas. In about 300 BC sour cherries were known to the Greek Theophrastus and proved so popular with the Romans, who developed at least half a dozen different varieties, that by the time of Pliny, in the first century AD, sour cherries had already long reached Britain. However, during the Dark Ages, the art of their cultivation was lost and the trees had to be re-introduced to England in the sixteenth century by Henry VIII, who had them brought from Flanders. They were soon adopted by the growers of Kent and by 1640 they had over two dozen varieties. The first cherries to reach the New World, the **Kentish Red**, were planted by the Massachusetts colonists.

**Fan-trained Morello, Kentish Red**

## VARIETIES

Before the Second World War more than fifty varieties of Morello and sour cherry were in cultivation, and almost every country had its own wide choice. Now few are grown commercially and only the generic **Morello** is offered by most suppliers. This last favourite, namesake for all its disappearing brethren, is deep crimson to black in colour with a richly bitter, slightly sweet flavour. Late flowering, it misses more frosts than sweet cherries so is more reliable and ripens in mid to late summer, towards the end of August in southern England. It is self-fertile, and would pollinate almost any other cherry of any type if the flowering period was not so late in the season. **Red Morellos**, **Amarelles** or **Griottes** are closely related, slightly more stubby trees with red fruits which are probably of mixed origin. The **Kentish Red** has endured since at least 1700. It is self-fertile with a scarlet skin, soft flesh and is only slightly bitter. It ripens in mid-summer. The **Flemish** is a similar cherry variety.

## CULTIVATION

Much the same conditions are needed as for pears, with an increased demand for nitrogen and even more water than needed by sweet cherries. Though the trees will do badly if they are waterlogged, they are more tolerant of poor drainage than sweet cherries.

## OTHER USES

The prunings make good kindling.

**Cherry jam**

**Red Morello cherries**

### Growing under Glass and in Containers
Although this would be possible, it would usually be more worthwhile to nurture sweet cherries, especially as Morellos will even crop on a cold wall in cool areas.

### Ornamental and Wildlife Value
Not as elegant or floriferous a tree as the sweet cherry, so less ornamental value. However, morellos are well-loved by birds and the early flowers are good for insects.

### Maintenance Calendar
As for sweet cherries.

### Propagation
As for sweet cherries.

### Weed, Pest and Disease Control
Morellos and sour cherries are particularly unbothered by pests or diseases other than losses to birds.

### Pruning and Training
Morellos fruit on younger wood than do sweet cherries and thus they can be pruned harder. However, it is usually more convenient to stick to removing dead, diseased and congested growths in spring or summer. Usually grown as standards, they are ideal as low bushes for picking and bird protection, although they can also be trained as fans. They will even crop well on cold walls.

### Harvesting and Storing
Cut the cherries off the tree rather than risk damage by pulling the stalks. Morellos were one of the first fruits to be stored frozen and are one of the best. They can be frozen without sugaring and retain their flavour superbly.

### Companion Planting
As for sweet cherries.

## CULINARY USES

They are primarily a culinary fruit and make fabulous pies, tarts, jams and cakes.

### Blacker Forest Gâteau
(Serves 6–8)

*500g/1lb black cherries*
*125g/4oz honey*
*4 tablespoons kirsch*
*little water*

For the sponge:
*100g/4oz butter*
*100g/4oz fine light brown sugar*
*100g/4oz white flour*
*2 large or 3 small eggs*
*1 heaped teaspoon baking powder*
*1 heaped teaspoon cocoa powder*

For the filling:
*600ml/1 pt double cream*
*1 heaped teaspoon sugar*
*1 heaped teaspoon cocoa powder*
*vanilla extract*
*100g/4oz dark chocolate*

Wash and stone cherries. Dissolve the honey and kirsch in sufficient hot water just to cover the stoned fruits. Simmer till they soften, then strain (keeping the syrup) and chill. Mix the sponge ingredients and divide between three oiled or lined sandwich tins. Bake in a pre-heated oven at 170°C/325°F/gas mark 3 for about half an hour. Turn out and cool, then soak the sponge cakes in the syrup. Whip the cream, then stir in the sugar, cocoa powder and vanilla. Build up alternate layers of sponge, cream filling and fruit. Finish off with a covering of filling and grated chocolate.

*Morus nigra* and *Morus alba* from the order *Moraceae*

# MULBERRIES

*Tree up to 9m/30ft. Long-lived, hardy, deciduous, usually self-fertile.*
*Fruits: 2–3cm/1½–2¼in, purple, also red through pink.*

Mulberry trees are medium-sized trees with a round domed crown, formed by their habit of having no terminal bud on their over-wintering twigs. They can become big, gnarled and picturesque in advanced old age. The leaves are heart-shaped, toothed and occasionally lobed, lightly downy underneath but rough on top. The Black Mulberry, *M. nigra*, fruits are like loganberries, of a blackish dark red through purple when ripe and stain all they touch. The White Mulberry, *M. alba*, fruits are red or pinkish white, and slightly inferior to eat. There is a Red Mulberry (which can be almost black), native to North America, and several similar species in hotter climates.

Black Mulberries are thought to be native to Western Asia. Known at least since the time of the Greeks, they failed to become popular until the Roman Emperor Justinian encouraged them for the production of silk. The trees appeared all over the Empire and *Morus nigra* was not superseded by *Morus alba*, the more productive variety for feeding silkworms, until the sixteenth century. Exceptionally long-lived, the Black Mulberry may attain some stature; giants found in many parts of the world were planted during the seventeenth and early eighteenth centuries in vain attempts to foster local silk industries. Some mulberries such as *M. alba* var. *tatarica*, the Russian Mulberry, seed freely and become weeds. The Red Mulberry was native to the Northern Missouri region and along the Kansas river system, where it was an esteemed fruit.

**White Mulberry trees**

## VARIETIES

There is a named **Black Mulberry** variety, **Chelsea,** otherwise buy the species. The **Red Mulberry** (*M. rubra*) has red/black fruits and lovely autumn colour with bright yellow leaves; it is said to have the preferable fruit. The **White Mulberry** (*M. alba*) has wider leaves up to 15cm/6in across and is grown for silkworm fodder, though the fruit is quite edible, often red or pinkish and sweet. *M. alba* is also popular as an ornamental in many varieties. Cultivated mulberries are mostly self-fertile with unisexual flowers, though the species tend to be dioecious when growing in the wild.

## CULTIVATION

Mulberries succeed in any well drained soil, but the roots are brittle so these need care during planting, which is best done in early spring. They prefer a warm site, as typical of southern Britain, to fruit happily in the open, and are rarely bothered by late frost damage as they are tardy coming into leaf and flower. Normally they are grown in a fine grass sward to enable the fruit to be collected reasonably cleanly as it drops from the tree.

**Growing under Glass and in Containers**
This may be feasible, but I've not heard or read of it.

## Ornamental and Wildlife Value

Mulberries become gnarled and attractively grotesque as they age. The traditional situation is in the middle of a lawn with a circular wooden seat around the trunk. The berries are much appreciated by birds and small children.

## Weed, Pest and Disease Control

No significant pests or diseases bother the trees, other than the usual hazards of birds and small children.

## Maintenance Calendar

*Spring* Cut grass and spray seaweed solution monthly.
*Summer* Pick the fruits as they ripen and drop.
*Autumn* Cut grass and enjoy the seat occasionally.
*Winter* Thin and remove dead and diseased growths.

**Black Mulberry in fruit**

## Propagation

25–30cm/10–12in cuttings of newly ripened growth with a heel taken in December are ideal. Layering is possible as are (supposedly) whole branch cuttings.

## Pruning and Training

Mulberries can be pollarded hard to give the maximum foliage needed for feeding silkworms. If left to themselves, they make congested heads, so thin out twiggy, dead and diseased growths. Their narrow forks, big heads and brittle wood mean old trees should be carefully inspected and excess weight removed by a competent tree surgeon.

## Harvesting and Storage

Mulberries are aromatic and mouth-watering when fresh and ripe, but decompose rapidly so are really only of use as they drop and will not store or travel, though they can be frozen.

**Mulberry wood tea-caddy**

## COMPANION PLANTING

Mulberries must be grown in a grass sward if there is to be any hope of getting clean fruit. They were one of the traditional trees to support grapevines in classical times.

## OTHER USES

Of course you can try silkworm production and the foliage is palatable to other animals. The fruits will certainly make dye!

## CULINARY USES

The fruits can be made into jams or jellies, though they are usually combined and bulked out with apples, and the wine is an old country favourite.

### Mulberry No Fool
per person

*Clotted or thick fresh double cream*
*some honey*
*a pot of tea*
*biscuits*
*a mulberry tree in fruit and a sunny day off*

Take a cereal bowl with a large portion of clotted or thick cream, and the tea and biscuits. Sit peacefully under the mulberry tree, savouring the tea and biscuits while waiting for enough fruits to fall to fill your bowl. Then eat them with the cream and honey. In emergencies tinned or fresh fruit of any sort and a patio umbrella can be usefully substituted for the mulberries and tree!

*Ficus carica* from the order *Moraceae*

# FIGS

*Tree/bush, up to 9x7m/30x20ft.*
*Hardy, self-fertile. Fruits: pear-shaped,*
*6x10cm/2x4in, browny green.*

Fig leaves are large and distinctive, but vary in exact shape with each variety. Although figs are deciduous, young plants tend to be almost evergreen and are then more tender. Figs can be grown as trees or bushes, but are most often trained on walls. Almost all fig cultivars set the fruit parthenocarpically, without actual fertilisation. However, some old and mostly inferior varieties in hot climates have female fruiting plants and male caprifigs that are separately and specifically cultivated to produce female fig wasps. These wasps will crawl through the minute end hole into the fruits to pollinate them.

Figs are indigenous to Asia Minor and were one of the first fruits to be brought into cultivation. They thus became an intrinsic part of the diet of the Mediterranean basin long before classical times, though the Greeks claimed they were given to them by the goddess Demeter. Cato knew of six different figs, and two centuries later, in about 60 AD, Pliny notes no fewer than 29 varieties! Figs were certainly brought to England by the Romans as remains have been found, though the plants were not officially introduced until the early sixteenth century. There are over 600 fig species. Many of the varieties that we encounter today are ornamentals such as the **India Rubber Plant** (*Ficus elastica*), the **Weeping Fig** (*F. Benjamina*) and the **Fiddle leaf plant** (*F. lyrata*).

**Brunswick**

## VARIETIES

In the UK figs ripen from mid-August. **Brunswick** produces large fruits which are most tasty a couple of days after picking; **Brown Turkey** is reliably prolific; **White Marseilles** has pale fruits. Also: **Angelique, Black Ischia, Bourjasotte Grise, Castle Kennedy, Negro Large, Osborne's Prolific, Rouge de Bordeaux, St John's, Violette Dauphine, Violette Sepor, White Ischia** and, in the USA, **Adriatic, Celeste, Kadota, King, Magnolia (Brunswick), Mission.**

**Brown Turkey**

## CULTIVATION

Varieties vary in hardiness, but even if the tops are lost many will regrow from the roots if these are protected from the frost. Thus figs may be planted a little deep to encourage stooling. Often grown against a wall, they can be cropped in the open in southern Britain, their main enemy being the excessive wet rather than the cold. It is traditional to confine the roots of figs grown against walls to promote fruiting. This appears unnecessary if excessive feeding is avoided, but too much nitrogen will promote abundant undesirable soft growth.

### Growing under Glass and in Containers
Figs fruit and ripen much more reliably under glass, and with heat and care three crops a year are possible. Figs can be grown confined in large pots and can make excellent foliage plants for house or patio, though they will need careful watering and training.

### Ornamental and Wildlife Value
The very attractive foliage adds a luxuriant touch to a garden. Of little use to wildlife in colder climes, figs are much more valuable in hotter countries.

### Maintenance Calendar
*Spring* Remove frost protection, weed, spray seaweed solution monthly, and thin the fruits.
*Summer* Protect the fruits carefully from wasps and birds, make layers.
*Autumn* Remove all fruits of all sizes before frosts arrive.
*Winter* Prune, take cuttings, protect from frost.

**Figs stuffed with mascarpone, glacé mixed peel, a little honey and brandy to taste are delicious**

**Wall-trained fig**

### Propagation
Layers can be made during summer. 20cm/8in well-ripened or old wood cuttings taken during the early winter root, especially if given bottom heat. Seeds produce plants which are unlikely to fruit well.

### Pruning and Training
The most fruitful wood is well ripened, short jointed and sturdy; long soft shoots are unproductive and better removed. Figs can be pruned any time during dormancy, but are best left until growth is about to start in spring. More importantly, remove any fruit or fruitlet in autumn to prevent these starting into growth, failing and thereby spoiling the second crop that could otherwise succeed.

## CULINARY USES

Figs are delicious fresh and they can be made into jams, jellies, cheeses and chutneys.

### *Savoury & Sweet Figs*
Serves 4 as a snack or canapé

*12 dried figs*
*90g/3oz mild hard cheese*
*pinch of celery seed*
*1 shallot*
*50g/2oz marzipan*
*25g/1oz each sultanas and raisins*
*25g/1oz dark cooking chocolate*
*a little Cointreau or sweet liqueur*
*honey*

Stuff half the figs with some small chunks of cheese, a sprinkling of celery seeds and a thin slice of the shallot.

Grate the chocolate and marzipan. Mix in the dried fruit and liqueur, then stuff the remaining figs with this mixture. Smear all the figs with honey and put them in an oiled dish in a preheated oven at 180°C/350°F/gas mark 4 for 10 to 15 minutes. Serve the figs hot or cold.

### Weed, Pest and Disease Control
Fig plants have few problems except birds and wasps. Weeding must be thorough near the trunks to prevent rodents nibbling the bark. Under cover, on walls or in pots they may suffer from red spider mites.

### Harvesting and Storing
The fruits are soft-skinned and do not travel or store well once ripe. In hotter regions figs can be dried and will then keep well.

## COMPANION PLANTING

One of the few plants to get on well with rue.

## OTHER USES

Figs are known by many for their syrup, administered as a laxative. Also valuable as a food, they contain nearly half their weight in sugar when dried.

# SOFT, BUSH AND CANE FRUITS

I prefer to group these fruits as fruitcage fruits because this accurately describes their most common factor: without a cage most of them cannot effectively produce fruits at all. The reasons for their other names are fairly self-evident: soft, because they are not hard fruits such as apples, bush is self-descriptive and cane refers to the slender branches. (The term vine is applied differently depending on region; in some places it is used solely for grapes, in others to plants with long flexible branches, even cucurbits.)

The fruitcage members are grouped together by the gardener because they must be netted or grown in a cage. However, as with orchard fruits, most of them come from the *Rosaceae* family. They are shrubby perennials, not tree-like, and thus fairly compact, or can be kept so, quick to crop, and small fruited. Most are found growing naturally on the woodland's edge and thrive given moist root runs with plentiful humus-rich mould and thick mulches of leafy material. Most will grow and even crop in light shade, though of course they usually produce sweeter, better tasting fruit given more sun. Grape-vines will most obviously require much more sun than do the other plants of this group.

Rhubarb is anomalous on almost every point – but is included here as it enjoys the same general conditions. It is consequently often grown by gardeners near these true fruits and it immediately precedes them in both culinary and garden usage.

The majority of these fruits have been gathered from the wild native species since prehistory and their 'cultivation' will have occurred inadvertently around sites of human habitation, from waste heaps and primitive latrine arrangements. (Both, of course, afford remarkably well fertilised ground, and thus select for strains that could use such conditions.) Being fast growing plants and quick to crop, the proximity and opportunity would have created more, but still inadvertent, selection. Such a process would have produced much improved 'cultivars', spread by migrating peoples, and these may well have influenced wild populations. Certainly now some wild fruits such as the blackberry are just such hybrids in most areas, and it may well be that some supposed native species are in reality escaped cultivars from our distant past.

Thus the cropping potential of some wild fruits may have been raised over the millennia by our own unintended selection. In any case, the wild forms of most of these fruits were so productive and available in such vast quantities that they were simply not brought into cultivation until the end of the Middle Ages, with the important exception of grapes, which have been tended since prehistory. Some, such as the strawberry, have undergone intense development and hybridisation and so have improved dramatically, while others, such as aronia, have remained almost unaltered. Many closely related edible species are available which could be crossed with cultivated forms, so improved fruits may be only be an experiment or two away. The Tayberry is the result of one such crossing, and is better by far than all its similar predecessors.

*Rheum rhaponticum* from the order *Polygonaceae*

# RHUBARB
## PIE PLANT

*Herbaceous. 1x2m/3x7ft.   Life span: perpetual.*
*Fruits:   the stems, 2x60cm/1x24in.*

Manifestly rhubarb is not a fruit, but after several protests it is now included. This most British of fruits is apparently craved by tourists to Britain seeking traditional cuisine, who flock to motorway service stations for the eponymous crumble and custard. The stems are long, succulent and red with a very acid taste. Rhubarb is absolutely uneatable raw but widely popular cooked, probably because it is available so early in the year before true fruits arrive.

The first rhubarbs to arrive in Europe were for medical use. *R. rhaponticum* is noted first in Italy during 1608. It had been brought from Siberia for its laxative effect and was never eaten for pleasure initially. However, people are adventurous, and though the leaves are poisonous the stems proved tasty when cooked with sugar, as did the unopened *ëpouchesí* or flower heads which we no longer consume.

### Growing under Glass
Most commercial rhubarb is grown in blacked-out sheds from roots originally grown in the open, and discarded after use. However, rhubarb could be also grown as a conservatory border plant.

### Growing in Containers
Rhubarb is not very happy cropping perpetually in containers, but it can be briefly forced once and then planted out to recover.

Victoria, strawed up

### VARIETIES

It is worthwhile buying virus-free stock as the growth is then much stronger than from old infected stools. There are a surprising number of varieties with some differences in colour and taste. **Glaskin's Perpetual** is green and has low oxalic acid levels, so it can be eaten later into summer. **Victoria** is a late, strong grower and crops till well into summer. **Timperley Early** is one of the earliest and best for forcing, but has thin stems. In their native Himalayas other species are also eaten and/or used medicinally. One, *R. ribes*, was the currant-fruited rhubarb. Sadly this appears now to have been lost.

Glaskin's Perpetual in flower

### CULTIVATION

Rhubarb is often a neglected crop, seldom getting any attention other than a cursory strawing up and much pulling. It responds to richer conditions by growing well. For forcing, dig good roots in early winter and leave them exposed to cold for a fortnight. Then pot up and keep them in a warm, dark place. These produce better stalks with pale leaves months earlier than outdoor plants, but they are useless and exhausted afterwards.

### Maintenance Calendar
*Spring* Pull stems as required, propagate.
*Summer* Remove the blanching pot and straw, weed and tidy.
*Autumn* Add compost or a good mulch.
*Winter* Cover roots with straw and blanching pots.

### Ornamental and Wildlife Value
There are some inedible ornamental varieties, but ordinary rhubarb is itself imposing enough to be used in the flower garden. Rhubarb provides useful ground cover and dry shelter for small creatures.

### Propagation
**Glaskin's Perpetual** and the species can be grown from seed, otherwise pieces of root with a bud are transplanted or potted in early spring.

## Weed, Pest and Disease Control

Remarkably free of problems, though occasionally the crown may rot. Starting a new bed elsewhere is the best solution.

## Pruning and Training

Longer, tenderer, sweeter stems are had by forcing them to grow up through straw towards the light in a blanching pot, bottomless bucket or chimney pot. Cut out flowering stems before they blossom. After pulling finishes, remove the pot, straw, any mouldy stems and leaves. Weed carefully and mulch well with compost in the autumn.

## Harvesting and Storing

The stems are pulled, not cut. Twist outwards as you pull and the stem will detach cleanly. Remove the leaf and top of stem immediately, or the stem will wilt. Stalks will only keep a few days once detached, but stay good on the plant till mid-summer. They can be kept longer if stood in cool, clean water which is changed daily. Roots can be dug up and forced many months early to spread the season.

**Strawing rhubarb and covering with forcing pots brings an early spring crop**

## CULINARY USES

Rhubarb is eaten stewed, in pies, tarts or as the famous crumble. It can be jammed successfully or made into chutney and even wine.

### Rhubarb Crumble
Serves 4-6

*500g/1lb rhubarb*
*75g/3oz light brown sugar*
*splash of elderflower wine*
*or cider*

*For the crumble topping:*
*175g/6oz flour*
*75g/3oz butter*
*50g/2oz light brown sugar*
*hint of cinnamon*

Chop the washed rhubarb into short chunks and put in pie dish with the sugar and wine. Mix the crumble ingredients with your fingers until they resemble breadcrumbs; add more butter or a drop of water if they do not bind. Sprinkle on top of the rhubarb and bake in the oven at 190°C/375°F/ gas mark 5 for approximately 30 minutes, until it starts to brown. Rhubarb crumble must be served with custard, and for a traditional feel this ought to be a bright yellow proprietary brand.

## OTHER USES

Rhubarb leaves are poisonous and were once boiled with water and soft soap to make an aphicide. Many of the other species are used medicinally. The leaves make cool packing for other fruits.

## COMPANION PLANTING

Rhubarb is reputed to deter clubroot and root flies if pieces are planted in the holes with brassica roots.

**Victoria**

*Fragaria* hybrids from the order *Rosaceae*

# SUMMER STRAWBERRIES

Royal Sovereign

*Herbaceous. 30cm/1ft. Life span: short. Self-fertile. Fruits: up to 5x5cm/2x2in, red, conical.*
*Value: some vitamin C and half as much iron as spinach*

This most delicious of fruits really needs no introduction! Modern strawberries are hybrids based on *F. chiloensis*, the **Chilean Pine**, and *F. virginiana*, the **Scarlet Virginian**. The first contributed larger fruit with a pineapple tang and was brought to Europe in 1712; the latter, first mentioned in Massachusetts in 1621, provides the superior flavour, and is still grown commercially as **Little Scarlet** for jam-making. These two were first combined in the nineteenth century, with intensive development since. Every region has its favourite varieties.

## VARIETIES

There are far too many to list and new improved ones are continually becoming available. My favourites are:

**Royal Sovereign** (mid-season), beautifully flavoured if light cropping, originally introduced in 1892; **Silver Jubilee** (mid) is tasty with some disease resistance; **Cambridge Vigour** (early) is a commercial variety, but has rich flavour; **Late Pine** is also simply delicious.

## CULTIVATION

All preparation is well repaid. Strawberries need a very rich soil, full of humus, and benefit from slow-release phosphates, such as bone meal. Well rotted manure or compost, and/or seaweed meal dressings, will be recouped with better cropping. The more space you give them the better they will do and the less work they will be! 60cm/2ft each way is the minimum.

### Growing under Glass
They do not like the hot dry conditions under cover, and these also encourage red spider mite. However, the advantages of protection from birds, prevention of rain damage and earlier crops mean that they are widely grown under glass and plastic. For winter cropping, the new Californian day-length indeterminate types are far superior.

### Growing in Containers
Many containers, often tower shaped, are sold specifically for strawberries. While a good idea, the small amount of root run, hot in an above-ground position, and usually dry because of low water-holding capacity, make these poor growing conditions for strawberries. The plants respond with low yields, all of which occur in a short period, which makes them neglected for much of the year.

However, strawberries can be grown successfully in pots and containers. They need regular feeding as well as copious automatic watering!

### Ornamental and Wildlife Value
Rather too straggly to be considered decorative, they would make effective but short-lived ground cover and would not be very productive. By the losses, one must assume that they are valuable to birds!

### Maintenance Calendar
*Spring* Weed, root first runners, spray seaweed monthly.
*Summer* Weed, straw, protect from birds and mould, pick.
*Autumn* Establish new plants, tidy up the best, eradicate old.
*Winter* Rake up old leaves and mulch and compost them well.

### Propagation
Some special varieties can be grown from seed, but otherwise seed generally produces poor results. Runners are the obvious replacement, usually available to excess. These

**Cambridge Vigour**

**Tamella strawberries displayed on a tiered stand**

### Weed, Pest and Disease Control

Major losses are from birds and mould. Individual bunches can be protected from both with jam jars. Netting is usually obligatory. Mould can be decreased by strawing up and removing fruits that rot, preferably before the mould goes 'fluffy'. After fruiting has finished, tidy the plants, shearing back surplus runners and dead leaves, and in winter tidy them again, removing old straw as well for composting. Aphids spread the dreaded virus diseases, so you should buy in fresh clean stock every ten years or so.

## OTHER USES

As for perpetual strawberries (see page 63).

### Harvesting and Storage

Strawberries must be used quickly as they only keep for a day or so – they will last better picked with a stalk. They can be juiced and made into syrup, or jammed and jellied – the addition of apple, red- or whitecurrant juice will help with the setting. If frozen they will lose their delicate texture, but are still delicious.

## COMPANION PLANTING

Before establishing a new bed, dig in a green manure crop of soya beans to help prevent root rots. Growing borage, any of the beans or onions nearby reputedly helps strawberry plants.

## CULINARY USES

*Wimbledon Fortune*

Fresh strawberries, sprinkled with sugar, cream, a shortbread biscuit or two – and a small mortgage, unless enjoyed at home!

are best taken from quality plants which have been reserved for propagation and deflowered; half a dozen good ones, or many more poor, can be had thus. The first plantlet on an early runner is chosen, pinned or held to the ground – or preferably rooted into a pot of compost for an easier transplantation. Start new beds in late summer or early autumn to allow them to establish; they can then crop well the next summer. Late autumn or spring plantings should be deflowered the first summer to build up their strength for a massive crop the next.

### Pruning and Training

Strawberries will become relatively unproductive after three or four years, so in practice a continual annual replacement of a quarter or a third of the plants is best. Replacing all every four years or so means years of gluts and years of shortages, as they are all the same age. Strawing up is essential for clean crops. Do not straw too early – only when the first green fruits are seen swelling. Remove surplus runners regularly.

*Fragaria* hybrids from the order *Rosaceae*

# STRAWBERRIES
## PERPETUAL AND REMONTANT

*Herbaceous. 30cm/1ft. Life span: short. Self-fertile. Fruits: up to 5x2cm/2x1in, red, conical.*
*Value: some vitamin C and half as much iron as spinach.*

The remontant or perpetual strawberries are just as much a mixture of, and very similar to, summer strawberries, except that they fruit continuously through the autumn. In fact they start to set early crops even before the summer varieties, but these are normally removed to ensure bigger crops later when the summer crowd has finished. Some have extremely good flavour, probably due to some *F. vesca* ancestry.

This particular group of strawberries has been improved far more in continental Europe than in America or the UK. Their development has been parallel to that of the summer strawberries, but with different mixes of species used in the hybridisation. Most of the strawberry family are greatly affected by the day-length, and this group perhaps most of all. Most strawberry varieties respond to a change of their native latitude, by producing primarily runners if they move north and fruits if they move south. It would thus seem that any variety would be a perpetual fruiter if cultivated at the 'right' latitude, and that perpetual fruiters are really just summer croppers enjoying a warmer latitude than nature intended.

Strawberries do well on windowledges in full sun

Aromel

## VARIETIES

My favourite and one of the finest flavoured is **Aromel**; this also does well under cover. **Mara des Bois** is a new French variety and is extremely well flavoured and crops well. Both of these varieties runner well. **La Sans Rivale**, an old French variety, and **Hampshire Maid** produce few runners. The Dutch have some runner-forming, climbing, remontant varieties. (They do not climb, but have to be pushed!) **Ostara** and **Rabunda** are good autumn croppers, especially if the first flowers are disbudded in the early summer months.

## CULTIVATION

Remontants need the same rich, moist conditions as summer strawberries. As they crop for longer and can give higher total yields they deserve even better treatment.

**Growing under Glass**
These are better value grown under glass than summer strawberries, as they use the space productively for longer. They benefit most from such cover at the end of autumn. They must have good ventilation or they mould rapidly, and they are prone to red spider mite attacks. Either use the commercial predators or suffer.

### Growing in Containers

These perpetuals are often recommended for growing in containers, as they are productive for far longer than summer fruiters and make better use of limited space. However, they will do much better in the ground, especially if erratic watering is a possibility!

### Ornamental and Wildlife Value

Climbing varieties can be trained well over trellises and can also be quite decorative, especially when in fruit. Their long flowering period makes these plants valuable to insects, and the fruits themselves are enjoyed by both birds and rodents!

### Maintenance Calendar

*Spring* Weed, mulch, spray with seaweed solution and deflower.
*Summer* Deflower, root some runners, remove rest.
*Autumn* Straw up and pick the fruits.
*Winter* Tidy bed, de-runner, plant out in late winter.

### Propagation

The perpetual fruited varieties cannot be reliably propagated by seed as they are such mixed hybrids. I have tried! Runners can be rooted in pots in summer and detached. They crop significantly more easily the first year than summer fruiters. This is because when planted out they have longer to establish before the fruiting commences, whether this happens in the preceding autumn, late winter or even early spring.

### Pruning and Training

Remontants are grown similarly to summer strawberries, but it pays to give them a sunny spot so their later fruits can ripen.

### Weed, Pest and Disease Control

Because they have such a long season, early mouldy fruits must be rapidly and hygienically removed, or later fruits will suffer exponentially. They are more prone to moulds because of the humidity in autumn and benefit from cloches. Bird damage is less as there are plenty of other attractive fruits around.

### Harvesting and Storing

Because the remontants crop late into autumn they are juicier than summer varieties, but not always so sweet, and often rot before ripening. They can be picked green if there is a hint of colouring, and are then fine for culinary use.

## COMPANION PLANTING

As with other strawberries, they do well with beans and are benefited by onions and borage. Most of all they love a mulch of pine needles.

## OTHER USES

Eating strawberries will supposedly whiten your teeth. Strawberry leaves have been used as a tea substitute.

**Strawberry tea**

## CULINARY USES

They can be used just like summer strawberries, but are conveniently fresh from summer till the frosts.

### Baked Strawberry Apples
Serves 4

*4 cooking apples*
*punnet of strawberries*
*a few raisins*
*a little sugar and butter*

Wash, dry and core the apples and smear with butter. Cut a thin slice off one end to ensure they sit flat in a greased baking dish. Setting aside the four best strawberries, eat some and pass the rest through a sieve. Fill the holes in the apples with strawberry purée. Push in raisins to bring the level over the top. Finish with the reserved fruits and a sprinkling of sugar. Bake at 190°C/375°F/gas mark 5 till the apples are bursting – for approximately 20 minutes. Serve hot with custard, cream or yoghurt.

*Fragaria vesca semperflorens* from the order *Rosaceae*

# STRAWBERRIES
## ALPINE AND WILD EUROPEAN

*Herbaceous. 30cm/1ft. Life span: short! Self-fertile. Fruits: up to 1 x2cm/½ x1in. Value: some vitamin C.*

Alpine strawberries differ from the common garden strawberries in two distinct ways. The fruits and plants are smaller and they do not form runners. The alpines form neat clumps about 30cm/12in across, with lighter green leaves, and flower all season almost from last to first frost. The other wild (European) strawberries, *F. vesca*, and **Hautbois**, *F. elatior/***moschata**, are more like miniature versions of garden strawberries. With smaller fruits than even the alpines, they do make runners. Indeed some of the wild woodland forms only produce runners and rarely fruit.

Alexandria

These wild forms were the earliest strawberries cultivated and are native to Europe, but only north of the Alps. They were thus unknown to the ancient Greeks, and although passing reference is given to them by Roman and early medieval writers, it is as wild, not cultivated fruits. In England the fruits are mentioned during the thirteenth century in the Countess of Leicester's Household Roll. By the reign of Henry VIII the fruit was highly esteemed and cost four pence a bushel. At the same time the **Hautbois** strawberry, *F. elatior/***moschata**, was also popular, especially on the Continent. It was one of the most fragrant of all and made few runners. The species from the Americas arrived during this period, but were considered not as good as these native wild varieties. It was not until the nineteenth century that the natives became superseded by 'modern' hybrids.

## CULTIVATION

Alpines are easier to grow, needing less richness and moisture than other types of strawberry, though they naturally will do much better given improved conditions. They can be spaced at 30cm/12in or so apart. Wild strawberries are better grown as ground cover in moist partial shade and allowed to run.

### Weed, Pest and Disease Control
Alpine and wild species are much tougher plants than conventional varieties and rarely suffer from pests or diseases. The fruits are also less appealing to birds, so they can often be cropped without protection.

### Pruning and Training
As with other varieties and species, it is best to replace the entire stock in stages normally running over a three- or four-year period.

### Growing under Glass and in Containers
Alpines can be cropped under glass to extend the season, but become more prone to red spider mite. Other wild species resent being under cover more. In pots they are easier than more conventional varieties, however, as they need less water and do not run.

## VARIETIES

Alpines are grown from seed. They are little improved on the true wild form, though yellow and white-fruited versions are available. **Baron Solemacher**

is a slightly larger-fruited selection; it needs nearly 60cm/2 ft of space each way. **Alexandria** is tastier, juicier and does better in moist half shade. Wild, runnering strawberries, known as **Fraises des Bois,** are obtainable on the Continent as seed or plants. The **Green Strawberry,** *F. collina/viridis,* has sadly vanished.

**Baron Solemacher**

**Delight is widely available**

**Maintenance Calendar**
*Spring* Weed, mulch, spray thoroughly with seaweed solution monthly.
*Summer* Pick regularly all through summer.
*Autumn* Remove old, worn-out plants.
*Winter* Sow seed in pots in coldframe in late winter.

**Ornamental and Wildlife Value**
Alpines make good ground cover and are more decorative than other strawberries, as they form neat mounds. The long flowering period makes them beneficial to insects and the almost evergreen clumps are good shelter and hibernation sites.

**Harvesting and Storing**
They can be picked under-ripe for culinary purposes. Pick and freeze them until sufficient quantities are gathered, then shake the frozen fruits in a dry cloth and many seeds can be removed. The fruits can be made into jams, jellies, sauces, syrups and compôtes.

**Propagation**
As true alpines make no runners, they are grown from seed. Sow early for plants to put out in spring. Sometimes the crowns can be successfully divided. The sixteenth-century poet Thomas Tusser suggested that strawberries should be obtained from the wild:
'Wife, into the garden, and set me a plot
With strawberry roots of the best to be got;
Such growing abroad among thorns in the wood,
Well chosen and picked, grow excellent good.'

## COMPANION PLANTING

Tusser also said:
'Gooseberries, raspberries, roses all three
With strawberries under do trimly agree.'
In the wild strawberries are sometimes found growing with vervaine.

## OTHER USES

Traditionally, the leaves of wild strawberries were used for medicinal purposes.

## CULINARY USES

Both alpine and wild strawberries are superlatively fragrant and delicious raw, if fully ripe. Cooking brings out even more flavour, from under-ripe fruits as well. These are less moist than ordinary strawberries, so require some water or redcurrant juice to make jam or jelly. They are also firmer after freezing and go well in compôtes.

*Alpine Strawberry Tarts*

Make individual sweet shortcrust pastry tart cases. Smear the insides with butter, then fill each tart with a mixture of both alpine strawberries and strawberry jam (alpine or otherwise). Bake in a preheated oven for ten minutes or so at 190°C/375°F/gas mark 5. Cool and top each with clotted cream before serving.

*Vaccinium* species from the order *Ericaceae*

# BLUEBERRIES AND BILBERRIES

*Bush. 30cm-4m/1-15ft. Life span: medium to long. Deciduous, self-fertile. Fruits: 1cm/¼ -½ in, spherical blue-black. Value: some vitamins C and B.*

Bilberries, blaeberries or whortleberries, *Vaccinium myrtillus,* are low shrubs native to Europe, found on heaths and moors in acid soils. They have slender, green twigs with myrtle-like leaves and spherical pink flowers followed by blue-black fruits in late summer. They are fiddly to pick and rarely cultivated. Highbush blueberries, *V. corymbosum,* and many near relations come from North America. The **Highbush** is a tall shrub up to 4m/15ft, so lower growing cultivars for garden use have been bred, though commercial growers still prefer the tall. Many similar species are used as ornamentals, because in autumn the leaves turn to some amazing reds and pinks. The **Rabbiteye Blueberries**, *V. virgatum/ashei* are similar. The **Lowbush Blueberry,** *V. angustifolium,* is different, only about 30cm/12in high, and is much hardier than the **Highbush**. The berries are large, sweet and early, so this has been crossed with the **Highbush**.

Bilberries were once highly popular. They would be picked from the wild and taken to market in the towns where they were esteemed for tarts and jelly. They were a staple food for the Scots Highlanders who ate them in milk and made them into wine. Bilberries went into oblivion when the better fruiting blueberries from America became available. Blueberries are a traditional American fruit, much loved by the native people, who ate many different species, preferring **Highbush**, or **Swamp**, and **Rabbiteye Blueberries** in the warmer areas and the **Lowbush**, **Early** or **Low**, **Sweet Blueberry** further north. The last was particularly useful as it was easily dried for preservation for winter. The dried berries were beaten to a powder and made into cakes with maize meal. In the north-west they even smoke-dried the berries for extra flavour.

## VARIETIES

Most of our garden varieties are of mixed American origin. Many of the better ones were bred in Maine, where the climate is similar to that of Britain. The early **Earliblue**, **Goldtraube** and **Jersey** are fairly compact. **Berkeley** is a spreader, **Blue Crop** more upright. All are commonly available and need planting 1.5m/5ft apart. Many of the species have edible berries. *V. ovatum,* the **Huckleberry** or **Box Blueberry**, is a small,

**Blueberries**

**Huckleberries**

attractive, evergreen shrub with tasty berries and can be used to make a hedge. The **Red Huckleberry**, **Red Bilberry**, *V. parvifolium* is a large deciduous shrub with red fruits. *V. membranaceum*, the **Big Huckleberry**, has big berries, is fairly drought resistant and one of the tastiest. *V. hirsutum*, the **Hairy Huckleberry,** is not very hardy with hairy fruits.

## CULTIVATION

An acid soil suitable for heathers or rhododendrons is essential; a substitute of peat and leaf mould will do. The tall species prefer wetter sites, the dwarfer ones will tolerate drier, but all crop better with moister positions. They prefer sunny sites though they will grow in partial shade. Partly self-fertile, they do better if several different varieties are grown together.

### Growing under Glass
They are sufficiently hardy almost anywhere, but glass protection may be worth-while temporarily while they are fruiting to prevent losses to the birds.

### Growing in Containers
Blueberries have to be grown in containers in many areas, as they die on lime soils. Ericaceous compost or a mixture of peat, sand and leaf mould is essential, as is

regular, copious watering with rain or acidic water. In limey areas avoid tap water!

### Ornamental and Wildlife Value
Stunning colours in autumn. There are countless ornamental species and varieties. All berry and are valuable to birds.

### Maintenance Calendar
*Spring* Weed and mulch.
*Summer* Make layers and pick fruit.
*Autumn* Take suckers and transplant once leaves fall.
*Winter* Prune if necessary.

### Propagation
The species come true from seed, but better varieties are layered in summer. Suckers can be detached in winter.

### Pruning and Training
Bilberries and blueberries need little pruning, except to remove dead or diseased growth, best done in winter.

### Weed, Pest and Disease Control
Apart from the usual losses to birds, this is a remarkably pest- and disease-free family. Any distress will probably be due to an alkaline soil or lime in the water supply.

### Harvesting and Storing
The berries should be picked when fully ripe and easily detached or they are too acid. They may be jammed, juiced, jellied or frozen and commercially are obtainable dried, resembling blue raisins.

**Highbush**

## COMPANION PLANTING

As these are ericaceous, they grow well near heathers.

## CULINARY USES

Blueberries and bilberries can be used in pies, tarts, jams, jellies and syrups. Blueberry cheesecake and blueberry muffins are very popular American dishes.

*Blueberry Grunt*
Serves 4-6

*500g/1lb blueberries*
*50g/2oz sugar*
*1 teaspoon allspice*
*1 small lemon*
*maple syrup to taste*
*125g/4oz white flour*
*pinch salt*
*1½ teaspoons baking powder*
*50g/2oz butter*
*300ml/½ pt single cream*

## OTHER USES

The leaves were used medicinally. Chewing dried bilberries was a cure for diarrhoea and mouth and throat infections.

Simmer the washed blueberries gently with sugar, spice and the lemon's juice and grated rind. Add maple syrup to taste. Meanwhile rub the flour, salt, baking powder and butter into crumbs and blend in enough cream to make a smooth creamy dough. Carefully spoon the dough on top of the blueberries, cover the pan and simmer till the crust puffs and sets. Serve with the rest of the cream and more maple syrup.

*Vaccinium* species from the order *Ericaceae*

# CRANBERRIES AND COWBERRIES

*Bush. Prostrate to 60cm/2ft. Life span: medium to long. Evergreen, self-fertile.*
*Fruits: up to 2cm/¾in, reddish orange. Value: some vitamin C.*

Cranberries are very similar and closely related to blueberries and bilberries, the most noticeable differences being that cranberries have red berries and are evergreen.

*V. oxycoccus*, the **cranberry**, is a native of most northern temperate countries and is found on bogs and moorlands. The low-growing, evergreen shrub is tough and wiry with long, sparsely-leafed stems. The leaves are longer and thinner than those of the blue-berried *Vaccinium* species. The flowers are tiny, yellow and pink, in early summer and are followed by the round red fruits, which are pleasantly acid to taste. The **American Cranberry**, *V. macrocarpon*, is much the same, but larger in size and berry. The **Cowberry**, **Crane** or **Foxberry**, *V. vitis idaea*, is also similar, more densely leafed, with rounded ends and clusters of berries which are more acid and less agreeable than cranberries.

The native cranberry has been gathered from the wild in most cool regions by native peoples throughout the northern hemisphere. The cowberry has not been enjoyed so widely as it is usually too acid to eat raw, though it is excellent after cooking. Strangely enough, the British never much liked either, although both the cranberry and cowberry were very popular in Sweden. When better North American cranberries appeared as a sauce to accompany the new dish of roast turkey, cowberries were also suddenly in demand – as now they could be sold to the unwary in London as 'cranberries'.

## VARIETIES

Apart from those already mentioned, there are several other *Vacciniums* that fall between cranberries and blueberries and have edible berries; *V. floribundum*, the **Mortinia**, is the least hardy and comes from Ecuador, but will survive in southern England. It is an attractive, evergreen shrub with heavy racemes of rose-pink blooms followed by masses of red berries. From East Asia and Japan comes *V. praestans*, a prostrate, creeping, deciduous shrub with sweet, fragrant, glossy, red berries. *V. nummularia* is one of the choicest little evergreens for an alpine house. It most resembles a prettier cowberry, with arching, hairy stems and small, black berries.

**Cranberry Fruit**

**The evergreen cowberry, V. nummularia**

## CULTIVATION

These really need moist boggy conditions, in lime-free soil and water. The best sites are made on the edge of a river or pond by slowly building up a layer of stones covered with a thick layer of peaty, humus-rich, acid soil. They must be moist but not drowned; they need to stand above the water! Most are small, needing as little as 60–90cm/2–3ft each way and even tolerating some light shade.

### Growing under Glass
As the usual varieties are hardy this is really only worthwhile for bird protection. *V. floribundum* and *nummularia* benefit from cool cover, such as that afforded by an alpine house, and are very beautiful small shrubs.

### Growing in Containers
Cranberries have to be grown in containers in many areas as they will die on lime soils. Ericaceous compost or a mixture of peat, sand and leafmould is essential, as is regular and copious watering with rain or acidic water. Avoid tap water in limey areas!

### Ornamental and Wildlife Value
On acid soils cowberries make excellent ground cover. Cranberries are not as dense, so they suppress weeds less well. The berries are loved by wildlife and, being evergreen, they will provide good shelter.

### Maintenance Calendar
*Spring* Weed, mulch, make the layers.
*Summer* Keep well watered.
*Autumn* Divide plants, pick fruit before frost.
*Winter* Protect less hardy species from frost.

### Propagation, Pruning and Training
The species can be grown from seed, by dividing in autumn, or they can be layered in spring. Only remedial tidying is required.

### Weed, Pest and Disease Control
Cowberries and most of the denser-growing species suppress weeds well. They are all pest- and disease-free in most gardens. Grown under glass they need to be kept cool or they suffer. Any problems are most often due to lime in the soil or water. Watering on sequestrated iron chelates will help but these are not available to organic growers.

### Harvesting and Storing
Cowberries are made sour by frosts so must be gathered promptly. In Siberia they were kept under water through the winter, so that they gradually became less acid, and were then eaten in spring.

## OTHER USES

The leaves and fruits of most of these berries have been used medicinally in the past. Cowberries have been eaten as a cure for diarrhoea.

## CULINARY USES

Invariably used for the jelly, but also in tarts and pies and added to many other dishes.

*Cranberry Jelly*
Makes about 3.75kg/7lb

*500g/lb cranberries*
*750g/1½lb apples*
*approx. 2kg/4lb sugar*

Wash the fruits, chop the apples and simmer both with enough water to prevent burning. Once the apples are soft, strain and add 500g/1lb sugar to each 600ml/1pt of liquid.

Bring the liquid back to the boil, stirring to dissolve the sugar. Cook briefly, skim and pour into sterile warmed jars. Seal at once. Serve with roast turkey.

## COMPANION PLANTING

They are ericaceous and enjoy similar conditions, root bacteria and fungi as rhododendrons and azaleas so can be used as ground cover between these.

**Coralling cranberries on the surface of a bog, Massachusetts, USA**

*Ribes sativum* from the order *Grossulariaceae*

# REDCURRANTS AND WHITECURRANTS

*Shrub 2m/7ft. Life span: long. Deciduous, self-fertile.*
*Fruits: 1–2 cm/½–¾in, globular, glossy red or white.*

Redcurrants are reliable, productive plants we rarely notice except when translucent, glossy red berries festoon the branches. Otherwise they are quite insignificant, similar to flowering redcurrant, *R. sanguineum*, which has such prolific pink tassels in early spring. (This sets inedible fruits occasionally.) Whitecurrants are varieties selected without the colour and with their own flavour. I find that the whites crop slightly less extravagantly than reds and are culinarily useful.

Redcurrants, *R. sativum* and *R. rubrum*, are native European fruits. They were not cultivated by the Romans. They gained garden notice in the sixteenth century when they rapidly became a stalwart of the cottager's garden. Long-lived, they often survive, neglected and unproductive, whereas, given a good site and bird protection, they produce prodigiously. Surprisingly little known in much of Europe and the USA, they are popular in Scandinavia and Russia.

**Raby Castle**

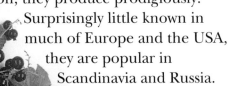

**Redcurrants**

## VARIETIES

**Earliest of Four Lands** is my favourite, but all are very amenable and productive,

varying little in taste, acidity and season – though this ma cover three months in a goo year. For example, **Raby Cas** has *R. rubrum* blood so is the most hardy of a really tough group; **Wilson's Longbunch** are crimson pearls, **White Grape** and **White Versailles** the equivalent whitecurrant

## CULTIVATION

Redcurrants respond best to a cool, well mulched soil. They do not need as rich conditions as blackcurrants or raspberries and will grow in partial shade and quite happily on cold walls. The berries are sweeter in the sun though. The main requirement is protection from birds. Without thorough netting, however, all else is useless, as these are the bird food supreme.

**White Versailles**

### Weed, Pest and Disease Control

The only major threat to the crop is the birds. Minor sawfly caterpillar attacks sometimes occur, but do little damage. Berries left to ripen fully mould in damp weather unless protected. The leaves regularly pucker with red and yellow blotches from the leaf-blistering aphis, though surprisingly this does not affect the yield. Indeed these leaves can be removed wholesale, with aphids still on board, during the summer pruning.

### Pruning and Training

These are the most easily trained and forgiving of plants. No matter how you misprune them, they respond with new growth and ample fruit. Redcurrants can be made to take any form, cordon, goblet, fan or espalier, and

moreover are quick to regrow. They will fruit best on a permanent framework with spurs and need every shoot, except leaders, cut back in summer and again harder in winter. Growing in good conditions, redcurrants can be trained over large walls, including north-facing ones. Moderately pruned as goblet bushes, they need to be nearly 2m/at least 6ft apart. As cordons they can be grown two to the metre/yard.

### Propagation

The easiest of all plants to root from autumn cuttings.

### Maintenance Calendar

*Spring* Weed, mulch and spray seaweed solution monthly.
*Summer* Pick fruit as required. After midsummer prune.
*Autumn* Take cuttings once leaves fall.
*Winter* Cut back hard to spurs on frame.

### Growing under Glass and in Containers

This can be worthwhile if you want pristine berries over a longer season or have no space for bushes. They do not want to get too hot!

**Wilson's Longbunch**

### Ornamental and Wildlife Value

Redcurrants have little value in the ornamental garden as the berries disappear so rapidly. Redcurrants are the most palatable bird snack and so they will be popular in wildlife areas, briefly.

### Harvesting and Storing

Currants can be picked from early summer as they colour, for use as garnishes, adding to compôtes and for the most acid jellies. Ripening continues into late autumn in dry years when the fruits become less acid and tasty raw. Being seedy, the fruit is conveniently stored juiced and frozen. Similarly currants are better as jelly rather than jam. Dry, cool berries keep very well.

## OTHER USES

Once popular with apothecaries, as they could be stored for months, packed fresh and dry into sealed glass bottles, and were thus available as 'vitamin pills' in bleak late winter and spring when fresh fruit and vegetables became scarce. The juice of redcurrants must be the best edible red dye you could want.

## COMPANION PLANTING

Redcurrants may benefit from nettles nearby, but the fruit picker will curse. *Limnanthes douglassii* is the best companion and ground cover once the bushes are well established.

## CULINARY USES

Redcurrants are immensely useful because of their colour and acidity. They add deep red to everything and their juice makes other fruit jellies set. Redcurrant juice adds tartness and flavour to other juices and can be used in many sweet and savoury dishes.

Whitecurrant juice is a substitute, if not an improvement, for lemon juice and makes even more delicious jellies.

### *Mint Sauce Supreme*
Makes about 1kg/2lb

*500g/1lb whitecurrants*
*approx. 500g/1lb sugar*
*125g/4oz fresh mint leaves,*
*finely shredded*

Simmer the whitecurrants till soft, then strain, or simply juice. Add the same weight of sugar to the juice and slowly bring to boil. Skim and remove from heat. Stir in the finely shredded mint and bottle in warm sterile jars. Cover immediately. This is the sauce for spring lamb roasts, for yoghurt dips and for barbecue glazes.

*Ribes grossularia* from the order *Grossulariaceae*

# GOOSEBERRIES

*Bush up to 1.5m/5ft. Life span: long. Deciduous, self-fertile. Fruits: up to 3cm/1in, oval, green to purple. Value: some vitamin C.*

Gooseberries you find in the shops are green bullets, for culinary use, nothing like the meltingly sweet, well-ripened dessert varieties. Compared to other *Ribes*, gooseberries have bigger, hairy berries and sharp thorns. They are easy to grow, but are often handicapped by being grown as a stool. Given attention and good pruning, large, succulent berries can be had, in almost any colour and with delicious flavour, which can range from a clean, acid-sweet taste to a deep and vinous plumness.

Unnoticed by classical writers but a European native, gooseberries, *Ribes grossularia*, are first mentioned in purchases for the Westminster garden of King Edward I in 1276. They became popular almost solely in Britain, and by the nineteenth century there were hundreds of varieties, and countless clubs where members vied to grow larger fruits, achieving berries the size of bantam eggs. One variety, **London**, an outstandingly large, not so hairy, red was the biggest exhibited every year from 1829 to 1867, 37 years unbeaten champion! The wild relation is found in rocky terrain as a small shrub, variable in berry colour, size and in habit of growth, with some being inconveniently lax. American gooseberries/ Worcesterberries are derived from *R. divaricatum*. They have smaller berries and are resistant to the American mildew disease that can damage European varieties.

Worcesterberries

## VARIETIES

**London** (mid-season) is biggest, and dark red. I love **Langley Gage** (mid-season) which has divine, bite-sized, syrupy sweet, translucent white globes hanging in profusion. **Early Sulphur** (very early) has golden yellow, almost transparent, tasty, medium-sized berries. For a substantial, dark olive green, strongly flavoured, large berry choose **Gunner** (mid), though it's not a heavy cropper. **Leveller** (mid) is, and has delicious yellow green fruits. The **Worcesterberry** is even meaner-thorned and is really an American species with smaller black berries more like blackcurrants. **Pixwell** is an improved, green-fruited form of gooseberry. *R. hirtellum*, the **Currant Gooseberry**, is another edible American species with small reddish fruits.

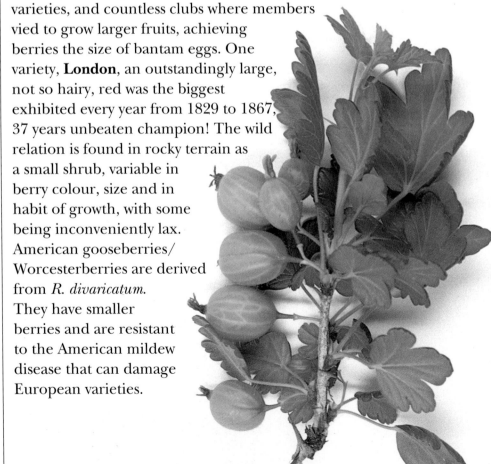

**Gooseberries**

**Langley Gage in flower**

## CULTIVATION

Gooseberries love rich, moist, loamy soil and do not like hot, dry, sandy sites or stagnant air, doing better with a breeze.

### Growing under Glass and in Containers

Gooseberries are so hardy they need no protection, and they are too thorny as well. They can be potted, but are easier in the ground.

### Ornamental and Wildlife Value

The bushes are drab, the flowers inconspicuous and the berries not brightly coloured - the ideal landscaping plant to go with modern buildings! The flowers benefit early insects and the berries disappear.

### Maintenance Calendar

*Spring* Weed, mulch, spray seaweed solution monthly.
*Summer* Thin and pick fruit, watch out for the hazards of sawfly and mildew.
*Autumn* Take cuttings.
*Winter* Prune hard.

### Propagation

Gooseberries are propagated by 30cm/1ft long cuttings. Disbud the lower end to prevent suckers.

### Pruning and Training

Often misgrown as a stool with many shoots direct from the ground, gooseberries are better hard pruned to spurs on a goblet-shaped frame with a short leg. I leave the pruning till late winter, so that the thorns protect the buds from the birds, which perversely delight in disbudding gooseberries. To get larger berries or more varieties in a confined space, gooseberries may easily be grown as vertical cordons, fans or even standards.

### Weed, Pest and Disease Control

American mildew is the worst problem, burning tips and felting fruits with a leathery coat that dries them up. Hygiene, moist roots, hard pruning and good air circulation reduce the damage. Sodium bicarbonate sprays and

*London*

sulphur-based ones (which burn some varieties) are available to organic growers. Occasionally, often in the third year or so after planting, gooseberries suffer damage from sawfly caterpillars. First appearing as a host of wee holes in a leaf, they move on to stripping the bush. However, vigilance and early action will prevent serious damage.

### Harvesting and Storing

Gooseberries do not have as much bird appeal as many fruits, and can even be got unripe without protection. Birds and wasps do steal them once they're ripe, otherwise the fruits mellow and will hang on till late summer if protected from such pests and damp.

## COMPANION PLANTING

Tomatoes and broad beans nearby are reputed to aid them and I always grow them with *Limnanthes douglassii* as ground cover.

## OTHER USES

Gooseberries make a powerful wine, much like that of the grape.

## CULINARY USES

Picked small and green, gooseberries make the most delicious acid jams and tarts – which turn red if overcooked. As they ripen they become less acid and fuller-flavoured for dessert purposes. Ripe fruits for cooking will combine well with redcurrants to keep up the acidity and are often jellied to remove the tough skins and seeds.

### *Gooseberry Fool*
Serves 4

*500g/1lb ripe green gooseberries*
*approx. 75g/3oz light honey or sugar*
*300ml/½pt thick cream*
*dark chocolate and grated nutmeg to garnish*

If the gooseberries are soft, press them through a sieve. If not, warm very carefully till soft first, or freeze and defrost first. Add sweetening to the purée to taste, and cool. Immediately before serving, whip the cream and fold in the purée. Garnish with grated dark chocolate and nutmeg.

*Ribes nigrum* from the order *Grossulariaceae*

# BLACKCURRANTS

*Bush 1.5m/5ft. Life span: short. Deciduous, self-fertile.*
*Fruits: 1–2cm/up to ½in, black, spherical. Value: very rich in vitamin C.*

Blackcurrants are quite different from the other types of *Ribes*, though they are often bundled in with redcurrants. They fruit on young wood, not old, and have dark purple, almost black, berries with a most distinct and unforgettable aroma which is similar to that of the aromatic foliage and stems.

These, like other *Ribes*, seem to have been unknown to the Ancient Greeks or Romans and were only used medicinally, as quinsy berries, for curing colds and throat problems until the sixteenth century. Then they became more popular as a garden crop and are now very widely grown commercially in Europe, but not so much in the USA. Their rise in fame was due to their very high vitamin C content, and probably also to the fact that sugar, needed to make this naturally sour fruit palatable, became available more cheaply. The native plants can occasionally be found in wild wet areas of northern Europe and Asia, but are now more likely to be garden escapes. Improvement has been done mostly by selection rather than producing hybrids with other *Ribes*, though the **Josta** is a good example of what is possible.

## VARIETIES

New varieties such as **Ben Sarek** (mid-season), **Ben Lomond** (late) and **Ben More** (very late) are numerous and generally more productive, with better disease resistance, than old favourites. **Laxton's Giant** (mid) is still one of the biggest, and **Seabrook's Black** (mid) is supposedly resistant to big bud. The **Josta** berry is a much larger hybrid, more like a thornless gooseberry, with heavy crops of large blackcurrant-flavoured berries. Some American species have been esteemed, such as the

**Ben More**

fragrant, bright-yellow-flowered **Buffalo Currant** or **Golden Currant**, *R. aureum/ odoratum*, which is also used as the stock for standard gooseberries. *R. americanum*, the **American Blackcurrant**, has yellowish flowers and inferior fruit, but turns glorious colours in autumn.

## CULTIVATION

Blackcurrants revel in rich, moist ground, the richer the better, and similarly respond to heavy mulching. They do not mind light shade. Late varieties are usually chosen to avoid frost damage during their flowering period.

### Growing under Glass and in Containers
The bushes prefer to be cool, so they are not happy for long under cover. They can be grown and fruited successfully in large pots.

### Ornamental and Wildlife Value
Rather dingy plants of little decorative appeal, though the smell of foliage and stems is most pleasing. However, the currants are as valuable to birds as to us, and thus form good subjects for wild gardens.

### Maintenance Calendar
*Spring* Weed, mulch, spray seaweed solution monthly.
*Summer* Protect, pick fruits.
*Autumn* Take cuttings.
*Winter* Prune back hard and compost heavily.

### Propagation
There are no easier cuttings! As blackcurrants are best grown as a stool, the main requirement is for multiple shoots from ground level. Thus cuttings have all buds left on and new bushes are planted deeper than is the standard practice for almost every other subject.

### Pruning and Training
In order to provide as much young fruitful wood as possible, the optimum pruning is to remove annually all shoots from a one-third segment of the stool. The lazy and less effective way is just to cut back one third totally, preferably of three or more, of the blackcurrant bushes once every three years.

### Weed, Pest and Disease Control
Weeds must be kept from encroaching on the stool, but rarely germinate there because of the intense shade. Birds are not so much of a problem, but will eat the currants eventually unless prevented. Mildew is aggravated by stagnant air and dry roots; hygienic pruning and vigorous growth is usually sufficient redress. Big bud is obvious. It is caused by microscopic pests that also carry virus diseases such as reversion. The simple solution is to replace old infected stock with new clean material after ten or fifteen years or when yields have dropped too far.

**Ben Lomond**

### Harvesting and Storing
Blackcurrants will keep for several days once picked as they are so firm and tough-skinned. They can be frozen, jammed, jellied and turned into the most delicious syrups and juices.

## COMPANION PLANTING

Nettles nearby benefit blackcurrants. In some parts of the USA, blackcurrants may not be grown as they are host to white pine blister rust.

## OTHER USES

The leaves have been used as tea for medicinal and tonic purposes and dried currants likewise, especially for throat infections.

## CULINARY USES

The currants have too little liquid to simmer down on their own, so they need water or other juices. Add redcurrant juice to make blackcurrant jams and dishes more pleasantly acid. Jelly is easier work than jam as de-sprigging the berries is tedious.

### Bob's Cunning Blackcurrant Jam
Makes about 3kg/6½lb

*1.5kg/3lb blackcurrants*
*500g/1lb redcurrants*
*a little water*
*approx. 2kg/4lb sugar*

De-sprig best quarter of the blackcurrants and set aside. Simmer the rest with the redcurrants and just enough water to cover, till they are soft. Strain, reserving the juice. Cover the pulp with water, boil up again and strain off another lot of juice. Weigh the combined juices, add reserved blackcurrants and two-thirds of the juice's weight in sugar. Bring to the boil, stirring until the sugar has dissolved. Boil briefly, skim and pour into warm sterilised jars. Cover the jars immediately.

*Aronia melanocarpa* from the order *Rosaceae*

# CHOKEBERRIES

*Bush up to 2m/7ft. Life span: medium. Deciduous, self-fertile.*
*Fruits: 2cm/½in, spherical, black. Value: very rich in vitamin C.*

With a name like chokeberry you can be sure the fruits are astringent and sour raw, though fine cooked and sweetened. They are hard, red, ripening to purple or almost lustrous black. They closely resemble blackcurrants in appearance and even in taste, though more acid and almost pine flavoured, making them a useful substitute where blackcurrants may not be grown, such as in some parts of their native USA. The bushes are easy to grow, reliable, highly productive, and compact with a height and spread of about 1.5m/5ft. White, hawthorn-like flowers and brilliant autumn leaf colours make this a most decorative fruit bush.

Distantly related to the pear and *Sorbus* genus, these berries came from eastern North America in 1700. They were relished by native Americans, who would mix the dried fruits with others to make 'cakes' for winter storage, but it was the autumn colouring that recommended them to European plantsmen. The Royal Horticultural Society Award of Merit was eventually granted in 1972, but still rather for their ornamental appeal than their taste. They are a fruit with great potential. I'm sure they would do better if called the tastyberry!

The dramatic autumn foliage of the Brilliant chokeberry

## VARIETIES

*Aronia melanocarpa*, **Viking** is available as bushes for fruit production and is self-fertile. Another similar cultivar of *A. melanocarpa*, **Brilliant**, is available but for ornamental plantings because it has exceptionally good autumn leaf colouring. *A. arbutifolia*, the **Red Chokeberry**, also has good autumn colour and produces red berries that were eaten by native American children for their aroma rather than for their taste. There is also a more erect form.

## CULTIVATION

Chokeberries are easy and do well on any reasonable soil other than very shallow chalk or in very boggy ground. Naturally they will respond to better conditions by becoming larger and more prolific, and are happier with well mulched peaty conditions. The bushes need to be 2m/7ft apart for effective cropping, but possibly closer for the massed displays of berries and autumn colour.

**Maintenance Calendar**
*Spring* Weed, mulch and spray with seaweed solution.
*Summer* Net to keep birds off and pick the fruit.
*Autumn* Prune out dead and diseased growths, take cuttings.
*Winter* Mulch with compost and straw, with leaf mould or bark.

**Propagation**
The species come true from seed, but named varieties are best reproduced from early autumn cuttings or division.

**Pruning and Training**
They can tend to sucker, turning them into a stool, but cultivation is easier if they are kept to a single stem. Pruning is mostly remedial, removing suckering, low-growing,

**Aronia**

**Viking**

congested and diseased growths. I suspect that chokeberries would be good trained on wires or a wall – they would certainly be most decorative.

### Weed, Pest and Disease Control

Other than the usual problems of choking weeds and losses to the birds, these plants are remarkably free from problems. One reason chokeberries are coming into cultivation is that they are as good a source of vitamin C as blackcurrants, but also more productive, with none of the potential problems of big bud, reversion or mildew.

### Growing under Glass and in Containers

There seems no need to grow chokeberries under glass as they thrive outdoors and are of little value fresh, only tasty once preserved. However, it is worth growing them in a container if you need a rich source of vitamin C and have no garden space available.

### Ornamental and Wildlife Value

The tough reliability, the profusion of spring flowers, immense quantities of glossy black berries and the colour of the autumn leaves make this an essential plant for any area, ornamental or wild, especially if you like birds.

### Harvesting and Storing

Chokeberries ripen in midsummer, but the flavour improves if they are left to hang. They will need good bird protection. The best and only sensible means of storage is turning them into preserves.

**Chokeberries ripening on the bush**

## COMPANION PLANTING

No good or bad companions are yet recognised as they have been little cultivated. I grow mine in a bed with rhubarb and seakale.

## OTHER USES

The berries can be used for an edible dye and I can vouch for their being a high-vitamin self-service food for my poultry, who head for them whenever they get out.

## CULINARY USES

They can be used in the same way as blackcurrants and indeed taste not dissimilar, if more piney and aromatic. However their preserve goes better with savoury dishes in the manner of cranberry jelly.

### Chokeberry Preserve

*1kg/2lb chokeberries*
*500g/1lb whitecurrants or*
*redcurrants if white*
*unavailable*
*1 small lemon*
*a little water*
*approx.1kg/2lb sugar*

Thoroughly wash the berries and currants, chop the lemon and simmer all three with just sufficient water to cover. Simmer till soft, then sieve out the skins and pips, weigh the juice and return it to the pan with three-quarters of its weight in sugar. Bring to the boil. Skim well, then pot in small jars. Store for six months before use. Serve with gammon steak, new potatoes and peas.

*Rubus idaeas* from the order *Rosaceae*

# RASPBERRIES

*Bush/vine. Life span: short. Deciduous, self-fertile. Fruits: up to 2.5cm/1in, red, yellow, black, conical.   Value: valuable amounts of vitamin C, riboflavin and niacin.*

Although many have described the strawberry as the finest fruit, others consider the raspberry to be as good, if not better. However, these exquisite berries are much less common by far, because the fruits perish so rapidly. Strangely, they are also little grown as garden fruits primarily, although they are amongst the easiest to care for and cultivate.

Raspberries vary considerably in size and are usually red, with black and yellow sorts also sometimes encountered. In good varieties, the conical fruit pulls off the plug easily, leaving a hole. Some are less easy to pick, and the berries may be damaged in the extrication as they are very soft and thin skinned.

Their young shoots are usually green, but soon go red or brown as they grow. Eventually the canes reach 1–3m/3–10ft high. They are often bristly and occasionally thorny. Individually the canes are short-lived, springing from a suckering root system one year, to die the following year after fruiting. The root systems could spread perpetually, though they most often fade away from virus infections. The flowers are small, usually white, with the fruitlet visible in the middle once the petals fall. While the flowers are usually unscented, the leaves have a slight fragrance. This is more pronounced in the North American wild species *Rubus odorata,* which has a resiny smell to the stems, though the pale reddish-purple flowers remain scentless. (Another, *R. deliciosus,* has large, rose-like flowers, which are deliciously perfumed.)

*R. idaeus* raspberries are native to Europe and Asia in hilly areas, heaths and on the edge of woodlands, especially those with acid soils. They are found growing wild in Scandinavia as far north as 70° and have long been gathered. Seeds and debris from the plants have been found preserved in the remains of the prehistoric lake villages of what is now Switzerland. Strangely, like other northern temperate fruits, raspberries went unregistered by the classical writers. The Romans were such ravenous gourmands that it seems unlikely they did not eat these delightful fruits when colonising cooler, wetter lands than their own. Perhaps because these were gathered from the wild in such profusion they needed no mention, being considered commonplace. Raspberries are included in the practical poetry of Thomas Tusser and noted by Gerarde in the sixteenth century. It seems that at that time the fruit of the closely related bramble was considered far superior, and raspberries were used more for medicinal and tonic purposes. There are many similar and wild species which are enjoyed in other temperate countries.

**Red raspberries are delicious but very perishable fruits**

**Autumn Bliss**

## VARIETIES

There are many *Rubus* species closely resembling raspberries and others very similar to brambles or blackberries. Some are so interesting they have been included as a separate group with wineberries (see page 88). In North America red and yellow raspberries, descended from *R. strigosa,* but similar to European raspberries, are grown. So are black raspberries, **Blackcaps,** *R. occidentalis,* which are less hardy and have fewer stouter canes, more given to branching. The **Rocky Mountain Raspberry,** *R. deliciosus,* is large-fruited and delicious, but a shy fruiter, especially in the UK.

Raspberries can be summer or autumn cropping and many cultivars vary more with the pruning method than inherently. **Autumn Bliss** is probably the best variety specifically for autumn fruiting.

As to choice, the new varieties of today are soon replaced by others at a great rate and no list can be complete. I still like the almost obsolete but tasty **Malling Jewel**. **Malling Joy** and **Admiral** are well flavoured. I also love the yellow raspberries. These originated alongside the reds and are less vigorous, with paler leaves. They naturally tend towards autumn fruiting. **Golden Everest** is superb, with richly flavoured, soft, sweet berries lacking the sharpness of many reds. **Fall Gold** is an autumn fruiter much like **Golden Antwerp**, which has the better flavour; one of the earliest known varieties, it is now rare. **Red Antwerp** is lost. **Norfolk Giant** is another good old variety now almost unobtainable.

## CULTIVATION

Preferring cool, moist conditions, raspberries do wonderfully in Scotland. Although they can be grown elsewhere, in most soils, they do considerably better given plentiful moisture, a rich neutral or acidic soil, or at least copious quantities of compost and very thick mulches. With hot, dry summers and wetter autumns the autumn-fruiting varieties can be much more productive, especially on drier sites, and these also suffer less from maggots. Summer-fruiters need a moist site, and do not mind quite heavy shade. They do not like the dry conditions against walls, but can be grown on cool, shady ones with a moist root run.

### Growing under Glass
Being mostly very hardy, raspberries need no protection. Under cover, however, providing they are kept cool and airy, they can

**White Raspberries**

produce good crops and benefit immensely from the bird protection. Growing them under glass also serves to spread the season. *R. niveus,* the **Mysore Black Raspberry**, comes from Asia and needs to be grown under glass.

### Growing in Containers
I have fruited raspberries in large pots. They resent it and do not crop well or flourish as they really need a bigger, cooler root run.

**Bob's own raspberry seedling**

### Ornamental and Wildlife Value

Cultivated raspberries are not very ornamental in themselves, and the fruit does not last long enough to be called a display! Some of the species are more decorative, and scented, so are worth considering, but they are nowhere near as productive as modern fruiting varieties. The birds adore raspberries and will get to them anywhere, so raspberries are good in wild gardens. However, you have a duty to others to eradicate the berries when they become virus-infected. The flowers are very beneficial to bees and other insects.

### Maintenance Calendar (Summer Fruiters)

*Spring* Weed, mulch heavily, spray seaweed solution at monthly intervals.
*Summer* Protect and pick fruit, thin shoots.
*Autumn* Cut out old canes, tie in the new.
*Winter* Add copious quantities of compost.

**A spray of raspberry flowers**

### Maintenance Calendar (Autumn Fruiters)

*Spring* Weed, mulch heavily, spray seaweed solution monthly, thin the shoots as they emerge.
*Summer* Tie in canes.
*Autumn* Protect and pick the fruit.
*Winter* Cut all canes to the ground, add copious compost to soil.

### Propagation

Varieties are multiplied by transplanting any piece of root with a bud or young cane in the autumn. Pot-grown ones may be planted in spring. Summer fruiters should not be cropped the first year but built up first; autumn fruiters may be cropped if they were well established early in the previous autumn. I have found that seed can provide very vigorous and productive, if variable, plants, but it is a better plan to buy new, named cultivars.

### Pruning and Training

Too lax to be left free, they are best restrained by growing between pairs of wires or winding the tips around horizontal ones. Alternatively, they can be grown as tripods, with three well spaced stools being joined to an apex. Pruning for summer raspberries is done in autumn; remove all old canes that have fruited or died and fix the new ones in place, selecting the biggest and strongest at about 12cm/5in apart. (It helps to pre-thin these when the shoots emerge in early summer.) Autumn fruiters are easier still: just cut everything to the ground in late winter. (Pre-thinning the canes in the spring is again quite advantageous.)

**Ripe raspberries are very tempting to birds and should be carefully netted**

**The Malling Jewel raspberry in training canes**

### Weed, Pest and Disease Control

Weeding must be done carefully because of their shallow roots. Thick mulching is almost essential. Birds are the major cause of lost crops – no protection, no fruit! The raspberry beetle can be controlled with hygiene and mulching (methodically rake thick mulches aside in winter to allow birds to eat the pupae) or the use of permitted sprays if necessary. These maggots are rarely a problem with autumn fruiters. Virus diseases may appear, mottling the leaves with yellow and making the plants less productive. Replacing the stock and moving the site is the only practical solution, but wait till the yields have dropped.

Interveinal yellowing is a reaction to alkaline soils; seaweed solution sprays with added magnesium sulphate are a palliative. Compost and mulching provide the most effective cure.

### Harvesting and Storing

Pick gently, leaving the plug; if it won't come easily, do not force it! They do not keep for long if they are wet, and less still if warm. If you want to keep them longest, cut the fruiting stalks with scissors and do not touch the fruits. They must be processed or eaten within a matter of hours, as they are one of the least durable or transportable fruits. Raspberries sold commercially are the toughest – and obviously also the least meltingly sumptuous!

## COMPANION PLANTING

They reputedly benefit from tansy, garlic or marigolds, and strawberries may be grown close by but not underneath them. Do not try to grow potatoes nearby, as they will then become more prone to blight.

## OTHER USES

Raspberry canes are bristly if not thorny. They have little strength or heat value, but can be useful for wildlife shelters. I find short lengths, bundled together, then 'Swiss rolled' in newspaper and jammed into a cut-open plastic bottle, will make superb dry but airy ladybird hibernation quarters, which I hide in evergreen shrubs. Raspberry leaves and fruits have been used medicinally and have often traditionally been used as a tea.

**Raspberry tea**

**Raspberry canes can be used for turnip down canes**

## CULINARY USES

Raspberries make wonderful juices, jellies, drinks and sorbets. They are often combined with redcurrant juice to add tartness. Their wine is delicate and beautifully coloured. Raspberries can be frozen, but have poor texture afterwards.

### Kitty Topping's Raspberry Conserve
Makes about 2kg/4lb

*1kg/2lb  freshly picked raspberries*
*1kg/2lb caster sugar*

Pick fresh raspberries and hurry straight to the kitchen. Wash them and immediately heat them in a closed pan, rapidly but gently, swirling the pan to prevent the fruit from sticking and burning. Once most berries have softened, but before they break down totally, add the same weight of pre-warmed caster sugar. Stir while heating. One minute after you are absolutely sure all the sugar has completely dissolved, pour into small, heated jars and seal. Keep in the cool and use quickly once opened as the aim of this recipe is the stunning flavour, not the keeping quality. Try to use freshly picked fruit!

*Rubus fruticosus* from the order *Rosaceae*

# BLACKBERRIES
## BRAMBLES AND DEWBERRIES

*Bush/vine. Life span: medium to long. Deciduous, self-fertile.*
*Fruits: up to 2cm/¾ in, black, drupe. Value: rich in vitamin C.*

Even without its glistening blackberries, the native bramble is known to everyone for the long, arching and scrambling stems, armed with vicious thorns. What may be appreciated more by the picker than the walker is that the fruits vary widely from plant to plant. In fact there is no single native bramble or blackberry, but hosts of them. These have occasionally been crossed deliberately, and often inadvertently, with each other and with other *Rubus* and then again with other garden escapes. Although in some remote areas the stocks remain as several distinct but variable species, they may nevertheless have been altered in prehistory by unconscious human behaviour, as has also been suggested for raspberries (see page 78). Certainly now, any blackberry found near enough to human habitation to be picked, is highly likely to be a hybrid. And those nearby will probably be different. Just by looking at the fruits or the flowers in any area you will usually see great diversity.

The common brambles have fern-like leaves, thin purple or green stems, white or light purple flowers and small hard berries. A better and recognisable type of wild blackberry is *Rubus ulmifolius*, which has strong-growing, plum-coloured branches with five-lobed leaflets which are very light on the underside. It is not self-fertile.

An improved form of this blackberry, *bellidiflorus*, is grown ornamentally for its pink double flowers. *Rubus caesius*, the **dewberry**, is another distinctive species with three-lobed leaflets on long, thin, creeping, almost tendril-like stems, which can form large mats. The dewberry is smaller than most blackberries, with fruits containing fewer drupelets that break up as you pick them. These come earlier in summer than the blackberries and do not have the same shiny glossiness, but are more matt, with a whitish bloom similar to a plum's.

Blackberry remains have been found in many of the earliest European habitations and have been an important autumn crop since before recorded history. They were known to the Ancient Greeks, as much for the herbal properties of their leaves as for the fruits. They have always grown in great profusion in woods and hedges, on heaths and moorlands and indeed on every site as soon as it has been vacated by us. So much fruit has always been available free that brambles have never been grown on a large scale, and even the markets were satisfied by gleaning the wild crop. More recently there has been some breeding, with improved varieties such as **Bedford Giant** and **John Innes**. Most work has gone into producing thornless and large-fruited varieties, in effect neglecting flavour, so many people prefer to pick wild berries rather than use cultivated sorts. Certainly there has been far more interest in the development of hybrids with other *Rubus.* The North American dewberries, which derived from *R. Alleghaniensis,* were introduced to Europe. They are less vigorous and larger fruited than the natives, but have unfortunately also proved more tender. Other introductions have been more successful. The **Himalayan Giant** is an exceptionally vigorous variety, which has encroached on the wild populations all over. Strangely enough, the thornless **Oregon Cutleaf Blackberry** is not American, as formerly thought, but an old English variety of *R. laciniatus,* or **Parsley-leaved Blackberry**. It has bigger fruits, is nearly evergreen and comes almost true from seed. It was discovered in Surrey in 1770.

**Oregon Thornless**

## VARIETIES

**Bedford Giant** has a good rich flavour and is early. It has very long canes which are not as thick and brittle as **Himalayan Giant's**. The latter is a heavier cropper, nearly as well flavoured, and the lower part of the 6m/ 20ft canes can be nearly as thick as a child's arm. It is not a plant for the faint-hearted pruner. **John Innes** is a later variety and not as vigorous as these. Of the thornless varieties, the best that I have tried is the **Oregon Cutleaf**. This is attractive and reasonably well-flavoured. **Merton Thornless** is not so good a cropper; it tends to have rather too many short canes.

**Ashton Cross**

## CULTIVATION

The whole bramble family are gross feeders and love rich, moist soils. They will crop in a light shade, but are sweeter in the sun. Their cultivation and control is more like a pitched battle – if you give way they will take over your garden! Each stem arches over, grows down and roots from the tip to form a new stool of stems. Their sheer size and exuberance make them too much for most small, modern gardens, though they do crop handsomely. Heavy dressings of compost and thick mulches will keep up the yields. They do well grassed up underneath, and left to themselves will exclude weeds and anything smaller than large trees.

### Growing under Glass and in Containers

They are so easy outside that it would be bizarre to grow blackberries under cover. Blackberries do not like the cramped conditions pots afford, and as most of them are thorny they are seldom grown this way. The thornless ones are still too vigorous to thrive in any reasonable pot.

### Ornamental and Wildlife Value

The fruiting species are all delightful in flower, with all a mass of blossom in early summer. There are also many ornamental varieties and species, though most are too vigorous for modern gardens. Their vast quantity of blossom is valuable for bees and other insects and the fruit is an immense feast for wildlife, fattening up the bird population for the winter. The thicket of the bushes makes a snug, dry home for many small creatures, from ladybirds and beetles up to small rodents and birds.

### Maintenance Calendar

*Spring* Weed, mulch, spray seaweed solution.
*Summer* Tie in new shoots.
*Autumn* Root tips or cut off, pick fruit.
*Winter* Prune, add copious amounts of compost.

### Weed, Pest and Disease Control

Remarkably tough and reliable, blackberries pose few problems. Even the birds find it hard to eat them as fast as they are produced. Weeds can get into the stool, but rarely succeed for long as the brambles are so vigorous a weed themselves.

### Propagation

Seedlings come up everywhere, but are variable. The tips readily root and form new plants in the few weeks at the end of summer and into autumn. At this time, make sure the tips go into pots of compost if you want extra plants, or cut them off if you do not.

### Pruning and Training

Blackberries can fruit on wood older than one year old and the canes do not always die, as with raspberries. However, the new wood is better and carries fewer pests and diseases, so it is best to cut all the old and dead wood out and tie in the new. The canes are much longer and carry heavier loads than raspberries, so strong supports are necessary. The young canes need tying in during summer. If new plants are not needed, they are best de-tipped in late summer to stop them from rooting wherever they hit the ground.

### Harvesting and Storing

Traditionally blackberries are picked as they ripen, from late summer up until Michaelmas, or the first frost, when the Devil was supposed to have spat on them and made them sour. They are unusable red, but turn soft to the touch as they blacken. Bedford Giant ripens one berry in each bunch way ahead of the others. The berries are fairly tough-skinned so can travel well and last longer than raspberries if picked dry and not so overloaded that they pack down. They are best used as soon as possible or frozen; the spoilt texture when they defrost is no problem if they are to be used in cooking anyway.

## COMPANION PLANTING

Blackberries benefit from tansy or stinging nettles nearby and they are a good companion and sacrificial crop for grapevines.

**Blackberry flowers and fruit**

## CULINARY USES

Blackberries are often too sour to eat raw, but once cooked they are much tastier and do not have such a deleterious effect on one's insides. They make excellent jams, though as they are rather seedy the jelly is more often made. Frequently apples are included in blackberry dishes, especially jams and jellies, to aid setting and also because the flavours combine so lusciously. Blackberry wine is made by country folk everywhere and the berries used to be added to wines and spirits to give a distinctive colour, such as with the Red Muscat of Toulon.

### Bob's Blackberry and Apple Pancake Supreme
Serves 4

*approx 300ml/½pt pancake*
  *batter*
*250g/8oz blackberries*
*golden syrup to taste*
*water*
*30g/1oz cornflour*
*a little milk*
*2 apples*
*knob of butter*
*sugar, lemon juice, lots of cream*
  *or yoghurt*

Prepare the pancake batter and set aside. Wash the blackberries and simmer with golden syrup till soft. Strain, reserving the juice, and keep the fruit warm. To the juice add enough water to make it up to 200ml/6fl oz, return to the heat and bring to the boil. Cream the cornflour in a little milk, pour it into the boiling blackberry juice, stirring all the time, and cook until the juice thickens. Set aside.
Peel, core and chop the apples into chunks. Heat them rapidly with a little butter till they start to

crumble at the edges, then remove from the heat and keep warm. Next preheat a grill and a frying pan. Oil the pan. Once it is smoking, pour in all the pancake batter. As the bottom sets, but while the top is still liquid, take the pan off the heat, rapidly spoon in apple chunks, blackberry blobs and stripes of sauce. Swirl slightly so that the liquid batter blends a little but does not mix or cover completely. Sprinkle sugar generously over the top, then lemon juice and put under the red hot grill. Serve immediately the top has caramelised. This goes well with yoghurt or cream.

**Bob's Blackberry and Apple Pancake Supreme**

## OTHER USES

Brambles make a secure and quick barrier to many four-legged animals, and to two-legged rats. There are few in the world who will try to come over or through a fence or hedge clothed in any of this thorny bunch. Himalayan Giant is so big and tough it will stop almost anything between the size of a rabbit and that of a tank! The prunings are vicious but do burn well and fiercely.

*Rubus* hybrids from the order *Rosaceae*

# LOGANBERRIES
## BOYSENBERRIES AND TAYBERRIES

*Bush/vine. Life span: medium. Deciduous, mostly self-fertile.*
*Fruits: 6x2cm/2x¾in . Value: some vitamin C.*

Tayberries

The loganberry resembles a blackberry in manner of growth, but the fruits are more like raspberries: cylindrical, dull red and firm with a more acid flavour than either, making them sour raw but exquisite cooked. Boysenberry fruits are sweeter, more blackberry-like, larger and reddish-purple. They can be savoured raw with cream, but also make the celebrated jam. The tayberry is bigger and sweeter than either, with an aromatic flavour. When fully ripe, the enormous loganberry-like fruits are dark wine red or purple, and nearly three times the size of most other berries.

Loganberries were reputedly a hybrid of the American dewberry and raspberry, raised by a Judge Logan of California in 1882. Introduced to Britain in 1897, loganberries have remained the supreme culinary berry for nearly a century. The boysenberry has a similar history. It is believed to be another hybrid dewberry, but is probably in fact a youngberry x loganberry. It is not as hardy as other hybrids and does better in a warmer site than the rest. The **Medana Tayberry** was developed by the Scottish Crop Research Institute, who crossed the Oregon blackberry **Aurora** with a tetraploid raspberry to produce this excellent fruit. It is outstandingly the best of all hybrids so far.

## VARIETIES

There are several varieties and many other similar hybrids. The **Thornless Loganberry LY59** is often thorny; the fruit does not pull off the plug easily, but it is a very heavy cropper and has a good flavour. The totally thornfree **L654** is better picking, but is not quite as productive. I similarly find the **Thornless**

**Boysenberry** not as good a cropper as the thorned. There are no thornfree tayberries so far. The **Tummelberry** is like a late tayberry. The **Marionberry** and the **Youngberry** have the habit and appearance of blackberries, but the fruits have more flavour. The **Youngberry**, sometimes called the **Young Dewberry**, is available as a thornless version. The **Black Loganberry** is a New Zealand variety; it has cylindrical, tapering fruits, and is slow to establish and crop. The **Black Raspberry** is close to the **American Black Raspberry**, *R. occidentalis*, in habit and fruit. The **Laxtonberry** has a round, raspberry-like fruit and is not self-fertile. The **Veitchberry** is a blackberry crossed with an autumn-fruiting raspberry. It is more mulberry-like, with a later fruiting season than that of other hybrids and large sweet fruits.

Thornless loganberries

## CULTIVATION

The hybrids all need much the same, cool conditions and rich moist soils. The boysenberry will cope well with drier sites and indeed prefers some shelter. They are generally quite happy on a cool shady wall if they have a moist root run.

### Growing under Glass and in Containers

They prefer cool, shady positions, so find the dry heat under glass too much and become prone to pests such as red spider mite. Generally needing a bigger, cooler root run than can be afforded in a pot, they will resent the confinement, sulk and crop poorly.

### Ornamental and Wildlife Value

Not really very useful ornamentally, and thorny, but their flowers and fruits are valuable in the wild garden, bridging the gap between raspberries and blackberries well.

### Maintenance Calendar

*Spring* Weed, mulch and spray seaweed solution at monthly intervals.
*Summer* Protect and pick fruit, tie in new canes.
*Autumn* Root tips in pots or cut them off.
*Winter* Cut out old canes and tie in the new. Add copious compost.

### Propagation

As these are hybrids, they will not come true from seed, though interesting results may be had. Tips can be rooted in late summer and early autumn and occasionally the roots can be successfully divided.

### Pruning and Training

They grow much like blackberries, but can have more brittle canes, like raspberries, so care must be taken when bending them. They mostly fruit on young wood which dies and is cleared completely after the second year. Canes may produce again a third year, as blackberries might, but are usually unproductive, so annual replacement of all the old by new is generally considered a better policy.

### Weed, Pest and Disease Control

The only common major problem is bird losses, which are high as these plants mostly crop after the summer fruits, but before the wild blackberries. Weeds choking the stool can reduce their vigour more than with blackberries.

**Tayberries**

**Boysenberries**

## COMPANION PLANTING

Tansy, marigolds and alliums are all beneficial.

## OTHER USES

These canes will make good additional barriers with fences and hedges.

## CULINARY USES

Generally best-flavoured when fully ripe, these fruits are not very acid and benefit from the addition of redcurrant juice to many recipes. Varieties from which the plug is not easily removed, or which even detach a thorny stalk with the fruit, are best used by straining or juicing them first. These fruits make excellent jams, jellies, tarts and pies. The juices are delicious as drinks and also make wonderful sorbets.

### Summerberry Squash
Makes about 2.5l/4pts

*1kg/2lb mixed berries*
*500g/1lb redcurrants*
*1kg/2lb sugar*
*1l/1¾pts water*

Wash the fruits and simmer them down with half the water till soft, then strain. Cover the fruit pulp with the rest of the water, bring almost to boiling point, and strain again. Combine the strained juices and the sugar, heating gently if necessary to make sure the sugar dissolves completely. Cool, then pour into plastic bottles when cold and freeze till required. Defrost and dilute with water to taste.

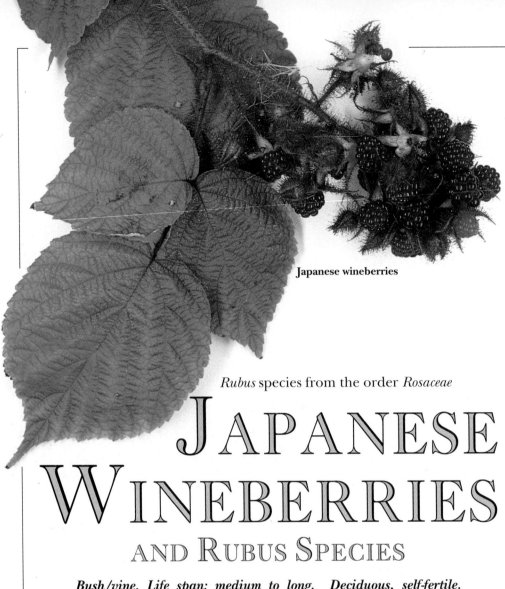

Japanese wineberries

*Rubus* species from the order *Rosaceae*

# JAPANESE WINEBERRIES

## AND RUBUS SPECIES

*Bush/vine. Life span: medium to long. Deciduous, self-fertile.*
*Fruits: variable. Value: some vitamin C.*

Rubus phoenicolasius, the Japanese wineberry, is the best of the vast raspberry/blackberry clan. This delicious and highly ornamental cane fruit resembles a vigorous raspberry covered with russet bristles and thorns. Unlike blackberries, these prick rather than jab, so are more pleasant to handle and pick. The fruits are smaller than blackberries, orange to cherry red, and they are generally far more palatable.

Japanese wineberries are not a hybrid, but a true species coming from north China and Japan. They certainly do come true, as you will find as they appear all over the garden once the birds spread the seed. Introduced to Britain around 1876, Japanese wineberries were considered worth cultivating and won a First Class Certificate from the Royal Horticultural Society in 1894. During the century since, however, they have not proved popular except with children of all ages who are lucky enough to find them.

There are no named varieties of any of these species, though there is some variation in leaf and fruit colour so there is some scope for improvement. *R. leucodermis*, **Blackcap**, has thorny, bluish stems with light green leaves, white underneath, on a medium-size bush, small white flowers and purple-black sweet fruits with a plum-like bloom. Yellow and red-fruited forms occur in its native north-west America. Another, *R. parviflorus*, the **Thimbleberry**, has large, fragrant, white flowers on strong, thornless stems and large, flattened, insipid, red berries. *R. parvifolius*, the **Australian Bramble**, was fruited in England in 1825 and has small, pink, tasty, juicy berries. The **Salmonberry**, *R. spectabilis*, has maroon red flowers on prickly erect stems and acid orange-yellow fruits. Apparently native Americans ate the cooked young shoots. *R. arcticus*, the **Arctic** or **Crimson Bramble**, has amber-coloured fruits that are said to taste mainly of pineapple. Very unusual is the **Rock** or **Roebuck Bramble**, *R. saxatilis*, which grows just like strawberry plants, and is eaten in much the same way. The Russians used to distil a spirit from the bramble berries.

## CULTIVATION

Although they will grow almost anywhere, the biggest berries come from plants growing in rich, moist soil well enriched with compost and leafmould. They will grow in moderate shade or full sun and are self-fertile.

Best grown on a wire fence or wired against a wall, after the manner of blackberries, they need a spacing of at least 3–4m/10ft apart and wires to at least 2m/7ft in height. Like most fruits, they do best when grown in well mulched, clean soil, but will still produce when grassed down around.

### Growing under Glass
These are mostly so easy to grow outside that there is little advantage to having them under glass except to extend the season.

### Growing in Containers
Growing them in pots will shorten their life and give greatly reduced yields, but it may be well worthwhile for both their snack and their garnishing value.

### Ornamental and Wildlife Value
Japanese wineberry leaves are a striking light green, with russet bristled stems, bright orangey-red fruits and a star-shaped calyx left over afterwards. They are highly decorative – probably the best fruiting plant to train against a whitewashed wall or up a pole for all-year-round interest and colour. Their value to wildlife is as immense as that of the whole clan.

### Maintenance Calendar
*Spring* Weed, mulch, spray seaweed solution.
*Summer* Protect and pick the fruit, tie in canes.
*Autumn* Pick the fruit and tie in canes.
*Winter* Cut out old canes, tie in the new, add copious quantities of compost.

### Propagation
These are species, so they come true from seed, and the tips can be layered in late summer and early autumn. Remove the old canes and tie in the new each autumn. Plants have a long life if well cared for. Prune out infections early.

### Weed, Pest and Disease Control
Choking and climbing weeds, such as nettles and bindweed, must be well controlled. There are no major problems other than the birds.

### Harvesting and Storing
Japanese wineberries are one of the most delicious of all fruits eaten fresh and also in quantity, though they will keep for a while in the cool of a refrigerator.

## COMPANION PLANTING

Tansy, garlic and French and pot marigolds are all potential good companions.

## OTHER USES

Their dense growth and prickly bristles make them attractive but impenetrable informal boundaries.

## CULINARY USES

Very valuable as garnishing for sweet and savoury dishes and simply eating off the plant. Some berries can be frozen to add to mixed fruit compôtes. Japanese wineberry jelly does not set, but forms a treacly syrup, ideal to accompany ice-cream.

### Wineberry Ripple
Serves 6

*1kg/2lb Japanese wineberries*
*approx 500g/1lb sugar*
*1kg/2lb superb vanilla ice-cream*

Freeze a few berries for garnishing. Simmer the rest till soft with just enough water to prevent sticking. Strain and weigh the juice. Thoroughly dissolve three-quarters of the juice's weight in sugar in the warm juice. Leave to cool completely. Once cooled, interleave scoops of ice-cream with the syrup, pressing it all down into a new container. Freeze the new rippled block and then scoop as required, garnishing well with the frozen berries.

**A cluster of Japanese wineberries**

*Vitis vinifera* from the order *Vitaceae*

# GRAPEVINES

*Vine up to any height. Life span: long. Deciduous, self-fertile.*
*Fruits: 2–3 cm/1in, ovoid, white, black, red. Value: generally beneficial.*

These scrambling vines have smooth, peeling, brown stems, large lobed leaves and bunches of grapes in autumn. The flowers are so insignificant they are rarely noticed, but are white and sweet-scented. The leaves colour well in autumn; red-berrying varieties will tend to go red and white ones yellow.

Grapes have been with us since Biblical times; Noah planted a vineyard. The Egyptians show full details of vineyards and wine-making in their relics from 2440 BC. The Romans spread vines all over Europe until, in the first century AD, Emperor Domitian protected his home market and ordered the extirpation of the grape from Britain, France and Spain. Two centuries later, Emperor Probus restored the vine, and long after the Roman Empire collapsed the monasteries kept vineyards going. By the time of the Domesday Book, in the eleventh century, there were still thirty-eight vineyards in Britain. But the climate was cooling and the last UK vineyards disappeared in the eighteenth century. During the nineteenth century grapes were widely grown in glasshouses and the Victorians raised grape cultivation to perfection, almost year round, in hothouses. Without the cheap labour and even cheaper fuel of Victorian times these hothouse grapes disappeared – though some survived, unproductive, on the sunny walls left when the glass had long gone. Since the Second World War there has been a revival of British viticulture and the vineyards are returning. Of course in Europe the grape has remained part of life, and in 1494 was already being grown in the New World. Over the last centuries the vine spread to almost every part of the world. Now most grapes are grown on American roots to prevent *Phylloxera* root aphids.

**Boskoop Glory**

## VARIETIES

Specific grapes for growing under glass or for wine-making are recommended in the next sections. The **Zante** or **Currant Grape** is nearly seedless. Introduced in 1855, it helped to make the Californian fruit industry, but is unsuitable in cooler regions. The hardiest and best grapes I have found for growing outside in a cool English climate are **Boskoop Glory**, a delicious, large-berried, dark purple grape; the **Strawberry Grape**, which produces rose-purple bunches in abundance, with a hint of American foxiness to them; and **Siegerrebe**, which has a rosé fruit with a sweet muscat flavour.

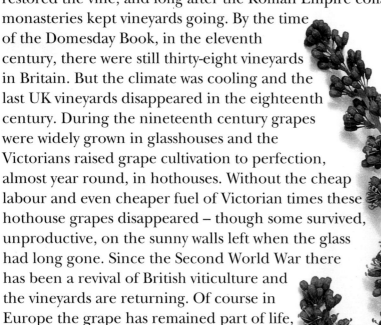

**Golden Chasselas**

## CULTIVATION

Grapevines are very easy to grow. They are usually too vigorous and do not need rich conditions to crop well. They need a hot, dry autumn to ripen well and thus are usually best grown on walls in cooler regions.

### Ornamental and Wildlife Value
Grapevines are quick to climb over and hide objects and turn bright colours in autumn, so they are valuable where space allows them to ramble. In the wild garden grapevines are useful both in flower and fruit.

### Growing under Glass and in Containers
These are so advantageous that there is a further section on page 95.

### Maintenance Calendar
*Spring* Weed, mulch and spray with seaweed solution at monthly intervals.
*Summer* Tie in and later nip out ends of shoots.
*Autumn* Protect and pick the fruit.
*Winter* Prune back hard.

### Propagation
In the UK we have no *Phylloxera* so we can grow grapes on their own roots; any ripe cutting will root in the autumn. Otherwise they are budded on resistant rootstocks.

### Pruning and Training
There are many ways to prune grapes and many sub-variations, enough to fill a book on their own. Left to themselves, vines will often produce rank growth and exhaust themselves with over-cropping; see sections on pages 93, 95 and 97.

**Netting is essential to keep birds off the grapes**

### Weed, Pest and Disease Control
Birds are the main cause of losses! Mould can be common in damp ripening seasons and mildews in dry ones. There are organic sprays to combat these but often the more resistant varieties crop unaided. The vine weevil may appear and is best treated with traps and by applying a parasitic nematode solution.

### Harvesting and Storing
Kept cool and dry, the grapes hang on the vines well. Cut bunches with a stalk, place the stalk in a bottle of water and keep the grapes in a cool, dry cellar for weeks. The less they are handled, the better they will keep!

## COMPANION PLANTING

Traditionally grown over elm or mulberry trees, grapevines are benefited by blackberries, sage, mustard and hyssop growing nearby, and inhibited by cabbages, radishes, Cypress spurge and even by laurels.

**Strawberry Grape**

## CULINARY USES

The best are excellent dessert fruits. They are easily juiced and the juice can be frozen for year-round use. They make good jellies and any surplus can be used for wine.

### *Love Nests*
per person

*individual meringue case approx 6 large dessert grapes, preferably muscat*

*marzipan, apricot conserve, clotted cream and dark chocolate to taste*

Peel and seed all but one grape per portion, and fill each with a pellet of marzipan. Smear the meringue bases with apricot conserve, then a layer of cream. Press in the filled grapes, cover with more cream, top with grated black chocolate and the perfect grape. Serve the nests immediately.

*Vitis* species from the order *Vitaceae*

# GRAPEVINE SPECIES

*Vine. Life span: long-lived.   Deciduous, sometimes self-fertile.*
*Fruit: up to 2cm/¾ in, in bunches, red or black.*

There are hundreds of true grapes, or *Vitis* species, which are mostly ornamental climbing vines. (Very closely resembling them are the *Ampelopsis* and *Parthenocissus*, of which the most common are known as **Virginia Creepers**. These resemble grapevines and even form bunches which are not edible.) These *Vitis* species are much grown for their covering capacity as they soon hide eyesores, and for their spectacular autumn colour. The vine fruits are often considered a bonus, but they offer different and exciting flavours.

Although the *Vitis vinifera* varieties are almost exclusively used for commercial purposes and wine-making, there are countless other *Vitis* species grapes eaten throughout the world, and have been since time immemorial. Their blood has also influenced the *V. vinifera* varieties on many occasions. These are but a few.

## VARIETIES

*Vitis aestivalis*, the **Summer**, **Bunch** or **Pigeon Grape** is from North America. It has heart-shaped leaves, downy underneath, scented flowers and early black grapes. It was first seen in Europe in 1656. *V. labrusca*, the **Plum**, **Skunk** or **Fox Grape** is another first brought to Europe in 1656. Its young shoots are covered in down and the leaves are thick, dark green on top, ageing to pink underneath. The fruits are rounded, blackish purple and have a distinctive musk or fox flavour, which some dislike. I enjoy it but not in wine! It has given rise to several good cultivars, such as **Concord**. *V. vulpina* is similar, with glossy leaves. Both have sweet-scented flowers. *V. rotundifolia* is the **Muscadine** or **Southern Fox Grape**, widely used for wine in the southern USA. It produces only half a dozen large fleshy grapes per cluster, usually black, though there are cultivated local white varieties. The **Winter**, **Chicken** or **Frost Grape** berry, *V. cordifolia*, is very hardy and does well on lime soils. The dark purple fruit has to be frosted before it is edible and is used for wine. Some local cultivated varieties have sweeter,

**Grapes on the vine**

tastier, red or black fruits. *V. riparia* is the high climbing **Riverbank Grape** from North America, with large, glossy, deeply lobed leaves and big panicles of male flowers that smell most distinctly and sweetly of mignonette. The fruits are black or amber and very acid. *V. coignetiae* comes from Japan and Korea. It has enormous leaves up to 30cm/1ft across. It is strong-growing; the leaves turn crimson and scarlet in autumn, so it is much used ornamentally, but the black grapes with a bloom are not very tasty. *V. davidii*, once called **Spinovitis** because it has spines on the shoots, stems and leaves, was brought from China for its glorious, rich crimson, autumn colouring. It also has edible black fruits. *V. californica* was originally cultivated by the native American Pueblo Indians. It must have been good because, to quote Sturtevant, 'The quantity of the fruit that an Indian will consume at any one time is scarcely credible.'

## CULTIVATION

Most species require much the same treatment as *V. vinifera* grapes. Over-rich conditions should be avoided. For most, a warm site is better, but they do not like warm winters and do best with some chilling in winter.

### Growing under Glass
The freedom from frost, rain and birds is valuable, but vines grown under glass become more susceptible to pests and mildew.

### Growing in Containers
Like *vinifera* grapevines, the species do not enjoy cramped conditions, but they can be grown in large pots. This shortens their life and gives small crops, but conveniently controls their vigour, allowing many to be grown in a small area.

### Ornamental and Wildlife Value
These are of the highest value as ornamentals and are useful for quick screens and coverings, though they can be too vigorous for small gardens unless hard pruned. Their bountiful flowers and fruit make them very good for wildlife gardens.

### Maintenance Calendar
*Spring* Weed, mulch and spray seaweed monthly.
*Summer* Tie in shoots, protect fruit, cut off tips.
*Autumn* Pick fruit.
*Winter* Prune well.

### Propagation
As these are species they can be grown from seed. Ripe wood cuttings, taken in late autumn, are best, and budding or grafting is possible.

### Weed, Pest and Disease Control
As these are species, they are generally resilient to most of the common grape pests and diseases. However, birds are still as much, if not more, of a problem.

## CULINARY USES

Most of these grapes are too small and pippy or sour to be used raw as dessert. They are best juiced or turned into jellies. The strong flavour of some, such as the Fox Grape, can make them unsuitable for wine.

### Grape Jelly
Makes approx. 2kg/4lb

*1kg/2lb grapes*
*approx.1kg/2lb sugar*

Simmer the grapes with only just enough water to stop them sticking. When they are soft, strain and weigh the liquid. Add the same weight of sugar to the juice and bring to the boil, skim until clear, bottle into hot jars and seal.

### Pruning and Training
See also sections on Grapes for Dessert and for Wine. There are many ways to prune grapes and many sub-variations, enough to fill a book on their own. The species are best treated much as regular vines which, left to themselves, often produce rank growth and nearly exhaust themselves with overcropping. For ornamental purposes that is no problem. However, for fruit they are best hard pruned and trained on a wall on wires about 50cm/1½ft apart, and on walls under cover for the more tender varieties. The main framework is formed in the first year, or so, covering the wires with stems that are furnished with fruiting spurs. Thereafter these shoot each spring and a flower truss appears between the third and fifth leaf. After another three or four leaves, each shoot is tipped, as are any replacements as they come. It is essential to thin the number of bunches, leaving no more than two per metre/yard run of cane. In winter, all shoots are cut back to one bud out from each spur, except for that of the leaders.

## COMPANION PLANTING

Species grapevines are probably benefited by blackberries, sage, mustard and hyssop growing nearby, and they are inhibited by cabbages, radishes, Cypress spurge and laurels.

## OTHER USES

As with other grapes, the grapevine prunings make great kindling.

*Vitis vinifera* from the order *Vitaceae*

# DESSERT GRAPES
## UNDER GLASS

*Vine.   Life span: exceptionally long-lived. Fruits: up to 3cm/1in, oval or round, any colour.*

Although most dessert grapes are grown in hot areas, the very best flavour, size and succulence come from grapes grown under glass in cooler regions. The varieties selected make bigger grapes with thinner skins than outdoor varieties. They are hardy, but depend on protection and warmth to ripen in time, so they will not crop outside except in favourable years.

Growing dessert grapes under glass was raised to an art by the Victorians, who could afford the heat and labour to produce perfect bunches of fine grapes almost every day of the year. Now, cheaper greenhouses and plastic-covered tunnels are within the reach of most gardeners and many varieties can be grown with little or no extra heat, so these gourmet fruits are once again achievable.

## VARIETIES

**Muscat Hamburg** is by far the best. It has oval black bunches of firm sweet grapes with a superb flavour. It is superior to **Black Hamburg**, though this too is a fine old variety, with bigger grapes in larger bunches. The **Black Hamburg** planted at Hampton Court Palace in 1796 still produces hundreds of bunches every year. Neither will crop outdoors save in an exceptional situation. **Buckland Sweetwater** has small, white, sweet and long-keeping grapes. **Chasselas Doré/ Golden Chasselas** is early, with translucent yellow fruits. It is most reliable and will even crop outdoors on a warm wall. **Perle de Czaba** and **Siegerrebe** are both speedier still and may crop outdoors, but they are better and reliable only on a hot wall or indoors. They both have the spicy muscat flavour; the **Perle** is yellow and **Siegerrebe** a rosé. The latter is a shy cropper, but has very choice berries.

## CULTIVATION

Amenable to almost any soil, they do not require rich conditions. The very best varieties need a long season with an early start. With Victorian heating they were started into growth in early spring. Heat was used to keep them frost-free through spring, and again in autumn to finish off a late crop. However, in a good season, many varieties can be cropped under glass just with the extra natural warmth afforded, the more so if they are grown in pots and brought in after chilling outside.

### Growing in Containers
This is most sensible with grapes. They resent the confined root system and need careful watering and pruning, but become controllable. Several varieties can go into a greenhouse too small for one planted in the ground. They are also conveniently moved outside for winter chilling and brought under for an early start, and again set outside for ripening in the warmth and protection.

**Warm sun is needed to ripen the grapes**

### Ornamental and Wildlife Value
Well pruned vines in pots or trained on walls are very decorative. The framework is easy to manipulate so almost any form can be achieved as long as all fruiting wood is kept at roughly the same level and in the light.

### Maintenance Calendar
*Spring* Bring in or heat greenhouse, spray with seaweed solution.
*Summer* Prune back tips, thin bunches, spray with seaweed solution.
*Autumn* Pick the fruits.
*Winter* Prune and put outside or chill glasshouse.

### Pruning and Training
In pots, vines are grown vertically or wound as spirals around a central supporting post. Grown in the ground under glass they are best planted outside, trained in through a hole and then treated the same as on a wall. This means wires about 50cm/1½ft apart and the same from the roof to allow enough space. The vine framework is formed over the first years, covering the wires with main stems furnished with fruiting spurs. Thereafter these shoot each spring and a flower truss appears between the third and fifth leaf. After another three or four leaves each shoot is tipped, as too are any replacements as they come. It is essential to thin the number of bunches, leaving no more than a two-metre/yard run of cane. In winter, shoots are all cut back to one bud out from each spur.

### Weed, Pest and Disease Control
Grapes can suffer many problems, but usually still produce. If the air is too humid when grapes are ripening they may mould. If they are kept too dry before then they get mildew and red spider mite. However, the permitted sprays and usual remedies work well with most problems. To exclude vine weevils from vines in pots, make a lid that fits snugly around the stem.

### Harvesting and Storing
Under cover they ripen early and hang longer as they are less threatened by pests or weather. Late varieties protected with paper bags may keep almost until the New Year.

**Vines in a pot need a central vertical support**

**Muscat Hamburg**

## COMPANION PLANTING

Grow French marigolds underneath the vines to deter whitefly.

## OTHER USES

Pieces of old vine, detached when pruning, will make good supports for climbers in their pots.

## CULINARY USES

The dessert fruit par excellence, their juice is delicious and freezes well.

For wine-making, the flavour and high sugar content will go well in combination with outdoor grapes which have lower sugar and higher acidity.

### *Recipe*
Just eat them as they come, sun warmed.

*Vitis vinifera* from the order *Vitaceae*

# GRAPES
## OUTSIDE AND FOR WINE

*Vine. Life span: long-lived. Deciduous, self-fertile.*
*Fruits: up to 2cm/1in. Some vitamin value.*

**Miguel Torres**

Wine grapes are as sweet, or more so, than dessert varieties. They have been bred to produce many small bunches rather than large berries, and this suits the vine's natural habit. The grapes are every bit as tasty, just smaller, and if you don't want the wine the juice is still valuable. They are hardier than dessert grapes and many are cropped commercially.

Although wine is predominantly produced in the Mediterranean region and areas with a similar climate, vineyards have been and are successful in many cool regions. The wines are usually light whites, but new hybrids now produce reds as well. Unfortunately European legislation does not permit commercial plantings of the new, high-yielding, disease-resistant hybrids, but they are still available to the amateur.

## CULTIVATION

Rich soils should be avoided as they will grow excessively. Obviously the warmer and sunnier the better: wires and supports should ideally run north–south, to give sun on both sides of each row.

### Growing in Containers
Although crops are light they can be grown in pots, see page 95.

### Ornamental and Wildlife Value
A vineyard is quite an accessory to any estate. Quote in bottles per year – it sounds bigger. The aim is two bottles per square metre/yard. The local wildlife are certainly going to like your vineyard unless you invest in netting against rabbits, rodents and birds.

### Maintenance Calendar
*Spring* Weed, spray with seaweed solution monthly.
*Summer* Thin and tie in new shoots, tip after flowering.
*Autumn* Protect fruit and pick when ripe.
*Winter* Prune back hard.

### Weed, Pest and Disease Control
The major losses are due to bird damage. Wet summers cause mouldy crops with little sweetness – little can be done about this. Mildew is easiest avoided by growing the more resistant varieties.

**Pinot Blanc**

**Chilean Riesling**

## VARIETIES

The classic wine grapes such as **Cabernet**, **Chardonnay/Pinot Blanc**, **Pinot Noir** and even **Riesling** are not suitable for cooler regions. **Mueller Thurgau/Riesling Sylvaner** is much planted for its excellent white wine, but mildew can be a problem. **Seyve Villard 5/276** is a white hybrid. It is more reliable, but lacks the character, so often both are grown. **Siegerrebe** is a light cropper of rosé berries which add flavour to blander grapes. The hybrids are by far the best croppers and most disease-resistant; **Triomphe d'Alsace**, **Leon Millot**, **Seibel 13053** and **Marshall Joffre** produce masses of dark black bunches which make good red wine or juice. The **Strawberry Grape** and **Schuyler** produce well and easily, but their flavour is not to everyone's taste. **Boskoop Glory** is the best outdoor dessert grape, a consistent producer of large, sweet black grapes.

**Chilean Cabernet-Sauvignon**

Vine weevils are controlled by having clean cultivation and keeping chickens underneath, except when the fruit is ripening.

### Pruning and Training

There are many different ways of treating vines outside. They can be grown with a permanent framework, as with indoor grapes or those on a wall, and this can be high or low, with benefits from air circulation or heat from the ground. You pays your money, and more for the higher methods! Strong posts and wires up to shoulder height are probably best, so the fruit is borne high enough up to avoid soil splash. Thus the bottom wire should not be less than 30cm/1ft high. A modified form of Guyot pruning is often used instead of spur pruning. A short leg reaches to the bottom wire and supports a strong shoot, or two, of last year's growth tied down horizontally to fruit from the buds along its length. Two replacements are allowed to grow from the leg and all other new shoots there are removed. Fruiting shoots are nipped out a few leaves after the flower truss, as with other methods.

### Harvesting and Storing

When the fruit has finally ripened enough, but before losses to the birds and mould have mounted, pick the bunches. A dry day after a rainy period gives cleaner bunches. Cut out mouldy bits as you go and press as quickly as possible for juice for drinking or for white wine. White wines can be made from black grapes; only certain Teinturier grapes have red juice. With most varieties the colour only comes from fermenting the skin. Red wines are fermented entire, with the grapes merely mashed. The juice is pressed from the pips and skins later. Extra pips and skins of those squeezed for juice can be added with benefit to the red wine mix as they serve to increase the tannins and sweetness.

**Harvesting Pinot Blanc grapes in Baden, Germany**

## COMPANION PLANTING

Asparagus is sometimes grown with the vines in France.

**Vineyards by the Mosel in Germany**

## OTHER USES

The vine prunings make good kindling. Big stems are often made into corkscrew handles.

## CULINARY USES

The juice is one of the most satisfying drinks. It can be used from the freezer throughout the year and is useful as a sweetener. The wine may be even better.

### Fruit Salad Soup
Serves as many as you like

Chop and slice finely as many fruits as available and serve in copious grape juice with cream or yoghurt and macaroon biscuits.

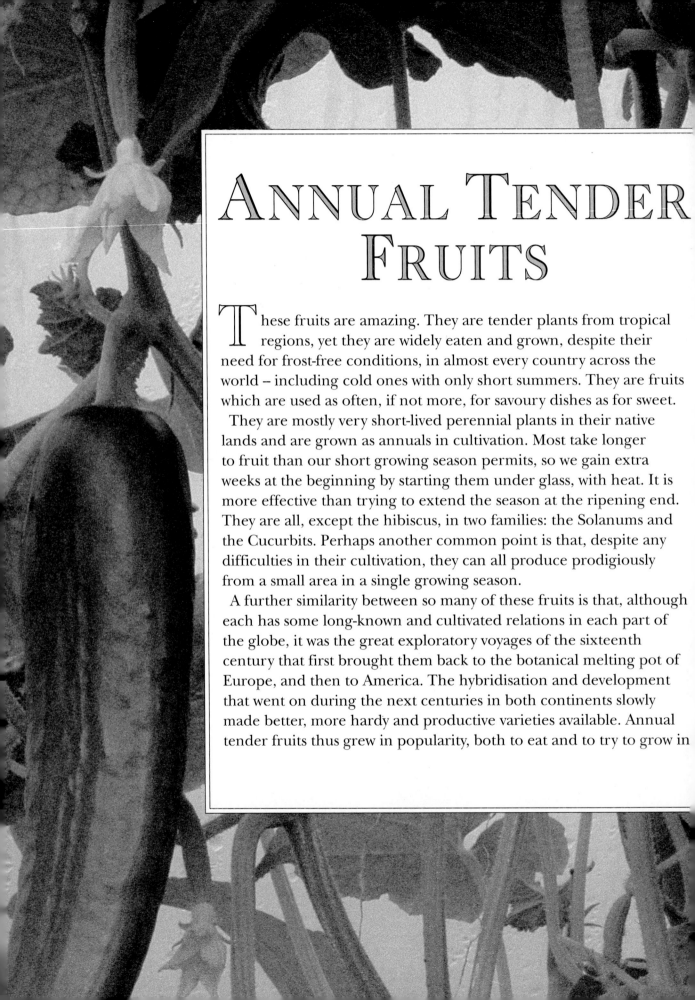

# ANNUAL TENDER FRUITS

These fruits are amazing. They are tender plants from tropical regions, yet they are widely eaten and grown, despite their need for frost-free conditions, in almost every country across the world – including cold ones with only short summers. They are fruits which are used as often, if not more, for savoury dishes as for sweet.

They are mostly very short-lived perennial plants in their native lands and are grown as annuals in cultivation. Most take longer to fruit than our short growing season permits, so we gain extra weeks at the beginning by starting them under glass, with heat. It is more effective than trying to extend the season at the ripening end. They are all, except the hibiscus, in two families: the Solanums and the Cucurbits. Perhaps another common point is that, despite any difficulties in their cultivation, they can all produce prodigiously from a small area in a single growing season.

A further similarity between so many of these fruits is that, although each has some long-known and cultivated relations in each part of the globe, it was the great exploratory voyages of the sixteenth century that first brought them back to the botanical melting pot of Europe, and then to America. The hybridisation and development that went on during the next centuries in both continents slowly made better, more hardy and productive varieties available. Annual tender fruits thus grew in popularity, both to eat and to try to grow in the adopted environment. In particular, the colonisation of the Canary Islands allowed the winter cultivation of many of these fruits within shipping distance of the European markets. Tremendous quantities began to be traded and even today the islands still supply much of the market. The development of cheaper glasshouses and steam boilers then allowed the Victorians to produce most of these fruits nearly year round in some of the more favoured sites nearer home, such as the Channel Islands. These won a large share of the business. Then the Dutch took over and for many years they dominated the market. Much of their trade still survives today, but long-distance air freight now brings in produce from further afield, and the tomatoes, melons or courgettes on sale at your local supermarket may well have ripened under some African, Israeli or South American sun.

Meanwhile, gardeners were happy to grow these plants at home, at first on rather a hit-or-miss basis, as they were so subject to the weather. However as glass became cheaper, greenhouses and cloches were used to make the crops more reliable. The plants were started, and the more tender grown to maturity, in frames on top of hotbeds. Faster fruiting and hardier varieties, developed for the commercial market, were sold and enthusiastic amateurs bred for flavour. From the original few native species we now have thousands of different varieties. So it is now possible to grow all of these fruits consistently, even in a cool country such as the UK, with only an amateur greenhouse and a sheltered garden or a warm wall.

Almost every garden seems to have a greenhouse with tomatoes in it, and young plants are on sale everywhere throughout late spring. At autumn Harvest Festivals the biggest marrow holds pride of place. Strange surroundings indeed for tropical South American plants!

*Lycopersicon esculentum* from the order *Solanaceae*

# TOMATOES

*Herbaceous. Life span: annual/short-lived perennial. Self-fertile. Fruits: from 1cm/½in to 10cm/4in weighing from a few grams/about ½oz to over 500g/1lb, red or yellow. Value: rich in vitamins A and C.*

A sprawling climber normally grown as an annual, the tomato is perennial but short-lived and only survives where the temperature does not fall below about 10°C/50°F. The racemes of yellow flowers are produced between leaf joints on the stems. Each flower is self-fertile, but better pollination is obtained by tapping the plant or by bees. The fruits have thick walls, making cells for the seeds in a thin jelly. In varieties such as **San Marzano**, an excellent culinary plum tomato, this jelly has been reduced; it is less watery and more flesh-like.

Once known as Gold, Peruvian or Love Apples, the tomato was originally golden, rarely red, but now the reds predominate, though yellow and striped varieties are sometimes grown. The early fruits were deeply ribbed and flattened; the beefsteak variety **Marmande** still sometimes exhibits such an appearance. Tomatoes are first recorded in 1554 in Italy, called Tomati. They had been found in Mexico, grown amongst maize, but had originated from the mountains of Peru and had already long been cultivated in South America. They remained only an interesting novelty for more than two centuries until becoming popular in Italy at the beginning of the nineteenth century and later throughout the USA and Europe.

## VARIETIES

There are many different types and varieties. There are those for greenhouse or outdoor culture; round or large ones with thin skins for salads, or thick-skinned ones for travel; plum varieties for juicing and cooking; cherry tomatoes for bite-size snacks. It is well to try several till you find what suits your site, soil and conditions.

## CULTIVATION

Tomatoes need warm, sunny sites, support, and rich, moist soil. They can be grown outside in cooler areas only if started off early under cover. Although most crops are rotated, many biodynamic gardeners grow tomatoes on the same site every year, and may feed them with compost made from tomato leaves.

**Growing under Glass**
Tomatoes are most reliably grown this way in colder areas (see page 104).

**Growing in Containers**
Tomatoes do best and are least work grown in the ground as they suffer many problems with the confined root run and sporadic watering in a pot. In the open garden grow tomatoes in the soil. Under glass, pots are still a poor alternative to the border soil, but see the greenhouse tomatoes on page 104.

**A spray of ripe tomatoes**

**Matador**

### Ornamental and Wildlife Value

Several tomatoes are useful decorative plants, for example, those designed to trail in hanging baskets, such as **Tumbler**, the patio or dwarf varieties such as the delicious **Minibel**, and those with brightly striped fruits like **Tigerella**.

### Maintenance Calendar

*Spring* Sow, pot up, disbud, tie up, spray with seaweed at weekly intervals.
*Summer* Disbud, tie up, pollinate flowers, pick fruit.
*Autumn* Disbud, tie in, top off, pick the fruit.
*Winter* Dig up and compost. Ripen the green fruits in warm dark.

### Propagation

Tomatoes are easily grown from seed and they usually come true unless they are F1 hybrids. To save tomato seeds, scoop the pulp into a jar of water and allow them to ferment for two days in a warm room, sieve, wash the seeds, sieve again and dry well. Tips, suckers and detached shoots can be rooted and the stems layered.

### Pruning and Training

Most tomatoes are grown on a single stem. This may be extended almost indefinitely, limited only by the growing conditions. A single stem cordon may be vertical or sloping, for convenience, but tomatoes can also be trained with more stems as fans or espaliers. The stems need support, tied to a cane or wound round a string. Each stem needs frequent pruning, nipping out all side shoots from the leaf joints while small to prevent crowding. Some varieties are determinate (i.e. they form bushes and do not grow well as cordons). These kinds are not pruned, and all shoots are left to form a rambling bush, best supported on netting or straw to prevent the fruits touching the soil.

**Golden Sunrise**

### Weed, Pest and Disease Control

Tomato plants may suffer several problems, but are reliably productive, given basically good conditions. Aphid attacks are a threat while the plants are small, but are easily remedied. Bird damage occurs to outdoor crops and several diseases may make the plants short-lived, but they should have set a good crop by then anyway.

### Harvesting and Storing

Red tomatoes start green, ripening to yellow orange then red. They ripen best if left to hang, but green fruits can be ripened in any warm place. They are sun-dried in hot regions and can be frozen whole without preparation, but take less space puréed. (Slip the skins off frozen tomatoes by putting them in hot water just for an instant.)

## OTHER USES

Surplus fruits feed poultry and many animals.

## COMPANION PLANTING

Tomatoes should be kept away from brassicas and potatoes as they mutually suffer blight. French marigolds, basil, carrots, onions, garlic and asparagus are beneficial grown nearby.

**Vine-grown tomatoes with marigolds and daisies in the foreground**

## CULINARY USES

Although definitely a fruit, tomatoes are now used predominantly in savoury dishes and as salad vegetables. The juice makes good stocks and sauces.

### Bob's Economical Marmalade

Makes about 2.5kg/5lb

*1kg/2lb yellow tomatoes*
*500g/1lb whitecurrants*
*1 lemon*
*approx.1kg/2lb sugar*

Chop the tomatoes and simmer with the whitecurrants till soft, then strain. Add the squeezed and very finely sliced lemon to the juice and weigh. Bring back to the boil, add the same weight of sugar, boil till the sugar has completely dissolved, then pour into warm, sterilised jars. Cover at once.

*Lycopersicon esculentum* from the order *Solanaceae*

# TOMATOES
## GROWN OUTSIDE

*Herbaceous. Life span: annual. Fruits: from 1cm/½ in to 10cm/4in weighing from a few grams/about ½ oz to over 500g/1lb, red or yellow. Value: rich in vitamins A and C.*

**San Marzano**

Outdoor varieties are much the same as indoor ones and some are dual purpose, such as the superb **Gardener's Delight**. Generally, however, outdoor plants are hardier, preferring more airy conditions, and may suffer in the close humidity of a greenhouse. Outdoor varieties from hot countries are often not suitable for the low light and close, damp conditions in an equally hot, but northern greenhouse, and are better off grown in front of a hot wall, having been started off under cover.

I grow two lots: one reliable crop under glass and plastic, but I always prefer the flavour of the crop grown and ripened outside, even if they are often beaten by the weather.

Much breeding has gone into making tomato plants hardier, so they can be grown further north, and faster, so that they can be cropped in a shorter time. This also helps us to grow them in the short summers at high latitudes, but even so they have to be started off under cover and planted out, so that the fruits can be ripening before the frosts of autumn kill the plants.

## CULTIVATION

A warm spot with rich, moist soil is needed, so incorporate copious quantities of compost beforehand. A shovelful of wood ashes per square metre/yard will provide the potash that tomatoes crave. Shelter is very beneficial, so provide a good site in front of a sunny wall or, failing that, in front of other, tougher plants. Strong supports are essential, but in cool regions tomatoes are unlikely to swell, let alone ripen, more than half a dozen trusses, so posts need only be shoulder high.

**Growing in Containers**
Tomatoes do badly in containers compared to growing in the soil, especially if they are unevenly watered. If no soil is available then a large, deep pot is better than a flat plastic bag, as it allows deeper roots with less risk of water saturation in the bottom. Grow plants singly. Do not plant several in a bag, as often suggested, as this produces fewer fruit for the same effort. Water religiously and feed frequently. Feed made from rotted down comfrey is perfect once diluted; seaweed and fish emulsion feeds are also beneficial.

## VARIETIES

Currently my favourite outdoor varieties for flavour are the small-fruited **Gardener's Delight**, **Sweet 100**, the dwarf **Minibel** and the orange **Sungold**. For outdoor productivity, the bush **Amateur** is reliable, the potato-leafed **Herald** is hardy and well-flavoured, and the yellow **Golden Sunrise** sometimes fools the birds, who wait for it to ripen. The big beefsteak **Marmande** types are wonderful even though you have to restrict each plant to only a couple of fruits. Plum tomatoes such as **San Marzano** and **Super Roma** are worth growing, even if they do fruit only poorly outdoors, as they are so tasty once cooked.

**Gardener's Delight**

### Ornamental and Wildlife Value

As suggested on page 101, tomatoes can also be used decoratively. Their value to wildlife is small, as the fruit often rots before it ripens. Self-sown seed also rarely lives long enough to reproduce itself.

### Maintenance Calendar

*Spring* Start off under cover, pot up, harden off and plant out after frosts, spray with seaweed solution fortnightly.
*Summer* Nip out sideshoots, tie up, protect and pick the fruit.
*Autumn* Cut stems off before frost and hang in dry, airy shed to ripen fruits.
*Winter* Prepare next year's site with plentiful compost and ashes.

### Propagation

Start off outdoor tomatoes four to six weeks before the last expected frost date. Sow them singly in small pots in a warm, light place. Pot them up regularly, make sure they are well hardened off, protect them the first few nights, and again on cold nights. Plant them deep to encourage basal rooting.

### Pruning and Training

Pot up often, support with a cane and nip out sideshoots. The first truss should be ready to flower when they go out. You should nip out the tip after six trusses.

**Shirley (foreground) and Gardener's Delight further back**

**Tomatoes need shelter and good support to grow well outdoors**

### Weed, Pest and Disease Control

The worst problems are cold weather and late frosts. In warm, damp seasons potato blight may cause problems, but it can be prevented with Bordeaux mixture. Birds eat the ripe fruits.

### Harvesting and Storing

Pick ripe fruit or protect it from the birds. Once frosts are likely, cut off the stems and hang them upside-down in a dry, airy shed to ripen the green fruit on the vines.

### OTHER USES

The poisonous leaves have been used as a pesticide.

### COMPANION PLANTING

Tomatoes should be kept away from brassicas and potatoes, as they mutually suffer blight. French marigolds, basil, carrots, onions, garlic and asparagus are beneficial grown nearby.

### CULINARY USES

Outdoor tomatoes have better flavour than those grown indoors, so I use them first for salads and then for drinking juice.

### *Stuffed Tomatoes*
Serves 4

*1 large onion*
*1 clove garlic*
*knob of butter*
*1 large carrot*
*1 large potato*
*a few French beans, topped and tailed*
*1 cob sweetcorn*
*1 bunch of peas*
*mayonnaise*
*black pepper*
*4 large tomatoes*

Chop and fry the onion and garlic in butter until transparent. Cool. Boil the carrot, potato, French beans, sweetcorn cob and peas till cooked. Drain and cool. Scrape the corn off the cob, cut the carrot and potato into pea-sized cubes and chop the beans into short lengths. Mix all together with enough mayonnaise to bind it, add plenty of black pepper. Cut a lid off each tomato and hollow out the centre. Fill with the vegetable mayonnaise mixture.

*Lycopersicon esculentum* from the order *Solanaceae*

# TOMATOES
## GROWN UNDER GLASS

*Herbaceous. Life span: annual, potentially perennial.*
*Fruits: from 1cm/½ in to 10cm/4in weighing from a few grams/about ½ oz*
*to over 500g/1lb, red or yellow. Value: rich in vitamins A and C.*

Greenhouse tomatoes are similar to outdoor varieties, but have been specially bred for rapid cropping in warm, low light conditions and for their disease resistance. Some will not grow outdoors at all, as they need shelter and warmth, but many varieties are dual purpose and grow happily in a favoured outdoor site.

It is quite amazing that a plant native to the mountains of tropical Peru could become a major commercial crop throughout the year in temperate countries of the world. The first winter tomatoes were brought from hotter regions such as the Canaries to the markets of Europe. Development of large glasshouses and heating allowed these tender fruits to be grown in favoured areas such as the Channel Islands. Eventually better varieties and improved technology made even the cool countryside of Holland one of the largest producers of salad tomatoes.

**Alicante tomatoes in gro bags**

## VARIETIES

The best and quickest varieties change yearly. **Counter**, **Cyclon** and **Shirley** are all excellent and the large **Dombito** is one of the best flavoured of all, rivalling **Ailsa Craig**. **Gardener's Delight**, **Sungold** and **Golden Sunrise** are dual purpose and very tasty.

**Super Roma** and **San Marzano** plum tomatoes prefer cool greenhouse conditions to hothouse, and produce masses of fleshy cooking fruits.

## CULTIVATION

The soil should be well enriched with copious compost, wood ashes and seaweed meal. Calcified seaweed or lime should be applied every other year and forked in. Ideally, automatic watering systems should be arranged, preferably to the roots to keep the foliage dry. Strong supports are also necessary for a good crop. Ensure ventilation and heating are adequate.

**Greenhouse tomatoes**

### Growing in Containers
It is said that tomatoes should be grown in containers as the greenhouse soil becomes unsuitable for them with regular use. For most gardeners, the work of changing the soil every six years or so, if this degradation does occur, would still be less than the six years of carrying in and out all the containers full of potting compost and the extra water and feed they require. Still, if containers you must have, use big ones, one plant to each, and arrange a religious watering and feeding regime.

### Ornamental and Wildlife Value
Patio and hanging varieties can both be used most decoratively, without taking up too much space, in either a conservatory or greenhouse. Tomatoes are happy in similar conditions to humans, while both find conditions for cucumbers and melons too humid.

### Maintenance Calendar
*Spring* Sow later crops, pot up, tie in, de-shoot.
*Summer* Tie in, de-shoot, pick fruit.
*Autumn* Clear early crops, stop late crops.
*Winter* Sow early crops for heated, lit greenhouses.

### Propagation
Best grown from seed for the cleanest plants, but shoots from existing stock can be layered or taken as cuttings. Plants for heated and lit greenhouses can be started at almost any time, although for heated greenhouses without lights, the earliest sowing time is late winter as otherwise there is not enough light to produce good growth or fruit as the plants mature. If the greenhouse cannot be heated, plants are best sown about six weeks before the last hard frost is expected.

**Totem tomatoes in a suitably large container**

## CULINARY USES

Tomatoes grown indoors seem to have less flavour and acidity than the same varieties grown outside. None the less, they are delicious and glass protection lengthens the season for fresh tomatoes to more than half the year. Plum tomatoes are the best both for purées and pasta sauces.

### Proper Breakfast
per person, all quantities to taste

*pork sausages*
*bacon*
*plum tomatoes*
*mushrooms*
*eggs*
*buttered toast*
*mustard*

First fry sausages and bacon and set aside to keep warm. Then slice the tomatoes in half lengthways before frying with the mushrooms in the meat fat. Set these aside and fry the eggs. Serve all together with some hot buttered toast and mustard.

### Weed, Pest and Disease Control

Aphids and whitefly can appear and require the usual remedies. The worst problems are usually caused by poor growing conditions. Tomatoes need warmth, light and a buoyant atmosphere to crop well under glass; if it is humid

**San Marzano plum tomatoes**

and close they may get moulds. Blossom end rot is a black corkiness of the flower end of the fruit, often caused by poor watering of plants with a confined root system. Green tops to fruits are similarly caused, especially with high temperature conditions.

### Pruning and Training

Good ventilation is essential under cover, so regular pruning is needed, usually to a single stem. Lower leaves are also removed, once they start to fade, to allow better air circulation. Obviously mouldy leaves, fruits and flowers should all be removed just as soon as they are spotted.

### Harvesting and Storing

Under cover, fruits can be left to hang but watch out for mould. With dry conditions in a frost-free but otherwise unheated greenhouse, they may still be usable off the vine in the winter. The fruits are said to ripen more quickly with bananas near them.

## COMPANION PLANTING

Always have plenty of French marigolds as they keep whitefly away. Alyssum is a good pollinator attractant and basil grows well with tomatoes, as they enjoy similar conditions.

## OTHER USES

Puréed plum tomatoes are an invaluable antidote to a dose of skunk perfume.

**Counter**

*Capsicum* species from the order *Solanaceae*

# HOT AND SWEET PEPPERS

*Herbaceous to semi-shrubby, up to 1m/3ft. Life span: annual or perennial. Tender, self-fertile. Fruits: from 2.5cm/1in to 15x7cm/6x3in, spherical to box-shaped, often with dented sides. Usually yellow, green or red. Value: very rich in vitamin C.*

A true fruit, though mostly used in a savoury manner, the sweet pepper has large, oblong fruits, which are green, ripening to yellow, purple or usually red. These have thick, crunchy walls enclosing a void and small seeds adhering to white ligaments. The fruits of hot peppers are much smaller and pointed, usually green ripening red, and thin-walled. The fruits are borne singly, following the white flowers which come from leaf axils and where stems divide. Both plants are tender, with a long growing season, so need starting under cover and, in most regions, are best staying there.

The hot and sweet peppers come from tropical America, and are not closely related to white or black peppercorns, which are the seeds of a South Asian native climber, *Piper nigrum.* The first fruiting pepper in Europe was recorded in 1493 as having been brought back from the so-called New World with Columbus. It was pungent and all early interest was in the fiercely burning hot or chilli form, now called *Capsicum frutescens.* It probably helped to disguise the putrid food of the times. The subtler flavour of the milder sweet peppers, *C. annuum,* were ignored until recent times, when they became particularly valued for salads, for flavour and for their high vitamin C content.

**Assorted hot and sweet pepper varieties**

## VARIETIES

Very much a matter of taste: **Canape F1** is very good, a reliable sweet fruiter. I like **Hungarian Hot Wax** which is yellow to crimson, depending when picked. It is mild and never gets too fierce. **Hero** is long, thin, red and hot; any chillies are evil. There are many carefully selected and fiendishly hot varieties around the world. Take care. If you come across **Bonnet Peppers**, you have been warned!

## CULTIVATION

Easier than tomatoes, peppers will require a moderately rich, moist soil, warmth and light. Some support is needed for the huge crops. Otherwise they rarely have any problems.

### Growing under Glass

I have succeeded in occasionally growing good crops outdoors, but these plants really require the shelter and warmth of a greenhouse. Safe inside, they are then both admirable and productive subjects.

### Growing in Containers

These are more suited than many plants to growing in pots. They must have careful watering and crops will be smaller, but they are neat and simple to look after. The pot size effectively controls that of the plant.

### Ornamental and Wildlife Value

The compact habit, glossy foliage and brightly coloured fruits make these very attractive. The long chilli varieties are smaller-leaved and fruit even more prolifically, making them extremely decorative for a long time.

**Chilli pepper**

**Triton**

### Maintenance Calendar

*Spring* Sow early, pot up often, spray seaweed, watch for aphids.
*Summer* Support bushes, take some fruits early.
*Autumn* Keep watch for mould and slug damage.
*Winter* Remove stumps and compost.

### Propagation

Start the seeds off singly in small pots, keeping warm, light and airy as for tomato plants, and pot up regularly. They can go in their final position once the warmth can be sustained, and outside after hardening off, but only in a very favoured spot. Cuttings can be taken and the seed will come true of non-F1 varieties grown alone.

### Pruning and Training

Nipping out the tips of leggy plants and supporting heavy crops are all that is needed. Take some fruits unripe to relieve any crowding.

### Weed, Pest and Disease Control

The worst problem is aphid attacks when the plants are seedlings, which may check growth. Slugs will eat them and damage the fruits. Mould may appear in humid conditions in late autumn.

### Harvesting and Storing

They can be eaten green, but are less challenging when ripe, which usually means dark red, when they have a rich, sweet flavour. Hot peppers are invariably cooked or pickled. The fruits can hang on the bushes for a while, especially the hotter varieties, but for long-term storage they are best sliced and dried or frozen. They travel well and should keep for days.

## OTHER USES

The seeds and fruits have been used medicinally.

## COMPANION PLANTING

These plants give off exudates that kill Fusarium moulds, so they benefit tomatoes grown nearby and enjoy similar conditions. Both will also get on well with basil.

## CULINARY USES

The seeds and white ligaments contain most of the pungent heat; removing them reduces it considerably. Paprika and pimento are made from hotter varieties of sweet pepper. Tabasco is made from fiery, small, chilli hot peppers, and cayenne pepper is made from powdered dried fruits. Just because they are grown in a cool country does not make them any less hot.

### *Sweet Starter*
per person

*1 dark red sweet pepper*
*equal measures of chopped celery, grated apple, grated carrot, peas and mayonnaise*
*a half measure of chopped onion*
*some paprika and a little parsley*

Cut off the tops of the pepper, remove the seeds and white ligament and fill with mixture of vegetables and mayonnaise. Garnish with a sprinkle of paprika and a sprig of parsley. (A measure of grated hard cheese can be included in the mix if wished.)

*Solanum melongena* from the order *Solanaceae*

# AUBERGINES
## EGGPLANTS AND HUCKLEBERRIES

*Herbaceous, up to 1.5m/5ft. Life span: perennial grown as an annual. Fruits: variable size and shape, from 1cm/½in spheres to 6x25cm/2½x10in cylindrical whoppers, purple, ivory or white.*

**Long Purple**

Bonica leaf and flower

### VARIETIES

The purple varieties dominate. Some, such as **Black Enorma**, produce, well, enormous fruits. Most varieties are similar in growth, so the larger-fruited ones make the best choice as there is much less waste when they are peeled. Avoid the white, egg-shaped and small-fruited varieties, except out of curiosity, as they are relatively poor croppers. **Huckleberries**, *S. intrusum*, are closely related and similar, but have small, insipid, sweet, black berries, remarkably like those of the poisonous *S. nigrum*, **Black Nightshade**. They come from Africa and are indeed sometimes eaten in parts of North America, though frequently confused in literature with *Viburnum* **Huckleberries**, and the far more popular *Gaylussacia* **Huckleberries** (which are *Ericaceae* much resembling *Vacciniums*).

*Solanum quitoense*, Naranjilla or **Quito Orange,** is a large, half-hardy, shoulder-high shrub which has decorative leaves and small, orange-like fruits, much esteemed in their native Peruvian Andes for their sweet, fragrant, green pulp.

Unlike tomatoes or peppers, aubergine fruits are not sweet or edible raw. The large, purple, glossy, smooth-skinned fruits are carried on waist-high, stiff bushes with large, soft, almost downy leaves. The flowers are purple, resembling the potato more closely than the tomato, and spring from the stems between leaf joints. They frequently have spines on the stems.

The aubergine is often called the eggplant as the early forms, which you may still find, are white or ivory and egg-shaped. It was also known formerly as the mad apple. It is a native of Asia and was unknown to the Ancient Greeks or Romans. Its first mention is in fifth-century Chinese writings. In the West,

**Huckleberries**

it became known in the Mediterranean region in the twelfth and thirteenth centuries from Arab sources, and finally reached northern Europe in the fifteenth and sixteenth centuries. However, it still was not widely grown in Europe until the nineteenth century. Even now, it is still not commonly appreciated.

**Black Enorma**

## CULTIVATION

Aubergines and similar species all need warmer conditions than tomatoes or peppers and a long growing season. They need a rich, moist soil and some support for the heaviest crops.

### Growing under Glass
Too difficult for outdoor cultivation in Britain and similar cool climates, cold-frames or cloches are not sufficient. Aubergines need a greenhouse, though I find they do better in a polythene-covered walk-in tunnel.

### Growing in Containers
Can be grown in large pots and are more amenable to this than tomatoes, but not as good as peppers. They need regular watering and feeding.

### Ornamental and Wildlife Value
Not very attractive plants, rather dingy in fact, but the fruits can be impressive. They have little value to wildlife.

### Maintenance Calendar
*Spring* Sow early, pot up, spray with seaweed, watch for aphids.
*Summer* Support heavy crops, pick as they ripen.
*Autumn* Use before the cold damages the fruits.
*Winter* Compost old plants and prepare for new.

### Propagation
Best grown from seed, which is, however, difficult to save. Cuttings may be possible.

Start the seed off early and keep potting up until their final position is warm enough. Aubergines prefer warmer conditions than peppers or tomatoes, but do not like it as humid or shady as cucumbers or melons.

### Pruning and Training
No pruning is needed. Removing dead leaves and any mould is good practice. The heaviest crops will benefit from support.

### Weed, Pest and Disease Control
Given good conditions and a long growing season they are usually productive regardless of the odd aphid or red spider mite attack. These necessitate only vigilance and the usual remedies.

### Harvesting and Storing
If left too long on the vine, the seeds form and make the fruit less desirable. Picked too small and young, they may be woody. They have a tough skin and travel well, keeping for a week or more. The fruits can be peeled, chopped, salted and fried in oil with garlic before freezing, when they are then useful for winter recipes.

## COMPANION PLANTING

Aubergines need similar conditions to peppers and tomatoes. They are benefited by peas, beans, tarragon and thyme nearby.

## CULINARY USES

The tough peel is probably best removed. The flesh is often salted, and rubbed with lemon juice or garlic before cooking. Aubergines will absorb lots of oil and thus acquire flavour in early cooking, and later will become a thick purée.

### Super Rat
Serves 6
(quantities are all approximate, add more or less according to taste and what is available)

*1 large aubergine*
*salt*
*garlic clove*
*1 large onion, sliced*
*olive oil*
*2 courgettes*
*1 red and 1 green pepper*
*1 ear of sweetcorn*
*6 plum or cooking tomatoes*
*red wine*
*bread, Parmesan cheese,*
*black pepper*

Peel and chop the aubergine. Salt and rub with garlic. Leave to stand for 10 minutes, then fry in the oil with the onion. Add the sliced courgettes, chopped red and green peppers, stripped corn and skinned tomatoes. Simmer slowly, adding a slug of red wine. When the vegetables have all softened, serve with bread, more wine and some grated cheese and pepper.

**A delicious aubergine soup and a curry from Kerala (above)**

*Physalis* species from the order *Solanaceae*

# CAPE GOOSEBERRIES
## AND GROUND CHERRIES

*Herbaceous. Life span: annual or short-lived perennial.*
*Fruits:   up to 6cm/2½ in, yellow to purple in papery husk. Value: rich in vitamin C.*

**Chinese Lantern**

The *Physalis* are all distantly related to tomatoes, peppers, aubergines and potatoes. Their best known member is the perennial **Chinese Lantern**, or **Bladder Cherry**, *P. franchetii/alkekengi*, which has straggling stems, heart-shaped leaves, inconspicuous flowers and bright orange, papery lanterns surrounding a red, edible but unpalatable fruit. The more palatable species are similar. The **Ground Cherry**, **Strawberry Tomato** or **Cossack Pineapple**, *P. pruinosa*, is low-growing, up to knee level, and has small, green fruits ripening to dirty yellow. Sweet and acid, they are vaguely pineapple-flavoured. *P. peruviana*, the **Cape Gooseberry, Ground** or **Winter Cherry**, is taller (about 1m/3ft) with yellower fruits. Both fruits are enclosed in similar, though duller, papery husks to those of the **Chinese Lantern**. Another similar fruit is the **Tomatillo** or **Jamberry**, *P. ixocarpa*, which is perennial, with much larger green or purplish berries filling the husk.

The first *Physalis* to be commonly eaten seems to be have been *P. alkekengi*, which was known to the Greek Dioscorides in the third century AD and was gathered from the wild. The annual *P. pruinosa*, which grows wild in North America, was popular with Native Americans and, apparently, also with Cossacks. It was introduced to England in the eighteenth century, but never caught on. The perennial **Cape Gooseberry**, *P. peruviana*, comes from tropical South America and became an important crop for the settlers on the Cape of Good Hope at the beginning of the nineteenth century. *P. ixocarpa*, the **Tomatillo** or **Jamberry**, comes from Mexico, but has become popular in many warm countries as it fruits easily and reliably and makes good sauces and preserves. Improved versions are now being offered for greenhouse culture elsewhere.

## VARIETIES

No varieties of any species are widely available except for *P. ixocarpa*, which has an improved form, **New Sugar Giant**, with fruits up to 6cm/2½in across, yellow or green instead of the usual purple. Many other *Physalis* species are cultivated locally in warm countries, but seed or plants are rarely available.

**Cape Gooseberries**

Leaves and fruit
of the Cape
Gooseberry

## CULTIVATION

The genus are all best
started under cover and
planted out. The
perennials can ripen
outdoors in a good season
in southern England, but
are far more reliable under
cover. *P. pruinosa* is tough
and may crop outdoors
without protection. They all
prefer a rich, light, warm soil
and a sunny position. Little
support is really necessary,
though they do flop.

### Growing under Glass
All the family give better and
sweeter fruits grown under
glass and present no major
problems; indeed they seem
to be designed for it.

### Growing in Containers
*P. pruinosa* is easily grown in
pots. The larger *Physalis* can
be grown likewise, but do not
do quite as well, preferring
a bigger root run. The
decorative *P. alkekengi* is
worth having in a pot just for
the show it provides.

### Ornamental and Wildlife Value
Most of the productive
species are nowhere near
as attractive as their more
ornamental cousin, the
**Chinese Lantern**. They have
small value to wildlife,
though the flowers are
popular with insects.

### Maintenance Calendar
*Spring* Sow indoors, pot up
and plant out once
hardened off.
*Summer* Support lax plants.
*Autumn* Pick fruits once
fully ripe, discard husks.

*Winter* Protect the roots of
perennials well for another
season.

### Propagation
Normally grown from seed,
the perennial varieties can
be multiplied by root
cuttings or division in the
spring. Start them off early
and pot up regularly to build
up a large root system.

### Pruning and Training
They need little attention
other than tying in the lax
growths and clearing away
the withered stems after
cropping. The roots of
perennial varieties can be
got through mild winters
under protection for earlier
crops the following year.

### Weed, Pest and Disease Control
They are remarkably pest-
and disease-free. The
**Tomatillo** is especially useful
as it can be used much like
a tomato, but can ripen as
early in cool conditions
and does not suffer blight
as tomatoes may.

### Harvesting and Storing
The fruits must be fully ripe
to be edible. They can hang
on the plant till required
as they are rarely attacked
by pest, disease or bird.
The husk is inedible and
must be removed.

## COMPANION PLANTING

There are no known
companion effects.

## OTHER USES

The ornamental Chinese
Lanterns can be dried for
winter decoration and have
been used medicinally.

**Cape Gooseberries in flower**

## CULINARY USES

Most *Physalis* berries are
relatively tasteless and
insipid raw but make
delicious preserves, sauces
and tarts. The **Cape
Gooseberry** often tastes
best on first acquaintance
and may rapidly lose its
appeal after the initial
elusive strawberry flavour.
It was once imported in
vast quantities from South
Africa, when it was known
as Tippari jam or jelly.

*Tippari Jelly*
Makes approx. 2kg/4lb

*1kg/2lb Cape Gooseberries
a little water
approx.1kg/2lb sugar*

Remove the husks from the
fruit and boil them with
just enough water to
prevent the fruit from
sticking. Strain the juice
and add its own weight in
sugar. Simmer till fully
dissolved, skim off scum,
then jar and seal.

*Hibiscus/Abelmoschas esculentas and sabdariffa from the order Malvaceae*

# OKRA

## LADIES' FINGERS, GUMBO AND ROZELLE

*Herbaceous shrubs, up to 2m/7ft. Life span: annual. Self-fertile.*
*Fruits: long green seedpod/fleshy sepal calyx. Minor nutrient value.*

Hibiscus, now properly *Abelmoschas*, species are related to cotton and mostly known for the opulent flowering sorts. However, two others provide fruits loved by culinary enthusiasts. *H. esculentus*, **okra**, **ladies' fingers** or **gumbo**, is the more common of the two. These are long, pointed, occasionally spiny, green seedpods that break down when cooked to a mucilaginous texture appreciated for thickening savoury dishes. The rozelle or **roselle**, the **Indian sorrel**, is a very similar plant, *H. sabdariffa*, commonly grown in India, Florida and its native West Indies. After the flower petals fall, the thick fleshy sepals remain, forming a swollen calyx around the short fruit. These are made into sweet dishes; rozelle jams and jelly are even sold commercially. Both hibiscus are tender, shrubby annuals with a long growing season. The rozelle has reddish stems. Okra flowers are usually yellow and live for only an hour or two; rozelle flowers are red or white.

Okra comes from tropical Africa and has long been cultivated in the Middle East and India. In the nineteenth century it was seen growing wild on the banks of the White Nile. Okra was probably first introduced to Europe by the Spanish Moors; Abul-Abbas el-Nebati, a native of Seville, described the plant in detail in 1216. As soon as the New World was discovered it travelled there and was known in Brazil by 1658. There are now many local varieties in the southern United States, where it is much appreciated, as well

Okra or 'Ladies' Fingers' (foreground)

as in Africa and around the Mediterranean. The rozelle, *H. sabdariffa*, travelled in the opposite direction, from the West Indies to Africa, and then on to India. In Asia they make a pickle from the petals of our familiar *H. rosa-sinensis*, the **Chinese Hibiscus**, and other species are used in much the same ways in many countries of the world.

**Flower and fruit of okra**

## VARIETIES

The fruits of **Clemson Spineless** are conveniently so. This is the most popular variety of okra. The fruits are best picked when small and the plant will then crop heavily. **Green Velvet** is also very good, velvet-fruited and heavy-cropping. The rozelle is found in both red- or white-flowered forms and a greenish-fruited form known as **White Sorrel**.

## CULTIVATION

They need a rich, moist, open soil and continuous unchecked growth. Stiff plants, usually only growing to waist height, the crops are light so no support is necessary and they can be planted at 75cm/2–3ft apart.

### Growing under Glass
In any other than a hot climate they must be grown under glass. Okra fails outside even in good English summers, and the rozelle needs hothouse conditions. Start them early as they have a long growing season, but only when you can give them enough warmth and light.

### Growing in Containers
Okra resents confinement in pots and does best on hotbeds, as is the case with melons and cucumbers.

### Ornamental and Wildlife Value
The flowers are brief and not showy and the fruits hard to spot. The okra flowers are valuable to insects in warmer climates.

### Maintenance Calendar
*Spring* Sow, pot on, mist daily and spray with seaweed solution fortnightly.
*Summer* Plant out on to hotbed, keep warm, pick the fruit.
*Autumn* Provide light and heat for late cropping.
*Winter* Compost the stems and stumps.

### Propagation
As these are annuals, they are grown from seed. They do best sown *in situ*.

### Pruning and Training
They need no pruning or training, but the fruits must be picked as they swell. If not they prevent others forming and become tough and fibrous.

### Weed, Pest, and Disease Control
They may suffer from aphids, but red spider mite is not often a problem as long as there are sufficiently humid growing conditions.

### Harvesting and Storing
Okra pods must be gathered while they are small or they prevent others forming and they get tougher. If there is a surplus they are best cut in half and dried. They can be stored thus in sealed jars or pulverised to a powder first.

## OTHER USES

The seeds apparently make the best substitute for coffee.

## CULINARY USES

Fresh or dried okra is added to soups, stews and casseroles especially in Egyptian, Indian and Creole cuisine. The seed pods may be battered and deep fried or, picked young, they can be pickled like capers. Rozelle fruits are made into delicious tarts, a beverage called sorrel drink, puddings, jam and jelly.

**In India okra in yoghurt is also known as Dahi Kadhi**

### *Gumbo*
Serves 4

*500g/1lb thinly-sliced okra*
*3 small onions, sliced*
*2 garlic cloves, crushed*
*25g/1oz butter*
*1 large red pepper, chopped*
*4 large cooking tomatoes, peeled*
*½ teaspoon cayenne pepper*
*salt to taste*
*1½pts good meaty stock*
*75g/3oz long-grain rice, pre-soaked in cold water for 1 hour*

Fry the okra, onions and garlic for 5 minutes in the butter. Add the chopped pepper, tomatoes, cayenne pepper and salt. Add the stock and simmer for an hour or two. Add the rice and simmer for at least 30 minutes before serving.

## COMPANION PLANTING

Okra gets on well with cucumbers and melons. The rozelle is often grown in hot countries as an intercrop between other slower plants while they are establishing. Both species must be kept away from cotton as they share pests and diseases.

**Okra growing under a protective cover**

*Cucumis melo* from the order *Cucurbitaceae*

# MELONS

*Herbaceous vine. Life span: annual. Self-fertile but requires assistance as separate male and female flowers. Fruits: 5–25cm/2–10in spheres or ovoids, whitish cream to green, netted or smooth. Value: rich in vitamins A and C, niacin and potassium.*

Melons belong to a very wide family of tender, trailing, annual vines, much resembling cucumbers in habit. They have broad leaves, softly prickled stems and small, yellow flowers, followed by fruits which can be any size from small to very large, round or oval. Melons are characterised by a thick, inedible rind covering succulent, melting flesh, which encloses a central cavity and a battalion of flat, pointed oval, whitish seeds.

The tasty, sweet, aromatic melons we know were apparently unknown to the Ancients. They certainly grew similar fruits, but these seem to have been more reminiscent of the cucumber. Pliny, in the first century AD, refers to the fruits dropping off the stalk when ripe, which is typical of melons, but they were still not generally considered very palatable. To quote Galen, the philosopher-physician, writing in the second century AD, 'the autumn (ripe) fruits do not excite vomiting as do the unripe'. By the third century melons had become sweeter and aromatic enough to be eaten with spices, and by the sixth and seventh centuries they were distinguished separately from cucumbers. The first reference to really delicious, aromatic melons comes in the fifteenth and sixteenth centuries, probably as the result of hybridisation between many different strains. The seeds were left wherever humans ventured. Christopher Columbus returned to the New World to find melons growing aplenty where his previous expedition had landed and eaten the odd meal of melons, liberally discarding the seeds. Likewise, both deliberately and inadvertently, melons have reached most warm parts of the globe and are immensely popular crops for the home garden in many countries. The Victorians developed reliable varieties that were successfully cropped year-round under glass, though most melons are now imported to Britain from warmer countries.

## VARIETIES

There are countless varieties, literally hundreds if not thousands, and many more go unrecorded world-wide. Most of those that are available, either as seed or commercially, fall into three or four main groups. **Cantaloupe** varieties usually have orange flesh. The fruits tend to be broadly ribbed, often with a scaly or warty rind, but not netted. The flesh is sweet and aromatic. A good typical variety is **Charentais**. They are the hardiest – well, the least tender – of the

**Honeydew melon**

**An Ogen variety of melon**

# CULTIVATION

Melons are not difficult as long as their particular requirements are met. They need continuous warmth, greater than that needed for tomatoes, peppers or aubergines, and must have a much higher humidity. This makes them difficult to accommodate with these *Solanum* glasshouse crops. They grow most happily with okra and other *Cucurbits* such as cucumbers, as these all prefer similar humidity and heat and likewise will thrive in slightly less light than the *Solanums*. Indeed, they do not like bright light and prefer diffuse to direct sun. The soil must be rich, very well drained and, like the air, kept continually moist. Melons really do best on hotbeds or heating-up compost heaps.

### Growing under Glass

This is almost essential in all but hot countries where they can be grown in the open. In some sheltered parts of southern England, in a good

**Gallia melons growing intertwined with cucumbers**

year, the new hybrid varieties such as **Sweetheart** may be grown in the open with some hope of success. Cold greenhouses can produce light crops, heated ones far more. A coldframe or curtained area in the greenhouse is better still, and the ease of providing extra warmth and humidity more than makes up for the diminished light. A coldframe set on a hotbed, or with soil-warming cables, in a greenhouse or polytunnel, is the best environment attainable by the average gardener and can produce an impressive crop. Indoors, pollination is advisable as a precaution.

### Growing in Containers

Melons are one of the easiest plants to crop well in a large pot, providing they are kept warm, watered well and fed regularly with a liquid feed. (I even grow them successfully in bags of fresh grass clippings topped off with a bucketful of sieved garden compost to seal in the heat and smell. The seed is sown direct in a mound of sterile compost set on top of that and then covered with a plastic bottle cloche. The bag stands in my polytunnel, a self-contained mini hotbed. When the plant is growing, the bottle is reversed to make a useful watering funnel.)

melons and **Sweetheart** is one of the most reliable. **Ogen** melons are an Israeli strain. These resemble a much improved but more tender **Cantaloupe**. The fruits are smooth, broadly ribbed and yellow when ripe, with very sweet, green, aromatic flesh. **Musk melons** are netted or nutmeg melons and have distinct netting, lighter in colour and raised from the yellow or green rind. These are the typical hothouse melons – large oval or round fruits with very sweet and aromatically perfumed flesh from green to orange. A good old variety is **Blenheim Orange**. Winter melons are round to oval, yellow or green, smooth or with a leather-like surface and hard yellow flesh that is not very sweet or perfumed. Often called **Honeydews**, these are long-keeping, up to a month or so, thus they are popular in commerce.

**Sweetheart melons in net supports**

**Countess of Caernarvon, a Cantaloupe variety of melon**

### Ornamental and Wildlife Value

These are not really very decorative plants, but can impress with their luxurious growth. The scent of ripening melons is heavenly. The fruits are well liked by rodents and birds, making these useful for the wild garden in warmer countries.

### Maintenance Calendar

*Spring* Sow as soon as warm conditions can be maintained, pot up, nip out tip after four true leaves, pollinate, reduce excess number of fruits, spray with seaweed solution weekly and mist frequently.
*Summer* Spray with seaweed solution weekly, mist frequently and support swelling fruits.
*Autumn* Continue as for summer.
*Winter* Melons can be grown throughout the year if sufficient heat is maintained.

**Musk melon with flower and fruit**

**Melons are highly suited to growing in pots**

### Propagation

Melons are normally started from seed, which does not come true when self-saved unless you are very careful, as *Cucurbits* are promiscuous cross-pollinators. The seed requires warm, moist conditions to start, and the plants need continuous warm, rich, humid conditions. Avoid the roots making a tight ball in the pot, but do not over-pot. The stems can be layered or even taken as soft cuttings to continue the season.

### Weed, Pest and Disease Control

Providing the growing conditions are just right, melons usually suffer from no major problems. The slightest drop in humidity and red spider mite may need controlling, as this can check the plants. It may well be worth introducing the commercially available predator *Phytoseuilis persimilis* if red spider mite or other pests are spotted. Aphids sometimes appear, requiring the usual remedies. Melons do suffer occasionally from neck rot where the stem enters the soil, usually during cold conditions. Sterile compost, warmth and clean, carefully applied water usually prevent any occurrence. Victorian gardeners always grew melons on little mounds to keep the neck dry. If neck rot appears, rub with sulphur dust and then earth up with moist, gritty compost to encourage rooting from the base of the stem. Rodents and slugs will attack the fruits.

### Harvesting and Storing

Their heavily perfumed, aromatic sweetness and luscious, melting texture make melons divine when ripened to perfection – though too often they are taken young to travel and are then not sweet, but woody and never well perfumed. For sybarites they really must be ripened on the vine until they are dropping – the nets are not there to support but to catch the fruits! Once they are ripe enough to scent a room, the fruit should be chilled before eating to firm the flesh and then removed from the refrigerator a short while before serving to allow the perfume to emerge fully.

## COMPANION PLANTING

Melons like to ramble under sweetcorn or sunflowers, enjoying their shelter and dappled shade, even in English summers! They also get on with peanuts, but do not thrive near potatoes. **Morning Glory** seed sown with melons is said to improve their germination. Most of all, melons need the same hot, humid conditions as cucumbers and there seems little problem with their pollinating each other. However, there might be if you want to save seed.

## OTHER USES

Melons accumulate a great deal of calcium in their leaves, which makes them especially useful for worm compost. The empty shells make good slug traps. *Cucumis melo dudaim*, **Queen Anne's Pocket Melon**, is grown for its strong perfume but the flesh is insipid.

## CULINARY USES

Quintessentially a dessert fruit, melons are nevertheless most often served as a starter in the place of savoury dishes. They may be combined with savoury or sweet dishes and are exquisite as chunks combined with Dolcelatte cheese and wrapped in Parma ham. Melons can be made into jam or chutney, added to compôtes, and used as bowls for creative cuisine.

### *Melon Sundae*
quantities to taste

*ripe melon*
*vanilla ice-cream*
*toasted flaked almonds*
*sultanas*
*honey*
*grated dark chocolate*
*glacé cherries*

Remove balls of melon with a spoon. Layer these in sundae glasses with scoops of vanilla ice-cream, almonds and sultanas. Then pour over the melon juice thickened with honey. Top with grated dark chocolate and a glacé cherry.

**Melon Chutney**

**Petita flowers and fruit**

*Cucumis sativus* from the order *Cucurbitaceae*

# CUCUMBERS

*Herbaceous vine. Life span: short.*
*Fruits: variable in size and shape, normally*
*4–5x25–30cm/1½–2x10–12in, but some 'mini'*
*ones are 2–4x12cm/1–1½x5in, green.*
*Vitamin value: poor.*

Cucumbers are tender, short-lived, perennial, scrambling vines, very closely related to, and resembling, melon plants but with matt, grapevine-like leaves and long, green fruits. These may be prickly, especially in the hardier outdoor varieties, and the very similar gherkins, *C. anguria.* We prefer these fruits to be green and unripe, not mature and bloated as we do those of most other crops.

Originally from southern Asia, cucumbers were grown by the Ancient Greeks and Romans. Early varieties were incredibly bitter and used more medicinally than culinarily. Breeding parthenocarpic fruits that swell without being pollinated has produced fruits with no bitterness, and their tendency to cause flatulence has been decreased. Recent all-female versions have been improved to the point of trustworthiness.

**Carmen is a new F1 variety**

## VARIETIES

Indoor cucumbers are smooth-skinned, if slightly wrinkly, and the all-female varieties remove the need to eliminate male flowers. **Pepinex**, and the smaller-fruited **Petita** are remarkably good, and like other new F1 varieties have excellent disease resistance. The old varieties **Conqueror** and **Telegraph** or **Telegraph Improved** are still useful for growing in cold greenhouses and frames. Japanese cucumbers such as **Kyoto** are usually longer and not as uniformly shaped as indoor varieties. They can do well indoors, though intended for outdoors, and are staggeringly productive! Outdoor or ridge cucumbers bear shorter fruits, very prickly. They are grown outdoors, but are started off earlier under cover. **Burpless Tasty Green** is very popular. **Crystal Apple** is an old variety that produces round, apple-sized fruits believed to be more digestible than others. Gherkins are very similar to ridge cucumbers and have prolific little fruits that are exceedingly prickly. These fruits must be picked while they are still small.

## CULTIVATION

All cucumbers need rich, moist soil, though outdoor varieties and gherkins demand less than indoor sorts. The indoor varieties require similar warm, humid conditions to melons; like the latter they do well on hotbeds and do not share well with *Solanums*. Despite the name, ridges are not at all necessary for outdoor varieties, but all cucumbers are best started atop small mounds to keep their necks dry and prevent neck rot.

**Petita, the smooth-skinned indoor cucumber**

### Growing under Glass
Indoor varieties must be grown under glass; they need heat and high humidity. Outdoor varieties, especially Japanese and gherkins, may be grown in coldframes and unheated greenhouses to advantage, with the opportunity of earlier and longer cropping.

### Growing in Containers
Cucumbers crop in large pots fairly easily, but need careful watering and feeding. The soil must always be moist but should never be wet, especially around the cucumber neck.

### Ornamental and Wildlife Value
Outdoor varieties can be grown over arches or a trellis, but have little wildlife value.

**Cucumbers need good support when grown in pots**

### Maintenance Calendar
*Spring* Remove male flowers, pick fruits, tie in, spray with seaweed solution weekly, mist regularly.
*Summer* Remove male flowers, pick fruits, tie in, spray with seaweed solution weekly, mist regularly.
*Autumn* Remove mouldy and dying foliage, pick the fruits.
*Winter* Sow next crop.

### Pruning and Training
No pruning is needed, but tying in must be done regularly as cucumbers scramble, needing support indoors. Outdoors they are best grown over straw or on a trellis. Indoor fruits must not be pollinated, so remove all male flowers; with the outdoor varieties, however, this does not matter.

### Weed, Pest and Disease Control
Cucumbers are susceptible to neck rot (see page 116 for treatment). They can get red spider mite badly if not kept humid enough and in fact commercial predator introduction is almost a necessity. Mildews and other diseases are rarely a problem with modern varieties. Leaves may scorch in bright sun, necessitating shading.

### Harvesting and Storing
The end swelling on indoor fruits means that they are pollinated and will be bitter, so the swellings should be removed before they prevent others setting. For the same reason fruits should be removed before they swell and turn yellow – though they were once preferred in this fully ripe stage. Gherkins are picked sooner and more frequently.

## COMPANION PLANTING

Indoor cucumbers grow well with melons. They will also benefit from tansy and dill, which goes well with them in pickles. Outdoor cucumbers will enjoy the light shade of sunflowers or sweetcorn. All prefer to be near peas, beans, carrots or radish, not near potatoes or strong herbs.

## OTHER USES

The fruits have long been used as a skin conditioner and medicinally.

**Small cucumbers, known as gherkins, are good pickled**

## CULINARY USES

Eaten raw with salads and savoury dishes, cucumbers may also be cooked or pickled. Outdoor cucumbers and gherkins are most usually pickled.

### *'More tea, Vicar?'* Sandwiches

*cucumber*
*malt vinegar*
*soft white bread*
*butter*

Slice the cucumber very thinly and leave it soaking in the vinegar. Thinly slice the bread, thickly butter it and sandwich the drained cucumber between. Remove the crusts and cut into triangles before serving.

*Citrullus lanatus/vulgaris* from the order *Cucurbitaceae*

# WATERMELONS

*Herbaceous vine. Life span: annual. Self-fertile. Fruits: variably large, green.*
*Value: rich in vitamins and minerals; a serving contains more iron than spinach.*

Watermelons are scrambling, climbing vines. Their leaves are darker, more bluey-green, hairy and more fern-like than melon leaves; the flowers are similar, small and yellow. Watermelon fruits vary in size from small to gigantic, from light to dark green or yellow in colour. The thin, hard rind is packed with red flesh embedded in which are small, dark seeds. Eating the very juicy flesh is like drinking sweet water.

This productive and nutritious, thirst-quenching fruit comes from Africa and India, but was first mentioned by botanists and travellers in the sixteenth century. The fruit became widely cultivated, but it appears to have been little improved until it reached North America. There it was developed to produce examples weighing over 45kg/ 100lb and many varieties with different coloured flesh, rind or seed. These included a sub-group with ornamental 'painted', 'engraved' or 'sculptured' seeds.

**A spray of watermelon leaves**

## VARIETIES

The flesh is always exceedingly juicy and sweet and red, but once it varied in colour with black, white, cream, brown, purple and yellow-fleshed forms. Now few varieties other than the reds are grown on any scale. **Charleston Gray** is long, oval and light-green-skinned with crisp red flesh. **Sugar Baby** is round, darker green and with very sweet red flesh, but needs an early start for maximum sweetness. I have unexpectedly grown good fruits from seed saved from tasty, ordinary, unnamed supermarket varieties.

## CULTIVATION

Warm, well aerated but moist soil is required. Although copious water is needed at the roots to swell the large fruits, watermelons prefer rather less humid conditions than melons or cucumbers. They also do not need the same high degree of fertility and thrive in any reasonable sandy soil, as they benefit from watering as much as from feeding. In temperate areas with hot summers, the watermelon can be grown outdoors as it produces more quickly than the melon does.

**Growing under Glass**
This is absolutely essential anywhere other than in a country with hot summers. The vines do not mind light shade, but need warmth and prefer a drier atmosphere to melons or cucumbers – although they do better with them than with the *Solanums*. They need plenty

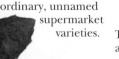

Watermelon
seeds are
contained
in the red flesh

of space: grow them at least
a metre/yard apart. Provide
support and train them up
if space is limited, but always
keep the fruits well
supported.

### Growing in Containers
Watermelons can be grown
in big pots although they
resent the restricted root run
and lack of aeration. Be sure
to use an open, gritty compost
and ensure religious watering
and feeding are maintained
throughout the season.

### Ornamental and Wildlife Value
The vines are much more
decorative than are those
of melons. The fruits are
appreciated by wildlife in
hotter countries.

### Maintenance Calendar
*Spring* Sow as soon as
warm conditions can be
maintained, pot up,
pollinate, reduce excess
number of fruits, spray with
seaweed solution weekly.
*Summer* Spray with seaweed
solution weekly and straw
under swelling fruits.
*Autumn* As for summer.
*Winter* Save the seeds for
spring sowing.

### Propagation
These are readily started
from seed, but they need
regular potting up. Watermelons are not as easy to
layer as melons. They will
prefer clay pots to plastic
ones and react very badly
to over-watering or to
compaction of the compost.

### Pruning and Training
Watermelons do not need
stopping like melons, but it

is a good idea to limit each
vine to one fruit to ensure
a decent size. The plants
are best allowed to ramble.
If they are trained up
anything, provide support
for the immensely heavy
fruits. On the ground they
are best laid on straw or on
a tile to keep them clean.

### Weed, Pest and Disease Control
Very prone to attack by red
spider mite under glass, so
the commercial predators
should be introduced early
before a major attack starts.
Although watermelons like it
as warm as melons, a similar
degree of humidity will
aggravate these attacks.

### Harvesting and Storing
Watermelons are ripe when
they sound taut and 'hollow'
to a tap from the knuckle. If
really ripe and well grown,
they will split open as soon
as the knife bites. However,
if left intact, they will keep
for a week or more.

**A good watermelon curry with chilli, turmeric and coriander powders, cumin seeds and lime juice is traditionally made in Rajasthan**

## COMPANION PLANTING

Watermelons do not object
to potatoes, as melons do,
and may run among the
plants to advantage in warm
countries.

## OTHER USES

The closely related *Citrullus
colocynthis*, **Colocynth**, **Bitter
Gourd**, is like a small,
intensely bitter watermelon.
It is used medicinally and
occasionally pickled or
preserved after many boilings.

**Young watermelon plants growing in an old deep-freeze**

## CULINARY USES

Watermelons are best
eaten fresh. Their seeds
may be eaten – they are
oily and nutritious. The
pulp can be made into
conserves, or reduced to
make a sugar syrup.

### *Watermelon Ices*
all quantities to taste

*watermelon*
*melted chocolate*
*grated desiccated coconut*

Freeze bite-size cubes of
watermelon on a wire tray.
Once they are frozen solid,
dip each quickly in cooling
melted chocolate, sprinkle
with grated coconut and
freeze again. Serve nearly
defrosted, but still just frozen,
with piped cream and
macaroon biscuits if liked.

*Cucurbita pepo* and species from the order *Cucurbitaceae*

# SQUASHES
## PUMPKINS, MARROWS AND GOURDS

*Herbaceous vine. Life span: annual. Fruits: variable, from 10cm/4in spheres to 1m/3ft flattened spheres, in yellow, orange or green. Value: riboflavin (vitamin B2), niacin, potassium and vitamin A.*

These are very vigorous, tender, rambling vines with enormous leaves and big yellow flowers followed by fruits in all sizes, shapes and colours, but usually green or yellow. There is an immense number of closely related and interbred species and varieties. Marrows are large and cylindrical; courgettes (zucchini) are the same but small. Most squashes are round or bottle-shaped; Custard or Scalloped Squashes have a distinctive pie-like appearance. Hubbard and Turban Squashes are keepers for winter use. They are richer in nutrients and vitamin A than the summer sorts. Pumpkins are very large, round and usually orange or yellow.

Various members were grown for millennia in Africa, the Americas and Asia. They only appeared in Europe in the sixteenth century, and over the next centuries developed into the myriad forms we know today. Marrows and courgettes are the English, French and Italian versions; squashes and pumpkins were developed more widely in North America. They are similar in most points save the fruits, and will hybridise all too readily.

**Prize-winning giant pumpkins**

**Courgette flowers are extremely good stuffed with ricotta cheese and herbs**

## VARIETIES

In these more than in most, variety is a matter of taste. Try them all for yourself. I believe courgettes give the best value. Avoid novelty spherical, coloured or tapered varieties if usable production is your aim. **Gold Nugget** keeps well with good flavour, but I find many squash, especially **Spaghetti**

**Marrows**, disappointing. If the American and European varieties are not enough, many more species are grown around the world. *Momordica charantia*, the **Balsam Apple** or **Bitter Gourd**, *Trichosanthes cucumerina*, the **Snake, Serpent, Viper's** or **Club Gourd**, and *Sechium edule*, the **Chayote**, are all very similar tropical *Cucurbits* used culinarily – the last for sweet as well as savoury dishes. **Chayote** also furnishes an edible farinaceous root rather like a yam to taste.

# CULTIVATION

A warm, rich, moist soil is needed for full cropping. They are all happiest growing on a compost or muck heap. Spacing depends on variety; compact bush courgettes need be only a metre/yard apart, but pumpkins will need much more room.

### Growing under Glass
Some of the more tender species such as **Loofahs**, *Luffa cylindrica*, **Lagenaria Gourds** and **Cushaw Pumpkins/ Crookneck Squashes**, *C. mixta/moschata*, can be grown under cover to advantage, if the space is available. Courgettes are often grown under glass for early crops, but produce mostly male flowers if kept too hot.

### Growing in Containers
These can be grown in large pots if given copious water and feed, but they are much smaller than when they are given a piece of ground to romp in.

### Propagation
These are started from seed. The plants hybridise, so it is best not to save seed. Old seed is said to give more female flowers. They are most reliable sown one per pot, potted up often, hardened off and planted out once the last frost is past, but sown *in situ* they tend to make better plants.

### Pruning and Training
These may be trained over a trellis or arches. Remove courgettes as fast as they form. No pruning will be necessary for these plants.

### Ornamental and Wildlife Value
Some colourful fruited varieties, especially the inedible gourds, are very attractive. The seeds are loved by rodents.

**Ornamental gourds in New Hampshire, USA**

### Maintenance Calendar
*Spring* Sow, pot up, plant out, spray with seaweed solution monthly.
*Summer* Pick courgettes and summer squashes.
*Autumn* Pick winter squashes and marrows before frost.
*Winter* Check stored fruits for rot regularly.

**Pumpkin seeds are very moreish**

### Weed, Pest and Disease Control

They are so vigorous that they rarely suffer from weeds. Virus infections may occur occasionally from dirty water. Generally, however, these are considered to be productive and trouble-free crops.

### Harvesting and Storing

Courgettes are best picked often and while small. Remove swollen large ones anyway, or they will prevent others forming. Summer squashes and marrows are best before full size is reached. Pumpkins and winter squashes need to ripen on the vine to store well and may keep over several months.

## COMPANION PLANTING

Grow these rambling under sweetcorn or near peas and beans, but not near any potatoes. Datura weeds may make the plants healthier.

## OTHER USES

*Luffa cylindrica* is very similar. Usually grown under glass in Britain, **Loofahs** are the prepared dried fruits. *Lagenaria siceraria*, is the **Bottle Gourd**, the dried fruits of which are used as containers.

**Top: Turk's Turban squash with French marigolds**

**Centre: Gold Nugget squash**

**Bottom: Turk's Cap squash**

**Marrows grow to enormous sizes. They can be cut in half, boiled and stuffed with a tasty mixture of minced beef, rice and herbs**

## CULINARY USES

These are used in a multitude of ways – baked, boiled, jammed, served in sauces, pickled, chutneyed or fermented. There are hull-less seeded varieties to make eating the nutritious kernels easier: these are good raw or fried and salted. Even the flowers are considered edible, stuffed or fried in batter.

### Marrow and Ginger Jam
makes about 2.5kg/5lb

*1.5kg/3lb marrow*
*1 large lemon*
*approx. 1kg/2lb sugar*
*7g/¼oz powdered ginger*

Peel the marrow, removing the loose flesh with seeds. Cut the firm flesh into bite-sized chunks and mix in the juice of the lemon. Weigh and add half the weight in sugar. Leave in a cool place overnight. Strain off the juice and bring to the boil.

Add the strained chunks, ginger and finely sliced lemon rind. Bring to the boil again and simmer for half an hour. Add the same weight of sugar again, bring to the boil, then skim and pot into sterilised jars.

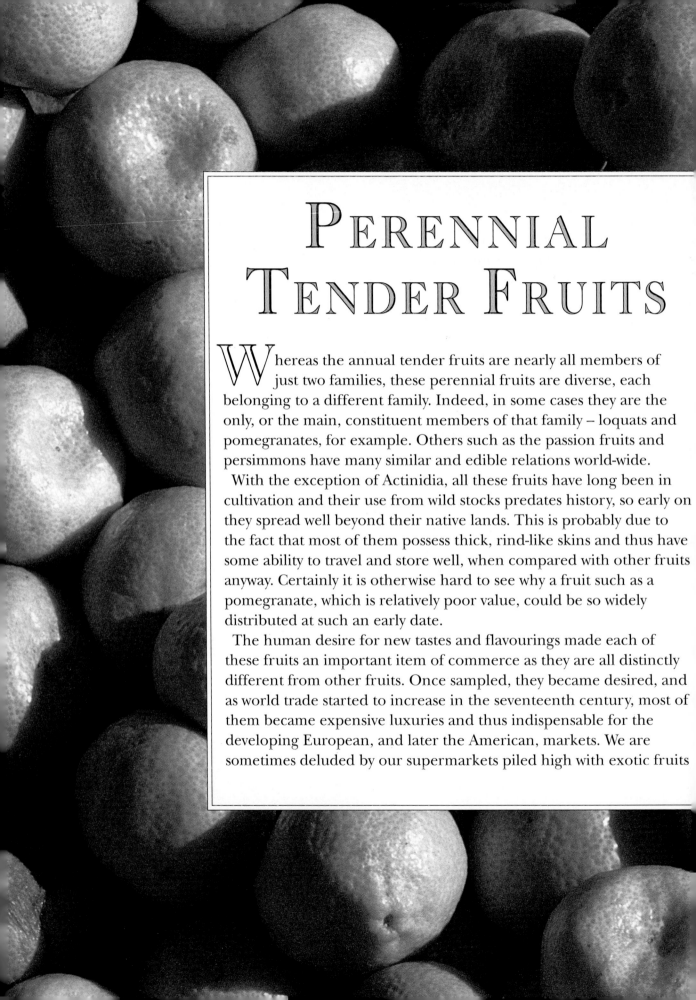

# PERENNIAL TENDER FRUITS

Whereas the annual tender fruits are nearly all members of just two families, these perennial fruits are diverse, each belonging to a different family. Indeed, in some cases they are the only, or the main, constituent members of that family – loquats and pomegranates, for example. Others such as the passion fruits and persimmons have many similar and edible relations world-wide.

With the exception of Actinidia, all these fruits have long been in cultivation and their use from wild stocks predates history, so early on they spread well beyond their native lands. This is probably due to the fact that most of them possess thick, rind-like skins and thus have some ability to travel and store well, when compared with other fruits anyway. Certainly it is otherwise hard to see why a fruit such as a pomegranate, which is relatively poor value, could be so widely distributed at such an early date.

The human desire for new tastes and flavourings made each of these fruits an important item of commerce as they are all distinctly different from other fruits. Once sampled, they became desired, and as world trade started to increase in the seventeenth century, most of them became expensive luxuries and thus indispensable for the developing European, and later the American, markets. We are sometimes deluded by our supermarkets piled high with exotic fruits

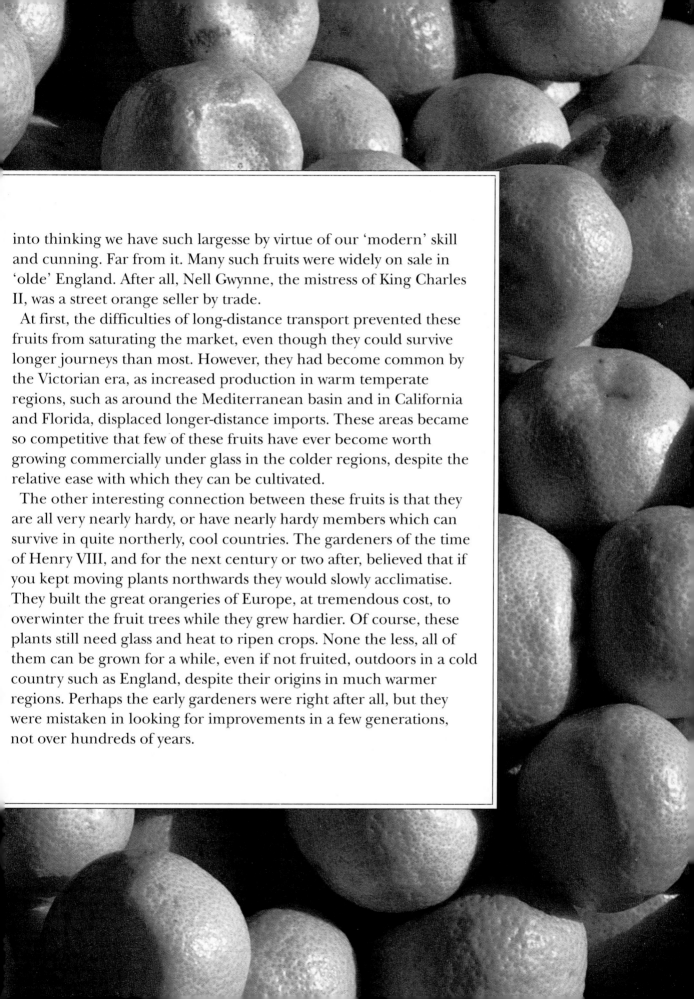

into thinking we have such largesse by virtue of our 'modern' skill and cunning. Far from it. Many such fruits were widely on sale in 'olde' England. After all, Nell Gwynne, the mistress of King Charles II, was a street orange seller by trade.

At first, the difficulties of long-distance transport prevented these fruits from saturating the market, even though they could survive longer journeys than most. However, they had become common by the Victorian era, as increased production in warm temperate regions, such as around the Mediterranean basin and in California and Florida, displaced longer-distance imports. These areas became so competitive that few of these fruits have ever become worth growing commercially under glass in the colder regions, despite the relative ease with which they can be cultivated.

The other interesting connection between these fruits is that they are all very nearly hardy, or have nearly hardy members which can survive in quite northerly, cool countries. The gardeners of the time of Henry VIII, and for the next century or two after, believed that if you kept moving plants northwards they would slowly acclimatise. They built the great orangeries of Europe, at tremendous cost, to overwinter the fruit trees while they grew hardier. Of course, these plants still need glass and heat to ripen crops. None the less, all of them can be grown for a while, even if not fruited, outdoors in a cold country such as England, despite their origins in much warmer regions. Perhaps the early gardeners were right after all, but they were mistaken in looking for improvements in a few generations, not over hundreds of years.

*Citrus* species from the order *Rutaceae*

# LEMONS, ORANGES

## AND OTHER CITRUS FRUITS

*Tree/bush, up to 8m/25ft. Life span: medium to long. Evergreen, self-fertile.*
*Fruits: variable size, orange, green or yellow. Value: rich in vitamin C.*

**Lemon**

Citrus fruits of the *Rutaceae* family are small, glossy-leaved evergreens with green stems which are occasionally thorny, especially in the leaf axils. Typical of this family, the leaves have glands which secrete scented oil. The small, white, star-shaped flowers are intensely and similarly perfumed, and are followed by the well-known fruits, which take up to a year to ripen. These swell to a size which ranges from that of a cherry to a human head, depending on the species.

They are yellow or orange with light-coloured flesh inside a tough, bitter and scented peel. The flesh is sweet or sour, always juicy, and segmented. Each piece may contain a few small seeds.

**Orange**

Originally from China and south-east Asia, some species and closely inter-related cultivars have been in cultivation since prehistory. They moved slowly westward to India and then on to Arabia and thus to the Mediterranean countries. The Ancient Greeks seem not to have been aware of any citrus. The Romans knew the citron, which was recorded in Palestine in the first century AD, but probably arrived several centuries before. The citron was widely planted in Italy in the second and third centuries, becoming especially popular near Naples.

The Romans were such gourmands that they would hardly have failed to notice a delight such as an orange. This fruit did not reach Arabia until the ninth century. It was recorded as growing in Sicily in the year 1002 and was grown in Spain at Seville, still famous for its oranges, while it was occupied by the Moors in the twelfth century. It is said St Domine planted an orange in Rome in the year 1200 and a Spanish ship full of the fruits docked at Portsmouth, England, in 1290; the Queen of Edward I received seven. These were probably bitter oranges, as many believe the sweet orange did not reach Europe till later. First seen in India in 1330, the sweet sort was first planted in 1421 at Versailles; another planted in 1548 in Lisbon became the 'mother' of most European sweet orange trees and was still living in 1823.

The lemon reached Egypt and Palestine in the tenth century and was cultivated in Genoa by the middle of the fifteenth century. The new fruits were soon spread around the warmer parts of Europe, and then further afield, with the voyagers of the fifteenth and sixteenth centuries. Columbus must have scattered the seeds as he went, for they are recorded as growing in the Azores in 1494 and in the Antilles in 1557. They had reached orchard scale in South America in 1587 and by then Cuba was covered in them. They are now mainly grown in California, Florida, Israel, Spain and South Africa, though every warm to tropical area produces their own and more.

**Pink grapefruit**

## VARIETIES

The various types are of obscure parentage and were most probably derived by selection from a distant common ancestor. *Citrus aurantium* is the **Seville**, **Bitter** or **Sour Orange**. Too sour to eat raw, this is the best for marmalade and preserves and was the first sort to arrive in Europe. *C. sinensis* is the **Sweet Orange**, often known by the variety, such as **Valencia Late**, **Jaffa**, which is large, thick-skinned and seedless, or the nearly seedless and finest-quality **Washington Navel**. **Blood Oranges**, such as the **Maltese**, are sweet oranges with a red tint to the flesh.

*C. limon* is the lemon. The fruits are distinctly shaped, yellow ovoids with a blunt nipple at the flower end and the characteristic acid taste. The commonest are **Lisbon**, **Eureka** and **Villafranca**; the hardiest and most convenient for a conservatory is the compact **Meyer's Lemon**.

*C. aurantifolia* is the lime. This makes a smaller tree of up to 3.5m/12ft. The small, green fruits do not travel well and are mainly consumed locally or made into a concentrate. Limes offered for sale are often small,

**The beautiful flowers of the Valencia Late orange**

**Lisbon**

unripe lemons, given away by the nipple, which a true lime does not have. Alternatively, they may be the similar *C. limetta*, **Sweet Lime**, which is insipidly sweet when ripe. True limes are grown mostly from seed and will require near-tropical conditions.

*C. paradisi* is the grapefruit. Not as acid as a lemon, this is relished for breakfast by many. It may be a hybrid of the **Pomelo** or **Shaddock**, *C. grandis*, which is similar but coarser. **Marsh's Seedless** is the commonest variety of grapefruit, with greenish-white flesh; but some prefer the Texan varieties with pink flesh.

*C. reticulata* is the **Mandarin**, **Satsuma**, **Tangerine** or **Clementine**. These names are confused and interchanged for several small, sweet, easily peeled and segmented sorts of small orange. *C. medica* is like a large, warty lemon and is now mainly produced in a few Mediterranean countries for making candied peel. There are many other citrus species and hybrids, **Uglis**, **Ortaniques** and **Tangelos**, to name but a few. The **Kumquat** is not a citrus, but belongs to the similar genus *Fortunella*. The fruits are very like small, yellowish, tart oranges, which are especially good for making preserves.

**Kumquats**

## CULTIVATION

Citrus need a warm, rich, moist soil, well aerated and never badly drained. They are all tender, though lemons and oranges have, despite the odds, been grown successfully outdoors in favourable positions on warm walls in southern England, and even cropped in some years. In warm countries they are spaced about 5–6m/15–20ft apart each way and are in their prime at ten years old. Trees with fruits of orange size will give a crop of about 500 each winter; small fruits, such as lemons, will crop more than 500; while big fruits, such as grapefruits, will crop less.

**Growing under Glass**
Frost-free protection in winter is necessary in northern countries. Citrus do not like being under glass all year round. They are much happier outdoors in summer and enjoy a rest in autumn. Thus they are best grown in large containers and moved under glass only for the frosty months, which conveniently are the months that they flower and crop. Limes and grapefruits are among the least hardy sorts and need more heat than the others.

**A grove of Jaffa oranges growing in Kos, Greece**

### Growing in Containers

This is ideal for citrus as it keeps them compact and makes it easy to give them winter protection indoors. They must have a well-aerated, well-drained, but rich compost. Avoid plastic pots or give them extra perforation. The 'old boys' always reckoned that diluted, fresh urine was the best feed for citrus.

### Ornamental and Wildlife Value

Very decorative in leaf, flower and fruit, all of which have a wonderful scent, these are ideal subjects for a conservatory and for a warm patio in the summer. The flowers are loved by insects; the fruits are less use to wildlife – which is fortunate for us.

### Maintenance Calendar

*Spring* Prune, spray with seaweed solution weekly, move outdoors.
*Summer* Prune, spray with seaweed solution weekly.
*Autumn* Prune, spray with seaweed solution weekly.
*Winter* Prune, move indoors, pick the fruit.

**Carved limewood, attributed to William Rogers**

### Propagation

Commonly, commercial plants are grafted or budded, often on *Poncirus* stock to dwarf them. Cuttings can be taken. I find some succeed quite easily in every batch. Seedlings are slow to bear fruit and may not be true; however, citrus seeds occasionally produce two seedlings, one being a clone copy of the original plant and the other normal. Seedlings are often more vigorous and longer-lived than worked plants, which may offset their slow development.

### Pruning and Training

Once these have grown tall enough they are best cut back hard to form a neat cone or globe shape. Regularly remove and/or shorten straggly, unfruitful, diseased and long shoots, cutting back hardest before growth starts in spring. They will generally need no support until they are in fruit, when heavy crops may even cause the branches to bend severely and tear.

### Weed, Pest and Disease Control

All manner of pests bother these plants under glass, but when they go out for the summer most of the problems disappear. The usual remedies work and soft soap sprays may also be useful against scale insects, which can particularly bother citrus, especially if ants are about to farm them. Bad drainage will kill them much more rapidly than cold weather will!

### Harvesting and Storing

Usually picked too young so they can travel, they are of course best plucked fresh off the tree and fully ripe. They do not all ripen at once and picking may continue over many weeks. The fruit rind contains the bitter oil which can be expressed to give a zest to cooking.

**The beautiful 'Citrus Allée' at the Villa Carlotta, northern Italy**

## COMPANION PLANTING

In warm countries citrus are benefited by growing rubber, oak and guava trees nearby. However, they are also said to be inhibited by *Convolvulus* or possibly by the *Ipomoea* species.

**Citrus cuttings are easy to grow in pots**

## OTHER USES

The leaves, flowers and fruits especially of *C. bergamia*, the **Bergamot** (*Monarda didyma*), are used in perfumery. The empty shells of the fruits make slug traps and firelighters if dried. *Citrus/Poncirus trifoliata* is hardier than the others and heavily thorned; it is used as a hedge in mild regions.

## CULINARY USES

The fruits can be juiced - much of the world's crop is consumed this way - or jammed or jellied and made into marmalade. The peel is often candied or glaceed. Small amounts of lemon juice prevent freshly prepared fruits and vegetables oxidising and gives a delightful, sharp, clean taste to most things, savoury or sweet. The Victorians grew the seeds for the young tender leaves to add to salads. The peels are much used for liqueurs and flavourings.

### Orange Sorbet
serves 4

*4 large unwaxed oranges*
*mace*
*sugar*
*egg white*
*parsley sprigs*

Cut the tops off the oranges and scoop out the contents. Freeze the lower shells to use as serving bowls. Strain the juice from the pulp and weigh and measure it. Simmer the chopped tops of the oranges with the pulp and a small piece of fresh mace in half as much water as you have juice, then strain out the bits and add half the juice's weight in sugar. Once it has dissolved, mix this sweetened water and the juice and partially freeze. Take it from freezer and beat vigorously, adding one beaten egg white per 450g/1lb of mixture, refreeze then repeat the beating. Serve, partially thawed, in the reserved shells with a garnish of parsley.

**Lemon jam**

**Orange flower water lends a wonderful perfume to the bath**

**Orange sorbet**

*Olea europaea* from the order *Oleaceae*

# OLIVES

*Tree, up to 10m/33ft. Life span: long. Evergreen, self-fertile.*
*Fruits: up to 2.5cm/1in, ovoid, green to black. Value: rich in oils.*

Cultivated olive trees are gnarled and twisted with long, thin, dark leaves, silvered underneath, though the wild species are bushier with quadrangular stems, rounder leaves and spines. The inconspicuous, sometimes fragrant, white flowers are followed by green fruits that ripen to brown or bluey-purplish-black, and occasionally ivory white, each containing a single large stone.

Found wild in the Middle East, olives have long been cultivated. They were amongst the fruits promised to the Jews in Canaan. According to Homer, green olives were brought to Greece by Cecrops, founder of Athens. They were certainly the source of its wealth. By 571 BC the olive had reached Italy and in the first century AD Pliny records a dozen varieties grown as far as Gaul (France) and Spain. These are still the major producing areas; olives are also grown in California, Australia and China.

Olives ripening on the tree

## VARIETIES

There are up to several dozen varieties of olive grown commercially in different regions, but only unnamed species are usually available. **Queen Manzanillas** are the biggest of the green pickling olive varieties.

## CULTIVATION

Olives grow well in arid sites that will not support much else. They prefer a well-drained, light, lime-based soil. They will grow, but rarely fruit well, outside Mediterranean climatic regions. Small strong trees, they need little support.

**Growing under Glass**
Olives are almost hardy but it is worth growing them in big pots so that they can be brought in for winter and put outside in summer. If kept indoors, they must not be too hot or humid.

**Growing in Containers**
Olives make good subjects for containers, though they are unlikely to be very productive. They must have a free-draining compost and then are fairly trouble-free.

**Ornamental and Wildlife Value**
Very attractive shrubs, these are worth having even if they never fruit, and they probably won't. The flowers are beneficial to insects, and some are fragrant. They are dense evergreens, making good shelter, and the fruits are rich in oils, so these are useful plants for wild gardens in warmer climes.

Olive branch and leaves

## Maintenance Calendar

*Spring* Prune, spray with seaweed solution monthly.
*Summer* Put outdoors, spray with seaweed solution monthly.
*Autumn* Spray with seaweed solution monthly.
*Winter* Take indoors or protect from frost.

## Propagation

Seeds may not come true, though they are often used, and the resulting plants can be slow to come into fruit. Cuttings with a heel can be taken in late summer, but like the seed need bottom heat to ensure success. Grow seedlings on for a year or two in large pots before planting out – they get tougher as they get bigger.

## Pruning and Training

As olives bear on the previous year's growth they must have only remedial pruning to remove the dead and diseased or crossing branches. This is best done in late winter or early spring. They can be trained as fans on walls for the extra protection. If the tops are frosted, they can still come again from the root and can be cut back very hard or pollarded. Old trees often throw suckers as replacements.

## Weed, Pest and Disease Control

Olives have very few problems in private gardens, though scale insects can bother them occasionally. Protection from frost and good drainage are more important.

**A ripe green olive**

**Nets are suspended below the olive trees to catch the ripe frut**

## Harvesting and Storing

In the Mediterranean region the trees bear when they are about eight years old. They produce about 25kg/60lb of fruit each, which reduces to about a quarter to half that weight in oil. The green fruits are ones picked unripe and pickled; the black fruits are ripe and ready for pressing for oil or preserving. The oil that is squeezed out without heat or excess pressure is called extra virgin (an interesting concept, rather typical of Latin thinking); cheaper grades are produced by heating or adding hot water to the mass.

## COMPANION PLANTING

Oaks are thought to be detrimental to olive trees.

## OTHER USES

The oil has many industrial as well as culinary uses. Much is used in cosmetics and perfumery and it was once burnt in lamps.

## CULINARY USES

The oil is used in many ways – in Mediterranean countries it is used in preference to animal fats – and the fruits are added to various dishes. The fruits are also eaten as savoury accompaniments pickled in brine, often stuffed with anchovy or pimento, or dried. If beaten to a paste, olives will make a delicious savoury spread.

### Olive Bread
makes 1 loaf

*500g/1lb strong white flour*
*1 x 6g packet dried yeast*
*water*
*60g/2oz black olives, stoned*
*olive oil*
*poppy seeds*

Mix the flour and yeast with enough water to form a dough. Knead and allow to rise until it is half as big again. Knead again and work in the olives. Rub the dough with olive oil; place it in an oiled tin to rise again with a sprinkling of poppy seeds. Once it has risen to half its size again, put it in a pre-heated oven at 220°C/425°F/gas mark 7 for half an hour or till brown on top. Serve as an entrée with a crisp green salad and a sharp dressing.

*Actinidia chinensis/deliciosa* from the order *Actinidiaceae*

# KIWI FRUIT
## OR CHINESE GOOSEBERRY

*Vine, up to 10m/30ft or more. Life span: medium. Deciduous, some not self-fertile. Fruits: up to 5cm/2in, flattened ovoid, brown, hairy. Value: very rich in vitamin C.*

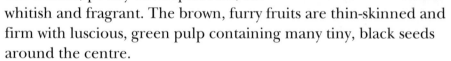

Kiwis, whole and sliced

The kiwi fruit or Chinese gooseberry is the best-known member of a small number of deciduous clambering and twining shrubs closely related to camellias. The kiwi has large, hand-sized, heart-shaped leaves, downy underneath, on softly bristled stems. The flower is like a small, poorly developed rose, off-whitish and fragrant. The brown, furry fruits are thin-skinned and firm with luscious, green pulp containing many tiny, black seeds around the centre.

These were not known in the West till the end of the nineteenth century when they were introduced from Japan and East Asia, more for their use as decorative climbers than for their fruits. Though now commonly known as kiwi fruit, they are not native to New Zealand, but were introduced there in the early years of this century and became more popular as a fruit when greenhouse growers needed to look for alternative crops to their oversubscribed tomato market. Recent breeding has developed self-fertile varieties. A dwarf, shrubby, form would be handy.

Leaf and flower of the kiwi vine

## VARIETIES

*A. chinensis/deliciosa* **Hayward** is the most widely available but is not self-fertile so needs planting with a male. **Tomari** is similar. **Jenny** and **Oriental Delight** are self-fertile. **Blake** is very high-yielding (up to 90kg/200lb per vine is claimed). It is self fertile and needs protection for the lower stems in cold regions. *A. arguta*, the **Siberian Kiwi** or **Tara Vine**, is very vigorous with deeply toothed leaves and fragrant, triple, white flowers with purple anthers, followed by green, sweet, slightly insipid fruits. The copious sap is drinkable. An improved self-fertile variety, **Issai**, is available which has hairless fruits. *A. kolomikta* is very attractive with large, oblong leaves which start green then go cream and pink. They are tapered at the end and hang from white, downy stems. The single, white flowers are sweetly perfumed and followed by long, yellowish, sweet berries. This is less vigorous than the other species and is thus more useful for cramped, modern gardens. It tolerates shade well. *A. polygama* is a native of Japan and has large, heart-shaped leaves which open bronze, maturing to green on red stems, with white, fragrant flowers and yellow fruits. There are many more sweet edible species.

## CULTIVATION

Kiwis require a warm site, preferably against a wall, as their young growths and flowers are easily damaged by late frosts. They need rich, loamy soil and strong supports. They will grow, but not crop, in shade. Some of the early varieties, such as **Hayward**, are female only and require one male to be planted to every half dozen females. Modern varieties are self-fertile, though they may perform better if planted with others to cross-pollinate. Some species similarly need pollinators, so it is often best to plant several (more than three) to be sure of getting one male for several female plants.

### Growing under Glass
If crops are wanted, kiwis have to be grown under glass to give them the warmth and long season they require. However, they take up a lot of space. They like similar conditions to tomatoes, so the two could possibly be grown together.

### Growing in Containers
These are too vigorous to be confined for long in a pot and are never likely to be very productive in one.

### Ornamental and Wildlife Value
Kiwis are very attractive climbers. The young shoots are particularly pretty as they are covered in many fine, red bristles. Kiwis are hardy enough to be used to cover eyesores, but they are not likely to crop unless they are given a warm site. The species are equally useful.

**The kiwi vine needs good support and training**

**Kiwi fruit makes a sooothing lip balm**

### Maintenance Calendar
*Spring* Prune and tie in, spray with seaweed solution monthly.
*Summer* Tie in new shoots.
*Autumn* Cut back sideshoots to shorter stubs.
*Winter* Pick the fruit – if you are lucky.

### Propagation
The species can be grown from seed, but varieties are grown from half-ripe summer or from hardwood autumn cuttings rooted with bottom heat in a frame.

### Pruning and Training
The fruits are borne on sideshoots. Unless these are left there are no fruits, so these must not be hard pruned but may be shortened. Kiwis must be well trained or they form an unruly thicket, therefore give them plenty of space. Old shoots die, so tie in replacements in spring. Good supports are necessary for these vigorous plants.

### Weed, Pest and Disease Control
There seem to be no major problems with these fruits, save dieback in cold winters. Give them extra protection if you are after fruits.

### Harvesting and Storing
The fruits ripen late; hang well with protection against frosts from the elements, ideally under glass.

## COMPANION PLANTING

There are no known companion effects.

## OTHER USES

These plants are useful for covering old trees and other eyesores.

## CULINARY USES

Kiwis can be eaten raw or made into juices, jellies and jams and are much liked for decorating other dishes, usually sweet but occasionally savoury. They contain an enzyme that breaks down gelatine, so should not be used to make dessert jellies. This enzyme can also tenderise meat.

### *Kiwi Meringue Pie*
serves 4

*4 individual meringue bases*
*green gooseberry jam or*
*  preserve*
*clotted cream*
*4 kiwi fruits*
*toasted chopped nuts*
*glacé cherries*

On each meringue base build a thick layer of jam, then a layer of clotted cream covered with very thin, overlapping slices of peeled kiwi. Top with nuts and a cherry or two.

*Passiflora* from the order *Passifloraceae*

# PASSION FRUIT

*Herbaceous vine, up to 10m/3ft. Life span: short. Semi-deciduous, self-fertile. Fruits: from 2.5cm/1in to 10cm/4in, spherical to cylindrical, yellow, orange, red, brown, black or green. Value: rich in vitamin C.*

Passion fruit are a family of perennial climbers with tendrils, deeply lobed leaves, amazing flowers and peculiar fruits. These vary in size from that of a cherry to a coconut, and in colour, coming in almost any shade from yellow to black. They are usually thick-skinned with a juicy, acid, fragrant, sweet pulp inside, almost inseparable from smooth, black seeds. The passion fruit, *Passiflora edulis*, is the most widely grown species. It has white or mauve flowers fragrant of heliotrope and purple-black fruits that are best when 'old' and wrinkled.

Passion fruit are native to America and were first recorded in Europe in 1699. The flowers caused quite a stir in European society, with many contemporary Christians claiming that they were a sign of Christ's Passion (the Crucifixion). The three stigmas represented the nails, the central column the scourging post, the five anthers the wounds, the corona the crown of thorns, the calyx the halo, the ten petals the faithful apostles, and the tendrils the whips and scourges of His oppressors. These delightful climbers, with their stunning flowers and delicious fruits, have now become popular in most warm countries. They are often grown in conservatories and in pots on patios for the flowers rather than the fruits.

**Passion fruit and leaves**

## VARIETIES

*Passiflora edulis* is the tastiest variety and hardy enough to survive in a frost-free greenhouse. Improved varieties such as **Crackerjack** are available. The **Giant Granadilla**, *P. quadrangularis*, needs more tropical conditions, but can produce fruits weighing many pounds; these are often used as vegetables in their unripe state. *P. laurifolia* is the **Water Lemon** or **Yellow Granadilla**, much esteemed in Jamaica. *P. incarnata* **Maypops**, comes from eastern North America. It has

**Banana passion fruit**

attractive creamy flowers, ornamental, three-lobed leaves and tasty yellow fruits. It is not self-fertile and spreads by underground runners. It can survive outdoors as it comes again from the roots. *P. caerulea* is the hardiest, with blue flowers and orange fruits which may be edible, but are not palatable, even after boiling with sugar. Dozens of edible-fruited passion flowers are grown locally, such as *P. antioquiensis*, with yellow, banana-shaped fruits, *P. foetida*, the goat-scented passion flower, *P. mixta* **Curuba di Indio** and *P. ligularis*, said to be the most delicious by connoisseurs.

**The passion fruit and its extraordinarily beautiful flower**

## CULTIVATION

A humus-rich, moist soil and a sheltered position on a warm wall suit the hardier varieties, with thick mulches to protect their roots. However, most of these plants are happier under cover.

### Growing under Glass
For edible fruit production, and to grow most of the more tender varieties, glass is essential. Fortunately, they can also be grown in pots, making them less rampant and allowing some to be put outside for the summer.

### Growing in Containers
Surprisingly, such rampant climbers take fairly well to pot culture, but require a lot of watering. They will crop in pots and, indeed, this is one of the better ways of growing them, so they can be taken indoors for winter. They need an open, free-draining, rich compost and regular feeding.

### Ornamental and Wildlife Value
Amongst the most attractive of all climbers in flower, foliage, or when festooned with fruits. The flowers are enjoyed by many insects and the fruits contain plentiful seeds for the birds.

### Maintenance Calendar
*Spring* Tie in new growth, spray with seaweed solution monthly.
*Summer* Tie in growths, spray with seaweed solution monthly.
*Autumn* Pick fruits after a long, hot summer.
*Winter* Prune before frosts and protect roots or take pots inside.

### Propagation
Passion flowers can all be grown from seed which can give good results for they are still relatively unimproved and most are true species. Propagate good varieties from heel or nodal cuttings in midsummer if they are given bottom heat.

### Pruning and Training
Pruning is remedial, removing dead and surplus growth. Strong wires are needed as these are quite vigorous and productive.

### Weed, Pest and Disease Control
Passion flowers tend to form rather dense stools which means they are prone to weed infestations which make the crown damp and short-lived. Occasionally they fail to thrive, but generally they are no problem save for frost damage: protect the roots and lower stems.

### Harvesting and Storing
Best ripen the fruit on the vine till they drop, though picked young for transport they keep well. As they ripen they will shrivel, appearing old and wrinkled, and the flavour is then at its best.

**Passion fruit vines are highly decorative and provide a dazzling splash of colour**

## OTHER USES

The empty shells make good slug traps for the garden.

**Passion fruit in flower**

## CULINARY USES

Thirst-quenching raw, passion fruit are made into juice which is a popular drink in many countries, much like orange juice and squash are in others. They can be made into jams, liqueurs and sorbets.

### Passion Fruit Sorbet
serves 4-6

*12 ripe passion fruit*
*approx.120g/4oz sugar*
*mint sprigs*

Scoop out the fruit pulp and seeds and sieve. Discard the seeds. To the juice, add half its weight in water and the same of sugar, stir till the sugar has dissolved and freeze. Partially thaw and beat vigorously, then refreeze. Serve partially thawed, scooped into glasses and decorated with mint sprigs.

*Punica granatum* from the order *Punicaceae/Moraceae*

# POMEGRANATES

*Bush, up to 4m/14ft. Life span: medium. Deciduous, self-fertile.*
*Fruits: up to 8cm/3in, spherical, orange. Value: little.*

Pomegranates have coppery young leaves that yellow in autumn, glorious orange or red, camellia-like blooms, and orange fruits with a rough nipple and thin, leathery rind. Inside they have bitter yellow pith and are stuffed with seeds embedded in pink, sweet pulp. They are infuriating to eat. Natives of Persia, the pomegranates were cultivated in Ancient Egypt and other Mediterranean countries. Some are now grown in California. They are easily transported, so were widely known in early times, even in most of the colder countries where they would not fruit.

**Pomegranate flowers are dazzling in full bloom**

## OTHER USES

They grow densely enough to be used for hedges in warm countries. A dye is made from the fruit peel. The peel and the bark are used as native cures for diarrhoea and dysentery.

**Weed, Pest and Disease Control and Companion Planting**
Pomegranates suffer from few problems and no companion effects have been noted.

## VARIETIES

Iraq is said to have the best pomegranates, large with perfumed flesh and almost seedless; such varieties have also been known in Kabul and Palestine. **Wonderful** is a Californian variety.

**Immature pomegranates and leaves**

## CULTIVATION

They will grow and flower outdoors but seldom set a crop in England, even on a warm wall. They prefer well-drained, limy soil.

**Growing under Glass**
This is the only way to have a crop. They need intense heat in summer to ripen and are more manageable in pots.

**Growing in Container**
Pomegranates are easily grown in pots, especially the dwarf variety, **Nana**. This is also hardier than the type.

**Ornamental and Wildlife Value**
They are as ornamental as any rose and several improved flowering varieties are available. The flowers are good for insects.

**Maintenance Calendar**
*Spring* Spray with seaweed solution, prune outdoor specimens.
*Summer* Keep hot to ripen the fruits.
*Autumn* Keep hot to ripen the fruits.
*Winter* Prune indoor specimens in early winter.

**Propagation**
By seed, layering or half-ripe summer cuttings using bottom heat.

**Pruning and Training**
They can be fan trained but, are easiest allowed to grow out as a bush from the wall. Old, diseased and weak wood is best pruned out in late spring. Prune indoor specimens in early winter and give them a reduced temperature for a few weeks afterwards.

**Harvesting and Storing**
They travel very well, keeping for weeks, so are easy to distribute.

## CULINARY USES

The juice is used for drinks, syrup, conserves and fermenting.

*Pomegranate Pastime*

Sit down under a shady tree with your ripe pomegranate. Cut open the rind, pick out the seeds individually with a pin and remove the pulp. The seed may be swallowed or rejected.

*Diospyros kaki* from the order *Ebenaceae*

# PERSIMMONS

*Tree/bush, up to 6m/20ft.   Life span: medium. Deciduous.*
*Fruits: 5-8cm/2-3in,  round,  orange-red.  Value: minor.*

Persimmons have lustrous, dark green leaves. The flowers are drab and the fruits look like large, orange tomatoes.

Japanese persimmons were first seen in 1776. Extremely popular in Japan and China, they are now grown on the French Riviera and in California. Other persimmons are eaten locally in hot countries.

## CULTIVATION

Persimmons are hardy, but need a well-drained soil and a warm wall to produce passable fruit. They grow better under glass, though the American species may crop well outdoors.

**Growing under Glass**
They need glass protection in northern Europe to extend the season long enough to ripen good fruits.

**Growing in Containers**
Persimmons are better in borders than pots, though these will do. Thin out the fruits to 25cm/10in apart, otherwise they overcrop and will not swell.

**Ornamental and Wildlife Values**
These are very attractive small trees, grown solely for their autumn colouring. In hotter climes the fruits are of value to birds.

**Maintenance Calendar**
*Spring* Weed, spray with seaweed solution.
*Summer* Disbud if over-vigorous.
*Autumn* Cut off fruit and store till ripe.
*Winter* Dress with compost and with copious amounts of straw.

**Japanese persimmons**

**Propagation**
By seed or grafting for the better varieties.

**Pruning and Training**
The branches split easily and are not easily trained. Only remedial pruning is needed, so plant at about 6m/20ft apart. Thin the fruits to get bigger ones.

**Weed, Pest and Disease Control**
There are few common pests or diseases, though a fungus has been known to kill wild trees in America.

**Harvesting and Storing**
Cut rather than pick to retain the short pedicel. This way they keep better. Store cool and dry until ripe – up to four months as they are best when somewhat shrivelled. When soft, they lose the astringency which makes unripe persimmons mouth-puckering and rather disgusting.

## COMPANION PLANTING

No companion effects have been noted.

## OTHER USES

The fruits are successfully used as pig food.

## VARIETIES

*Diospyros kaki* is the **Japanese Persimmon**. There are many varieties from the East, some of which are parthenocarpic. However, you should plant several to ensure pollination. *D. virginiana* is the **American Persimmon**, which has smaller, redder fruits and crops as far north as the Great Lakes. *D. lotus*, the **Date Plum**, is grown in the East and Italy, and many other species are eaten world-wide.

## CULINARY USES

Persimmons are eaten fresh, dried or candied, but rarely cooked.

*Percinnammons*
serves 4

*4 soft, ripe persimmons*
*cinnamon*
*apricot conserve*
*cream*
*4 glacé cherries*

Peel the fruit and cut in half. Dust each half with cinnamon, cover with conserve and top with cream and a cherry.

*Eriobotrya/Photinia japonica* from the order *Rosaceae*

# LOQUATS

## JAPANESE MEDLARS OR PLUMS

*Tree/bush, up to 10m/33ft. Life span: medium to long. Evergreen.*
*Fruits: up to 5cm/2in, pear-shaped, orange. Value: minor.*

Loquats have very large, leathery, corrugated leaves, woolly white underneath, and fragrant, furry, yellowish flowers. The fruits are orange and pear-shaped with a big, brown-black seeds and sweet, acid, chewy pulp.

First reported in 1690, these were imported from Canton to Kew Gardens in London in 1787. Widely cultivated in the East, they are now popular in the Mediterranean countries and in Florida.

## COMPANION PLANTING

These are dense evergreens which will kill off any plants grown underneath.

## OTHER USES

These shrubs make tall and attractive screens in countries with warmer climes.

## VARIETIES

Only the species is generally available, though improved sorts are now grown in Japan and China.

## CULTIVATION

They grow outdoors well enough in northern Europe, but do not fruit. Any reasonable soil and a warm, well-drained site will suffice. They do best on a warm wall, but it needs be a big one. They will crop only under glass or in countries with warm winters.

**Growing under Glass**
As they flower in autumn and the fruits ripen in late winter and spring, loquats need to be grown under glass if they are to fruit in any country that does not have a warm winter.

Loquats ripening on the tree

**Growing in Containers**
Loquats make big shrubs, so they are usefully confined in large pots.

**Propagation**
Loquats can be grown from fresh seed, or layers, or softwood cuttings taken in spring with bottom heat.

**Ornamental and Wildlife Value**
Very architectural plants with a lovely scent, they will also make good shelter for birds and insects.

**Weed, Pest and Disease Control**
Few problems with these.

**Maintenance Calendar**
*Spring* Prune if needed, spray with seaweed solution, pick fruit.
*Summer* Move outdoors for the summer.
*Autumn* Bring indoors.
*Winter* Protect outdoor plants from frosts.

**Pruning and Training**
Only remedial pruning is needed. They are best trained on a wall and allowed to grow out from it or grown as bushes in pots. Trim back any dead and diseased growths in spring.

**Harvesting and Storing**
The fruits need warmth and protection to ripen in late winter/early spring, so they must be grown under glass in cold countries.

## CULINARY USES

Loquats are eaten raw, stewed, jammed or jellied. They are made into a liqueur in Bermuda.

*Loquat Jam*
*makes approx. 2.4kg/5lb*

*1.4kg/3lb loquats*
*approx.1kg/2lb sugar*

Wash and stone the loquats, then simmer till soft with just enough water to prevent burning. Weigh and add three-quarters of the weight in sugar. Stir to dissolve the sugar, then bring to the boil. Skim and pot in sterilised jars. Store in a cool place.

*Opuntia ficus indica/dillenii* from the order *Cactaceae*

# PRICKLY PEARS
## BARBERRY FIGS

*Herbaceous, up to 2m/7ft. Life span: medium to long. Evergreen, self-fertile.*
*Fruits: 5-9cm/2-3½in, ovoid, red, yellow or purple. Value: minor.*

These are typical cacti, with round or oval, thick, fleshy pads covered with tufts of long and short spines. The flowers are large, 5-7cm/ 2-3in, yellow, with numerous petals, stamens and filaments. These are followed by red, yellow or purple, prickly, oval cylinders which are the fruits. Under the skin the flesh is very acid and sweet.

These are natives of the Americas where they have long been used. They have naturalised in the Mediterranean basin and almost every hot, dry country, even flourishing on the lava beds of Sicily.

## CULTIVATION

*Opuntia* need a well-drained, open, limy soil and a warm position. They are remarkably hardy, for cacti. Several survive outside at the Royal Botanic Gardens at Kew in England, and I have had them for many years in eastern England.

### Growing under Glass
This is necessary if fruits are to be produced, and you will also need extra artificial light.

### Growing in Containers
Providing the pots are large and free-draining, prickly pears are happy enough.

### Ornamental and Wildlife Value
Very decorative and quite a talking point in an English garden. They are more reliable under glass and just as attractive. The flowers are good for insects.

### Pruning and Training
No pruning is required. When the pads become heavy they may need propping up.

### Weed, Pest and Disease Control
Weed control needs to be good as these are nasty to weed between. Slugs and snails may develop a taste for the pads.

**Prickly pears thrive in arid, Mediterranean areas**

### Maintenance Calendar
*Spring* Keep weed-free.
*Summer*
*Autumn*
*Winter* Protect outside plants during coldest weather.

### Propagation
These can be grown from seed, but are slow. Detached pads or pieces root easily and are much quicker.

### Harvesting and Storing
This is a thorny task. Wrap a piece of bark round to pick the fruit, which will keep for several days. The peel is best skinned off completely before eating.

## COMPANION PLANTING

I grow them outside in front of evergreen hedges of leylandii and holly. They survive, but unfortunately have never fruited.

## VARIETIES

*Opuntia maxima* is very similar to *Opuntia*. **Burbank** raised a spineless variety.

## CULINARY USES

Prickly pears are usually eaten raw in place of drink and are occasionally fried or stewed. The red varieties will stain everything.

## OTHER USES

After ensilaging or pulping with salt, prickly pears make a useful animal feed.

# TROPICAL AND SUB-TROPICAL FRUITS

S ome of these fruits are the tastiest and most luscious in the
world. Strong sunlight and hot conditions produce sweeter,
stronger flavours (indeed often excessively so) than in temperate
zones. The natural conditions change little during the year, usually
being hot, bright and dry, followed by hot, bright and wet, or by
more of the same, rather than the fluctuating heat and light and
winter chilling of cooler regions. Tropical plants therefore often set
fruit several times a year, or continuously throughout it. Thus
tropical fruits are a more reliable source of food than those of cooler
areas and less reliance has to be put on storage till the next harvest.

The original species of many tropical fruit have disappeared, to be
replaced, even in the wild, by our partially selected stock. This
happened far back in prehistory; there is no wild date or banana that
corresponds to the cultivated varieties. Many of these long-cultivated
plants have been turned into clones, superior varieties propagated
vegetatively, often without seed, or not coming true from seed. This
handicaps the gardener as only inferior forms can be had from seed;
to get better sorts, living plant material has to be obtained. With
international restrictions this can be difficult.

However, some tropical fruits are still species, little changed from
the original, and useful to the gardener, for if the fruits can be
obtained, it may be possible to grow the plant. We can find some
fruits in ethnic shops and even occasionally in more adventurous
supermarkets. Modern refrigeration and air travel now permit us to
enjoy a tremendous range of fresh exotic fruits. The availability and

range is constantly extended, but of course our predecessors discovered and enjoyed these fruits before us, and they also wanted them back home after travelling abroad.

The first tropical fruits probably reached northern Europe in Roman times, but were then forgotten until rediscovered by late medieval travellers. To be enjoyed fully, many needed to be ripened longer on the plant than early long-distance transport allowed. The colonisation of the Canary Islands during the Renaissance enabled exotic fruits to be cultivated within reach of the European market, and this was given further impetus by the newly discovered New World fruits.

These new, expensive, luxury fruits were so desirable that owners of large estates in colder countries encouraged their gardeners to try them even though they needed more than a frost-free greenhouse or simple winter protection to grow, let alone fruit. Surprisingly, just as they had succeeded with orangeries, they met with more success; for example, pineapple plants were grown in Britain as early as 1690. However, it required the Industrial Revolution to provide the iron, glass and heat for serious home production.

The stove house was just that – a large glass greenhouse with a massive stove keeping the temperature tropical, different sections were arid and dry or steamy moist. With steam- or water-heated pipes, the stove could be moved to a separate boiler room. The Victorian age saw British-grown pineapples, bananas and mangosteens gracing many a table. Nothing seemed impossible to these horticultural pioneers.

Along with private extravagance, public botanic gardens were built, and specimens were obtained of many plants. Of course when kept some grew far too big to be considered, in pots. Many were successful, but others could not be persuaded to fruit even with extra heat. Now we are more fortunate: with electric light to replicate sunlight we can give these plants the brightness and day length they need. We also have automatic heat and humidity control, so it is easy to grow many exotic fruits ourselves. And if they still will not fruit, they always make attractive house plants.

*Ananas comosus* from the order *Bromeliaceae*

# PINEAPPLES

*Herbaceous, 1x1m/3x3ft. Life span: short-lived, perennial. Fruits: average 10x20cm/4x8in, dull orange or yellow. Value: rich in vitamins C and A.*

Pineapples need little description; they are the most distinctive of fruits – there is nothing else like them. They are Bromeliads, like many houseplants. They resemble common garden yuccas, being nearly cylindrical with a tuft of narrow, pointed leaves emrging from the top. The skin of the fruit is green to yellow, with many slightly raised protuberances. Wild species have serrated, thorny-edged leaves and set seed. Modern cultivars are seedless, with smoother leaves and smaller fruits; those of traditional varieties weighed up to 8kg/20lb.

Cultivated and selected from the wild by the people of Central America for thousands of years, the fruits were sensational in 1493 to the crew of Columbus. The first fruit, surviving the voyage back, was regarded as nearly as great a discovery as the New World itself. Pineapple motifs appeared, sometimes distorted, throughout European art – often as knobs on pew ends. By 1550 pineapple was being preserved in sugar to be sent back to the Old World as an exotic, and profitable, luxury. By the end of the sixteenth century pineapples had been spread to China and the Philippines and were naturalising in Java, and soon after were colonising the west coast of Africa. An enterprising M. Le Cour of Holland succeeded in growing them under glass in1686 and was supplying plants to English gardeners in 1690. Within a few years there was a craze for pineapples with noblemen's gardeners growing them under glass on deep hot- beds of horse dung and leather wastes as far north as Scotland. British-grown pineapples were sold in the markets at a guinea apiece. The Victorians raised the  cultivation of pineapples to a high level  with the regulated heat from steam boilers. A photograph of English pineapples from the turn of the century is a humblingly impressive display.

**Pineapple fields in Hawaii**

## VARIETIES

There have been hundreds of varieties, but most have disappeared as a few commercial cultivars monopolised trade. Pineapples are now grown most intensively in Hawaii, but also in Australia, Malaysia and South Africa. **Smooth Cayenne**, or **Kew Pine**, was widely grown for many years, but connoisseurs preferred **Queen** and **Ripley**. Long gone is the favourite British hothouse variety **Enville**.

## CULTIVATION, GROWING UNDER GLASS AND IN CONTAINERS

A tropical plant, the pineapple is happiest in Hawaii. It needs very high soil and fairly high air temperatures, high humidity during the growing season except when ripening, as much light as possible and a very rich, open, fibrous compost in quantity. In plantations pineapples have about a square metre/yard of ground each, so generous pots are required! Never let them chill below 21°C/70°F or 'cook' above 32°C/90°F.

### Ornamental and Wildlife Value
They are easy to root and grow as house plants, but require lots of heat and care to fruit well.

### Maintenance Calendar
*Spring* Pot up cuttings and mature plants.
*Summer* Root cuttings or crowns.
*Autumn* Tidy plants for the winter.
*Winter* Keep warm!

**Pineapples grow on a central stem which rises out of the crown of the fruit**

### Propagation
Suckers from healthy plants are best, fruiting in a year and a half or so. Gills, the shoots produced at the base of the fruit, seeds and even stem cuttings can be used, but take longer to grow and fruit. The crown from a fruit is easily rooted; cut it off entire with a thin shoulder, prise off the shoulder and pull off the lower withered leaves individually. Root over heat in a gritty compost. Keep the foliage moist in a plastic bag, but be careful of mould.

### Pruning and Training
Young plants rooted in summer need potting up in spring, growing on for a year and repotting the following spring to fruit that summer or autumn. Pot up annually, and remove superfluous shoots and fruited stumps if you have any. If happy, pineapples may grow and produce for five to ten years.

### Weed, Pest and Disease Control
The main pests are white scale and mealy bugs, controlled by sprays of soft soap or commercial predators.

## COMPANION PLANTING

A secret of success is apparently to grow them with a light top dressing of banana skins.

## HARVESTING AND STORING AND CULINARY USES

Picked under-ripe and kept cool, they can be stored for several weeks. They make tasty jam, delicious juice and are best-known canned. Although a fruit, they add sweetness and texture to many savoury dishes, from Chinese to curry, and can even be fried with gammon.

### *Pineapple-baked Ham*
serves 4

*1 very large tin of ham*
*1 larger pineapple*
*garlic (optional)*

Carefully empty the meat from the tin in one piece. Sharpen the open end of the can and use it to extract the pineapple from its skin, first slicing off the top shoulder. Leave the skin intact. (Slice and chill the pineapple flesh for dessert, cutting out the tough central core.) Insert the ham in the hole created, pin the shoulder back on to seal, and bake for at least an hour in a pre-heated oven at 200°C/400°F/gas mark 6. (Garlic lovers may rub the ham over before insertion.) To serve, turn the pineapple on its side to cut circles of ham with a pineapple rind. Serve with puréed sweetcorn and baked sweet potatoes.

*Musa* species from the order *Musaceae*

# BANANAS

*Tree/herbaceous plant, 3-9m/10-30ft and nearly as wide. Life span: perpetual as vegetative clones but sterile. Fruits: up to 30cm/12in, green to yellow or red. Value: nutritious and rich in starch.*

Banana plants form herbaceous stools of shoots like small trees. Each enormous shoot unfurls sheaths of gigantic, oblong leaves up to 4.5m/ 15ft long. A mature shoot disgorges one flower stalk which hangs down under its mighty bunch of many combs or hands of bananas. The hands point upwards, sheltered by succulent, purple bracts the size of plates, along the length of the stalk, and a mass of male flowers adorns the end. One bunch can hold about a dozen combs, each with over a dozen fingers. Bananas are the most productive food crop, giving about forty times the yield of potatoes. The fruits are green, ripening yellow, sweet, notoriously shaped and unforgettably scented.

The Ancient Egyptians had the culinary Abyssinian banana (*Musa ensete*), but early travellers from Europe soon discovered sweeter, more edible bananas in most tropical and semi-tropical regions. The hardiest, the smaller Chinese banana, was brought from the East Indies for cultivation in the Canary Islands by 1516 – and, it has been suggested, was introduced to the Americas from there but evidence of indigenous bananas discounts this. Most cultivated bananas are probably descendants of *M. sapientum, M. acuminata* and *M. balbisiana*, wild bananas thought to come from eastern Asia and Indo-Malaysia. *Musa maculata* and *M. rosacea* descendants are popular in parts of Asia and world-wide there exist many other species. In prehistoric cultivation, seed-bearing species were replaced by selected hybrids with big, seedless fruits propagated vegetatively. These superior sorts multiplied and by the nineteenth century there were countless local varieties of bananas in most hot countries. Many of these have now been lost and replaced by a few high-yielding commercial cultivars.

## VARIETIES

Common cultivars are **Robusta**, **Lacatan** and **Gros Michel**, the latter pair being old varieties that survived the Panama disease which destroyed many. However, they are tall and need hot, moist conditions such as those of Jamaica where **Gros Michel** was introduced in 1836. The **Chinese Banana** (*M. cavendishii*), also known as **Dwarf** or **Canary Island Banana**, is hardier, smaller and particularly tasty with shorter, delicate fruits, making it widely grown for domestic use, and well suited for greenhouse culture. A new, medium sized and more productive hybrid, **William**, is taking over commercially.

Plantains are separate varieties, possibly descendants of *M. paradisiaca*, larger and slightly horn-shaped. Plantains are most often used for cooking, not dessert purposes thus cooking bananas are sometimes referred to as plantains.

**Bob's own Abyssinian banana, which thrives outside in Norfolk**

## CULTIVATION

In warm climates bananas need a rich, deep, heavy, and well-drained soil with copious moisture. Freedom from strong winds is also essential. The smallest varieties are usually planted about 3m/10ft apart; the larger proportionately more.

### Growing under Glass and in Containers

In cooler climates the Canary/Chinese/Cavendish is best, as it is very compact and fruits at less than 3m/10ft high. Keep the temperature above 65°F/19°C in winter and under 85°F/30°C in summer. Potted plants can go out for summer.

### Maintenance Calendar

*Spring* Pot up or top dress, thin and root suckers.
*Summer* Top dress and thin any suckers.
*Autumn* Cut fruits, remove old shoot, thin suckers.
*Winter* Keep warm.

**Banana trees need large pots, so growing them in the ground under cover is best.**

### Propagation

Some ornamental and inferior varieties grow from seed. The best edible plants are bits of rhizome with a bud or sterile hybrids, propagated by suckers. Viable buds will resemble enormous, sprouting bulbs. They root easily in a gritty compost over heat in a moist atmosphere.

**The medium-sized hybrid, William, is becoming popular**

## HARVESTING AND STORING, CULINARY USES

Bananas are best matured off the tree and kept in a warm room. Most are at their best when yellow. They can be dried, made into flour or fermented to produce a sweet liqueur.

In hot countries, bananas are a staple food, being used as a vegetable and a useful source of flour, as well as a fruit.

### *Banana Custard Pie*
serves 4

*175g/6oz digestive biscuits*
*75g/3oz butter*
*30g/1oz strawberry jam*
*300ml/10 fl.oz milk*
*60g/2oz honey*
*15g/½oz cornflour*
*dash of vanilla essence*
*3 or 4 bananas, sliced and chilled*
*nutmeg*

Crush the biscuits and mix with most of the butter. Press into a pie dish and freeze. Spread the frozen surface with the remaining butter, paint with the jam and refreeze. Heat the milk and honey, mix the cornflour with a drop of water and the vanilla, then pour the hot milk on to the flour mixture. Return to the heat, stirring continuously, till thickened, then allow to cool. Put chilled banana slices into the cooled custard, mix together and pour into the biscuit case. Top with grated nutmeg and chill till required.

### Pruning and Training

Bananas fruit continuously if growing happily. A stem will flower and fruit in about a year and a half. Only one main shoot and a replacement are allowed; all others should be removed, and once the main shoot has fruited it is cut out. The clump or stool may live as long as a human being, but is replaced commercially every dozen years or so.

### Weed, Pest and Disease Control

No major problems for private gardeners.

## OTHER USES

Often used in beauty preparations and shampoos (below). The foliage will provide good animal fodder.

*Phoenix dactylifera* from the order *Palmae*

# DATE PALMS

*Tree, 25x6m/80x20ft. Life span: as long as a human being.*
*Fruits: just under 2x5cm/1x2in, blue, brown or yellow.*
*Value: rich in vitamins A, B1 and B2 and some B3.*

A tall tree with ferny leaves, the russet dead leaf bases protecting the trunk. Separate male and female plants are required for fruiting, which is prolific. Each tree annually bears several bunches of three or four dozen strings, each string carrying two or three dozen dates, the total weight being up to 68kg/150lb.

Dates have been cultivated in the Middle East for at least 4000 years and all wild forms have disappeared. They have always been one of the staple foods of the Arab peoples, much of whose lives were centred around the oases where the palms were found.

**Fresh dates**

## VARIETIES

Numerous local varieties exist. **Deglet Noor** is from north Africa and is the world's most popular variety. **Saidi** is the common date, **Fardh** is a favourite in Arabia, **Weddee** a feed date for

**A date palm laden with unripe fruit**

donkeys and camels, **Farayah** a choice, long, blue.

## CULTIVATION

One of the few crops to revel in hot, even scorching, dry places, date palms still need irrigation to fruit well, but can use brackish water.

### Growing under Glass and in Containers

They are well suited to indoor life, though they may find it too humid with other fruits, and they get too big and need too much heat to produce good fruit. Date palms are easy to distribute as the small rootballs will transplant with ease.

### Ornamental and Wildlife Value

Choice ornamentals, not quite hardy enough for planting outside in Britain, they are popular in hotter climates both with people and wildlife.

### Propagation

For choice fruit, offshoots or suckers have to be potted up; however, for ornamental use, seedlings are easily germinated but grow slowly. Large trees are easily transplanted with small rootballs. One male palm will be needed to every fifty females.

## OTHER USES

The palms have their sap extracted for sugar or fermenting. They may also be used as lumber.

## HARVESTING AND STORING, CULINARY USES

Soft dates are partly dried, stoned and pressed into cakes, then exported all over the world. Semi-soft dates are those we find in packs at Christmas. Dry dates are hard, ground to a flour and commonly found only in Arab markets. Dates can be used in cakes, biscuits and confectionery and with curries and savoury dishes. They are also made into wine.

### Stuffed Date Chocolates

*1 box of dates*
*1 pack (225g/8oz) real marzipan*
*150g/5oz bar of dark chocolate*
*icing sugar*

Stone the dates and stuff with marzipan. Dip in melted chocolate and cool on a tray dusted with icing sugar.

**A ripe avocado**

# AVOCADOS
*Persea americana/gratissima* from the order *Lauraceae*

## ALLIGATOR PEAR, VEGETABLE MARROW

*Tree, up to 9m/30ft by 6m/20ft. Life span: short, self-fertile. Fruits: 15x8cm/6x3in, green. Value: very rich in fats, protein, vitamins C and A, vitamins B3, B2 and thiamine, B1.*

Medium-sized, bushy tree with large, green, often rough but shiny, pear-shaped fruits. Each is filled with an enormous stone and a morsel of greeny-yellow flesh next to the leathery skin. (Large avocados are better value than small ones!) The small, greenish-cream, hermaphroditic flowers are especially fragrant.

Natives of tropical America, avocados soon spread to Australia, India and other tropical areas. They were naturalised on Mauritius by 1758, but also north as far as Florida, California and even Madeira.

## VARIETIES

Each tree can yield 500 fruits a year weighing up to 1kg/2lb, but smaller ones are preferred for supermarkets. Mexican or Canary varieties generally withstand the lowest temperatures, so use these to grow from stones. Jamaican and Guatemalan are less hardy.

## CULTIVATION

Rich soil, full of humus, and good drainage with plentiful moisture are necessary. Be generous with pot size, but avoid excessively nitrogenous composts.

### Growing under Glass and in Containers
If fruits are produced in northern areas, they ripen late, through autumn and into winter, so are best under glass They can be grown in large pots, surviving easily, but are harder to fruit.

### Ornamental and Wildlife Value
Avocados are attractive and often grown as house plants.

## Propagation, Pruning and Training
Easily grown from fresh stones kept warm and moist. The best fruiting varieties are layered, or grafted on seedling stock. Little pruning is needed; nip out the centre shoot if you want a more squat shape!

### Weed, Pest and Disease Control
Under glass they may get attacks of common pests, but are usually robust.

## HARVESTING AND STORING, CULINARY USES

The fruit is best picked a week or so under-ripe and ripened in the cool, say at 7°C/45°F. The colour lightens and the flesh softens and becomes like butter. It is very susceptible to bruising. More savoury than sweet, an avocado is best with vinegar, pepper and salt, but is usually overwhelmed with prawns and mayonnaise. Containing up to 25% fat, it adds body (and calories) to dips.

### *Avocado Dip/ Guacamole*
serves 6

*3 avocados*
*1 large or 2 small hard-boiled eggs*
*1 plum tomato, skinned and seeded*
*1 small sweet pepper (I prefer red)*
*3 spring onions*
*1 or more garlic cloves (optional)*
*1 tablespoon lemon or lime juice*
*dribble of olive oil*
*salt and pepper in moderation*
*a little ground coriander*
*as much chilli powder as you like*

Scoop out the flesh of the chilled avocados and blend with all the other ingredients. Chill and serve immediately with raw vegetable sticks (crudités).

*Monstera deliciosa* from the order *Aroideae*

# CERIMANS
## SWISS CHEESE PLANTS

*Herbaceous vine, may ramble or climb to over 12m/40ft.*
*Life span: appears perpetual and invulnerable.*
*Fruits, about 2.5x22cm/1x9in, green. Value: some vitamin C.*

The Swiss cheese plant is one of the commonest and most enduring house plants, somehow surviving hostile conditions in dark, dry rooms the world over. The leaves are dark green, large, scalloped and, uniquely and curiously, have natural holes in them, presumably to let tropical winds pass with less damage. In its native habitat it is an epiphytic climber, rambling on the forest floor and climbing up vigorously, clothing the trees and throwing down masses of aerial roots. It is a close relation of the arum lily and the flowers are similar. The long, cone-like, spadix fruit, or ceriman, is green, cylindrical and leathery with tiny, hexagonal plates for skin. The flesh is sweet and richly flavoured, resembling a cross between a pineapple and banana. It is absolutely delicious if completely ripe, otherwise the texture is spoilt by spicules and it is inedible.

Swiss cheese plants are native to Central America, but have been spread world-wide for their attractive leaves and amazing durability. This fruit was discovered in Mexico and was originally known as the Mexican bread fruit. It became known as the shingle plant and classed as *Philodendron pertusum*, then *Monstera acuminata* and now as *M. deliciosa* but is known world-wide as the Swiss cheese plant. In 1874 the fruits were exhibited before the Massachusetts Horticultural Society. The fruits are as delicious as the name suggests, but the spicules make unripe fruits unpleasant, so they have never become widely popular.

**A distinctive Swiss cheese plant**

## CULTIVATION

One of the most enduring and robust plants discovered, but will only fruit if given warmth and moisture. It does not need as much bright light as most tropical fruits, and has been grown successfully under glass in most countries.

### Growing under Glass and in Containers
Ideally suited to almost any treatment! For fruits, give better conditions, eg copious watering and syringing.

### Ornamental and Wildlife Value
Superb ornamental value almost anywhere frost-free.

### Propagation, Pruning and Training
They can be air-layered, or easily rooted from cuttings. They are happy climbing up a stout, rough-barked tree or log, or wired on a wall.

## HARVESTING AND STORING, CULINARY USES

When the fruit is ripe the inside appears to swell and the leathery skin plates loosen up; they can be eased off like tiny buttons. Then the flesh can be eaten off the stem. Try it with care – the tiny spicules of calcium oxalate irritate some people's throats, but appear harmless. Do not worry about the spicules if you eat only ripe fruits: many people regularly enjoy them. Cerimans are used only as dessert fruit and are widely popular in native markets.

**Fruit of the Swiss cheese plant**

## OTHER USES

The vines make a good, quick-growing screen in warm regions.

*Cyphomandra betacea* from the order *Solanaceae*

# TREE TOMATOES

*Shrubby tree, up to 5m/17ft. Life span: generally short.*
*Fruits: 4x6cm/1½x2½in, ovoid, purple. Value: some vitamin C.*

The tree tomato is not a tomato but an evergreen, semi-woody shrub from the same family. The leaves are large and lightly felted and smell muskily aromatic. Greeny-pink, fragrant flowers are followed by copious fruits similar to tomatoes but more pointedly egg-shaped and more purple. Each fruit is thick-skinned with two lobes containing about a hundred seeds. They are tasty raw only if well ripened, usually being too acid when they require cooking. The fruits start green and ripen to reddish-yellow or purple.

Native to Peru or Brazil, they are widely cultivated in most warm zones. They fruit conveniently during much of the year, even when the true tomato does not, making them a good substitute.

## VARIETIES

Only the species is widely available.

## CULTIVATION

Tree tomatoes prefer medium to high altitudes in the tropics and demand deep, well-manured soils to produce dessert fruits. For culinary purposes they can be grown anywhere frost-free and are obliging as to soil, preferring well drained sites.

## WEED, PEST AND DISEASE CONTROL, COMPANION PLANTING

More prone than many to the usual pests, requiring the usual remedies. I suspect these need to be grown with French marigolds to keep away the whitefly.

### Growing under Glass and in Containers

The plants need a lot of light and heat for tasty dessert fruits, but easily give high yields for cooking purposes during the winter months, as they prefer warm days and cool nights.

### Ornamental and Wildlife Value

They resemble daturas in many ways, including the smell of the foliage and delicious flowers. Much loved by whitefly!

### Propagation, Pruning and Training

Tree tomatoes are easily grown from seed or cuttings, fruiting by their second year. They are best trained as a short standard; pruning then is mainly needed to nip out growing points to keep the bush compact.

### Immature tree tomatoes

A young tomato ripening on the tree

## HARVESTING AND STORING, CULINARY USES

The fruits are fairly robust till fully ripe and keep for several days. When ripe they are purple and can be eaten raw, but tend to be sour and better stewed.

### Tree Tomato Jam
makes approx. 2kg/4lb

*1kg/2lb tree tomatoes*
*approx.1kg/2lb light brown*
*  sugar*
*1 small lemon*

Stew the tomatoes in a little water till soft, sieve and return to the heat. Add the same weight of sugar and the lemon's grated rind and juice. Bring to the boil, bottle in warm, sterilised jars and seal.

*Mangifera indica* from the order *Anacardiaceae*

# MANGO

*Tree, variable size. Life span: as long as a human being. Fruits: variable in size, flat ovoids, green/yellow or red. Value: mangoes are rich in vitamins A, B and C.*

Medium to large trees, with luxuriant masses of narrow leaves, these carry fruits which weigh anything from a few grams/ounces to a kilogram/2lb. The fruits have an inedible, tough skin and an enormous, flat stone to which the fibrous flesh adheres.

Mangoes are native to India, where they exist in countless variety. Doubtless early Europeans came across them, but they were first recorded by a Friar Jordanus in about 1300. Mangoes have now spread to most hot regions, including Florida.

## VARIETIES

India's favourite varieties are **Alphonso**, large and of fine quality and flavour, and **Mulgoa**, medium-large, green and blotchy. The West Indies prefer **Bombay** (**Peters**), round, flat, yellow when ripe and very juicy, and **Julie**. Cuba once exported one rated very highly called **Biscochuelo**.

## CULTIVATION

Mangoes want a hot, dryish climate and deep, well-drained, rich soils. Excessive rain spoils pollination and drought spoils the quality of the fruit. They want exceptionally deep and wide planting holes dug about 10m/33ft apart.

**A well-developed mango tree in the sunshine of St Lucia**

## Growing under Glass and in Containers

As they are large when fruitful, the glasshouse would have to be big. They may be grown in pots for ornamental use but fruiting success seems unlikely.

## Propagation

Mangoes raised from seed are often polyembryonic, giving several seedlings. Some are near-clones of the original, and some produce poor fruits with stringy texture and a turpentine taint! The best varieties are grafted or layered and will bear in about four years.

## HARVESTING AND STORING, CULINARY USES

Mangoes soften and turn yellow or red as they ripen, and do not keep. Picked unripe, they travel well and are fine for culinary use. They are very messy to eat raw! They are widely used for chutneys, jams, tarts, pickles and preserves.

### Mango Chutney
makes approx. 1kg/2lb

*1kg/2lb green mangoes*
*175g/6oz salt*

## Pruning and Training

Remedial pruning of thin and poor growth is necessary once a head has formed, plus root pruning if the tree persists with strong, unfruitful growth.

## OTHER USES

The seeds have been boiled and eaten in famines. The wood is poor but used for packaging crates and firewood.

*600ml/1pt vinegar*
*75g/3oz each peeled chopped garlic cloves; sultanas; chopped dates*
*50g/2oz each chopped fresh ginger; chopped blanched almonds*
*2 teaspoons hot chilli powder*
*500g/1lb brown sugar*

Peel, stone and chop the mangoes, sprinkle them with salt and keep cool overnight. Rinse and drain thoroughly. Mix all the ingredients except the sugar and simmer for several hours till soft. Add the sugar, bring to the boil and bottle in clean, sterilised jars. Store for six months before use.

*Carica*

# PAWPAWS
## PAPAYA

*Herbaceous, up to 6m/20ft.   Life span: very short.*
*Fruits: up to 30x15cm/12x6in.*
*Value: rich in papain.*

Pawpaws (also known as papaya) are small herbaceous 'trees' which resemble palms as they are unbranched with ornate, acanthus-like foliage clustered on top and up to fifty green 'melons' underneath. There are male, female and hermaphrodite plants. The fruits uncannily resemble melons, turning yellow-orange as they ripen. The flesh is usually pink with a central hole full of small round seeds and can weigh up to 5lb/2kg.

**Pawpaw seeds are embedded securely in the orange flesh of the fruit**

Although it is indigenous to Central America, the pawpaw has rapidly spread to every warm country. Seeds were sent to Nepal as early as 1626 from the East Indies.

## VARIETIES

**Solo** is a commercial dwarf, but most pawpaws are local varieties selected from seed and varying considerably. Grow them from fruit you like. *Carica candamarcensis,* or the **Mountain Papaw**, is hardier with coarser leaves and smaller fruit which have blunt ridges and an apple-like aroma. They are too acid to eat raw, but good cooked or as jam.

## CULTIVATION

Pawpaws prefer deep, humus-rich soil, and to be about 10ft/3m apart. They need support while young. You should eliminate most males and replace the whole lot every five years.

**A pawpaw tree in fruit**

**Growing under Glass and in Containers**
They are practical for tall heated greenhouses, and highly ornamental, so also well worth growing as pot plants, but they do not fruit well easily.

**Ornamental & Wildlife Value**
Their foliage is very attractive and they're so easy to grow they are worth trying anywhere frost-free and else-where as summer bedding!

**Propagation**
Variable from seed, but they are usually grown by sowing several to a hole and eliminating the poorest seedlings. (Only one male is needed to fifty females, but in fact they can only be differentiated when flowering.) Fruiting occurs within a year.

## CULINARY USES

Pawpaws are in season all year, and unripe ones keep for many days. Eaten as dessert or cooked as a fruit or vegetable, pawpaw is delicious, especially the first time. However, most importantly, the fruit and leaves contain papain which tenderizes meats cooked with them.

*Pawpaw breakfast juice*
serves 2

*1 ripe pawpaw*
*1 small lime*
*honey or sugar to taste*

Scoop out the flesh and sieve out the seeds of the pawpaw. Add lime juice and sweetener and liquidize. Serve immediately in frosted glasses with sugared rims as breakfast starters.

## OTHER USES

Papain is used medicinally, and for chewing gum.

*Psidium* and *Feijoa* from the order *Myrtaceae*

# GUAVAS
## AND FEIJOAS

*Tree, 3-9m/10-30ft.　Life span: short.*
*Fruits: 5-8cm/2-3in, yellow or red.*
*Value: very rich in vitamin C.*

Guavas are small trees or spreading shrubs with leathery leaves. The bark peels off the smooth, ruddy branches in flakes. The fruits are round, ripening from green to yellow or red, full of acid yellow or red pulp and many hard, round seeds.

Native to tropical America, guavas soon became popular the world over and were grown in orangeries.

**Feijoa leaves**

## VARIETIES

There are many species of guavas. *P. guajava* is the commonest, with yellow

**The Pineapple Guava flower**

fruits. Many varieties of it are pyriferum - bearing somewhat pear-like fruits which are a little acid and better for cooking. Some varieties are pomiferum, bearing apple-shaped fruits which are thought better. For dessert, gourmets choose *P. cattleianum*, the **Strawberry Guava**. This has a reddish-purple, plum-size, sweeter fruit on a hardier, grey-barked tree. *P. araca, P. montanum, P. pigmeum* and *P. polycarpon* are all reputed more delicious still. *Feijoa sellowiana* is so similar as to be a variety of guava. It is smaller, with crimson and white flowers and fragrant fruit. It is almost hardy and not self-fertile, and grown in California. Feijoas are rich sources of iodine.

**Guava fruit on the tree**

## CULTIVATION

Any good soil and a sunny site is all they require. In a warm climate they are normally planted at about 4-5m/15ft apart.

### Growing under Glass and in Containers
*Feijoa* is most reliable, the **Strawberry Guava** next, but all guavas are easily grown under glass and/or confined in pots. They can be put outdoors during the warmer months of the year.

### Ornamental and Wildlife Value
Attractive pot plants even if they never fruit, in the wild they are loved by birds which spread the seeds.

### Propagation, Pruning and Training
Propagate by seeds for the species but also by suckers, layers or grafts for better varieties. Some plants occasionally produce seedless fruits: note these and propagate from them. Nip out top shoots to promote bushiness, otherwise prune only remedially.

## OTHER USES

The heavy wood is used for agricultural implements. The leaves and bark are a native cure for dysentery.

**Sliced, ripe guava fruit**

## HARVESTING AND STORING, CULINARY USES

Guavas are best fresh off the tree, or if picked early, then as they soften. They are good for dessert, and cooked as tarts, jam and of course the infamous jelly.

*Guava Jelly*
makes approx. 2kg/4lb

*1kg/2lb guavas*
*1 large lemon*
*approx. 1kg/2lb sugar*

Simmer the washed, chopped guavas for 2 hours with a little water. Strain, weigh and bring back to the boil. Add the same weight of sugar and the lemon juice, reboil, pour into warmed sterilised jars and seal.

*Artocarpus* from the order *Moraceae*

# BREADFRUIT
## AND JACKFRUITS

*Tree, up to 28m/90ft. Life span: medium.*
*Fruits: up to 20cm/8in diameter, leathery balls. Value: mostly starch.*

Both breadfruit and jackfruit are attractive, tall trees with large, deeply incised leaves. From the branch ends hang green, round to ovoid fruits which have a thin, warty rind and are white and starchy within. Some have about 200 fleshy, edible seeds or more, some have none.

Breadfruits are native to the Pacific and East Indies, jackfruits come from the Asian mainland and Indian sub-continent. They were first noted in the voyages of the sixteenth century and soon taken to other hot regions, but never proved really popular. Breadfruit plants being taken to the West Indies played a part in the famous 1787 mutiny on the *Bounty*. When the water supply ran low, the valuable cargo was given water in preference to the crew.

## VARIETIES

*Artocarpus communis* (*incisa* or *altilis*) is the **Breadfruit** proper, bearing a remarkable resemblance, once cooked, to bread. From the West Indies comes the bread-nut tree, which, when cooked, is claimed to rival a new loaf in both taste and texture. *A. integrifolia* (*heterophylla*) is the **Jackfruit** or **Jakfruit**. The fruit is much bigger, weighing up to 30kg/65lb. These largest of fruits strangely spring from

**Breadfruit and leaves**

older branches and direct from the trunk. When ripe they give off a strong odour of very ripe melon. *A. odoratissima*, the **Johore Jack,** is smaller and esteemed for its sweetness and flavour.

## CULTIVATION

Any reasonable soil and site in a hot and moist climate.

### Growing under Glass and in Containers
The size of the fruiting tree makes it impractical to grow these in pots or under glass except for ornamental value.

### Ornamental and Wildlife Value
Very handsome trees, the fruits are valuable to wildlife.

### Propagation, Pruning and Training
They can be propagated by seed, but the best varieties come only by root suckers or by layering. Little pruning is required except remedial.

### Harvesting and Storing
Breadfruit is eaten fresh after cooking, but used to be stored in pits where the pulp was fermented to make a nauseous soft 'cheese' which would keep for several years.

## COMPANION PLANTING

The jackfruit tree is often used to support **pepper** (*Piper nigrum*) and as a shade tree for coffee plantations.

## CULINARY USES

Breadfruit are usually eaten roasted, boiled or fried as a vegetable. The edible seeds are often preferred, when they occur. Jackfruit are eaten in the same way and have a stronger flavour. Breadfruit can be dried and ground to a flour.

*Baked Breadfruit*
serves 2

Bake a breadfruit in a pre-heated oven at 190°C/375°F/gas mark 5 until you can push a knife through it easily. Extract the pulp, seeds and all, and serve with curry or a savoury sauce.

## OTHER USES

Jackfruit wood is like mahogany, valuable and useful. A yellow dye for clothing is extracted from the wood in India and the east. Breadfruit wood is light and used for box manufacture, and in Hawaii for surfboards.

**Breadfruit leaf**

*Durio zibethinus* from order *Malvaceae/Bombacaceae*

# DURIANS
## CIVET FRUIT

*Tree, 30m/100ft. Life span: fairly long. Fruits: about 25x20cm/10x8in, ovoid, green to yellow. Value: a little protein, a little fat; one quarter to a third is fat and starch*

Durian fruits taste delicious, but smell revolting!

This is an infamous fruit, banned from airlines and loathed by most people on first acquaintance. It has an aroma similar to that of an over-ripe Gorgonzola cheese in a warm room. The flavour was long ago described as 'French custard passed through a sewer pipe'. The texture is like that of blancmange or custard and the sweet flavour, delicious and addictive. Once bravely tasted, the durian is unforgettable and 'the sensation is worth a voyage to the East'.

The trees are very large and upright with leaves not dissimilar to a peach's. The fruits are round to ovoid, very large, weighing up to 4-5kg/10lb, green initially, yellowing as they ripen, with a long stalk. They are covered in short, sharp spikes and resemble some brutal medieval weapon. The pulp is white with up to a dozen big seeds.

Durians come originally from Malaysia and spread to south-east Asia in prehistoric times. Widely grown all over the region, they have never managed to become more than a curiosity elsewhere.

## VARIETIES

Local varieties exist with variation in size, shape and flavour, but no widespread commercial clones are available.

## CULTIVATION

The large trees need a deep, heavy soil to secure them, but they are not too difficult to please.

### Propagation, Pruning and Training

Seeds, if fresh, germinate in about a week and come nearly true. Only remedial pruning work is necessary.

### Growing under Glass and in Containers

Their size and their need for tropical heat and moisture make them difficult. They may make good pot specimens if fresh seed can be obtained.

### Ornamental and Wildlife Value

Attractive trees in their native climate.

## OTHER USES

Durians help get railway compartments to oneself. They are also reputed to be an aphrodisiac.

The Durian tree has a truly majestic stature

## HARVESTING AND STORING, CULINARY USES

Durians must be eaten fresh and they quickly go off due to a chemical change (and the aroma gets worse!). They are best eaten raw but may be made into ice cream or jam or juiced and drunk with coconut milk. The large, fleshy seeds are boiled or roasted and eaten as nuts.

### *Durian Delight*
serves 6

*225g/8oz each unsweetened durian purée, honey, natural set yoghurt, cream dash of vanilla essence*

Mix the ingredients and beat till smooth. Partially freeze, beat again and repeat this two or three times before freezing firm. Keep well sealed until immediately before eating!

*Anona* from the order *Anonaceae*

# CHERIMOYAS
## CUSTARD APPLES AND SOUR SOPS

*Tree, up to 6m/20ft. Life span: short.*
*Fruits: variable in size, green and scaly.*

A family of small trees, known as custard apples or sour sops, from the flavour and texture of the better fruits. Many have aromatic leaves and/or fragrant flowers. Despite the varying appearance of each species, the common names are often swapped or confused in different countries. The flesh is usually white, sweet and acid, with up to 30 black seeds embedded in it and covered with a thin rind, which breaks off like scales when ripe.

Natives of the Americas, they are most popular there but have spread to other tropical and warm zones. They are grown in Madeira and the Canaries for the European trade.

## OTHER USES

Corossol tea, shown above, was traditionally made from the leaves of *A. muricata*.

## HARVESTING AND STORING, CULINARY USES

Picked under-ripe they keep for up to a week or so. They are usually eaten raw or used to flavour drinks and ices.

## VARIETIES

*Anona squamosa* is the true **Custard Apple** or **Sweet Sop** and is most common in the West Indies. *A. cherimolia* is the **Cherimoya**. This is deciduous and more hardy, growing at high elevations in the hotter areas. The leaves are deliciously scented and downy underneath; the flowers are fragrant, fleshy, green and yellow; the fruit resembles a small artichoke with a banana/pineapple flavour. *A. muricata*, or **Sour Sop**, is evergreen with leaves that smell of blackcurrants and large (up to 3.5kg/8lb), green fruits with soft spines in ridges and a taste sourer. *A. reticulata* is the **Bullock's Heart**, so-called because of its ruddy colour. It has firm, sweet, yellow pulp. Numerous other species are grown all over the Americas.

## CULTIVATION

They will thrive in poor soils but give better crops with better treatment and prefer dryish, hilly conditions.

### Growing under Glass and in Containers
The cherimoya is worth growing even if it never fruits and custard apples are probably worth trying. Sour sops may not crop, but all are good value as pot specimens.

**A ripening Cherimoya fruit**

### Propagation, Pruning and Training
They grow from seed, but best varieties are budded. Only remedial pruning and nipping out is required.

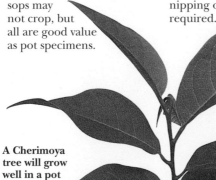

**A Cherimoya tree will grow well in a pot**

*Sour Sop Sorbet*
serves 6

*500g/1lb sugar*
*1 large ripe sour sop*
*60g/2oz crystallised ginger*

Dissolve the sugar in 450ml/16 fl oz boiling water and chill. Squeeze the juice from the sour sop pulp and strain. To each cupful add half a cup of sugar syrup. Partly freeze, beat and refreeze. Repeat twice. After the final beating, mix in the chopped ginger.

*Averrhoa carambola* from the order *Oxalidaceae*

# CARAMBOLAS

*Tree, up to 11m/35ft. Life span: medium. Fruits: up to 5x15cm/2x6in.*
*Cylindrical, star-shaped in cross section, yellow. Value: sugar, some*
*oxalic acid.*

Averrhoas are small trees with delicate, pinnate (walnut-like) foliage. A profusion of sprays of little white or pinkish flowers are followed by huge quantities of yellow, cylindrical, star-shaped fruits with five prominent angles, which weigh down the branches.

Natives of Indonesia and the Moluccas, averrhoas are still mostly grown in south-east Asia and the Indian sub-continent. However, because of their decorative value, and being quite robust, they are now exported and appear almost everywhere.

**The distinctive, star-shaped Carambola fruit**

## VARIETIES

**Carambolas** are variable in taste. Some are much better than others, though they are all juicy. I have eaten them from European supermarkets, when they were like yellow soap, and also fresh, when they were amber and a joy. *Averrhoa bilimbi* or **Billings** are similar, resembling gherkin cucumbers, but are used more as vegetables and in curries, and for the popular billings jam.

## CULTIVATION

Adaptable to most warm, moist climates, and any reasonable, well-drained soil, they fruit prolifically with little attention.

### Ornamental and Wildlife Value
Burdened with yellow fruit, they are impressive.

### Growing under Glass and in Containers
Carambolas are pretty plants, so make good specimens. If they fruit they will put on a terrific show.

### Propagation
Usually they are grown from seed, but better varieties are grafted. Only remedial pruning is needed.

**The delicate sprays of the flowers are very attractive**

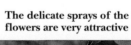

They travel fairly well if picked just under-ripe and then keep for a week or two. **Carambolas** are more often used for making jelly and preserves than as dessert fruits. Their star shape makes excellent decorative garnishes in compotes and fruit salads. **Billings** are used for pickles and preserves and billings jam is made after soaking overnight and straining to remove the acid bitterness. The flowers of both species were once made into conserves.

### *Camaranga or Carambola Jam*
makes approx. 2kg/4lb

*1kg/2lb carambolas*
*1kg/2lb white sugar*

Cut the fruit up into finger-thick pieces and discard the sharp edges. Do not discard the seeds as they improve the flavour of the jam. Add water to cover them and boil till the pieces are softening – about 15 minutes should be sufficient. Add the sugar and bring to the boil again for another 15 minutes, then bottle and seal.

## OTHER USES

Carambola juice removes stains from linen and can be used for polishing brass. Billings also polishes brass.

*Achras sapota/Manilkara zapota* from the order *Sapotaceae*

# SAPODILLAS

## OR SAPOTA, NASEBERRIES, BULLY TREES, CHIKKUS

*Tree, 4-16m/14-52ft. Life span: medium.*
*Fruits: about 6cm/2½in, rounded, brown.*

Sapodilla makes a medium to big tree with long, glossy leaves. The fruit is a large, round berry with a rough, brown skin over luscious pulp similar to a pear's but containing a core with up to a dozen seeds much like an apple's – black, shiny and inedible. The tree's milky sap can be tapped in the same way as rubber. Once collected, it is coagulated with heat and the sticky mass produced is strained out and dried to form chicle gum.

Still mostly grown in its native region of Central America, sapodilla is still found wild in the forests of Venezuela. Sapodillas were more extensively planted when chicle gum started to be used for a booming new commodity – chewing gum. Now it is an important crop for Mexico and Central American countries.

**Fruit on the Sapodilla tree**

## VARIETIES

Local varieties are cultivated for fruit, but there is little commercial demand, as it must be eaten absolutely ripe. However, there is a big demand for chicle gum; varieties selected for sap production can give up to 3kg/6½lb gum per year.

## CULINARY USES

Perfectly ripened, they are considered superb dessert fruit. The fruits keep up to a month or more in a cold refrigerator.

### Chewing Gum

*120g/4oz each of chicle gum, glucose, caramel paste, icing sugar*
*225g/8oz sugar*
*spearmint or mint flavouring to taste*

Melt the gum carefully in a bain-marie. Meanwhile boil water, 100ml/4 fl oz, the sugar and glucose to exactly 124°C/255°F.

Remove from the heat, add the caramel and boil again. Off the heat, mix the syrup into the melted gum, beating steadily and briskly. Add the flavouring and pour on to a cold surface thickly coated with icing sugar. Roll flat. When cold, cut into strips, wrap and label.

## CULTIVATION

Sapodilla prefers very hot, moist climates with rich soil.

### Propagation, Pruning and Training

Propagate by seed or preferably by grafting for better varieties. Only remedial pruning work seems necessary.

### Growing under Glass and in Containers

The trees are variable in size and unlikely to crop well under glass, but they are attractive so should make good specimen pot plants.

### Ornamental and Wildlife Value

Sapodilla has very attractive foliage and the fruits are enjoyed by wildlife.

### Harvesting and Storing

Best finally ripened off the tree, when the fruit softens and mellows in a few days to a treacly, gummy consistency. Left on the tree, the fruits become veined with milk, which makes them too acid until bletted like medlars (see page 169).

## COMPANION PLANTING

Sapodilla trees are normally grown for the first five years with underplanted legume crops.

## OTHER USES

Sapodilla wood is hard and durable, so it is used for handles and tools.

*Nephelium lappaceum* and *N. chinensis/litchi* from the order *Sapindaceae*

# RAMBUTANS AND LITCHIS

*Tree, up to 18m/60ft. Life span: medium to long. Usually not self-fertile; male and female flowers often on separate trees. Fruits: 2.5-5cm/1-2in, round, reddish or yellow.*

Rambutan or ramtum trees are large and spreading, with pinnate leaves, and festooned with hairy, chestnut-like conkers. These fruits are apricot-sized, covered with red or orange-yellow, soft spines like tentacles. Underneath the skin the flesh is wrapped around the single, inedible, brown seed. The flesh is sweet, acid, almost like pineapple with a hint of apricot – shame there is so little, as it is one of the best fruit I've ever tried.

Very similar and more perfumed are litchees, lychees or litchis. These have a prickly, crackly shell and grow on a smaller tree.

Originally from the Malay archipelago, rambutans are greatly appreciated in South-east Asia where they are often grown in gardens, but, surprisingly, have never proved popular anywhere else. Litchis have long been a Chinese speciality, so they followed their people to many other suitable areas, even to Florida.

## VARIETIES

Many different varieties of rambutan and litchi are grown in their regions. The **Pulassan**, *Nephelium mutabilechryseum*, is another species, native to Java. It is similar but covered with warts instead of tentacles. *N. longana*, the **Longan**, is popular in southern China. It is smaller, brownish-yellow and nearly smooth-skinned, with similar chewy flesh.

## CULTIVATION

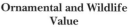

They need tropical conditions. Litchis prefer lower humidity, rambutans more.

## HARVESTING AND STORING, CULINARY USES

Both will ripen if picked early off the tree, so they are often found in temperate country shops.

### Growing under Glass and in Containers

Sadly they are too large. They may possibly do as pot specimens for foliage, but are unlikely to fruit.

### Ornamental and Wildlife Value

Handsome trees, they are often planted in gardens and parks in South-east Asia and the Indian sub-continent. The fruit is exceptionally attractive to birds and also bats.

### Propagation, Weed, Pest and Disease Control

They come nearly true from seed, but the best varieties are budded. Bird and bat damage is a severe problem.

**Litchis have tiny, soft spines**

Litchis are often preserved in syrup or dried to perfumed 'prunes'. All the fruits are superb desserts. Litchis are often used to close a Chinese meal.

### *Litchi Sundae*
serves 4-6

*1kg/2lb litchis*
*600ml/1pt real vanilla ice cream*
*60g/2oz blanched toasted almonds*
*nutmeg*
*30g/1oz coarse brown sugar*
*4-6 glacé cherries*

Peel and stone the litchis, then chill them. Layer the fruit in tall glasses with ice cream and almonds and top with a flourish of nutmeg, sugar and a cherry.

*Garcinia mangostana* from the order *Clusiaceae (Guttifereae)*

# MANGOSTEEN

*Tree, 14m/45ft. Life span: long. Fruits: 6cm/2.5in, round, brownish. Value: small amounts of protein, mineral matter and fat; approx. one seventh sugar and starch.*

The trees are small to medium-sized, cone-shaped and have large, leathery leaves somewhat like a lemon's. The fruits are round, purplish-brown, about apple size, with a rosette of dead petals around the stalk and an odd 'flower'-shaped button the other end. If you cut the rind around the fruit's circumference, the top can be lifted off to reveal about half a dozen kernels of melting white pulp, tasting between grape and strawberry, tart and sweet, almost treacly and chewy. There is a seed contained in many kernels, which is not eaten.

Mangosteens are natives of Malaya and were described by Captain Cook in 1770 in detail, and with delight. They were introduced to Ceylon (now Sri Lanka) in 1800 and were successfully fruited in English greenhouses in 1855. Widely held to be the world's most delicious fruit, they may be found in gardens in every tropical area, but are nowhere grown on a commercial scale.

**Mangosteen trees**

**Ripe mangosteens**

## VARIETIES

There are many local varieties and also close relations, most of which are found in the East Indies. *Garcinia cambogia* has a smaller, yellow-pulped, yellow fruit. *G. cowa* is the **Cowa-Mangosteen**. Bigger, ribbed and apricot-coloured, it is generally too acid for dessert but makes good preserves. Another, *G. indica*, the **Cocum**, **Conca** or **Kokum**, has a sour, purple pulp used to make a vinegar, and the seeds are pressed for cocum oil. *G. dulcis* is a yellow-fruited variety found in the Moluccas. *G. morella* is common in South-east Asia and the plant also provides an orange-red resin, gamboge.

## CULTIVATION

Mangosteens need deep, rich, well-drained soil, a sheltered site, shade when young, a hot, moist climate.

### Growing under Glass and in Containers

If it can be done in England in the mid-nineteenth century, it can be done now.

### Propagation

They are slow and unreliable from seed. They are then slow-growing, reaching only to the knee after two or three years. The best varieties are layered.

## COMPANION PLANTING

Mangosteens benefit from light shade, especially when young, preferring tropically bright but not direct light, so they are planted in the shade of taller trees.

## HARVESTING AND STORING, CULINARY USES

Use a ladder to climb up and pick mangosteens as they bruise if they fall. They can be picked unripe and kept for a few days or may be made into conserves.

*Mangosteen Ecstasy*
If you are fortunate enough to have a mangosteen, just eat it!

## OTHER USES

The thick rinds are rich in tannic acid and dyes.

# TRAVELLER'S TALE TROPICAL FRUITS

There are many more fruits the inveterate traveller may come across in tropical and semi-tropical countries. Some of these are of more practical or commercial interest, such as the spices, while others are of such purely local interest they rarely if ever get recorded. Many may be unknown, as they are unpalatable by 'modern' standards, or they may be delicious but difficult to cultivate. As we move relentlessly into a homogenised world of mass consumption, the numbers of varieties of even the most popular fruits are declining. Quaint, difficult and unusual fruits have already disappeared from all but local native markets and botanic and private gardens. If you travel far off the beaten track, you may come across the following, and others – but do not rely on my identification.

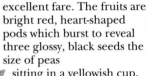

Tamarind pods

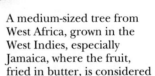

*Blighia sapida*, **Akee, Sapindaceae**.

A medium-sized tree from West Africa, grown in the West Indies, especially Jamaica, where the fruit, fried in butter, is considered excellent fare. The fruits are bright red, heart-shaped pods which burst to reveal three glossy, black seeds the size of peas sitting in a yellowish cup, which is the tasty bit. The seeds are inedible, the pink flesh highly poisonous and even the edible bit is poisonous if under- or over-ripe. One wonders how this ever became popular!

*Borassus flabellifer*, **Borassus** or **Palmyra palm**, **Palmaceae**.

A tall palm like a date palm but with shorter, fan-shaped leaves. It is widely distributed in the drier regions of Africa and Asia. The fruits contain much sap this is also tapped from the trunk for boiling down into sugar or for fermenting.

*Aberia gardneri*, **Ceylon Gooseberry**, **Bixineae**.

Native to what is now Sri Lanka, this is a small, shrubby tree with large, purplish-brown, round berries mostly used for making jams and preserves. Closely related is *A. caffra*, the **Kai**, **Kau** or **Kei Apple** of South Africa, which is yellow and so acid it is used as a pickle, omitting the vinegar.

*Baccaurea dulcis/Pierardia motleyana*, **Rambeh** or **Rambei**, **Euphorbiaceae**.

Found in Malaysia, especially Sumatra, and China, this has long, hanging bunches of large, yellow berries that are reputedly sweet-tasting, juicy and luscious.

*Bactris/Guillielma utilis*, **Peach Nut** or **Pewa**, **Palmaceae**.

A native of Central America, similar to a date palm, this has fruits like large dates. Usually cooked in salted water before eating, they taste of chestnuts. The best varieties are seedless. Other relations are the **Prickly Palm**, *B. Major*, and the **Tobago Palm**, *B. minor*.

**The Borassus or Palmyra palm**

*Carissa grandiflora*, **Natal Plum**, **Apocynaceae**.

This and *Carissa carandas* are large, thorny shrubs used as hedges in Natal. They have purple, damson-like fruits tasting of gooseberry which are widely used for tarts and preserves. *C. carandas*, which is also used for pickling, prefers drier areas.

**The exotic Natal plum**

*Chrysophyllum cainito*, **Star Apple**, **Sapotaceae**.

Noted by Cieza de Leon in Peru in 1532–50, this is a large, evergreen tree with purple-brown 'apples', which, when cut through, have a star shape in the middle with about half a dozen shiny, brown seeds in a sweet/acid pulp.

*Coccoloba uvifera*, **Seagrape**, **Polygonaceae**.

A coloniser of tropical shores, this is a very salt-tolerant, small, evergreen shrub or tree found from Florida to Venezuela. The 'grapes' are up to half an inch across, mild and sweet. They are eaten raw or jellied. The wood is hard and takes a polish well. It is often used as hedging or for good windbreaks.

**This banana tree from the Canary Islands thrives in Bob's own garden**

*Elettaria cardamomum*, **Cardamoms**, **Scitamineae**.

These are the fruits of a perennial herbaceous Indian plant used in curries and liqueurs.

*Eugenia caryophyllus*, **Cloves**, **Myrtaceae**.

Cloves are the dried flower-buds of this Indonesian tree. Other *Eugenia* species such as the **Malay Apple**, *E. Malaccensis*, the **Rose Apple**, *E. Jambos* and, the **Surinam Cherry**, *E. uniflora* have edible fruits varying from yellow to red or purple. They are eaten raw and made into jams and liqueurs in tropical and sub-tropical countries.

*Mimusops elengi*, **Sapotaceae**.

This large East Asian tree has fragrant flowers, the 2.5cm/1in yellow berries are eaten when ripe and an oil is expressed from the seed. Other *Mimusops* are also grown for their similar fruits. *M. elata* of Brazil is the **Cow Tree**. Its apple-sized fruits

contain a milk-like latex that resembles milk, when fresh, and is drunk with coffee, but soon congeals to a glue.

*Pimenta dioica*, **Allspice**, **Pimento**, **Myrtaceae**.

This small, evergreen, West Indian tree has pea-size berries that are dried unripe for their mixed spice flavour.

*Piper nigrum*, **Pepper**, **Piperaceae**.

Black and white pepper are the unripe and ripe (and de-corticated) seeds of this Indian climbing vine.

*Spondias*, **Spanish**, **Hog** or **Brazilian Plum**, **Anacardiaceae**.

Distantly related to cashews and pistachios, the *Spondias* have edible fruits, most of them only when made into preserves, but some are eaten raw. They are purple to yellow, resembling a plum with a central 'stone'. The stone of the **Spanish Plum**, *Spondias purpurea*, is eaten by some people.

**Black and white peppercorns, allspice, cloves and cardamoms**

*Tamarindus indica*, **Tamarind Tree**, **Leguminoseae**.

This large, handsome tree has brown pods containing very acid pulp used for beverages and in chutneys, curries and medicine.

*Vanilla planifolia*, **Orchidaceae**.

Vanilla is the fruit of an orchid which is native to Central America but is mostly grown in Madagascar. The bean-like pods are cured and dried for flavouring.

*Zizyphus jujuba*, **Jujube**, **Chinese Date**, **Rhamnaceae**.

An East Indian native, this reached China and was improved to dessert quality. In China it is popular dried or preserved in syrup. Jujubes resemble large, yellowish or reddish cherries with thick, tough skin, a hard kernel and a pithy, acid pulp, rich in vitamin C. The thorny, shrubby trees survive in cooler climates and have been in Mediterranean countries since biblical times. *Z. vulgaris*, a native of the Middle East, is similar but less agreeable. *Z. lotus* is like a sweet olive and is thought to be the lotus Odysseus had trouble with.

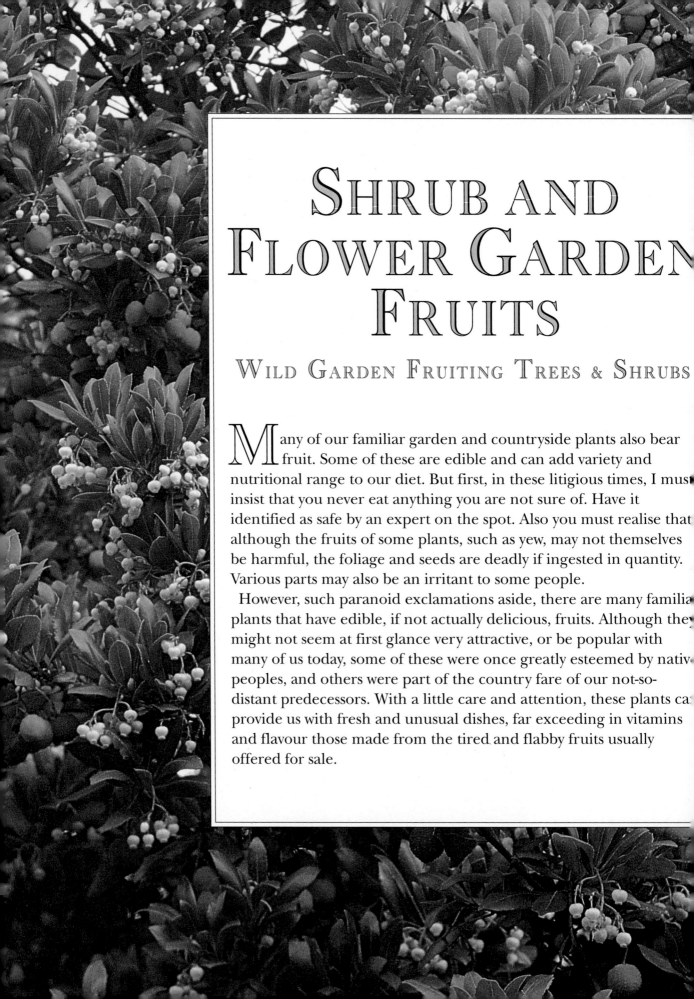

# SHRUB AND FLOWER GARDEN FRUITS

## WILD GARDEN FRUITING TREES & SHRUBS

Many of our familiar garden and countryside plants also bear fruit. Some of these are edible and can add variety and nutritional range to our diet. But first, in these litigious times, I must insist that you never eat anything you are not sure of. Have it identified as safe by an expert on the spot. Also you must realise that although the fruits of some plants, such as yew, may not themselves be harmful, the foliage and seeds are deadly if ingested in quantity. Various parts may also be an irritant to some people.

However, such paranoid exclamations aside, there are many familiar plants that have edible, if not actually delicious, fruits. Although they might not seem at first glance very attractive, or be popular with many of us today, some of these were once greatly esteemed by native peoples, and others were part of the country fare of our not-so-distant predecessors. With a little care and attention, these plants can provide us with fresh and unusual dishes, far exceeding in vitamins and flavour those made from the tired and flabby fruits usually offered for sale.

The plants at the beginning of this section are all excellent garden subjects, worthy of anyone's attention, which incidentally bear edible fruit. Some of the other plants with edible fruits are not attractive enough, or grow too big, for most gardens, but are of interest or value to insects or birds, and are more often planted in larger, public or wildlife gardens.

The ideal picturesque garden, often called the cottage garden, is typified these days by extravagances rushed up at flower shows with odd mixtures of flowers, half of them out of season, grown elsewhere in pots and jammed cheek by jowl, with a camouflage of bark. The true cottager's garden was indeed a mixture of plants, but all with a purpose – to provide medicines, herbs, flavourings, fruits and, last of all, flowers.

Fruiting trees and shrubs can be fitted in easily with other plants underneath, and were the backbone of a true cottage garden. A mixture of plants which were found to grow happily together for both production and ornament was sensible as it produced a mixed ecology so there were rarely pest or disease problems. In addition, the plants grown in flower, shrub and wild gardens are often innately more reliable than those especially cultivated for fruits, as they are closer to the wild forms, with natural pest and disease resistance.

The biggest handicap for some of these plants has probably been their very attractiveness. If they had been a little less pretty, they might have been developed further for their fruits and have remained part of our diet. Few of them are palatable raw, at least not to most people's taste, and all are better made into jams, jellies and preserves, but they have appealing and interesting flavours and are of inestimable value to the adventurous gourmet or those wishing to expand their dietary range. And for those looking for a breeding programme, they offer plenty of opportunity for rapid improvement towards bigger, tastier and better fruits.

*Amelanchier canadensis* from the order *Rosaceae*

# JUNEBERRIES
## SNOWY MESPILUS, SHADS, SWEET/GRAPE PEARS

*Tree/bush, up to 6-9m/20-30ft. Life span: medium. Self-fertile. Fruits: 1cm/½ in, round, purple-black, rich in vitamin C.*

The amelanchiers are small, deciduous trees or shrubs tending to suckering growth, most noticeable when absolutely covered with white blossoms. The fruits are purplish, spherical and about pea-size, but can be larger.

*A. canadensis* is the best species and a native of North America. Though there are relatives in Asia and Europe, these are not as palatable. *A. vulgaris* grows wild in European mountain districts and was long cultivated in England, as much for the flowers as the fruits.

**Amelanchiers look beautiful covered in white blossom**

## HARVESTING AND STORING, CULINARY USES

They can be eaten raw, but are better as jams or tarts, or dried like raisins.

*Snowy Mespilus Sponge Cakes* makes about 10

60g/2oz each butter, castor sugar and white self-raising flour
1 large or 2 small eggs
dash of vanilla essence
splash of milk
120g/4oz dried amelanchier berries

Cream the butter and sugar, beat in the egg and vanilla, fold in the sifted flour, then add enough milk to make a smooth mixture. Stir in the berries; pour into greased paper cups. Stand the cups on a metal tray and bake in a pre-heated oven at 190°C/375°F/gas mark 5 for 20 minutes or till firm.

### VARIETIES

*Amelanchier canadensis* was a favourite fruit of native Americans. It was adopted by the French settlers and became **Poires** in Canada and **Sweet** or **Grape Pear** in what is now the USA. It has small, purple berries which are sweet and tasty. *A. alnifolia*, or **Western Service Berry**, is larger and found wild in the states of Oregon and Washington. All cultivars are supplied for ornamental rather than fruiting purposes.

### CULTIVATION

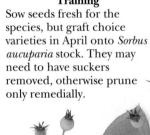

Amelanchiers do best in moist but well-drained, lime-free soil. They are slow-growing, tending to sucker.

**Ornamental and Wildlife Value**
Neat, compact, floriferous, good autumn leaf colours, excellent shrub border plants. The berries are much liked by birds.

**Propagation, Pruning and Training**
Sow seeds fresh for the species, but graft choice varieties in April onto *Sorbus aucuparia* stock. They may need to have suckers removed, otherwise prune only remedially.

**Growing under Glass and in Containers**
They are so hardy that they hardly seem worth the space under cover. They could be delightful small specimens in pots.

**Weed, Pest and Disease Control**
No particular problems affect these tough plants.

**A spray of juneberries and leaves**

### OTHER USES

Can be used as rootstocks for pome fruits.

*Myrtus communis from the order Myrtaceae*

# MYRTLE

*Tree, up to 4.5m/15ft. Life span: medium. Fruits: 1cm/½ in, usually black-blue.*

Myrtle is one of sixty small evergreen shrubs which are densely and aromatically leafed, with white flowers.

*Myrtus communis* has long been grown in southern Europe and western Asia. It was highly revered and much enjoyed by the Ancient Greeks whose mythology held myrtle sacred to Aphrodite, the Goddess of Love. As all other myrtles are native to South America or New Zealand, common myrtle may indicate a prehistoric link between the continents.

## VARIETIES

*Myrtus communis* is grown for fruit and has ornamental forms such as *microphylla* and *tarentina* which are small, rarely reaching more than 60cm/2ft high. Their foliage is aromatic when crushed, making them good for small patios or sunny windows, but they rarely fruit well. *M. ugni* is the **Chilean Guava Myrtle** which has delicious, mahogany red, pleasantly fragrant berries which are used to flavour water. These apparently fruit well in English greenhouses.

## OTHER USES

Used in medicine. The dried leaves and wood are fragrant. The flowers are made into perfume and toilet water.

## CULIVATION

Myrtles need full sun and a well-drained soil. They are not averse to lime and are also good by the seaside. *M. communis, chequen* and *nummalaria* are the hardiest.

### Ornamental and Wildlife Value
Very attractive evergreens for mild regions. The flowers and berries are attractive to wildlife.

### Weed, Pest and Disease Control
As myrtles are very tough there are no real problems.

### Propagation and Training
The species can be grown from seed, or half-ripe cuttings can be taken in late summer with some success. Myrtle is best grown as a bush against a wall for the shelter and warmth. In early summer, clipping is usually preferred to pruning.

## HARVESTING AND STORING, CULINARY USES

Myrtle berries are eaten raw or in tarts and jams or dried. The jam has an aromatic flavour which goes well with savoury dishes. The fresh flowers can be added to a salad. Mediterranean, especially Tuscan, cooking uses the dried fruits and flower buds as a spice. In Chile, **Temo**, *M. molinae*, seed was used to make a coffee.

*Myrtle Jam*
makes approx. 2kg/4lb

*1kg/2lb myrtle berries*
*1kg/2lb sugar*

Wash the berries and prick them with a darning needle. Simmer them until soft with just enough water to prevent burning. Add the sugar and bring to the boil then bottle in warm, sterilised jars and seal.

### Growing under Glass and in Containers
Very good subjects to have under glass and/or in containers, especially *M. ugni* or *M. communis tarentina.*

**Myrtle leaves and fruit**

*Berberis vulgaris* from the order *Berberidaceae*

# BARBERRIES
## MAHONIAS, OREGON GRAPES

*Bush, up to 4x4m/14x14ft. Life span: short.*
*Fruits: under 1cm/½ in, white, yellow, scarlet, purple or black.*

The *Berberis* family contains hundreds of small- to medium-sized, spiny shrubs that have masses of berries in many colours. The leaves of most deciduous varieties turn bright shades in autumn and the wood is usually yellow.

Various species are found all over the world. Our common barberry is now seldom relished, but was once widely popular. Indeed the settlers in Massachusetts grew so many that in 1754 the province had to forbid further planting.

### VARIETIES

*Berberis vulgaris* is the **Common Barberry** which once existed in a host of local forms and colours. One found in Rouen was seedless. Other species are enjoyed all over the world: *B. darwinii* is popular; *B. buxifolia*, the **Magellan Barberry**, is large and said to be the best raw or cooked. *Mahonia* is now a separate genus, but is very similar in many ways, only lacking the spines and having pinnate leaves. The flowers are yellow, usually scented, and the blue-black berries of *M. aquifolium* were made into preserves as Oregon grapes.

**A cluster of barberries**

### CULTIVATION

They will grow almost anywhere not actually dark, bone-dry or waterlogged, and are even fairly tolerant of salt spray.

#### Growing under Glass and in Containers
They are hardy enough not to need protection, but do make good plants in containers.

#### Ornamental and Wildlife Value
Some ornamental varieties are very attractive, though not as productive of berries, which are exceedingly well liked by birds. Most varieties are excellent when used for wildlife gardens.

#### Propagation, Pruning and Training
The species grows from seed, layered or grafted. They can usually be cut to the ground and will recover.

**Barberry flowers**

### WEED, PEST AND DISEASE CONTROL, COMPANION PLANTING

Barberries are an alternate host for wheat rust, so care should be taken not to plant them near wheat.

### OTHER USES

They make good hedges and game cover. They were used for a yellow dye.

### HARVESTING AND STORING, CULINARY USES

The berries can be pickled in vinegar, preserved in sugar or syrup, candied or made into jam. The leaves were once used as a seasoning.

*Colonel Flowerdew's Bengal Chutney*
makes approx 3lb/1.4kg

*1kg/2lb grated apples*
*120g/4oz each of following:*
*dried barberries, soft brown*
*sugar, Demerara sugar,*
*mustard seed and*
*golden syrup*
*60g/2oz each of the following*
*chopped onions, chopped*
*garlic, chopped fresh ginger*
*and salt*
*15g/½oz cayenne pepper*
*600ml/1pt vinegar*

Mix all the ingredients and simmer till soft, say 2–3 hours. Bottle in small jars for six months.

*Mespilus germanica* from the order *Rosaceae*

# MEDLARS

*Tree, up to 9m/30ft. Life span: medium. Self-fertile.*
*Fruits: 2.5–5cm/1-2in, green to russet.*

Medlars resemble pear trees but are smaller, have bigger leathery leaves, single, large, white flowers and fruits like giant, distorted rose hips. The brownish-green fruits have a rough 'leafy' end which shows the seed chambers. Medlars seldom ripen fully on the tree in cool regions and were eaten 'bletted' – stored till at the point of decomposition. The taste is somewhat like that of rotten pear and they are now disdained.

Originally from Persia, medlars became naturalised over much of Europe. Theophrastus mentions them in Greece in 300 BC and Pliny refers to the Romans having three sorts. Once very popular, they are now planted infrequently.

**Medlar flower and leaves**

## VARIETIES

There are only a few left. Generally the bigger the tree, the larger the fruit tends to be. **Dutch** and **Monstrous** are the largest, **Royal** and **Nottingham** the tastiest and smaller. The seedless **Stoneless** has disappeared.

## CULTIVATION

Medlars are obliging and will grow in most places, generally preferring a sunny spot in a lawn or grass.

**Medlar trees are beautiful in their autumn colours**

### Growing under Glass and in Containers
The tree is hardy, so it is a waste to grow it under cover, but the twisted framework and general attractiveness make it a good specimen plant for pot growing.

### Ornamental and Wildlife Value
Pretty flowers, large leaves and gorgeous autumn golds make this a delightful specimen tree, with a twisted and contorted dark framework for winter interest. The fruits are useful to the birds late in winter.

### Propagation, Pruning and Training
Medlars can be grown from seed, but are usually grafted on pear, quince or thorn stock. They are best pruned only remedially as they fruit on the ends of the branches.

### Weed, Pest and Disease Control
Medlars rarely suffer from any problem.

## HARVESTING AND STORING, CULINARY USES

The fruits should be left on the tree till winter and then stored in a cool, dry place till they soften (blet). The pulp was once popular raw, mixed with liqueur and cream, but is better jammed or jellied.

*Medlar Fudge*
makes about 2kg/4lb

*1kg/2lb medlars*
*1 large or 2 small lemons*
*3 cloves*
*600ml/1pt cider*
*approx.1kg/2lb light brown sugar*
*honey or maple syrup to taste, cream and macaroons to serve*

Wash and chop the fruit, add the cloves and cider and simmer until the fruit is soft. Sieve and weigh the pulp. Add three quarters of its weight in sugar and bring back to the boil, then bottle and scal. When required, whip the fruit cheese with honey or maple syrup till soft, spoon into bowls and top with whipped cream and broken macaroons.

*Chaenomeles japonica* from the order *Rosaceae*

# JAPONICA QUINCES

*Shrub, up to 3x3m/10x10ft. Life span: short. Self-fertile.
Fruits: 2.5–5cm/1-2in, round, green/red/yellow.*

A tangled mass of dark, occasionally thorny branches covered with red, white, orange or pink blossom in early spring. This is followed later in the year by hard, roundish fruits, green flushing red or yellow.

Often just called japonica, this shrub arrived in Europe from Japan as late as 1800. It was rapidly accepted and is now widely planted in many varieties and hybrids, for its flowers not the fruits. There is opportunity for developing a better culinary or even a dessert form.

## CULTIVATION

Hardier than **Cydonia Quinces**, these are easy almost anywhere, even on shady walls.

**Growing under Glass and in Containers**
Tough and unruly plants, they are better outdoors. However, I've found them dependable in pots to force for early flowers.

**Ornamental and Wildlife Value**
The displays of early flowers and long-lived fruit are exceptional, making these valuable shrubs. The flowers come in late winter, benefiting early insects, but the hard fruits often rot before the birds take them.

**Propagation, Pruning and Training**
Unlikely to come true from seed. Better varieties are

**Japonica quince flowers provide a marvelous splash of colour**

easily layered or can be grafted. Winter cuttings may take; softwood cuttings are better but trickier. The shrubs have a congested form and are best left alone or tip pruned in summer to control their size. I weave young growths like basket work to produce a tight surface that can be clipped.

**Weed, Pest and Disease Control**
Other than weeds and congestion, they have no common problems.

## VARIETIES

The botanical *C. japonica* has orange flowers and is not common. The true japonica is *C. speciosa*. There are many ornamental hybrids and varieties that also fruit. **Boule de Fer** is my favourite and is a heavy cropper. A related species, *C. cathayensis*, is larger, with green fruits up to 15cm/6in long, and is a thorny brute!

## OTHER USES

Chaenomeles make good, sturdy hedges.

## HARVESTING AND STORING, CULINARY USES

Inedible, well impenetrable anyway, until cooked, when they have an aromatic scent similar to but different from Cydonia quinces. They can be used for tarts, baked or stewed or made into cheese or jelly.

*Japonica Jelly*
makes approx. 4kg/8lb

*2kg/4lb chaenomeles fruits approx. 2kg/4lb sugar*

Chop the fruit and simmer in 3 litres/5pt water till tender, then sieve and weigh the pulp. Add 500g/1lb of sugar per 600ml/1pt of pulp and return to the heat. Bring to the boil, bottle and seal. Store for 3 months before use.

*Arbutus unedo* from the order *Ericaceae*

# STRAWBERRY TREE

## CANE FRUIT, ARBUTE

*Tree, up to 6m/20ft. Life span: long. Fruits: about 2cm/1in, spherical, red.*

*Arbutus unedo* is a small evergreen tree often with gnarled, shedding bark, rich brown underneath. It has white, heather-like flowers in late autumn as the previous year's crop of spherical fruits ripens. These are stubbily spiky, resembling litchis. The pulp is really no good raw, especially in cool regions such as Ireland, but may be better in warmer climes.

*Arbutus unedo* is native to the Mediterranean. The Ancient Greek Theophrastus knew it was edible, but three hundred years later, the Roman Pliny did not regard it as worth eating. Ever since it has been planted for its beauty, yet not really for the fruit, which have remained undeveloped. I gather the descriptive name *unedo* means 'I eat one only'.

**A colourful display of autumn fruit on the tree**

**Strawberry tree leaves and fruit**

### VARIETIES

The ordinary **Killarney Strawberry Tree** is commonest and in few varieties; **Rubra** has pink flowers and abundant fruits. Other species are *A. canariensis,* whose berries are made into sweetmeats, and *A. menziesii.* **Madrona**, from California, has cherry-like fruits that are said once to have been eaten.

### CULTIVATION

*A. unedo* is, surprisingly, not particular as to soil, but prefers a mild climate or a warm site. Although ericaceous, it does not mind some lime, but does better in a leaf-mould-rich woodland or acid soil. The other species are not as compliant.

### Ornamental and Wildlife Value

One of the most highly prized, small, ornamental evergreens. Of slight value to wildlife, though the flowers are handy for insects late in autumn.

### Weed, Pest and Disease Control

Few problems occur.

### Growing under Glass and in Containers

So ornamental it is worth having under cover, but only if confined in a pot. Be careful to use rain water.

### Propagation, Pruning and Training

Seed of the species comes true, layers are possible and winter cuttings may take. The strawberry tree needs little pruning and usually recovers if cut back hard.

### OTHER USES

The hard, tough wood is turned into carved souvenirs of Killarney, especially small cudgels.

### HARVESTING AND STORING, CULINARY USES

Harvested a year after the flowers, the fruits are made into sweets, confections, liqueurs and sherbets, but never eaten raw.

*Killarney Strawberry Surprise*
serves 6

*225g/8oz wheatmeal biscuits*
*120g/4oz butter*
*120g/4oz strawberry jam*
*225g/8oz strawberries*
*30g/1oz gelatine*
*1 large cup water*
*Killarney strawberries*
*(arbutus fruits) to garnish*

Break up the biscuits and mix them with most of butter. Press into a tart dish and chill. Once set rub the biscuit crust with the rest of the butter, line with half the jam, then fill with strawberries. Dissolve the gelatine and the rest of the jam in a cup of hot water, then cool. Pour the jelly over the fruit, swirl and chill. Garnish with Killarney strawberries and serve with cream.

*Viburnum triloba* from the order *Caprifoliaceae*

# HIGHBUSH CRANBERRIES

**Shrub, 4m/14ft. Life span: relatively short. Fruits: 2cm/1in, round, scarlet.**

A large, spreading shrub with maple-like leaves that give good autumn colour, and scarlet, glossy, translucent berries in mid-summer, very similar to the European guelder rose.

*Viburnums* is an immense genus of many species, some of which have berries which were once considered highly edible. The guelder rose (snowball tree, whitten, water elder, *V. opulus*) is now forbidden fruit and as children we are warned how dangerous it is. Though the foliage is poisonous, the fruit was cooked and eaten by the poor for millennia. A native European fruit, it thrives in wet soils and damp hedgerows. Similar conditions suit most species.

## VARIETIES

*V. trilobum*, **Highbush Cranberry**, which is very similar to *V. opulus*, is one of several edible wild North American species; *V. lentago* (**Sweet Viburnum**, **Nannyberry** or **Sheepberry**) has sweet black berries; *V. nudum* (**Naked Viburnum** or **Withe Rod**) is similar, with a deep blue berry; *V. prunifolium* (**Black Haw**) is sometimes good enough even to eat raw.

**Leaves and unripe fruit**

**The elegant flower of the highbush cranberry**

### Growing under Glass and in Containers
Tough individuals, these are mostly hardy and need no glass, though other viburnums may be grown in pots so that their scented flowers may be enjoyed.

### Ornamental and Wildlife Value
Most viburnums are grown for their pretty or scented flowers. The berrying sorts are often as decorative and both fruit and flowers are very useful for attracting insects and birds.

### Propagation, Pruning and Training
Species come true from seed but are slow. Most varieties can be layered and some will strike from hardwood cuttings taken in winter.

### Weed, Pest and Disease Control
No common problem other than weeds and bird losses.

## CULTIVATION

Very easy to please. Most species do best in moist, humus-rich soil; many, except *V. nudum*, like lime.

## OTHER USES

The berries are used to make a spirit in Scandinavia. The bark of the black haw is a source of medicinal drugs.

## HARVESTING AND STORING, CULINARY USES

The berries are not eaten raw, save occasionally after frost, but can be made into sharp-tasting jams and jellies.

*American Highbush Chutney*
makes approx 1.25kg/ 2½lb

680g/1½lb highbush cranberries
300ml/10 fl oz distilled vinegar
120g/4oz each currants, sultanas, raisins, sugar
15g/½oz salt
2 teaspoons each cinnamon, allspice
pinch of nutmeg

Wash the fruits and then remove each of the stalks. Simmer with enough water to prevent burning until soft. Add in the vinegar and the other ingredients, simmer until the chutney thickens. Jar and store for 3 months.

*Fuchsia* from the order *Onagracieae*

# FUCHSIA

*Semi-herbaceous shrub, to 2x2m/7x7ft. Life span: short.*
*Fruits: 1cm/½in, round/oval purple-black.*

This gloriously flowered plant needs little description, and most of us must have noticed the roundish-oval, purple fruits it occasionally sets. As I have always searched for new fruits from far places, I was amused when I first saw fuchsia jelly, and learned that these berries I had overlooked so close at hand were often edible and as delicious as many from distant shores.

The first fuchsia was recorded in 1703. Over the following century a few species arrived from South America with little remark, but in 1793 James Lee astutely launched his *F. coccinea*, the first with impressive flowers, and took the world by storm. Other species were introduced from New Zealand and now there is an amazing range of colours and forms of hybrids of many species.

A mixture of royal ferns and fuchsia forms this rich Irish hedge

**Fuchsia flower and leaves**

## HARVESTING AND STORING, CULINARY USES

Some are tasty raw, but all are best jellied or in tarts.

*Fuchsia Jelly*
makes approx. 2kg/4lb

*1kg/2lb fuchsia berries*
*approx.1kg/2lb sugar*
*juice of 1 lemon*

Simmer the berries with sufficient water to cover. Once they have softened, sieve and weigh. Add the same weight of sugar and the lemon juice. Bring back to the boil, then jar.

## VARIETIES

Fuchsia species *corymbiflora* and *denticulata* were eaten in Peru and *F. racemosa* in Santo Domingo. Fuchsia clubs and societies often have jelly competitions. There appears to be no known poisonous variety – and I have tried many. As they are all bred for flowers, the berries are neglected and should be easily improved – there is enough variety to start with! *F. magellanica* is the hardiest, but rarely fruits.

## CULTIVATION

Even many less hardy species can be grown in cold regions if the roots are well protected as fuchsias usually spring again from underground to flower and fruit. Make back-up plants to be safe and keep these indoors. Fuchsias are amenable to almost any soil but prefer a sunny site.

### Propagation, Pruning and Training
Seed produces mixed results; cuttings are easy to train to any shape. Control growth by nipping out tips in summer; cut back in winter.

### Ornamental and Wildlife Value
Fuchsias are appealing. They can support large numbers of unwanted wildlife.

### Growing under Glass and in Containers
One of the ideal plants for a cool or heated greenhouse or conservatory. Can be grown for many years in large pots.

### Weed, Pest and Disease Control
They suffer from common pests requiring the usual remedies (see page 228).

## OTHER USES

Fuchsias are used as hedges in mild regions.

*Rosa* from the order *Rosaceae*

# ROSE HIPS

*Clambering shrub, up to 9m/30ft. Life span: short to medium. Usually self-fertile. Fruits: up to 2.5cm/1in, ovoid, red, yellow or purplish-black. Value: very rich in vitamin C.*

There can be none of us who does not know roses and few who have never nibbled at the acid/sweet flesh of a rose hip. These are so rich in vitamin C that they were collected on a massive scale during the Second World War for rose-hip syrup for expectant mothers and babies. Rose stems are commonly thorny with a few exceptions such as the divine Zéphirine Drouhin. The deciduous leaves vary from glossy to matt, the flower colour is any you want save black or blue, though wild roses are almost all white or pink. The **Eglantine** rose leaves smell of apples after rain.

Rose hips and flowers are eaten in countries all over the world. The brier or dog rose, *Rosa canina*, and eglantine or sweetbrier, *R. rubiginosa*, are natives of Europe and temperate Asia. Their fruits have been eaten by country folk since time immemorial, but are now regarded with some disdain. However, eglantine sauce was made at Balmoral Castle from sweetbrier hips and lemon juice and was considered good enough for Queen Victoria. Roses are bred for flowers, not for their hips, so most varieties have small hips. However, a little selective breeding could produce hips as large as small apples within a few generations.

## VARIETIES

The **Brier** and **Eglantine** rose hips are the commonest varieties used for hips, though *R. rugosa*, the **Ramanas Rose**, offers larger hips, so is more rewarding. *R moyesii* has large flask-shaped hips and *R. omiensis* has pear-shaped, yellow and crimson fruits that ripen early. *R. spinosissima/ pimpinellifolia*, the **Scotch** or **Burnet Rose**, is another European native, often found in maritime districts. It has a very sweet, purplish-black fruit.

**Ripe rosehips are a glorious red**

## CULTIVATION

Most roses are accommodating but they prefer heavy soil, rich in organic matter, and need to be kept well mulched with their roots cool and moist yet not wet.

### Propagation
Some species can be grown from seed. Cuttings taken in early autumn are reliable for many varieties and most species.

### Ornamental and Wildlife Value
Roses are *the* garden plant. At least one or more can be fitted into almost any garden anywhere to good effect. Single-flowered roses are valuable to insects and the hips are choice meals for winter birds and rodents.

**A spray of rosehip flowers and leaves**

**Growing under Glass and in Containers**

Only tender roses such as *R. banksiae* are happy under glass. Hardier varieties tend to become soft and drawn and suffer from pests. They must be kept moist at the roots, well-ventilated and shaded against scorch.

**Maintenance Calendar**

*Spring* Weed, mulch heavily and spray with seaweed solution often.
*Summer* Dead head regularly, watch for aphids.
*Autumn* Take cuttings.
*Winter* Cut back or tie in.

**Pruning and Training**

This requires a chapter on its own just to list the methods. Basically, for most roses, plant them well apart, prune as little as possible and wind in growths rather than prune. Reduce tall hybrid bushes by a third to a half in height with hedgetrimmers annually in late winter.

**Weed, Pest and Disease Control**

Roses suffer from a host of common diseases, but providing they are growing reasonably well the only real threat to flower and hip production is aphids. Control these with jets of water and soft soap.

**A mixture of immature and ripe hips**

## COMPANION PLANTING

Underplantings of alliums, especially garlic or chives, help deter blackspot and pests. Parsley, lupins, mignonette and lavender are beneficial catnip and *Limnanthes douglassii* are good ground cover underneath roses.

## OTHER USES

Strong-growing roses such as *R. rubiginosa, R. spinosissima* or **The Queen Elizabeth** make excellent stock- and people-proof hedges. The flower petals are dried for pot-pourri and used in confectionery, medicinally and in perfumery. The seeds are covered in hairs that itch when put down the back of other children's collars . . .

**A bowl of rosehip pot-pourri**

## HARVESTING AND STORING, CULINARY USES

The berries need to ripen fully on the bush before being eaten raw, but are best taken before they soften for culinary use. All seed hairs must be removed! Hips can be made into jellies, preserves and the famous syrup. The flower petals may be used as garnishes, preserved in sugar or syrup, used for rose-water flavouring, honeys, vinegars and conserves, pounded to dust for lozenges and they make good additions to salads. The leaves of *R. canina* have been used for tea (in desperation, one suspects).

*Rose Hip Tart*
serves 6

Pastry
*225g/8oz self-raising flour*
*150g/5oz butter*
*1 large egg yolk*
*30g/1oz fine brown sugar*
*pinch of salt*
*splash of water*

Filling
*500g/1lb rose hips*
*60g/2oz each fine brown sugar, honey, chopped stem ginger preserved in syrup*
*1 saltspoon cinnamon sprinkling of sugar and grating of nutmeg*

Rub together the ingredients for the pastry, making it a little on the dry side, and use it to line a tart dish. Wash, top, tail and halve the rose hips, extract every bit of seed and hairy fibre, rinse and drain. Mix with the sugar, honey, cinnamon and ginger and spoon on top of the pastry. Decorate with pastry offcuts and sprinkle with sugar and nutmeg before baking at 180°C/ 350°F/gas mark 4 for half an hour or untill the pastry is light brown on top.

*Cornus mas* from the order *Cornaceae*

# CORNELIAN CHERRY, SORBET

*Tree/bush, up to 8m/25ft. Life span: medium to long. Deciduous, self-fertile.*
*Fruits: 1cm/½ in, ovoid, red.*

Cornelian cherry fruits resemble small, red cherries but are generally too sour to eat raw, except for the occasional better one. The trees or large bushes are tall, deciduous, densely branched and suckering, common in hedgerows and old grasslands. The stems are greyish and the leaves are oval, coming to a point with noticeable veins. The flowers are primrose yellow and appear in small clusters early in spring before the leaves.

The cornelian cherry is one of a genus of about a hundred, mostly small, shrubby plants up to 3m/10ft high but ranging from creeping sub-shrubs to small trees. One of the two species native to Europe and western Asia, *Cornus mas* was once widely cultivated and rated very highly, though now it is rarely eaten even by country folk. There are species from North America and the Himalayas and it seems a shame they have not been cross-bred for better fruits. The cornelian cherry really is a fruit that has stalled in development and probably would not take much further work to improve immensely.

*suecica* used to be gathered by native Americans, who froze them in wooden boxes for winter rations. *Cornus kousa chinensis* comes from China via Japan and is a smaller tree than *C. mas*. The flowers are greyish-purple backed by immense pale bracts, the fruits are more strawberry-like and juicy with better flavour. This species needs a moist, acid soil. *C. macrophylla* and the tenderer *C. capitata* come from Asia and the Himalayas and are eaten raw and made into preserves in India. *C. canadensis* (*Chamaepericlymenum canadense*), **Bunchberry** or **Dwarf Cornel**, is a different type altogether. A lime hater more resembling a soft dwarf raspberry in manner of growth, it has white flowers on low, soft shoots with vivid red fruits which are pleasant enough, if tasteless, and can be added to summer puddings.

**The distinctive primrose yellow flowers of the Cornelian cherry**

## VARIETIES

The variety *C. mas macrocarpa* has somewhat larger fruits and is still available. There used to exist many other improved forms, now apparently lost. In France and Germany there are records of several varieties of sorbets, as they were called – one that had a yellow fruit, some with wax-coloured fruits, white fruits and even one with a fleshy, rounded fruit. Other cornus such as *C. stolonifera*, the **Red Osier**, and *C. amomum*, **Kinnikinnik**, are found in North America and are edible. The former was eaten more in desperation than for pleasure; the latter, found in Louisiana, is said to be very good. The berries of *C.*

The flowers of the Cornelian cherry appear before the leaves in spring

## CULTIVATION

C. mas is easy to grow almost anywhere but prefers calcareous soil. Some species need acid conditions. Generally they are amongst the most reliable of shrubs, requiring little attention.

### Maintenance Calendar
*Spring* Cut back ornamental stemmed varieties, weed, mulch and spray with seaweed solution.
*Summer* Make layers.
*Autumn* Preserve fruit for winter.
*Winter* Take cuttings or suckers and prune.

### Growing under Glass and in Containers
They are hardy, so are hardly worth growing under glass unless perhaps you wish to force them for their early flowers. They will grow well in pots.

### Ornamental and Wildlife Value
Many species are liked particularly for their autumn colour and some species and varieties are grown for their brightly coloured stems. The flowers are early, benefiting insects, and birds and rodents love the berries. One of the best backbone shrubs of a wild garden.

### Propagation
The species come true from seed with some variation, but are slow. Suckers taken in autumn are best, hardwood winter cuttings may take, but layering is more sure.

### Pruning and Training
Generally only remedial pruning is needed, though, as these plants sucker, some root pruning may become necessary. Ornamental coloured-stem varieties are best sheared to ground level in early spring.

### Weed, Pest and Disease Control
No common problems bother these tough plants.

## OTHER USES

*Cornus sanguinea*, the **Cornel Dogwood**, **Dogberry** or **Pegwood**, is a common European relation, not really edible, though the fruits were once used for oil and in brewing. *C. alba* varieties tolerate wet or dry situations and can be used to reinforce banks. Dogwoods grow stiff and straight, so were used for arrows.

## HARVESTING AND STORING, CULINARY USES

In Germany the fruits were sold in markets to be eaten by children (who presumably liked them). They were widely made into tarts, confectionery and sweetmeats, even used as substitutes for olives. In Norway the flowers were used to flavour spirits and in Turkey the fruits were used as flavouring for sherbets. It is noticeable that fruits vary on different bushes and some are more palatable raw than others.

*Sorbet Sorbet*
serves 4

*1kg/2lb cornelian cherries*
*1 small lemon*
*approx. 600g/1¼lb sugar*
*2 or 3 small egg whites*

Wash the fruits, slit the cherries, chop the lemon and simmer them till soft, just covered with water, in a deep pan. Strain and measure the juice, then dissolve 200g/7oz sugar per cup of juice. Bring back to the boil, cool and partially freeze. Remove from the freezer and beat, adding one beaten white of egg for every two cups of sorbet. Repeat the freezing and beating one more time before freezing till required.

*Sambucus nigra* from the order *Caprifoliaceae*

# ELDERBERRIES

*Bush, 10m/33ft. Life span: short. Deciduous, self-fertile.*
*Fruits: 7mm/¼in, purple clusters. Value: rich in vitamin C.*

These well-known, large, many-branched shrubs are loved by children as they have hollow stems good for all sorts of illicit purposes and the strong vertical shoots are easy to break off for mock battles. The plants have a distinctive, rank smell to them and they grow most happily in dank places and on waste ground. The flowers hang in great creamy clusters, varying in smell from sweetest honey to cat's urine. Elderberries themselves are still widely used, but the foliage and stems are slightly poisonous and can be an irritant.

**Elderflowers and leaves**

Closely related to the viburnums, elderberries are native to Europe and Asia. They have been a resource for the poor, but not loved by many, since pre-history. Elder is almost sacred and surrounded with many superstitions which may have protected it, but cynics believe it was because the berries were useful for making fake 'imported' wine or for upgrading cheap local wines.

**Delicate white elder blossom**

## VARIETIES

*Sambucus nigra* is the common wild elder with purple fruits. There are several ornamental forms with coloured, filigreed or variegated foliage, though most of these are poor fruiters. *S. nigra fructaluteo* has yellow fruits, but there is no known large-berried form. This is a shame as elder is a prolific fruiter, tough and easy to propagate. There are several related North American species. *S. canadensis*, **Canadian Elderberry**, was once found good for wine and the unopened flower buds were used as a substitute for capers. The **Blue Elderberry**, *S. caerula*, is from Utah and produces enormous clusters of fruits, rather preferable to *S. canadensis*, and popular in California for tarts and jellies. Another, *S. mexicana*, apparently bears flowers and green and ripe purple fruits simultaneously in its native land of Mexico. The fruits are said to be as good as blackberries. *S. xanthocarpa*, **Australian Elder**, is reportedly edible. These last two are probably too tender for outside cultivation in Europe, if you could find them. There are several other species that berry. Some of these may possibly be inedible or even poisonous, such as *S. ebulus*, so be careful with identification.

## CULTIVATION

Elderberries are too easy for words. They thrive almost anywhere in sun or shade. They prefer a moist spot and rich soil, but then tend to make too much foliage and wood growth at the expense of flowers and fruit.

**Elderberries**

## Growing under Glass and in Containers

There seems no reason to grow elder under glass as it is very hardy. It sows itself in pots of other plants, so clearly also makes a good subject in one!

## Propagation

Elder certainly comes up from seed everywhere. The best varieties have to be propagated by cuttings, but this is no problem as they will root like magic.

## Maintenance Calendar

*Spring* Cut back hard, weed, mulch and spray with seaweed solution.
*Summer* Protect fruit from the birds.
*Autumn* Take cuttings.
*Winter* Cut out diseased wood once leaves fall.

## Ornamental and Wildlife Value

Some of the cut-leafed, golden and variegated forms make attractive garden shrubs, but are not generally popular – probably as they grow large quickly and smell rank. In the wildlife garden, the flowers and fruits are essential, an important part of the natural ecology.

## Pruning and Training

Hard pruning in late winter or early spring keeps them confinable, and produces fewer, bigger flower heads and larger trusses of fruit.

## Weed, Pest and Disease Control

They do suffer from black aphis attacks, but this is cured with soft soap sprays. Ironically the leaves used to be boiled with soft soap as an aphicide. Bird losses are high unless they are netted.

## COMPANION PLANTING

Elder bushes aid composting and should be planted near the bins. They leave a good soil, probably due to leaf litter, if you can lose them.

## HARVESTING AND STORING, CULINARY USES

The berries can be dried, used in tarts or jellied. In Portugal large quantities were cultivated for adding a deep red colour to wines, especially to port. The flowers of sweet-perfumed common elderberries can be dipped in batter and fried to make delicious fritters; the berries make excellent wine.

### Elderflower Fritters
serves 4

*120g/4oz flour*
*30g/1oz butter*
*2 small eggs*
*up to 1 cup milk*
*gallons of fresh elderflowers*
*caster sugar, salt and lemon juice to taste*
*sunflower oil for deep-frying*

Mix together the flour, butter, eggs, salt and a little of the milk and stir to a uniform paste. Add the rest of the milk slowly, mixing well. Beat vigorously, then leave in a cool place for an hour. Wash and trim the elderflowers, leaving a long stalk. Using this stalk, dip the flowers in the batter, drain off the excess, then immerse in boiling sunflower oil and deep-fry until tanned. Drain and dry on absorbent paper and remove the stalk. Dredge with castor sugar and a squeeze of lemon juice before serving hot.

## OTHER USES

Elder makes quick but poor hedges and good screens for summer. The wood is useful for fishing floats and blow-pipes but is otherwise useless and even poor for kindling or firewood. The berries are a source of dye (see right).

*Crataegus azarolus* from the order *Rosaceae*

# HAWTHORN AND AZAROLE

*Tree/bush, up to 8m/25ft. Life span: long. Deciduous, self-fertile.*
*Fruits: up to 2.5cm/1in, roundish, usually orange.*
*Value: rich in vitamins C and B complex.*

The azarole is a more palatable relation of the well-known hawthorn and is cultivated in many of the Mediterranean countries for its cherry-sized fruits. These are usually yellow to orange, but can occasionally be red or white. They are larger than a hawthorn haw and have an apple-flavoured, pasty flesh with two or three tough seeds. Small, spreading trees or large shrubs, these are typical of the thorn genus, with clusters of large, white flowers which do not have the usual family scent.

**Characteristic yellow azarole fruits on the tree**

The thorn family are remarkably hardy, tough plants for wet, dry, windswept or even coastal regions. They are survivors and various species can be found in almost every part of the world, many of which bear similar small, edible, apple-like fruits. Native to North Africa, Asia Minor and Persia, the azarole, *C. azarolus*, may be the mespile anthedon about which Theophrastus wrote. More popular in the Latin countries, it was brought to Britain in 1640. In 1976 it got an award of merit from the Royal Horticultural Society, but it has never really caught on, most probably because other more floriferous varieties and species were readily available.

**Red azarole fruits**

The azarole is the more productive of the species and is grown commercially for flavouring liqueurs. It is probably the best choice for a tree for preserves. The Armenian *C. tanacetifolia*, the **Tansy-leafed Thorn** or **Syrian Hawberry**, is another good choice. The berries are almost relishable raw as dessert and have an aromatic apple flavour, which is surprising as they also closely resemble small yellow apples. They are pale green to yellow, with slight ribs like a melon, and a tassel of 'leaves' at the end. The **Common Hawthorn** or **Quickthorn Haw**, *C. monogyna*, has one seed and is edible but not at all palatable, so is seldom eaten save by curious children. Reputedly it was eaten raw when fully ripe by Scots Highlanders. The fruits are dark red and hang in immense festoons in autumn. The flowers have a sweet perfume when new, but go fishy as they age – on some trees more than others. Equally common, *C. oxycantha/laevigata* is very similar, usually with dark red flowers. There are several edible North American species. *C. tomentosa*, **Black Thorn** or **Pear Thorn**, has hard, orange-red, pear-shaped fruits; *C. flava* has yellow fruits; *C. douglasii* is a better species with small but sweet, black berries with yellow flesh. One identified as *C. coccinea* (now *mollis*, *sub mollis*, *pedicellata* or *intricata*) was very popular with native Americans, who dried the large scarlet or purple fruits for winter use. Sometimes these fruits were mixed together with choke cherries and service berries before they were dried and pressed into cakes for storage.

**A hawthorn or may bush in full flower**

### Maintenance Calendar
*Spring* Weed, mulch and spray with seaweed monthly.
*Summer*
*Autumn* Collect fruits before the birds do.
*Winter* Prune if necessary.

### Pruning and Training
Very little is needed. Do not over-thin the branches as thorns will naturally have a congested head.

### Weed, Pest and Disease Control
Thorns rarely suffer badly from problems, though they are occasionally defoliated by caterpillar attacks. These attacks may be easily avoided by diligent observation and prompt action.

## OTHER USES

Thorns make the best and most traditional hedge with a trimmed surface like fine tweed. The wood is heavy and hard and will burn with a good heat.

**Paul's Double Scarlet hawthorn in flower**

## CULTIVATION

The thorns are all extremely easy to please and require little skill or attention. They tend to lean in the more exposed situations.

### Growing under Glass and in Containers
Because they are so hardy they do not need protection, but several of the ornamental varieties can be grown in pots for forcing to produce early flowers.

### Ornamental and Wildlife Value
The shows of blossom and masses of bright fruits make these an excellent choice for larger shrub borders and informal gardens. The flowers, fruit and foliage are useful to all manner of wildlife. The common thorn flowers attract over 150 different insect species.

### Propagation
This is more difficult than for many fruits. The haws need stratifying for winter and a year before sowing the next spring, and may also produce mixed offspring unless they are from a true species grown far from any others. Cuttings are difficult, so choice varieties are best obtained budded in May or grafted in April on to common stock.

## HARVESTING AND STORING, CULINARY USES

The flowers of common hawthorn once made a heady liqueur or wine. The young leaves and buds, known to schoolchildren as bread and cheese, had a nutty taste and made a welcome addition to salads. We are now told that both are slightly poisonous. However, the berries of azarole, common thorn, and especially the Armenian or Syrian, will make excellent preserves, wines and jellies.

### *Hedge Jelly*
makes approx. 3kg/6lb

*1kg/2lb haws*
*500g/1lb crab or cooking apples*
*225g/8oz elderberries*
*approx. 1.5kg/3lb sugar*

Wash the fruits, chop the apples and simmer the fruits together, just covered with water, for about 2 hours, till softened. Strain and weigh the juice. Add the same weight of sugar to the juice and bring back to the boil. Skim off the scum, jar and seal.

*Sorbus aucuparia* from the order *Rosaceae*

# ROWAN, WHITEBEAM AND SERVICE BERRIES

*Tree, up to 15m/50ft. Life span: short. Deciduous, self-fertile.*
*Fruits: up to 1cm/½in, spherical, scarlet, in clusters. Value: very rich in vitamin C and pectin.*

Rowans are most attractive, small trees with distinctive, pinnate leaves, dark green above, lighter underneath. They have big heads of foamy, cream flowers like elderflowers, but smelling unpleasant. In autumn the branches bend under massive clusters of bright red to scarlet berries, which would hang through the winter if the birds did not finish them so quickly. The Latin name *aucuparia* means 'bird catching' and refers to the fruit's early use as bait.

The *Sorbus* family is large and includes dwarf shrubs and large trees. They are spread all over the world and the majority are quite hardy. They colour richly in autumn and are widely grown for their attractive shows of fruits, also in yellow and white. Many new ornamental species were introduced from China during the nineteenth century, but little advance has been made in fruit quality since *S. aucuparia edulis* (*moravica* or *dulcis*) was first introduced in about 1800.

**Whitebeam tree in blossom**

## VARIETIES

*Sorbus aucuparia*, the **Rowan** or **Mountain Ash**, has scarlet berries that birds love and which are generalyy too sour and bitter for our tastes. There are many other ornamental species and varieties, for example *S. aucuparia xanthocarpa* which has yellow fruits. However, the common rowan is still the frequent favourite choice from the genus and much planted in metropolitan areas. The best variety by far for the gourmand is *edulis* which has larger, sweeter fruits carried in heavy bunches. *S. aria*, the **Whitebeam,** has similar red berries to a rowan and they were once eaten and used for wine. *Sorbus domestica*, the **Service Tree**, is a native of Asia Minor and was also once widely liked, but is now less common. It has smaller clusters of larger fruits of a brownish-green, resembling small pears. They need to be bletted like medlars (see page 169) before they are edible. There were pear-shaped and apple-shaped versions; the flavour and texture were improved after a frost and they were commonly sold in London markets. In Brittany they were used to make a rather poor cider. The **Wild Service** or **Chequer Tree**, *S. torminalis*, has smaller, still harder fruits, that would pucker even the hungriest peasant's mouth, but were once eaten by children.

**Rowan flowers and leaves**

**Fruits on the Wild Service tree**

**A Mountain Ash tree covered in berries**

### Pruning and Training
Pruning should be only remedial once a good head has formed, but watch for overladen branches and prop in time. The strongly erect growth of young trees can be bent down and into fruitfulness: pull them down gently with weights tied near the ends.

### Weed, Pest and Disease Control
Apart from bird losses, and being rather short-lived on alkaline soils, the members of this genus need little care and rarely suffer problems. They are thus well liked for amenity planting.

## OTHER USES

Rowan bark was used in dyeing and tanning. The wood is strong and was used for handles. Service wood is tough and resists wear well. The berries of the wild service tree, *S. torminalis*, were also used medicinally.

**Mountain Ash jelly**

## HARVESTING AND STORING, CULINARY USES

Rowan berries make a delicious jelly, almost like marmalade, which goes well with venison, game and fatty or cold meats. They can be used in compôtes, preserves and syrups, and are sometimes added to apple dishes to liven them up. They have been used for fermenting and distilling liquor, and in emergencies the dried berries have been ground into meal to make a substitute for bread. Service fruits were used traditionally in quite similar ways.

### *Mountain Ash Jelly*
makes approx. 2kg/4lb

*1kg/2lb firm ripe rowan berries*
*1 small lemon*
*approx.1kg/2lb sugar*

Wash and de-stem the berries, add the chopped lemon and 425ml/15fl oz water and simmer till soft (for about an hour). Strain and add 450g/1lb sugar to each 600ml/1pt juice. Bring back to the boil, skim and jar.

## CULTIVATION

Rowans are tolerant of quite acid soils and do not like chalky or limy ones, protesting by being short-lived. They generally prefer drier to wetter sites but, strangely, are commonly seen growing naturally by mountain streams and in wet, hilly country.

### Growing under Glass and in Containers
They are hardy and rather too large for growing inside. They can be grown, and fruited, in pots if only a small crop is desired.

### Ornamental and Wildlife Value
Almost all the species and varieties are very attractive to us in flower and fruit, turning glorious shades of crimson in autumn, but most unfortunately do lack a sweet scent. Rowans are valuable to the birds and insects and are pollinated by flies and midges.

### Maintenance Calendar
*Spring* Weed, mulch and spray with seaweed solution.
*Summer*
*Autumn* Pick fruit before the birds get them.
*Winter* Prune as necessary.

### Propagation
Seed from the species may come true if the tree is isolated, but it must be stratified over winter first. Cuttings are rarely successful, so selected forms are budded in midsummer or grafted in early spring on to seedling rootstocks. The fruits of rowans are thought to get larger if the trees are grafted on to service stock.

**Rowan berries in autumn**

*Prunus* species from the order *Rosaceae*

# SLOES, BIRD CHERRIES, BEACH PLUMS

*Tree/bush, up to 9m/30ft. Life span: medium. Deciduous, self-fertile.*
*Fruits: up to 2.5cm/1in, ovoid, single stone, red to black. Value: rich in vitamin C.*

**Ripe sloe berries have a sharp, bitter taste**

Closely related to orchard plums and cherries, the wild *Prunus* species remain very much tough, hardy alternatives for difficult spots or wild gardens. Sloes are the fruits of the blackthorn, *P. spinosa*, which is a medium-sized shrub, many-branched, very thorny, with blackish bark. The fruits are black ovoids with a bloom that resembles plums, and hard, juicy, green flesh that is usually far too astringent to eat raw. However, like many children, I forever searched for a sweeter one.

Sloes are native to Europe, North Africa and Asia. The stones have been found on the sites of prehistoric dwellings, so they have long been an item of diet. They may be one of the ancestors of the damson and some of their 'blood' has probably got into many true plums. The bird cherry is a native of Europe and Asia, especially grown in the north of England. The sixteenth-century herbalist Gerard claimed it was in 'almost every hedge'. Many ornamental *Prunus* species were later introduced in the eighteenth and nineteenth centuries; *P. maritima* was introduced by Farrer in 1800.

**Sloe berries and leaves**

## VARIETIES

*Prunus padus*, the **Bird Cherry** or **Hag Berry**, is a small tree with white, fragrant flowers in late spring; the double-flowered form, *P. padus plena*, is more heavily almond-scented. The leaves and bark smell of bitter almonds and contain highly poisonous prussic acid. *P. maritima*, the **Beach Plum,** comes from the eastern seaboard of North America, from Maine down to the Gulf of Mexico. It is a small, compact shrub with masses of white flowers and red or purple juicy fruits up to 2.5cm/1in across. These can be eaten raw, but are better if preserved. Another North American species is *P. virginiana*, the **Choke Cherry**. This is a tall shrub with glossy, green leaves and variable red to purplish-black berries. The **American Red Plum**, **Goose**, **August**, **Hog** or **Yellow Plum**, *P. americana*, was the native American's favourite and is good for eating raw, stewing or jamming. It is reluctant to fruit in the British Isles, apparently preferring a more continental climate. *P. simonii*, the **Apricot Plum** from China, has large, attractive, red and yellow, scented fruits.

## CULTIVATION

Sloes and bird cherries are very hardy and good for making windbreaks. They like an exposed site and thrive on quite poor soils, even one packed with chalk, while *P. maritima* does best in coastal regions, and is happy with salt winds and sandy soils. Do mulch these heavily; water well while establishing on very sandy soils as these hold little water.

### Growing under Glass and in Containers

Most of these are hardy and not tasty enough to merit space under cover. *P. americana* may be more fruitful if pot-grown, wintered outside and brought in for the spring through to autumn.

### Ornamental and Wildlife Value

All *Prunus* are good at flowering time, but few are worth space in most small, modern gardens. They are more use to the wild garden as the flowers are early, benefiting insects, while the fruits are excellent winter fare for birds and rodents.

### Pruning and Training

Minimal pruning is required and is best done in summer to avoid silver leaf disease. As hedges, blackthorn

**Bird Cherry blossom**

**Flowers and leaves of the Bird Cherry tree**

should be planted at forty-five degrees, staggered in two or three close rows, each laid in opposite directions. Most species can be trained as small trees, but leave beach plum bushes alone.

### Maintenance Calendar

*Spring* Weed, mulch, spray with seaweed solution.
*Summer* Prune if any pruning is needed.
*Autumn* Protect fruits from the birds.
*Winter* Pick fruits.

### Propagation

The species usually come true from seed. Choicer varieties have been developed for ornamental use and must be budded in summer or grafted in spring. Cuttings do not take.

### Weed, Pest and Disease Control

These wildest members of the *Prunus* family suffer least from pests or diseases.

## OTHER USES

Sloes are good hedging plants. Their leaves were formerly used to adulterate tea. Bird cherries do well in a hedge. Their wood is hard and used for carving and especially liked for rifle butts. Sloe bark was once used for medicinal purposes.

**Blackthorn bush in flower**

## HARVESTING AND STORING, CULINARY USES

Sloe berries are much used for liqueurs, especially gin-based ones, and to add colour to port-type wines. All over Europe they are fermented for wine or distilled to a spirit. In France the unripe sloes are pickled like olives. They can be made into juice, syrup or jelly. Bird cherries have been used in much the same way but are inferior. The American species are used similarly. The apricot plum seems strangely under-rated.

### *Sloe Gin*

*sloes*
*brown sugar or honey*
*peeled almonds*
*gin, brandy or vodka*

Wash and dry the sloes and prick each several times. Pack the sloes loosely into bottles. To each bottle add 120g/4oz brown sugar or honey and a couple of almonds, then fill with gin (or brandy or vodka). Leave for several months before drinking.

*Juniperus communis* from the order *Pinaceae*

# JUNIPER BERRIES

*Tree/bush, almost any size. Life span: long.*
*Evergreen, self-fertile.*
*Fruits: 1cm/½in, green ripening black, oily.*

The juniper is naturally a small tree or shrub with aromatic, evergreen, needle leaves of blue-green. Many ornamental species and varieties are in cultivation and junipers now may be found as ground cover, specimens or hedging plants.

Juniper is native to Europe, but is being displaced by other more profitable trees. Other species come from all over the world.

**Juniper berries and leaves**

## VARIETIES

The common juniper berry is used as a flavouring; other species can be more palatable. The berries of *J. scopularium*, the **Rocky Mountain Juniper**, have been eaten raw and boiled, used to flavour meat and even roasted to make a coffee substitute. The **Syrian Juniper** is dioecious (having separate male and female flowers), columnar-growing, with broad, prickly needles. It fails to ripen fruit in the UK, but in its native lands produces edible, blue-black fruits up to 2.5cm/1in across. A Mexican species, *J. deppeana pachyphlaea*, is said to be sweet and palatable.

## CULTIVATION

Found wild on lime-rich hillsides and moorlands, also on heaths and scrubs, juniper surprisingly survives in acid soils and will grow in heather gardens.

### Growing under Glass and in Containers
It does not like being under glass, especially in dry air. It can be grown in containers.

### Ornamental and Wildlife Value
Valuable conifers for year-round colour and form, junipers will also provide shelter for insects, small creatures and birds.

### Propagation
Seed is slow and needs stratification. Autumn cuttings may take, but spring layering is best.

### Weed, Pest and Disease Control
Junipers have few problems.

**Ripening juniper berries on the tree**

**A juniper wood in Scotland**

### Pruning and Training
Trim if needed in early spring.

## OTHER USES

Juniper wood and berries were used medicinally, for smoking hams and for making an olive-brown dye. *J. virginiana*, the **Pencil Cedar** is used for that purpose. *J. recurva* twigs are burnt as incense in India.

## HARVESTING AND STORING, CULINARY USES

Juniper berries are usually not eaten themselves, but used to flavour meats, sauerkraut and liqueurs. They were used so much for flavouring a spirit made in Holland it became gin, from the Dutch word *genever*, in turn from the Latin *juniperus*. Dried berries have been used as a substitute for pepper and roasted to make a coffee. In France, Genevrette is a beer made from barley and juniper berries.

### *Porc au Genievre*

Before roasting a pork joint, make incisions all over and push in juniper berries, garlic cloves and black peppercorns. Rub with salt and cook as usual.

*Pinus pinea from the order Pinaceae*

# PINE KERNELS

## PIGNONS, PINONS, PINOCCHI

*Tree, up to 25m/80ft. Life span: long. Evergreen, self-fertile.*
*Fruits: up to 1cm/½in long, ivory-white seeds inside a cone.*
*Value: high in minerals and oils.*

**Pine cones (above) contain the edible kernels (left)**

Pine kernels are more nuts than fruits as we eat the seed and not the surrounding part (in this case, the cone), but they are softer than true nuts. Most pine kernels come from the stone or umbrella pine. It is an attractive, mushroom-shaped tree with glossy, brown cones which expand in the sun, and drop the seeds. Each is in a tough skin which needs to be removed before they are eaten.

The stone pine is indigenous to the Mediterranean region. Loved by the Ancient Greeks, it was dedicated to the sea god Poseidon. The kernels of other species are eaten almost anywhere they grow.

**Ornamental and Wildlife Value**
Very attractive if the space is available. Pine kernels will provide excellent food for many species of bird.

**Weed, Pest and Disease Control**
Pines need companion bacteria and fungi, so do better if soil from around another pine is used to inoculate new sites.

**Pruning and Training**
Pines are best left well alone.

**Propagation**
They can be grown from seed or grafted (with skill).

## HARVESTING AND STORING, CULINARY USES

Pine nuts are roasted and salted in the same way as peanuts, and also used in marzipan, confectionery, salads and soups.

*Pinon Truffle Salad*
quantities to taste

*pine kernels*
*butter*
*truffles*
*walnut oil*
*vinegar*
*lettuce*

Gently fry the kernels in butter till light brown. Remove from the heat; add finely sliced truffles, oil and vinegar. Cool the mixture and toss it with clean, dry lettuce leaves.

## VARIETIES

*Pinus pinea* grows happily in northern regions, but without enough sun the cones do not ripen. *P. cembra*, the **Arolla Pine**, is native to Central Europe and Asia and the seeds are a staple food in Siberia. *P. gerardiana*, **Gerard's Pine**, comes from the Himalayas. *P. cembroides* is a native of North America and has pea-sized kernels that taste delicious roasted. *P. edulis*, from Mexico, is the best variety, but unlikely to fruit in Britain. Likewise the **Araucaria Pine** or **Monkey Puzzle Tree**, *A. aurucana*, which has edible kernels and grows but rarely fruits in cool climates (see page 209). The **Parana Pine**, *A. angustifolia*, from South America, is not hardy and equally is too big for glass-house culture.

## CULTIVATION

Stone pines will need shelter to fruit in cold regions. They prefer to grow in sandy soils and acid conditions.

**Growing under Glass and in Containers**
Most pines grow too large unless confined and are unlikely to crop. *P. canariensis*, however, is a particularly pleasing indoor pot plant.

**A Colorado Pine, Arizona, USA**

## OTHER USES

Pines are a source of turpentine and resin.

**The bright-coloured Mexican Stone Pine flower and needles**

# VERY WILD FRUITS

A Hottentot fig in flower

There are many other edible, if not palatable, fruits in our gardens and parks, just waiting for breeders to improve them. What could be more gratifying and worthy than to present the world with new and improved fruits that can be grown in almost anyone's backyard? The following are a few of the many which are occasionally eaten by some, but are not widely used. Please remember *not* to eat anything you are not 100 per cent sure of and which you have had identified on the spot by an expert!

Flower and leaves of the Hottentot fig

### *Asimina/Anona triloba*, Northern Pawpaw, Anonaceae

Introduced to Britian in 1736, the Custard Banana is a bottle-shaped fruit with fantastic potential. Closely related to the papaya, it is much hardier. In its native America it is found as far north as Michigan and New York. A large, attractive, long-leafed, suckering bush, it is pest-resistant with fragrant, purple flowers. It prefers moist, not wet soils. Male and female plants are needed; pollination is by flies. The fruits vary from 5 to 15cm/2 to 6in long, are green, ripening yellow to bronze, with yellow pulp, big brown seeds and a resinous flavour, best cooked. Slow-growing, slow-bearing and long-lived, they are most likely to fruit under glass.

### *Carpobrotus edulis*, Hottentot Fig, Aizoaceae

This resembles the mesembryanthemums, with which it was once classed. Native to South Africa, it is a low-growing succulent, found wild in maritime south-west England and southern Europe. Large, magenta or occasionally yellow flowers are followed by small, fig-like fruits which can be eaten raw or cooked, pickled or preserved. The fleshy, triangular leaves can be eaten as saladings as also can those of the similar *Mesembryantheum crystallinum*.

### *Ceratonia siliqua*, Carob Tree, Leguminosae

The Locust Bean or St John's Bread is an edible, purple-brown, bean-like pod that tastes so much like chocolate it can be ground up and used as a substitute. The seeds are not eaten, but are so exact in size and weight they were used for weighing gold and were the original 'carat'. This tree is native to the Mediterranean region and preserved pods have been found at Pompeii. Nowadays the pods are used as animal feed.

### *Elaeagnus umbellata*, Autumn Olive, Elaeagnaceae

A strong-growing, spreading, deciduous shrub from Asia with fragrant, yellow flowers and small, orange or red berries used like redcurrants or dried to 'raisins'. Many species in this genus bear edible fruits, and most of these have fragrant flowers. *E. commutata*, the Silver Berry, has pasty, silver berries and silver leaves. *E. angustifolia*, Oleaster or Wild Olive, has sweet berries, and is still popular in south-eastern Europe.

### *Akebia quinata*, Berberidaceae

A hardy climber from China with attractive, five-lobed leaflets and scented, chocolate-purple flowers in two sizes. These are followed by weird little purple sausage fruits, surprisingly edible – sweetish but pasty and insipid. This needs a warm spot to ripen the fruits, which have a yellowish pulp full of black seeds. *A. trifoliata/lobata* is similar.

### *Hovenia dulcis*, Japanese Raisin Tree, Rhamnaceae

I remember having this as a child. Resembling brown, candied angelica, it is the dried, swollen flower stalk from behind the pea-sized seed of a small, attractive, Asian tree with glossy foliage.

Pods hanging from the carob or locust tree

*Humulus lupulus,*
**Hop, Cannabidaceae**

**The common hop in flower**

I have to include this strange fruit or I will never be forgiven by my beer-swilling compatriots! A rampant climber closely related to cannabis, this is a hardy native of southern Europe with maple-like leaves. Twining stems produce drooping, greenish-yellow, aromatic flower clusters that enlarge as they set. These are boiled to add their bitter, aromatic flavour to good ale and make it beer. The youngest shoots can be eaten in the manner of asparagus in early spring.

*Rhus glabra,*
**Scarlet Sumach, Vinegar Tree, Anacardiaceae**

This small, easily grown, hardy shrub was introduced to the UK from North America in 1622. It is often grown for its spectacular foliage, which turns scarlet in autumn. However, it can produce masses of fruits if both males and females are grown, and these were eaten by native Americans and children. They have a sour taste and were used as a substitute for vinegar. Dried and crushed, they were sprinkled over meat and fatty dishes as a seasoning. Some other members of the *Rhus* family have apparently had their fruits or foliage eaten, but as they are closely related to poison ivy, *R. toxicodendron*, great caution is advisable!

*Taxus baccata,*
**Yew, Taxaceae**.

The foliage is deadly without cure, the seed may be poisonous but for centuries children have eaten the red, fleshy aril. However, it is advisable not to try this one.

*Yucca filamentosa,*
**Adam's Needle, Liliaceae**

A well-known, spiky, garden perennial, this flowers occasionally in Britain and rarely sets fruit. This can be as large as a peach in the plant's homeland, south-western North America. The native Americans were fond of the fruit fresh or dried and ate the flower-buds roasted or boiled.

*Hippophae rhamnoides,*
**Sea Buckthorn, Elaeagnaceae**

Often grown as an ornamental for its silver leaves, this tall, thorny shrub produces acid, orangey-yellow fruits if both sexes are planted. The fruits are too sour for most tastes, but have been eaten in famines and by children and are apparently widely collected in Russia as they are very rich in vitamin C. They are used as a sauce with fish and meat in France, and in Central Europe they are made into a jelly that is eaten with fish or cheese.

*Tilia species,*
**Limes, Lindens, Tiliaceae**

These enormous, well-known trees have sweet sap which was formerly boiled down to sugar. The fruits were once ground into a 'chocolate', but this never caught on as it kept badly.

*Smilacina racemosa,*
**Treacle Berry, Liliaceae**

This delectable, herbaceous garden plant has scented, foamy, white flowers followed by apparently edible, sweet, red berries. One of the best unknown of fruits!

**Harvesting lime flowers**

*Gaultheria procumbens,*
**Checkerberry, Teaberry, Ericaceae**

A low-growing, evergreen native of North America with white flowers and red berries, needing moist, acid soil and partial shade. The berries are odd raw, but can be cooked for jellies and tarts and were once popular in Boston. Ironically the leaves were once used as 'tea'. *G. humifusa* was also used, as was *G. shallon*, another taller, shrubbier version with great clusters of purple, berries which were eaten dried by native Americans.

**Colourful checker berries and leaves**

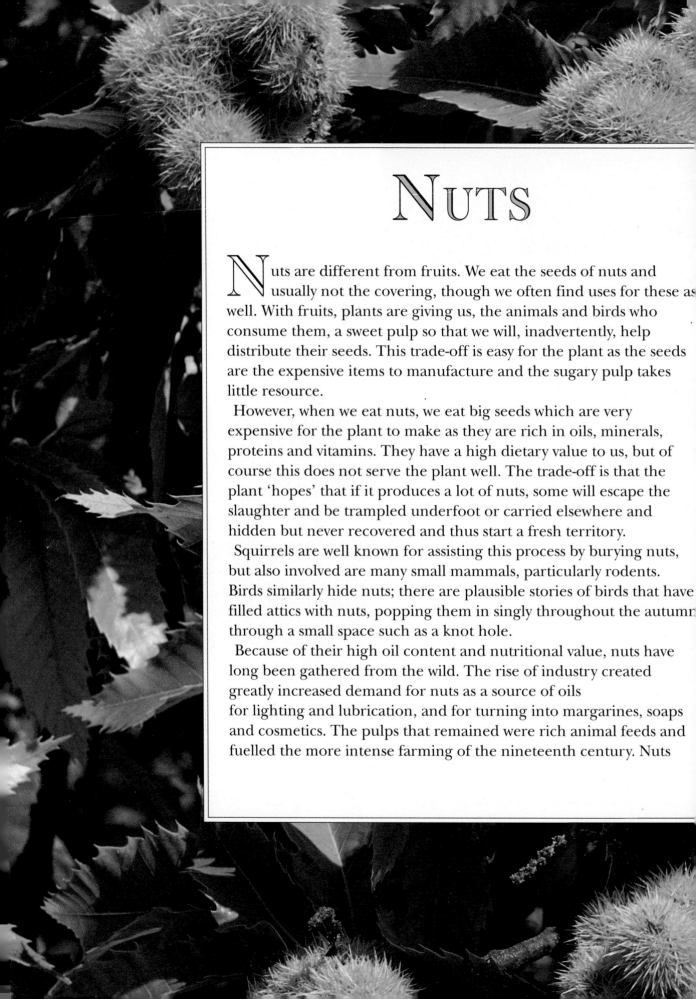

# NUTS

Nuts are different from fruits. We eat the seeds of nuts and usually not the covering, though we often find uses for these as well. With fruits, plants are giving us, the animals and birds who consume them, a sweet pulp so that we will, inadvertently, help distribute their seeds. This trade-off is easy for the plant as the seeds are the expensive items to manufacture and the sugary pulp takes little resource.

However, when we eat nuts, we eat big seeds which are very expensive for the plant to make as they are rich in oils, minerals, proteins and vitamins. They have a high dietary value to us, but of course this does not serve the plant well. The trade-off is that the plant 'hopes' that if it produces a lot of nuts, some will escape the slaughter and be trampled underfoot or carried elsewhere and hidden but never recovered and thus start a fresh territory.

Squirrels are well known for assisting this process by burying nuts, but also involved are many small mammals, particularly rodents. Birds similarly hide nuts; there are plausible stories of birds that have filled attics with nuts, popping them in singly throughout the autumn through a small space such as a knot hole.

Because of their high oil content and nutritional value, nuts have long been gathered from the wild. The rise of industry created greatly increased demand for nuts as a source of oils for lighting and lubrication, and for turning into margarines, soaps and cosmetics. The pulps that remained were rich animal feeds and fuelled the more intense farming of the nineteenth century. Nuts

were no longer wild crops, but had become cultivated crops on a vast scale.

Although nut trees generally require little work, they mostly grow too big for the garden and are best grown agriculturally. (Of course they then suffer from a build-up of pests and diseases – problems associated with all crops if they are grown as monocultures.) They are slow to come into production, though on the plus side they are mostly long-lived and make good timber. Many nut trees produce very hard or oily wood that lasts well. Walnut is one of the most prized of all timbers, so precious that it is mostly used only as veneer.

Nuts suffer different pests from those that attack fruits. Bigger birds and rodents are more of a threat and, as nuts are larger, they are harder to protect or grow under cover (indeed, except as bonsai, many are almost impossible to keep small). Also, they are unfortunately more tender and susceptible to frost damage than many fruits. This, plus the need for a hot summer and autumn to ripen the nuts, means that most nut trees are best grown in warmer countries than Britain.

One interesting connection between many of these nut trees is how many of them have catkins and are wind-pollinated, even though these nut trees belong to entirely different families. This also means that they do not generally have scented flowers and give little nectar to insects, but they are, of course, a rich source of pollen.

From a commercial point of view, it is curious how almost all retail nut sales take place at Christmastime, the period which serves to outsell the rest of the year put together.

*Prunus dulcis/amygdalis* from the order *Rosaceae*

# ALMONDS

*Tree, up to 6m/20ft. Life span: short. Deciduous.  Fruits: 5cm/2in, pointed oval, in brown skin.
Value: rich in protein, calcium, iron, vitamins B2 and B3 and phosphorus.*

Almond trees resemble and are closely related to peaches, with larger, light pink blossoms appearing before long, thin leaves. Flowering a fortnight earlier than peaches, they are often affected by frost. The wild varieties sometimes have spiny branches. The almond fruit has tough, inedible, leathery, greenish-brown, felted skin with a partition line along which it easily splits. The skin peels off a smooth, hard stone, full of small holes which do not penetrate the shell, containing the single, flat, pointed oval seed.

Originally from the Middle East, almonds were known to the Ancient Hebrews and Phoenicians. Long naturalised in southern Europe and western Asia, they are now widely grown in California, South Africa and south Australia. Almond trees were introduced to England in 1548.

**Almond blossom**

## VARIETIES

*Prunus dulcis dulcis* is the **Sweet Almond**, *P. dulcis amara*, the **Bitter Almond**. The former is the much-loved nut; the latter is used for producing oil and flavourings and is too bitter for eating. It contains highly poisonous amounts of prussic acid. In Spain, a light-cropping old variety, **Jordan**, is still grown and commercial varieties are available in some regions. The variety **Texas** is especially tasty roasted and salted with the skin on. Ornamental varieties rarely bear fruit.

## CULTIVATION

Almonds want well-enriched, well-aerated, light soil, and to be at least 3m/10ft apart. They need no staking after the first year. They want copious quantities of compost and mulches. Usually grown as a bush, they can be planted against walls. They should not be planted near peaches as they may hybridise, resulting in bitter nuts. Hand pollination is recommended. They are not usually self-fertile, so several trees should be planted together.

### Growing under Glass

Almonds are rarely grown under glass because the necessary extra efforts of replenishment pruning and tying in are not usually well rewarded. The greenhouse must be unheated in winter to give them a dormant rest period. More problems occur under cover and red spider mite can be troublesome unless high humidity is maintained.

### Growing in Containers

Almonds can be grown in large pots as they can take heavy pruning if well fed and watered. Pots enable them to be kept under cover during winter and through flowering and then brought out all through the summer, thus avoiding peach leaf curl and frost damage. The flowers must be protected from frosts and so too must the young fruitlets.

### Ornamental and Wildlife Value

The almond is a real beauty – the fruiting tree as much as the many ornamental varieties. In hot, dry countries they are useful to birds, insects and rodents.

### Propagation

Almonds can be raised from stones, but take years to fruit and may produce a mixture of sweet and bitter fruits. Budded on to St Julien A in the UK, for example, almonds will normally fruit in their third year. Seedling almond or peach rootstocks are better.

**Maintenance Calendar**
*Spring* Protect blossoms from frost, hand pollinate, weed, mulch and spray with seaweed solution monthly.
*Summer* Thin fruits early.
*Autumn* Remove ripe and mummified fruits from the trees.
*Winter* Prune hard, spray with Bordeaux mixture.

**Pruning and Training**
Almonds fruit on young shoots, like peaches, but need to carry more fruits, so the trees are not pruned as hard. Commercially, every third year or so a few main branches are cut back hard and the top end of the remaining higher branches is removed to encourage prolific growth from the lower branches and stubs. This is best done in late winter, though it may let silver leaf disease in. It also keeps the bushes lower and more manageable. On walls and under cover, almonds may be fan trained, as for peaches. Thinning the fruits is not essential, but prevents biennial bearing.

**Almonds ripening on the tree**

**A grove of almond trees**

# OTHER USES

The wood is hard and makes good veneers; the oil is used in cosmetics.

### Weed, Pest and Disease Control
Earwigs can get inside the fruits and eat the kernel, but are readily trapped in rolls of corrugated paper around each branch. Protect the bark from animals such as rabbits and deer. Almonds' main problem is peach leaf curl, see 'Peaches' (page 43) for treatment. Rainy weather in late spring and summer may cause fruits to rot.

Dieback and gummosis are symptomatic of poor growth and are best treated by heavy mulching and hard pruning.

### Harvesting and Storing
Once the nuts start to drop, knock them down, peel and dry. Commercially they are hulled, but the nuts will keep better intact. They can be stored even in dry salt or sand for long periods.

# COMPANION PLANTING

Almonds are benefited by *alliums*, especially garlic and chives. Clover or alfalfa and stinging nettles are also reputedly helpful.

# CULINARY USES

The nuts are left with the brown skin on, or are blanched to provide a cleaner-tasting product. They may be eaten raw, cooked or turned into a milk, *Sirop d'Orgeat.*

*Sirop d'Orgeat Milkshake*
quantities to taste

*Sirop d'Orgeat*
*ice-cold full-cream organic milk*
*grated nutmeg*

To one part Sirop d'Orgeat add approximately seven parts milk, mix well and top with the grated nutmeg.

*Carya* species from the order *Juglandaceae*

# PECAN AND HICKORY NUTS

*Tree, up to 30m/100ft. Life span: medium to long. Deciduous, partly self-fertile.*
*Fruits: up to 5cm/2in, green-skinned, hard-shelled nuts. Value: rich in oils and vitamins B1 and B2.*

Pecans are very large, fast-growing trees with pinnate leaves, male catkins and insignificant flowers followed by pointed, rounded, cylindrical fruits.

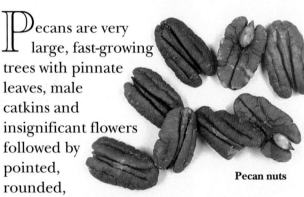

**Pecan nuts**

These have a leathery skin which peels off to reveal a reddish, smooth shell enclosing the walnut-like kernel. Hickories are similar, though not as large in tree or fruit, with non-aromatic leaves and peeling bark, while the pecan has grey, resinous leaves. Hickories also prefer more humid conditions than pecans.

These are natives of North America and have been long enjoyed by native Americans. They are grown in Australia, but rarely crop well elsewhere, though they are widely grown for their timber. The first trees were introduced to Britain in 1629.

## VARIETIES

*Carya illinoensis* is the **pecan**, a fruit much like a walnut in most ways save that the reddish shell is smooth, not embossed, and is also more cylindrical. The trees grow up to 21m/70ft high, so are not very suitable for most modern gardens. Burbank developed new varieties of pecan with very thin shells, but these are not widely available. The hickories are similar to the pecan, with more flattened nuts. The trees generally grow up to half the pecan's height again, which is pretty big anywhere. The **Shellbark Hickory**, *C. laciniosa/alba*, and *C. ovata*, the **Shagbark**

Hickory, are the more popular and productive sorts. *C. tomentosa*, the **Mocker** or **Square Nut** has a tasty nut, but is very difficult to shell. *C. cordiformis* is the **Bitternut Hickory**, and *C. porcina/glabra* is the **Pignut**. As their names suggest, these are suitable only for pigs and, of course, hungry children. *C. sulcata* is the **King Nut**, considered the best variety by the native Americans, but not yet developed commercially. Many other minor species are also occasionally eaten from the wild.

## CULTIVATION

They will grow in the British Isles, but rarely fruit here. The pecan prefers a hotter, drier, more sub-tropical climate; the hickories prefer one that is warmer and wetter, so may produce crops in a favourable site in certain western regions.

**Immature pecan nuts growing on the tree**

The pointed, cylindrical pecan fruit contain the edible kernel

## Growing under Glass and in Containers

There is little practical possibility of getting these huge trees under cover. They resent being confined in pots and are unlikely to crop, though they may make good bonsai subjects.

## Ornamental and Wildlife Value

Given a suitable setting, these are large, attractive trees with decorative foliage that turns a rich yellow in autumn. They are not of any significant wildlife value except in their native woods.

## Maintenance Calendar

*Spring* Weed, mulch, spray with seaweed solution.
*Summer* Prune, but only when needed remedially.
*Autumn* Collect nuts if it has been a long, hot summer.
*Winter* Cut out coral spot if any is seen.

## Propagation

Normally grown from seed, they are best pot-grown and then planted out as soon as possible in their final site as they do not like to be transplanted. They are slow to establish and then fast-growing. Improved varieties are grafted or budded on seedling stock.

## Pruning and Training

Minimal pruning and training are required. Large specimens need staking for the first few years, as they are slow to take.

## Harvesting and Storing

Ripe fruits are knocked down from the tree, peeled (if the peel has not dropped off already) and dried. They do not store as well as walnuts, though they may keep up to a year if they are stored in a cool, dry place. Commercially they are hulled before storage and will keep up to two years at 5°F/–15°C.

# WEED, PEST AND DISEASE CONTROL, COMPANION PLANTING

Very few pests or diseases are problems for the hickories in European gardens. The pecan finds Britain too cool to ripen its wood and suffers from coral spot, which needs pruning before this spreads. In America pecans suffer from many pests and diseases. No companion effects are known about for either tree.

# OTHER USES

Hickories are planted for their tough, elastic timber and are renowned as fuel for smoking foods. Hickory bark was used for a yellow dye.

# CULINARY USES

Pecan nuts taste much like mild, sweet walnuts and to my taste are preferable. They are used raw or cooked in savoury and sweet items, especially cakes and ice-cream. Pecan pie is a legendary dessert. Hickory nuts are used similarly and can be squeezed to produce nut milk or oil.

### *Pecan Pie*
serves 4–6

*175g/6oz shortcrust pastry*
*60g/2oz shelled pecans*
*90g/3oz brown sugar*
*3 small or 2 large eggs*
*225g/8oz golden syrup*
*30g/1oz maple syrup*
*½ teaspoon vanilla essence*
*¼ teaspoon salt*

Roll out the pastry and line a wide, shallow pie dish. Bake blind, weighed down with dried peas or similar, at 190°C/375°F/gas mark 5 for 20 minutes or until cooked. Cool and fill the case with pecans, arranged aesthetically. Beat together the other ingredients till the sugar is dissolved and pour over carefully without disturbing the nuts, which may float. Bake at 220°C/450°F/gas mark 8 for 10 minutes, then reduce the temperature to 180°C/350°F/gas mark 4 and cook for another 30 minutes. Cool and chill well before serving in slices with lashings of cream.

*Juglans* species from the order *Juglandaceae*

# WALNUTS

*Tree, 45m/150ft. Life span: long. Deciduous, partially self-fertile. Fruits: up to 5cm/2in, green sphere enclosing nut. Value: rich in oil; the husks contain much vitamin C.*

Walnuts are slow-growing, making massive trees up to 45m/150ft eventually, with aromatic, pinnate foliage, silvery bark, insignificant female flowers and male catkins. All parts have the distinct sweet, aromatic smell. The fruits have a green husk around the nut enclosing a kernel wrinkled like a brain.

*Juglans regia*, the common or Persian walnut, is native to western Asia. Introduced to the Mediterranean basin before the first century BC, it became an important food in many regions and was also grown for timber. Walnuts reached Britain in the sixteenth century, if not in Roman times. The black walnut, *J. nigra*, comes from north-east America and was introduced to Britain in 1686. It is even bigger than the common walnut and widely grown for timber. The nuts are large, very hard to crack and a valuable dietary source of phosphorus.

more you beat them the better they'll be' is advice which puzzles many. It is not to encourage fruitfulness, but rather to give the walnut a damaged bark which then produces a more valuable distorted grain in the timber. As to dog or wife, I suggest attention and treats probably develop better relationships with either.

### Growing under Glass and in Containers

Huge trees, these can hardly be housed; they're fairly hardy anyway. I've a fifteen-year-old bonsai, but I doubt that it will ever fruit!

### Ornamental and Wildlife Value

Very attractive and sweetly aromatic trees, but they grow too big for most gardens. They are not in general very valuable to wildlife save to rodents and squirrels.

### Maintenance Calendar

*Spring* Weed, mulch and spray with seaweed solution.
*Summer* Take young fruits for pickling.
*Autumn* Collect nuts, prune.

## VARIETIES

Named varieties of common walnuts such as **Franquette** are hard to find in Britain, though may be available elsewhere. France had one called the **Titmouse**, because the shell was so thin that a titmouse could break in to eat the kernel! Black walnuts are usually offered as the species here, but there are several named varieties available from the USA. They can grow half as high again as common trees, up to 45m/150ft. Another American species, the **White Walnut** or **Butternut**, *J. cinerea*, introduced in 1633, is grown for timber and ornamental use. The nuts are half as big again as common nuts, strong-tasting and oily. *J. sieboldiana cordiformis* is the **Heartnut** from Japan. Fast-growing, fruiting after only five years or so, it has leaves up to 1m/3ft long and small, easily shelled nuts which hang on strings.

## CULTIVATION

Walnuts prefer a heavy, moist soil. They should not be planted where late frosts occur. As pollination is difficult it is best to plant several together. The old saying 'The wife, the dog and the walnut tree, the

The fruit opens as it ripens to reveal the kernel inside

**Walnut wood, fruit and leaves**

### Propagation

The species can be grown from seed, but are slow. Improved varieties are grafted or budded, and still take a decade to start to fruit, finally maturing around the century. They are best started in pots and moved to their final site while still small, as they resent transplanting.

### Pruning and Training

Walnuts must be pruned only in autumn as they bleed in spring. Minimal pruning is required, but branches become massive, so remove badly positioned ones early. They need no stake after the first years.

**The common walnut tree**

### Weed, Pest and Disease Control

There are few problems. Late frosts damage them, otherwise they are slow reliable croppers, each averaging 68kg/150lbs annually.

### Harvesting and Storing

The nuts are knocked down and the sticky staining peel is removed before drying. Walnuts can then be stored for up to a year. For pickling, pick the nuts green when a skewer can still be pushed through.

## COMPANION PLANTING

Varro, in the first century BC, noted how sterile the land near walnut trees was. Walnut leaves give off exudates that inhibit many plants and prevent their seeds from germinating. The American species are more damaging than the European and they are particularly bad for apples, *Solanaceae*, *Rubus* and many ornamentals.

## OTHER USES

Other image

The foliage and husks have long been used as brown dyes and the oil as a hair darkener and for paints. The wood has always been valued for veneers and gun stocks, the more gnarled the better. Walnut trees were often planted near stables and privies as their smell was thought to keep away flies. The walnut sap has traditionally been boiled to produce sugar.

## CULINARY USES

Walnuts may be eaten either raw or cooked, often in confectionery or cakes, and associate particularly well with coffee or chocolate. They yield an edible, light oil. The young fruits may be pickled before the stone forms.

### Walnut Aperitif

*young green walnuts*
*brandy*
*red wine*
*sugar as required*

Wash and prick enough nuts to fill a wide-necked bottle. Fill with brandy, seal and store in a cool, dark place. After a year, decant the brandy into another bottle, refill the original bottle with red wine and reseal. After another year, decant the wine into the brandy, refill the walnut bottle with wine and reseal. After another year decant again, fill the walnut bottle with white sugar and reseal. After a year (making four in total,) discard the nuts and add the sugar syrup to the wine and brandy. Serve in sherry glasses before meals.

*Corylus* species from the order *Corylaceae*

# HAZELS, COBS AND FILBERTS

*Tree/bush up to 6m/20ft. Life span: medium to long. Deciduous, partially self-fertile. Fruits: up to 2.5cm/1in, pointed round, or oblong oval, brown nuts. Value: rich in oils.*

These are shrubby trees, typical of woods and thickets, with dark stems, leaves rounded to a point and magnificent, yellow, catkin male flowers in early spring. The gorgeous, carmine-red, female flowers are tiny, sea-urchin-like tentacles that protrude on warm days. The nuts are a pointed round or oblong oval. Hazels and cobs have a husk around the base, while filberts (full-beards) are completely enveloped by the husk. The shell is thin and the kernel sweet. Wild hazels are *Corylus avellana*, but, being wind-pollinated, these have often been influenced by *C. colurna*, cobs, also known as Turkish or Barcelona nuts, and *C. maxima* or filberts.

Hazelnuts of wild species were known in ancient times and filberts were introduced by the Romans from Greece. Pliny claims they came there from Damascus. The Romans may have brought filberts to Britain, but they were not noticed officially till introduced in 1759. Cob nuts were introduced earlier, in 1582, and the American hazelnut, *C. americana*, a similar, smaller nut with a thicker shell and heart-shaped leaves, arrived in 1798. Any appellation no longer signifies true breeding, as these all became interbred during the nineteenth century, which gave us most of our current varieties.

**Immature hazelnuts**

planted severally to ensure pollination. They are an immensely easy crop for the lazy gardener, requiring even less effort than most.

### Growing under Glass and in Containers

These are so hardy there seems no reason to grow them under cover and I suspect they would not like it anyway. They survive in pots quite well, looking attractive but seldom cropping.

### Ornamental and Wildlife Value

These are not generally noticed, save when their catkins make a welcome display. The **Twisted Hazel** is attractively distorted and deformed and still crops well. The hazels will support many life forms, both large and small, and are also excellent plants for wild or native gardens.

### Maintenance Calendar

*Spring* Weed, mulch and spray with seaweed solution at monthly intervals.
*Summer* Cut close underneath if grassed.
*Autumn* Clear mulch or cut the grass close to disclose any fallen nuts.
*Winter* Prune, mulch well if not under grass.

## VARIETIES

I adore **Red-skinned Filberts**; they are certainly small and fiddly, with tight, russet husks, but they are so delicious. **Cosford Cob** is thin-shelled and a good pollinator of others. **Kentish**

**Cob** (**Lambert's Filbert**) is a prolific cropper of large nuts if pollinated by Cosford or **Pearson's Prolific** (**Nottingham Cob**). This last is compact, a good pollinator and has large nuts. For the best flavour, however, you can't beat the wild hazelnut.

## CULTIVATION

Hazels prefer stony, hilly ground. A well-drained, loamy soil will do, but heavy, damp, rich soils cause too much rank growth and few female flowers. Hazels need no support and are best

### Propagation
These can be grown from seed but do not come true. Layering or grafting is possible, but root suckers are best, detached in autumn and potted up or planted *in situ* or a nursery bed for a year before their final move.

### Pruning and Training
Traditionally hazels were grown on a low, flat, cartwheel frame. They are probably best trained to spurs on goblets, but are often left to be bushes or thickets. It is worth keeping them on a single trunk, uncongested, and removing the suckers, to prevent losing any of the nuts.

### Weed, Pest and Disease Control
Weedy growth underneath makes it hard to find nuts, so hazels are best grassed down or mulched. In gardens they suffer few problems on a scale sufficient to damage crops other than the attentions of pigeons, rooks, pheasants, rodents, children and especially squirrels.

**Male and female hazel flowers**

### Harvesting and Storing
The nuts can be eaten a little unripe, but have to be fully ripe to keep. Ideally they should be allowed to fall off, but many are stolen by wildlife. They need to be dehusked and dried to keep well, though I never dehusk my red-skinned filberts. They will keep best, and for years, if packed in salt.

### Companion Planting

They seem to associate naturally with bluebells and primroses, and truffles can be grown on their roots.

### Other Uses

**Hazel growing in the wild**

Hazels make good hedges and windbreaks. The foliage is eaten by many animals, including cows. The stems are tough and flexible, so are good for baskets and hurdles, and forked branches make divining rods. The wood is used for smoking fuel and I smoke my cheese with the shells.

### Culinary Uses

Hazelnuts of all varieties are used in savoury dishes, but more often in sweet dishes and confections. They are used for liqueurs and can be squeezed to express a light, edible oil.

*Hazelnut Macaroons*
makes about 12

*120g/4oz hazelnuts*
*120g/4oz light brown sugar*
*1 egg white*
*drop of vanilla extract*
*thick or clotted cream to serve*

Grind three quarters of the nuts in a food processor, then add the other ingredients and cream them together. Pour rounds of the mix on to rice paper on a baking tray, place the remaining nuts on top and bake for 15 minutes at 180°C/350°F/gas mark 4. Serve sandwiched with thick or clotted cream.

*Castanea sativa* from the order *Fagaceae*

# SWEET OR SPANISH CHESTNUTS

*Tree, up to 37m/120ft. Life span: long. Deciduous, rarely self-fertile. Fruits: 5cm/2in, prickly burrs containing two or three nuts. Value: rich in oils.*

Sweet chestnuts make massive and beautiful trees. They have very large, serrated-edged leaves. The male flowers are long, yellow catkins, different from walnut or hazel catkins as they are divided like pearls on a string. The fruits are brownish-russet, softly spiny burrs usually containing three brown nuts with thin, tough, leathery shells, flattened on one side and pointed.

Sweet chestnuts are native to the Mediterranean region. They were highly valued by the Romans for food and timber and became widely distributed. They fruit well only after hot summers in Britain, but are still capable of reaching a large size, so they have been planted for timber and were often coppiced. The major exporter of nuts has always been Spain, though most southern European countries have their own production as chestnuts have become a staple food. Madeiran nuts are said to be the biggest and traditionally served to sustain the peasants for months each year.

has been almost wiped out by a fungus, chestnut blight. Now American growers are breeding hybrids from the resistant *C. mollissima*, the **Chinese Chestnut**. *C. pumila*, the **American Chinquapin**, is rare in cultivation and unlikely to fruit in Britain, but the nut is said to be very sweet. Other *Castanea* species are widely grown and the delicious nuts eaten with appreciation all around the world.

## CULTIVATION

Sweet chestnuts are far too big for most gardens, rapidly reaching 30m/100ft or even more. They do not like thin chalky soils, but are not calcifuges and will grow on an alkaline soil if it is also a light, well-drained loam or light, dry, sandy soil. They need no staking after the first year or so. If nuts are required rather than timber, plant on the sunny side of woodlands or windbreaks, ideally of yew or holm oak.

**Maintenance Calendar**
*Spring* Weed, spray with seaweed solution.
*Summer* Hope for hot weather.
*Autumn* Collect nuts if following a hot summer.
*Winter* Enjoy the nuts toasted over the fire.

## VARIETIES

*Castanea sativa* is usually available only as the species or ornamental selections, though better varieties exist, such as *C. sativa macrocarpa*, **Marron de Lyon**, from France. *C. dentata* was the **American Sweet Chestnut**, with smaller, richly flavoured, sweeter nuts, but

**Sweet chestnut leaves and ripening fruit**

### Ornamental and Wildlife Value

Sweet chestnuts make statuesque trees and the large leaves colour well in autumn. The nuts are often rather too useful to wildlife.

### Growing under Glass and in Containers

Far too big to grow under glass, they resent being confined in a pot and they are unlikely to ever fruit in one, but there's a challenge.

### Propagation

They can be grown from seed and are fast-growing but still slow to fruit. The best varieties are budded or grafted, but are hard to find in the UK.

### Pruning and Training

Minimal pruning is required and is best tackled in winter. Chestnuts get very large, so care must be taken to remove unsound branches.

**The elegant shape of the sweet chestnut tree**

### Weed, Pest and Disease Control

Generally they are problem-free in Britain and will set crops in the south following hot summers. In America, chestnut blight wiped out their best species, but this is no problem elsewhere. Rodents, birds (especially rooks and pheasants) and squirrels soon take the nuts.

### Harvesting and Storing

The nuts are beaten down, the husks then removed and dried. They will keep for a year in cool, dry conditions; longer if totally dried first.

## COMPANION PLANTING

Chestnuts are considered healthier when they are grown near oak trees.

**The brown chestnut is contained within a tough, leathery shell**

## CULINARY USES

Chestnuts are not eaten raw, but are delicious roasted. They are made into *marrons glacés* (crystallised chestnuts), ground into flour and then made into porridge, puddings, breads, cakes, muffins and tarts and they are also much used for savoury dishes such as pâtés and in stuffing for meats. Sweet chestnuts are even made into liqueurs.

### Chestnut Amber
serves 4

*225g/8oz chestnuts*
*300ml/10fl oz milk*
*1 lemon*
*1 vanilla pod*
*60g/2oz breadcrumbs*
*30g/1oz butter*
*60g/2oz caster sugar*
*2 eggs, separated*
*120g/4oz shortcrust pastry*

Roast the chestnuts for 20 minutes, cool and remove the skins. Simmer gently, with sufficient water to cover, until tender, then drain and sieve to a purée. Simmer the milk with the lemon peel and vanilla pod for 15 minutes, then strain on to the breadcrumbs. Blend the butter and half the sugar, mix in the egg yolks and lemon juice and stir in the puréed chestnuts, breadcrumbs and milk. Line a deep dish with pastry and fill with the mixture. Bake at 200°C/400°F/gas mark 6 for 25 minutes, or until firm and brown. Whisk the egg whites to a stiff froth, add a teaspoon of sugar, whisk again and spoon on top of the pie. Dredge with more sugar and then return to the oven until the meringue turns a delicious amber.

## OTHER USES

Sweet chestnut has long been used for cleft paling. The wood is durable, but has 'shakes' or splits in it. Often used for rough or external timber, such as coffins and hop poles, it makes a poor firewood but superior charcoal. The nuts were traditionally esteemed for the self-service fattening of swine.

*Pistacia vera* from the order *Anacardiaceae*

# PISTACHIOS

*Tree, up to 9m/30ft. Life span: medium. Deciduous, not self-fertile.*
*Fruits: 2.5cm/1in, pointed oval nuts. Value: rich in oil.*

Pistachios are small, tender trees with grey bark and grey-green, slightly downy, pinnate leaves. The male and female flowers are borne on separate trees in the wild, but some cultivated varieties may be unisexual. It is hard to tell as the flowers are inconspicuous though carried in panicles which later become masses of small, pointed, red fruits. These have a thin, green husk covering the thin, smooth, twin-shelled nut, housing a small, oval, green kernel which has a most appealing taste, especially after roasting and salting. Pistachios are usually the most expensive variety of nuts to buy.

Pistachios are natives of the Middle East and Central Asia and, with some close relations, have been cultivated since ancient times. They were grown in Italy in the late Roman period but were not introduced to Britain till the sixteenth and seventeenth centuries and then never proved hardy enough. The seed was distributed by the US Patent Office in 1854 and the trees proved successful in many southern states where the nuts are now produced in quantity, rivalling the output of the Mediterranean and Turkey.

## VARIETIES

Pistachios, *Pistacia vera*, are not hardy enough for outdoors in Britain except in a very favoured site, for example against a hot wall or under glass. The variety **Aleppo** is an old favourite, but probably unobtainable. *P. terebinthus*, the **Cyprus Turpentine Tree** or **Terebinth,** is similarly not hardy. The whole plant is resinous with nuts which start coral red, ripening to brown, and have edible, oily kernels, also green and pointed but smaller. It was used as a pollinator for pistachios as these shed pollen too early to fertilise themselves. Thus most seedling pistachios became hybrids of these two species. This has prevented much improvement of the pistachio nut. *P. lentiscus* is the evergreen **Mastic Tree**. The nuts yield edible oil, but this tree is grown mainly for the resin obtained from bark incisions, used in turn for chewing gum and medicines.

**Pistachio trees are grown in warm, arid countries for their edible nuts (above)**

**A spray of pistachios and leaves**

## CULTIVATION

Pistachios are not particular as to soil, but will require a protective wall in Britain. In warmer countries they are useful for growing on poor, dry, hilly soil where other nuts will not thrive. Their greater value commercially also encourages this. One male staminate tree is needed for six female pistillate trees, but as the pollen is shed early it needs to be saved in a paper bag until the pistils are receptive.

### Growing under Glass and in Containers
Pistachios have been grown under glass and they make very attractive shrubs in large pots. However, good provision must be made for their pollination.

### Ornamental and Wildlife Value
In warm countries or on a warm wall these are not unattractive, small trees. The unproductive **Chinese Pistachio**, *P. chinenis*, is a small, very pretty and hardy shrub. Pistachio nuts are readily taken by maurauding birds and mammals.

### Maintenance Calendar
*Spring* Put out pots or uncover trees, weed, mulch, spray with seaweed solution. *Summer* Water plants in pots regularly but minimally. *Autumn* Gather nuts if the summer has been hot. *Winter* Bring in pots or protect trees.

### Propagation
Although better varieties could be grown, pistachios seem to lack development. Continual cross-hybridisation with terebinths has prevented improvement, but means that nuts come as true as their parents, which is not claiming a lot. Better varieties can be layered, budded or grafted.

### Pruning and Training
Only remedial pruning is required and this is best done in midsummer. They can be trained against walls and are then best fan trained initially, then allowed to grow out to form a bush.

### Weed, Pest and Disease Control
No common pests or diseases are a problem for pistachios in garden cultivation, though under glass and on a warm wall they may suffer red spider mite attacks.

### Harvesting and Storing
As these hang severally on panicles they can be cut off to be dried and husked. They are best stored in their shells, which open automatically if they are roasted.

## OTHER USES

*P. terebinthus* was long ago cultivated for producing first terebinth, the resin which oozes from the tree, and later turpentine. The wood is dark red and hard and used in cabinet making.

## CULINARY USES

Pistachios can be eaten raw, but are most commonly roasted and salted, the shelling being left to the purchaser. They are much used as a colouring and flavouring for a wide range of foods, some savoury and many sweet, including nougat and ice cream.

### Pistachio Ice Cream
serves 6

*3 small or 2 large egg yolks*
*175g/6oz honey*
*1 teaspoon vanilla extract*
*600ml/1pt cream*
*120g/4oz shelled pistachios*
*natural green food colouring*
*candied lemon slices and glacé cherries to taste*

Whisk the egg yolks, honey, vanilla and half the cream. Scald the remaining cream in a bain-marie, add the egg mixture and stir until the mixture thickens. Remove from the heat, cool, chill, then partially freeze. Remove from the freezer, beat vigorously and return. Repeat but after the second beating mix in the nuts and colouring, then freeze again. Partially defrost before serving the ice cream scooped into glasses, garnished with lemon slices and cherries.

*Anacardium occidentale* from the order *Anacardiaceae*

# CASHEWS

*Tree, up to 12m/40ft. Life span: medium.*
*Semi-evergreen. Fruit: up to 8cm/3in long, weird.*
*Value: kernels are nearly half fat*
*and one fifth protein.*

Cashews are medium-sized, spreading trees with rounded leaves related to pistachios. The cashew comes attached underneath the bottom of the much larger and peculiar fruits, cashew apples, which are juicy and astringent. The nut is grey or brown, ear-shaped and contains a white kernel within the acrid, poisonous shell.

Indigenous to South America, cashews were planted in the East Indies by the sixteenth century and are now grown in many tropical regions, especially India and eastern Africa.

## VARIETIES

Other cashews are eaten: *A. humile*, the **Monkey-nut**, and *A. nanum* are from Brazil and have similar nuts. *A. rhinocarpus* is the **Wild Cashew** of Columbia and British Guyana.

## CULTIVATION

These are best grown by the sea in moderately dry tropical regions and will thrive in any reasonable soil.

**The cashew (shown here in Kenya) looks like an English country park tree**

### Growing under Glass and in Containers
Plants dwarfed by large pots could probably be grown in a hot greenhouse or conservatory, if the seed could be found.

### Ornamental and Wildlife Value
Cashews make interesting subjects for a collection or botanical garden.

### Propagation
They are normally grown from seed, but this is difficult to obtain.

### Pruning and Training
Only remedial pruning is necessary.

### Weed, Pest and Disease Control
No problems are known. The trees exude a gum obnoxious to insects which was used in book-binding.

### Harvesting and Storing
Once the nuts are picked from underneath the fruits they have to be roasted and shelled which, despite mechanisation, is labour-intensive. This is because all the shell must be removed as it contains an irritant in the inner membrane around the kernel, though this is rendered harmless by heat.

## OTHER USES

The shells of the nuts contain an oil used industrially. The 'apples' are then fermented to make a liquor. The sap makes an indelible ink.

## CULINARY USES

Cashew nuts are popular raw, i.e. already partially roasted, or roasted and salted. They are used in many sweet and savoury dishes and can be liquidised to make a thick sauce. Cashews are fermented to make wine in Goa.

### *Cashew Tarts*
makes 12

*225g/8oz marzipan*
*a little icing sugar*
*120g/4oz cashew nuts*
*60g/2oz honey*
*1 teaspoon vanilla extract*
*a little milk*
*glacé cherries*

Roll the marzipan as pastry and form individual tart cases in a tray dusted with icing sugar. Liquidise the other ingredients, adding just enough milk to ensure success. Pour into the marzipan cases, set a cherry in each and chill them to set.

*Macadamia ternifolia* from the order *Proteaceae*

# MACADAMIAS

## OR QUEENSLAND NUTS

*Tree, up to 14m/45ft. Life span: medium. Semi-evergreen.*
*Fruits: up to 2.5cm/1in, grey-husked nuts. Value: over 70% fat.*

Macadamia trees are densely covered with long, narrow, glossy, dark green leaves. The tassels of whitish flowers are followed by strings of small, hard, roundish, pointed nuts in greyish-green husks. The kernel is finely flavoured and of exquisite texture.

These nuts, despite the Greek-sounding name, are natives of north-eastern Australia. Not widely appreciated, they are mostly consumed in the United States from plantations in Hawaii. They were introduced to Ceylon, now Sri Lanka, in 1868.

**The distinctive foliage of the macadamia tree**

## VARIETIES

No species or varieties are available in Britain.

## CULTIVATION

Macadamia nuts prefer tropical or sub-tropical, moist conditions. They are not particular as to soil and do best on the volcanic slopes of Hawaii. They thrive at medium elevations.

### Growing under Glass and in Containers
If the seed could be obtained they might be grown under glass, in pots to constrain growth, though it is doubtful they would crop.

### Ornamental and Wildlife Value
They are attractive, glossy, dark trees, but too tender for growing successfully outside sub-tropical zones.

**Propagation**
They are propagated by seed, but as they are usually sold roasted and salted this may be difficult to find.

**Pruning and Training**
Only remedial pruning is necessary and they will form bushy trees.

## CULINARY USES

Most macadamia nuts are eaten roasted and salted, but they are also used in certain baked goods and confectionery.

### Macadamia Slice
serves 8-10

*120g/4oz macadamia nuts*
*icing sugar*
*225g/8oz marzipan*
*1 dessertspoonful apricot*
*   conserve*
*30g/1oz chopped candied peel*

Rinse and dry the macadamia nuts if they are salted. Dust a rolling board with icing sugar and roll out the marzipan thickly.

**Harvesting and Storing**
The shells are very hard to crack, so the bulk crops are collected mechanically and taken to factories to be de-husked, shelled, roasted and salted before packaging and storing, when they will keep for a year or so.

Coat thinly with conserve and cut into two equally shaped pieces and an approximate third. On one piece spread a layer of nuts and peel, then place the scrappy third of marzipan on top, sticky side down. Smear the top with conserve and add another layer of nuts and peel. Then put the last third on top (also sticky side down). Carefully press and roll this sandwich flatter and wider until the nuts almost push through. Trim, cut into small portions and dredge the mixture with icing sugar before presenting.

*Cocos nucifera* from the order *Palmae*

# COCONUTS

*Palm, up to 28m/90ft. Life span: medium to long.*
*Evergreen, not usually self-fertile. Fruits: 30cm/12in plus, green-brown,*
*oval husk containing the nut. Value: 65% oil.*

These attractive palms, so typical of dreamy, deserted islands, are spread by their floating, oval-husked nuts. The thick fibrous husk is contained in a rind and itself encloses a thick-shelled, oval nut with a hollow kernel that is full of milk when under-ripe.

Venerated in the islands of the Pacific as a sacred emblem of fertility, coconuts are distributed and known around the world.

## VARIETIES

The **King Coconut** of Ceylon is esteemed for its sweet juice. The **Dwarf Coconut**, **Nyiur-gading**, of Malaysia has small fruits, but crops when young and at only about a metre/a few feet high. The **Maldive Coconut** is small and almost round; the **Needle Coconut** of the Nicobar Islands is triangular and pointed.

**The King Coconut**

## CULTIVATION

Coconuts thrive by the sea in moist, tropical heat and rich, loamy soils and are planted about 10m/33ft apart.

### Growing under Glass and in Containers

These are very attractive, easy plants to start with, rapidly outgrowing most places. The **Dwarf Coconut** may fruit, given good conditions, in only four years – thus while still small enough to stay indoors!

### Ornamental and Wildlife Value

Very attractive trees, these can be used for indoor display until they grow too large.

### Propagation

Ripe nuts which are laid on their side and barely covered with compost will germinate readily in heat.

### Pruning and Training

Dead leaves need removing.

### Harvesting and Storing

The nuts are used as they drop, but for milk, processing or cooking are picked by climbing or by using trained monkeys.

**A coil of coir rope in Sri Lanka**

## COMPANION PLANTING

Coconuts are often grown in alternate rows with rubber trees, and with cacao while young. Climbing peppers, *Piper nigrum*, are grown up the coconut trunks.

## OTHER USES

The trunks are used as timber, the leaves for thatch, the husk is coir, used for ropes and matting. The sap makes sugar or is fermented to toddy or distilled to arrack. Dried nuts are copra, used for oil for cosmetics, soaps and detergents. The pressed waste is animal food.

## CULINARY USES

The milk is drunk fresh or fermented. The nut eaten raw or cooked, often as desiccated, shredded coconut.

*Coconut Biscuits*
makes approx. 10

*1 egg white*
*150g/5oz caster sugar*
*75g/3oz desiccated coconut*
*rice paper*
*glacé cherries*
*crystallised angelica*

Beat the egg white until stiff, then beat in the sugar and coconut. Spoon blobs of the mixture on to rice paper on a baking tray. Garnish each with a cherry and angelica and bake at 180°C/350°F/gas mark 4 for 15 minutes or until they are browning.

*Bertholletia excelsa* from the order *Myrtaceae*

# BRAZILS
## PARA OR SAVORY NUTS

*Tree, up to 30m/100ft. Life span: long. Semi-evergreen.*
*Fruits: up to 15cm/6in, brown, spherical shell containing many nuts.*
*Value: 65% fat and 14% protein.*

**The Brazil nut tree enjoys a warm tropical climate**

These are tall handsome trees found on the banks of the Amazon and Orinoco Rivers. They have large, laurel-like leaves and panicles of white flowers which drop brown, spherical bombs with thick, hard cases. These need to be smashed to reveal inside a dozen or more nuts shaped like orange segments, each with its own hard shell enclosing the oval, brown-skinned, sweet, white kernel.

Natives of Brazil, these are still mainly produced there and also in Venezuela and Guyana. They are grown ornamentally in other countries such as Ceylon, but rarely on a commercial scale.

**Pruning and Training**
These need no special attention, but are slow. They are often not cultivated, but are gathered from the wild as they take fifteen years to start fruiting.

**Propagation**
The nuts can be started off in heat, but actually take months to germinate.

## OTHER USES

The oil expressed from the kernels is used industrially; bark once caulked ships.

## VARIETIES

Many consider the **Sapucaya Nut** superior; it is similar, though it comes from a different tree, *Lecythis zabucajo*.

## CULTIVATION

Brazil trees thrive in deep, rich, alluvial soil in tropical conditions.

**Ornamental and Wildlife Value**
Very attractive trees, but too large and requiring too much heat and warmth for widespread use.

**Growing under Glass and in Containers**
These can be grown from seed and kept dwarfed in containers, making interesting specimens, but are unlikely ever to fruit.

**Harvesting and Storing**
The individual nuts are obtained by cracking the spherical containers, which are sealed with wooden plugs. Inside their shells the nuts will keep for up to two years.

## CULINARY USES

Most often Brazil nuts are eaten raw at Christmas time but are also widely used in cooking, baking and confectionery.

*Treacly Brazil Pie*
serves 6

*225g/8oz shortcrust pastry*
*75g/3oz Brazil nuts*
*60g/2oz breadcrumbs*
*75g/3oz golden syrup*
*juice and grated rind of 1 lemon*
*cream to serve*

Roll out three quarters of the pastry and line a pie dish with it. Use dried peas to weigh it down, and bake blind at 190°C/375°F/gas mark 5 for 10 minutes. Remove the peas and put a layer of nuts around the base of the case. Mix the other ingredients together and pour on top. Decorate with strips of pastry and then bake for 20 minutes at 190°C/375°F/gas mark 5. Serve the pie with lashings of thick cream.

*Arachis hypogaea* from the order *Leguminosae*

**Groundnuts**

# GROUNDNUTS OR PEANUTS

*Herbaceous, 60cm/2ft. Life span: annual. Self-fertile.*
*Fruits: 1cm/½in small oval seeds. Value: rich in oil, protein and vitamins B and E.*

Peanuts are always known and used as nuts, although they are in fact the seeds of a tropical, pea-like, annual plant. After pollination of the yellow 'pea' flower, the stalk lengthens and pushes the seed pod into the ground, where it matures. The light brown husks shell easily to reveal a few red-skinned, whitish-yellow seeds.

Natives of tropical America, peanuts were brought to Europe in the sixteenth century and remained curiosities until the nineteenth. Useful for oil, animal feed and 'nuts', they are now grown world-wide.

### VARIETIES

**Spanish Bunch** or **Virginia** varieties average fewer kernels than the better **Valencia** varieties, which have up to four. **Mauritius** peanuts are believed to be of superior quality.

### CULTIVATION

Peanuts prefer loose, dryish, sandy soil. Cool, wet, British summers are unfavourable and they do better under glass, but can be raised indoors and planted out, and will then produce light crops. They are normally grown on ridges to make digging the crop easier.

### Ornamental and Wildlife Value

Too pea-like to be attractive, they have curiosity value. The seeds are only too valuable to wildlife!

### Pruning and Training

These require no care. The old, runnering varieties were more difficult.

### Weed, Pest and Disease Control

On a garden scale these are problem-free, save for rodent thefts.

### Harvesting and Storing

The pods are dug in autumn, thoroughly dried and shelled before storing. Commercially the bulk is pressed for oil and feedcake.

### Propagation

Sow in pots in heat for growing on in large pots to fruition, or planting out in favourable areas. In warm countries they are grown outdoors sown 8cm/3in deep, about 60cm/2ft apart each way.

### Growing under Glass and in Containers

Peanuts are good subjects for greenhouses, or in large pots which can be kept under cover at the start and end of the season and put out on the patio during the summer months.

### COMPANION PLANTING

Peanuts have been grown with rubber and coconuts.

### OTHER USES

Peanut oil is used industrially.

### CULINARY USES

Peanuts are commonly roasted and salted, and are much used in baking and confections, savoury sauces and for their butter and edible oil. They should be kept dry until required.

*Roast Peanuts*
makes 1kg/2lb

*1kg/2lb peanuts*
*30g/1oz garlic*
*1x50g/2oz tin anchovies*
*7g/¼oz oregano*

Boil the peanuts for 2 minutes and slip off their skins, then dry the nuts. Blend the garlic, anchovies and oregano. Coat the peanuts with this mixture and roast at 180°C/350°F/gas mark 4 for 10 minutes or so. Stir and cool.

# OTHER NUTS

*Araucaria Araucana,*
**Monkey Puzzle** or **Chile Pine**, Auracariaceae
These well-known trees, with spiny, overlapping, dark green leaves festooning the long, tail-like branches, rarely fruit in the UK, it seems, as they are usually planted singly. Where they have been planted severally, as at a school in Sussex, they reportedly set seed and the nuts were shed most years. In Chile the seeds are eaten raw, roasted or boiled. Closely related trees are also grown in Brazil and in Australia.

*Castanospermum australe,*
**Moreton Bay Chestnut**, Leguminosae
These poisonous Australian nuts are relished by native Australians, who leach them in water before drying and roasting the nuts to render them edible.

*Coffea arabica,*
**Coffee**, Rubiaceae
Small, evergreen trees which once grew wild in Arabia and are now cultivated in most hot countries. Coffee 'beans' are seeds from the cherry-like berries, roasted to oily charcoal, then leached with hot water.

*Cyperus esculentus,*
**Tiger Nut**, Cyperaceae
Also called **Ground-almond** or **Chufa**, this is not a nut at all but the edible, underground rhizome of a small, perennial, grass-like sedge. It is grown in dry, sandy soils in western Asia and Africa.

*Fagus sylvatica,*
**Beech**, Fagaceae
A well-known tree that can reach 30m/100ft and chokes out everything underneath with heavy, dry shade. Although parts of the tree are poisonous and have been used medicinally, an edible oil can be extracted from the seeds and they have been eaten raw and roasted to make 'coffee'. In sheer desperation, beech sawdust has been boiled, baked and mixed with flour to make 'bread'. A worthy subject for parks on acid or alkaline soil, but far too large for most gardens! The **American Beech**, *F. grandiflora*, is similar.

*Ginkgo biloba,*
Maiden Hair Tree, *Coniferae*
This 'prehistoric' plant is grown ornamentally for the strange, leathery, fan-shaped leaves which turn bright yellow in the autumn. In the UK the gingko rarely sets fruits, which resemble unpleasant-smelling, yellowish plums, as it is usually planted singly whereas both male and female forms are necessary. In the Far East the seeds, which resemble round, vaguely fishy almonds, are eaten, especially by the Chinese at weddings.

**Ripe coffee beans on bushes in Costa Rica**

*Myristica fragrans,*
**Nutmeg**, Myristiceae
These nuts are only ever used as a spice. They are natives of the Moluccas Islands in Indonesia and are commercially grown in few other places save Grenada in the West Indies. The trees reach 18-21m/60-70ft and have fruits resembling apricots or peaches which split, like almonds, revealing a nut surrounded by a reddish-yellow aril. This is the spice, mace. Inside the thin shell is the brown nutmeg kernel which rattles when ripe. If still alive, they will germinate in heat after three months or so.

*Pterocarya fraxiniflora,*
**Caucasian Wing-nut**, Juglandaceae
Native to the Caucasus and Persia and introduced to Britain in 1782, these are strong-growing relations of the walnut. They have large, non-aromatic, pinnate leaves, catkins and small, edible nuts surrounded by semi-circular wings. They are hardy, though sustain some dieback after hard frosts, and succeed in damp places. They could be improved, perhaps by crossing with other species such as the **Japanese Wing-nut**, *P. rhoifolia,* or the large-fruited Chinese *P. stenoptera.*

*Theobroma cacao,*
**Cocoa**, Sterculiaceae
The cocoa beans, known as nibs in the trade, are fermented, dried and ground to make chocolate. The trees, which are small natives of the Americas, are now mainly grown in West Africa. The melon-like pods are green, ripening to red or yellow. They spring directly out of the trunk and main branches of the tree after the delightful pink flowers.

**An open, ripe cocoa pod showing the beans and flesh**

# PLANNING THE FRUIT GARDEN

Planning your fruit garden means deciding on your priorities – what do you want most? A little thought beforehand can save you a lot of wasted effort and ensure that you actually get what you are after. With vegetables and bedding plants we have the luxury of burying our mistakes annually; with our trees and bushes we need to be more certain.

Although most of us get our garden fortuitously with our house, we usually have quite a wide choice of what we actually do with it, though the tendency is rarely to make radical changes. However, if we spend as much time and effort planning and remaking the garden as we do on decorating and furnishing the rest of our home, it will turn out a mighty fine place!

Obviously the soil, climate, large trees, buildings and the rest of the hard landscape have to be worked around. But with skill and cunning, and modern materials, we can have almost any fruit we desire. Which fruits we actually choose to grow must depend on our budget as much as our climate. Obviously growing fruit in the open garden is easiest and cheapest, but a heated greenhouse allows for more.

I think the first criterion for choosing fruit must be taste. After all, if you are growing for yourself, there is no point in having poorly flavoured varieties or ones that are widely available commercially. Go for those with flavour and sweetness

**Apples grown as single-tier espaliers**

even if they are poor croppers. If you find you especially like a particular kind, you can always grow more.

Freshness is invaluable and one's own fruits are the most truly fresh. It makes sense to choose fruits and varieties that are best eaten straight off the plant and thus rarely found in shops. Likewise dessert are preferable to cooking varieties as we eat them with all their vitamins and flavour, while culinary fruits lose some in the cooking.

Of course growing your fruit yourself guarantees freedom from unwanted chemical residues, and applying plentiful compost will ensure a good internal nutritional balance in the fruit. However, when choosing fruits, bear in mind that their dietary value can vary as much with variety

as with type or growing conditions. For example, **Golden Delicious** apples contain a third or less vitamin C than **Ribston Pippins,** while **Laxton's Superb** has only one sixth!

Economy must always be considered. Fruit growing requires higher investment initially than vegetables, but running costs are lower.

Similarly, soft fruit is cheaper than tree fruit individually, but requires netting from birds in many areas. For maximum production, tree fruits produce as much weight from fewer plants per hectare usually require less maintenance, and live longer, but are slower to crop. Likewise vine fruits

**Dwarf peaches in a courtyard garden**

and cordons need more posts, ties and wires than trees or bushes. Any form of greenhouse or cover is costly and requires upkeep, and of course heating uses much expensive energy.

The seasonal implications, and the time needed to maintain different fruits, need to be considered, although in general fruit requires much less labour per yield than vegetable production. Initially the preparation and planting make heavy demands on time and energy, but afterwards the workload is light, at least for the amateur if not for the professional. Fruit trees and bushes will generally need mulching, thinning, picking and pruning, which are all light tasks and can be done upright in pleasant conditions – unlike digging in the mud for roots.

Growing the fruit is only half the battle, though. After picking we need to process and store the fruit and this takes more time than the growing. Don't plan to grow fruits that mature just when you leave on your holiday!

**Apples trained over interlocking arches leading to an apple tunnel**

# SOIL, SITES, PREPARATION AND PLANTING

**Commercial strawberry growing on polythene**

Drainage is occasionally necessary to prevent water-logging, as no fruiting trees or bushes survive for long with drowning roots. But for most gardens, water is more often a problem in its absence. Growing on raised areas is preferable to draining away the water, in areas with dry summers.

In regions of high summer rainfall some fruits, such as cherries and strawberries, rot rather than ripen. In hot, dry areas fruits such as apples may fail to swell or ripen too quickly and have poor flavour and texture. The temperature may get too cold in winter and freeze unprotected plants to death, or just enough to destroy fruit buds. Areas with late frosts can regularly have complete blossom loss, or the growing season may be too short or too cool for a plant to complete its cycle or

Most old gardening books started off with instructions to make a garden on a well-drained, south-facing slope of rich, loamy soil. If only we had such choice! We must often take what comes. And as we get small gardens with modern houses we rarely have much choice of positioning within.

Shelter is the best help we can give our plants – good hedges, fences, windbreaks, warm walls, cloches, plastic sheets and even old curtains on frosty nights. But be careful not to overdo it, as this will make the air around the plants stagnant.

To a limited extent we can control our soil. This is preferably as friable, moist and rich as we can make it for most fruiting plants. Of course it is very difficult to alter the basic soil type: a clay soil is always going to be heavy and a sandy soil will always be well-drained and hungry. The best cure for most soil difficulties is to incorporate more humus from compost, green manures, mulches and well-rotted muck.

Excessive fertiliser, organic or chemical, is not required and can be detrimental, causing soft, rank growth and

poorly ripening wood. Lime is needed by many plants and is often of more value in old gardens than more manure!

The natural acidity of the soil must be taken into account. A few fruits such as blueberries require acid conditions. They resent lime in the soil and need to be cultivated in pots of ericaceous compost and watered with rain not ground water. On the whole, though, we have unwittingly selected plants that grow happily in the average soils most of us have in our gardens, which are mildly acid to slightly alkaline.

**Sinking a tree stake to support a fruit tree**

**Young pear and apple trees protected by a hedge**

ripen the fruit. We can get around this by growing many plants under glass.

A more difficult climatic problem to solve comes in mild maritime regions where there are too few cold days to make the plants go dormant. Without this dormancy period some plants fail to thrive or fruit successfully. This need for dormancy is why it can be difficult to grow some plants under cover. Others may be sensitive to day length. For example, strawberries can be persuaded to grow happily throughout the year but are difficult to fruit when the days are short and the nights are long.

However, we commonly grow the plants we do because they are so easy and reliable. It is only when you venture to explore the more exotic that you encounter some of the more varied and interesting difficulties.

Preparation and planning are everything. The more you plan in advance and the more carefully you prepare the site, the better the results and the more pitfalls avoided. Always work out schemes on paper. Draw a map of existing features and plan how you will fit in the new. Then imagine walking round after five years when all the plants have grown up.

Remember that once the planting is done the future is determined. So do a good job and do not skimp on the digging or preparation of the hole. In this case, bigger is always better! Mix in garden compost with the soil and, whatever the final intention, do not allow a weed or grass within a circle as wide as the tree or bush is high for three years.

For trained, tall and lax subjects, the stakes or supports must be in place beforehand, must be strong enough to do the job and must last for a reasonable number of years. It is false economy to be mean on these, as they will be hard to correct when the plants are fully grown.

Do not bury plants too deep. Almost all wish to be planted at the same depth as they have grown, and keep their roots in their respective and different layers. Do not force them doubled up into a cramped hole and never pack them all down in a flat layer unless they grew like that. Gently pack soil around the roots, filling and firming as you go. It is better to over-firm than otherwise! Then attach the support if needed.

I prefer to mulch heavily from the second year, making the roots go down initially by regularly hoeing. However, a plastic sheet or carpet mulch is equally good at retaining moisture and suppressing weeds. Generous watering in dry spells for the first year is absolutely crucial.

**Fruit cage mulched with leaf mould**

# BUYING PLANTS AND PROPAGATION

To fill an average garden with plants does not require an immense investment, but the outlay is still quite enough to warrant care and budgeting. If you plan and choose carefully, a wide variety of good plants can be found. Specialist mail order nurseries usually provide a greater choice, and often more cheaply as well, than most local suppliers. They also generally give excellent service and are convenient. Get several catalogues and compare them carefully before ordering, and do so in good time.

Buying plants has the advantage of ease and speed over growing them yourself, but is relatively costly and incurs a high risk of importing weeds, pests and diseases, especially with pot-grown specimens. I prefer bare-rooted plants to pot-grown for all but difficult subjects as they are easier to inspect. I do not trust the hygiene of potted specimens and now always investigate them carefully. Bare-rooted subjects are dormant, so they are much easier both to inspect and clean.

The root systems on well-grown, bare-rooted trees are usually more extensive than those of pot-grown plants. Furthermore, for larger-growing trees, I believe it is unsafe to plant pot-grown specimens with the first metreof each root coiled round in a ball! However, for most smaller subjects, containerised plants are more convenient and will give good results from reputable suppliers.

Propagating your own plants is very satisfying, often cheap, hygienic and can give excellent results, but for some fruits it is a long, slow process, and with others, difficult or impossible.

Some plants are remarkably easy to multiply. Most suckering and clump-forming, fruiting plants can be divided in spring, as can most herbaceous plants. Strawberries and raspberries throw new plants all the time and we do well to prevent this waste of resource by removing them early on. The blackberry tribe root their tips anywhere they can in autumn, and many plants will root where they touch

**Plants should always be carefully inspected before purchase**

the ground to form natural layers which easily detach with roots in autumn.

Many of our annual fruits, such as tomatoes and melons, are quickly, easily and usually grown only from seed. Indeed almost all fruits can be grown in an original wild form or as a semi-improved form from seed. However, no plant will fruit until mature, and if started from seed this can take many decades for most trees. Until the fruit is produced there is usually no way of telling what it will be like – and it may not be very good.

Almost all the best varieties of fruiting plant are not species that come true from seed but need growing from a bit of an existing

specimen. If you can get a live piece of a desired plant with a bud on it, it can usually be grown into another fruiting plant, commonly by taking cuttings, or by layering, grafting or budding.

Many fruiting plants can grow from a hardwood cutting, a piece of their dormant wood stuck in the ground. For some, such as blackcurrants, this is nearly infallible; others need more care. Ideally, push cuttings into a slit trench lined with sharp sand in moist ground, firm well and keep them weed-free and protected from drying winds – a cloche is usually advantageous. Most success is had with new wood that has not flowered, is well ripened and is cut

**Young fruit plants in containers**

**A plastic bag is useful to protect tall, stiff plants**

Layering is most successful. Select a shoot as for a cutting, damage the bark and then surround it by moist, sterile, gritty compost. This can be as simple as weighing down the stem and burying a bit of it in compost under a heavy stone. A year or so later it will probably have grown roots and can be detached and grown on elsewhere. Many evergreens and difficult subjects are thus easily propagated. Alternatively a plastic bag or pot of moist compost can be made to enclose a section of shoot which is likewise detached when rooted – handy for vines and tall, stiff plants (see accompanying illustration – a cunning Victorian way to have grapes stay fresh at the table).

Softwood cuttings are usually taken in midsummer, small and in leaf. They need

and set in autumn when it is still full of sap. The lower cut is usually made through or just below a joint and a piece selected which has a healthy bud at the top. Usually all buds below ground level are removed to leave only the main stem.

**A swollen graft point**

a shaded cloche or a coldframe, preferably with bottom heat, to do well. Many plants may be multiplied in this way, especially evergreens. It requires more skill, but more plants can be produced from less material than with hardwood cuttings.

Some plants are propagated by only grafting or budding small pieces on to more easily grown rootstocks; however, often these are done with special rootstocks simply to influence growth or to get the maximum number of plants from limited material. Budding and grafting techniques, although apparently simple, are profoundly difficult to master without much practice and are beyond the scope of this book. (I'm not being patronising, just try it for yourself, if you doubt it!)

**This grape cutting is set well in its container**

**Strawberry runners**

# GROWING FROM SEED

Growing from seed is the most rewarding method of propagation. Almost every fruit you buy has seed within, though it may not always be viable. Specialist seedsmen offer rare and unusual seed and, providing regulations do not forbid it, seed can be obtained from friends or travel abroad. Seed may be slow to germinate, may require warmth or a period of cold first, but sooner or later, given the right conditions, viable seed will germinate, free of pests and disease. Given growing conditions reasonably like the original, eventually it will flower and fruit, though you may need a male and a female for this result!

The drawbacks are that plants grown from seed do not come true and can take many years to grow to maturity and fruit, and by then they are often far too big. Grafting the seedling on to a dwarfing rootstock is beyond the skill of most of us. However, we can constrain many plants by growing them in containers, which prevents their forming extensive root systems and thus limits their top growth.

Most seed, however you obtain it, should be sown as soon as possible. Seed that is fresh, with fruit attached, is usually cleaned first, but occasionally it may need the pulp to be fermented away before sowing.

Although some seed may succeed best in a seed-bed, more reliable results come from sowing in pots in a coldframe. For seeds from warmer climes, a heated propagator is needed. Do not cook them, though. A few seeds germinate best if they are chilled for a period first, though they rarely need freezing. Similarly most seeds need to be soaked to germinate, but few can stand water-logging for longer than an hour or two.

The compost in which you sow the seeds is important.

**Passion flowers are quick and easy from seed**

**Seedlings in pots and a propagator**

Sterile compost is best if the seed is small or slow to germinate. Most seeds do best in a gritty, well-aerated, humus-rich compost but some have special needs. Obviously use an ericaceous compost for plants that dislike lime. Most seeds do not want the initial compost to be very rich in fertiliser as this burns their tender roots. Indeed they often germinate better in a mixture of sharp sand and peat.

Do not sow too densely or too deeply. Be patient. Remember that some seeds naturally take a long time to emerge. When all else fails, reread the sowing instructions on the packet.

Once seeds do germinate and emerge they should be divided and repotted as soon as is practicable. Also, you should repot plants regularly as they grow to fill each pot, or they will be dwarfed prematurely.

# CONTAINER CULTURE

Many plants which would be difficult otherwise can be grown in containers. Containers cramp their root system and thus prevent them growing too big or too quickly. Allied with pruning, this allows us to dwarf plants we would find too large to handle. Often this restriction is resented by the plant and, perversely, may result in earlier fruiting.

With attention to feeding and watering, almost any plant can be coaxed to grow in a container, although it may not be persuaded to bear fruit, or at least not prolifically. Grapevines in the ground are rampant growers that crop heavily. In a large tub they are far less vigorous, but can still be expected to give several bunches. Many different varieties can thus be squeezed into the space otherwise occupied by one, allowing greater variety and a longer season.

Containers are particularly useful for plants that would not survive in the ground. If you have a chalky soil, the lime-hating plants can be grown in containers of ericaceous compost. Don't forget to water the plants with rain water, not tap water, as the latter is often as limy as the soil.

Conveniently, plants in containers can be taken under cover during hard weather and kept growing over a longer season. This makes it practical to grow more tender plants than would otherwise be possible. Likewise plants in fruit can easily be moved under cover for more secure protection from birds or damp.

Watering plants in their containers is very important. Most plants need moist soil but drown if water-logged

**Lemons in terracotta pots, Lemon Garden, Villa Torrigiani, Tuscany, Italy**

and wilt if dry. If you cannot be sure you can maintain religious watering devotion, install an automatic system of irrigation. Stand the plants on capillary matting, or at the least stand them in drip trays of gravel.

No matter how good the compost originally, with time it gets used up. Re-potting into a larger container is usually the best solution, but eventually this becomes difficult. The alternatives are top dressing with an enriched mix of compost and organic fertiliser, or feeding with a diluted liquid feed such as fish emulsion or comfrey and nettle extract. It is invariably better to administer these additions little and often rather than all in one go.

The container itself is important to some plants. Normally plastic pots are as good as porous earthenware, but the latter are preferred by some plants, such as citrus. Indeed plants which prefer really well-aerated soil do best in lattice timber or basket-work containers, though these may not last long and may be prone to drying out the compost.

# GROWING IN GLASSHOUSES AND CONSERVATORIES

There is no substitute for walk-in cover, which is more valuable if heated and frost-free; more so if kept warm or even hot. If it is maintained as warm as a living room all year round, many exotic fruits become possible such as oranges, lemons, passion fruits, even bananas (see page 163).

I grow exotics such as passion fruits under cover as they would not crop otherwise. The extra heat ripens the fruit and also the wood which often cannot ripen outdoors. Some plants take many months to crop each year and without cover they would never ripen before the frosts come. Extra warmth and shelter allows us to have tender or delicate plants which would not otherwise survive in the open, but it also means we can have the same crop earlier than outdoors – for example, strawberries.

Often it is best to grow plants in containers which are to go under cover as this allows for more variety in the same area, though each plant will necessarily yield less than if it was in the ground. Containers not only control the vigour of the plants but also make them portable: they can be moved under cover and outside as convenient. This suits many fruits such as the citrus which really prefer to be outside all summer but need frost protection in winter. By contrast, many varieties of grapevine are best under cover for an early start and for ripening but need to be chilled in winter to fruit well.

This is why some fruits are difficult. They need hot summers and warm autumns and also cold winters to go dormant. Without dormancy they do not ripen wood or fruit well and often just fade away. It is quite easy to chill a greenhouse in a cold area for the couple of months required, but not of course if other tender plants are kept there also.

The other requirement may be for extra light. Many plants need more light than can be had in winter through dirty glass. The physical barrier reduces light intensity by half. Fortunately, artificial lights are cheap to fit and run – compared to heating anyway. Some plants are very demanding; not only do they want more light and heat but they want enough hours of complete darkness every night as well. This requires the fitting of blinds to exclude daylight and also if you have a streetlight nearby! Similarly some plants find bright light too intense and need shading.

Fortunately most fruits are remarkably easy to grow. The biggest problems are usually the cost of heating and the eventual size of the plants.

**Grapevine in a conservatory**

# FRUIT CAGES

**Fruit cage with wild strawberries being grown as ground cover**

gives welcome shade and cooler conditions.

A fruit cage can even be reversed in principle to enclose all of a small garden and to confine ornamental seed- and insect-eating, but hopefully not inadvertently fruit-eating, birds. On a more prosaic level, it is practical to grow plants on a tall leg and then run chickens underneath for their excellent pest control. Similarly it is sensible to arrange it so that, if you have chickens, they can at least be running in the cage during most of the year when the plants are not in fruit.

Fruit cages can be hand-crafted from second-hand materials; easily assembled custom-made ones are also available. In areas of high wind, obviously, the most substantial materials have to be used. Permanent sides of wire mesh and a light net laid on overhead wires for the roof are most practicable. Make sure you can remove the roof net easily if snow is forecast as

a thick layer on top will break most cages.

Most fruit cage plants are natives of the woodland's edge and do not mind light shade, but few of them relish stagnant air, so do not overcrowd them. Fruit is sweeter if ripened in the sun. A few fruits such as grapes must have full sun to ripen at all well, so give these a prime position. You should always provide each plant with more space than seems reasonable.

Because most fruit cage plants grow naturally at the woodland's edge, they also prefer a richly mulched, cool, undisturbed and often shallow root run. Most of them will respond well to thick mulches and summer pruning to improve the fruit quality and stop the plants growing too large. Generally fruit cage plants do not like having vegetables around them if this involves digging or hoeing. However, some companion flowering plants such as *Limnanthes douglassii* are invaluable.

**Fruit cage protecting redcurrants, gooseberries and raspberries, mulched with straw to control weeds**

Fruit cages are cover with netting. They are necessary to protect soft fruit in areas with many birds. The most troublesome birds, such as blackbirds and pigeons, can be excluded with coarse 2.5cm/1in mesh, while smaller, insectivorous birds, such as wrens and bluetits, can still gain access. If all the net is wire, squirrels and rodents can also be

stopped. If a finer mesh, down to about 1cm/⅓in, is used then bees can still enter, but large moths and butterflies are excluded.

Fruit cages have other advantages. The netting itself makes a more sheltered environment enjoyed by the plants. Light frosts are kept off, and chill winds are reduced. In very hot regions, denser netting

# ORCHARDS

Orchards are devoted to the production of top or tree fruits, most frequently, privately and commercially, for apples, pears and plums. Other fruits are less common, being widely grown only in suitable areas – for example, cherries are little grown in wetter, maritime regions but are common in drier zones such as Kent, in south-east England.

Orchards were always grassed down for convenience and soil preservation, though recent practice has been for bare cultivation, but this has been shown to be irresponsible. Initially weed-free conditions must be maintained in the orchard, but in general the preserving of bare soil is counterproductive. Most home orchard fruits will be most successfully grown with the aid of a heavy mulch, ground cover or companion plants, or a grass sward.

For comfort and least cost, private orchards are still customarily planted with standard or half-standard trees on strong rootstocks. Though more intensive plantings with more dwarfing stock are more productive, they also require much more pruning and training and are difficult to mow underneath!

Grass clippings are an excellent mulch if put on in thin layers, and are a good fertiliser if returned to the sward. However, orchard, and indeed most other swards, should not be composed solely of grasses, as these compete strongly for resources in the topmost layers and do not contribute much to the mineral levels. Include clovers, alfalfa and chicory seeds in your sowing mixture. Special blends are now available ready mixed.

**Mistletoe growing on an old apple tree in a cider orchard**

Traditionally orchards were often combined with grazing livestock. Though no longer done on a commercial scale, the practice is still useful for amateurs. Running chickens underneath gives interest and fertility, and almost guarantees freedom from most pest problems. Cynics might add, 'Especially if you don't overfeed them!' Ducks will control slugs and snails better than hens and they do not scratch and damage so much. Nor, fortunately, do the drakes crow. Geese are superb natural lawnmowers, converting grass into fertiliser and eggs as well as being the most noisy of watchdogs. Be warned, however, as geese may serve to damage young plants with thin bark if they are hungry.

Other forms of livestock are more dangerous to the home orchard. I suggest that no four-legged, herbivorous animals are allowed anywhere near valued plants unless each one of them is individually and securely fenced and protected.

Orchards are also an enticement to two-legged rats and it has long been established best practice to surround them with a thick, impenetrable hedge of thorny plants such as quickthorn or blackthorn. This, and a narrow verge of long grass and native plants, simultaneously provides a good background ecology to help control all the other pests of the orchard. A fence or wall does not contribute in the same way, and is usually more expensive and surmountable.

**Groves of almonds, olives, oranges and lemons**

# ORNAMENTAL FRUIT GARDENS

Trained fruit trees and bushes which can be bought ready-made in a host of interesting and architectural forms, such as espaliers and fans, create interest out of season as the framework of the plants becomes revealed. Attention to the appearance of the supports is essential, as they are also disclosed for much of the time. Neatness and uniformity of support are thus of the greatest moment. Pergolas can look as beautiful clothed in grapevines as they do with any climber, and even a fruit cage can be fashioned ornamentally from the right materials.

It is important in a fruit garden to allow for plentiful light and air, more than perhaps might be granted with a shrub garden. Wide paths aid such design and can be of grass sward where wear is light. Gravel is the next choice for practicality and economy, and concrete or stone flags where the area is small or budget large.

More colour and interest, with benefit to the main planting, is obtained by having suitable companion plants to provide shelter, ground cover, flowers for nectar and pollen for the beneficial insects, and sacrificial plants that give up their fruits so that others may not be eaten. However, vegetables are not easily mixed in. They do not grow well surrounded by vigorous competitors, such as fruiting plants. Nevertheless most of the culinary herbs can be grown to advantage and use.

## Wildlife Fruit Gardens

Although these may be as stylised and neat as any purely decorative garden, an accurate description of many so called wild gardens is 'unkempt'. Indeed the term is often used to justify total neglect.

However, if the aim is truly to provide more and better habitats for endangered native flora and fauna, neglect is not enough. A wild garden needs to be managed so that we maximise the number and forms of life supported. The more fruiting and berrying plants we include, the more wildlife we attract, and we need to ensure other basic necessities for wild creatures.

The fruit helps immensely, but shelter for nesting and hibernation, water and peace are also required. Dense brambles, shrubs and evergreens are mandatory, but do ensure the gardener can still gain access. Paths should be maintained to permit various tasks, but of course excess traffic will soon serve to drive away most of the wild animals.

Many garden soils are too rich for the more appealing wild flowers. To establish these it is frequently necessary to start them in pots and plant them out into sites prepared by removing the turf. Thus they should be kept away from the fruiting plants which require richer conditions.

**Flowering pear on the garden wall of a country house**

# MAINTAINING THE GARDEN

**Trained Catillac pear tree**

## Pruning and Establishment of Trained Forms

We prune for two main reasons: to remove diseased, damaged and ill-placed growths and to channel growth into fruit production. We may also prune to reduce the size of a plant as it becomes too large for the space available, which is really cause for replanning.

Excessive pruning, especially at the wrong time, is counterproductive. In general, pruning even moderate amounts from a tree or bush in autumn and winter stimulates regrowth, proportionately as much as the amount removed. This is usefully employed when the plant is young and we wish to form the framework by stimulating the growth of some young and vigorous replacement shoots.

However, such autumn and winter pruning is not so suitable for more mature fruiting plants whose structure is already formed and from which we wish to obtain fruit. Most respond much better to summer pruning, which is cutting out three-quarters of every young shoot, bar the leaders. This redirects growth and causes fruit bud production on the spurs or short sideshoots formed. These may be further shortened and tidied in the winter, but then, as only a little is removed, vigorous regrowth may be avoided.

The majority of our perennial, woody, fruiting plants can be trained and pruned to make a permanent framework which carries these spurs, preferably all over. Growing just one such single stem, branch or cordon on a weak rootstock allows us to squeeze many varieties into the same space as one full-sized tree. Obviously such single-stemmed cordons do not produce very much fruit, especially as they are hard to support if they reach more than head height. Sloping these cordons will serve to make them longer without going too high.

Growing two, three or more branches is a better compromise. These can be arranged as espaliers (in tiers), fans (where they radiate from the centre), or gridirons of almost any design. However, for the vast majority of trees and bushes, the actual shapes most commonly employed are the expanding head, and the open bowl or goblet arrangement, on top of a single stem or trunk.

If you give a woody plant space and freedom, it tends

**Well-spaced fruit bushes with post-and-wire supports**

**Fan apricot**

to make an expanding mounded head like an upturned bowl or vase of dense growth on the surface and an almost empty space inside. This is least work and looks after itself, but it keeps getting bigger, and much of the fruit grows in shade. For the best fruit it is necessary to maximise the surface area of fruiting growth exposed to the sun and air. To do this, you should try to invert the natural bowl or vase shape by removing the main leader from the middle and training the branches as a bowl with a hollow centre open to the sky. The number of main stems is customarily about five or six which divide from the trunk and redivide to form the walls of the goblet. The stem or trunk may be short, as is common with gooseberries, or taller, which is often more convenient.

Where the branches of a tree divide from the trunk on a short trunk they are termed bushes, at waist to shoulder height they are called half-standards, and standards where they will start higher still. Bushes, especially those on the more dwarfing stocks, tend to be too low to mow underneath but can always be mulched instead. Half-standards grow large, depending on stock, and are tall enough to mow underneath. Full standards make very big specimens and are usually planted only in parks and meadows.

Young, unformed plants (maidens) can be bought more cheaply than those with a good shape already trained by the nurseryman. It is very satisfying to grow your own espalier or gridiron from a maiden, but the result will depend on your skill and foresight. These may be better used elsewhere. Therefore buy your trees ready-made unless you feel gifted. Soft fruits are quicker to respond and more forgiving, so are worth trying for yourself.

**A wall of Morello cherries**

**Raspberries before pruning (top) and afterwards**

Some fruits need to be pruned on the renewal principle. Whole branches or shoots are continually replaced as they reach a year or two old and after they have fruited. Raspberries are typical, the old shoots being removed at ground level as the young are tied in.

Grapevines can be constrained to two young branches emerging from the trunk, replaced each year.

Peaches on walls similarly have young shoots tied in and old fruited ones removed. Blackcurrants have a third of growths from the ground removed each year.

A few plants are pruned only at certain times of year. Hollow-stemmed, tender and evergreen plants are pruned in spring once the hardest weather is over and *Prunus* are pruned in summer to avoid disease.

Although it may seem complicated, pruning is easy once you have done it a few times. Providing that you do not get carried away and remove excessive amounts you are unlikely to do much harm to the plant. Be sure to use clean secateurs which have been sterilised with alcohol; rarely use a saw and cover any large wounds with a proprietary sealant to stop any water getting in.

# FERTILITY AND WATER MANAGEMENT

Fruiting plants need sufficiently fertile soil and water to grow and yield well, but ordinarily most are not as demanding as vegetable crops. Providing they are thinned, fruit yields can be surprisingly good in soils and seasons when many vegetables fail. Indeed excess fertility or moisture will frequently result in too much vegetative growth and little, or poorly ripening, fruit as a result.

The main advantage of the majority of fruiting plants is that they are perennial. Growing in open ground, they make extensive root systems which find the water and nutrients required. Annual and short-lived crops generally need much more attention to soil fertility and water provision because they have limited root systems. Plants in containers similarly require much care, and because of the confinement they will also readily suffer from any excess.

Fertility is best provided organically from materials that slowly convert to a usable form in the soil. Well-rotted farmyard manures, good compost, seaweed meal, hoof and horn meal, blood, fish and bone meal, or bone meal and fish emulsions are all suitable materials for mulches.

If mineral shortages are suspected, ground rock dusts provide cheap, slow-release supplies; potash, phosphate, magnesium (dolomitic) limestone, calcified seaweed and lime are all widely available, cheap and pleasant to apply. Wood ashes are extremely valuable to most fruiting plants. Seaweed extracts sprayed on the foliage can give rapid relief from mineral deficiencies.

Bulkier materials such as well-rotted manure and compost also provide much humus which is essential for the natural fertility of the soil, its water-holding

**Bottle-watering a young apricot**

**Leaf-mould mulch**

capacity and its buffering action (preventing the soil being too acid or alkaline). The humus content is conserved by minimal cultivation and refraining from using soluble fertilisers.

More humus can be provided by growing green manures. These occupy the soil when other plants are dormant throughout winter. Nutrients and water that would have leached away are combined with winter sunlight to grow dense covers of hardy plants. These also protect the soil surface from erosion and rain impaction. When the weather warms up, green

manures are incorporated *in situ* by digging in or composting under a plastic sheet. Or remove and add to the compost heap.

Organic mulches such as well-rotted manures, composted shredded bark, leaf mould, mushroom compost, straw or peat are all advantageous to most plants. They rot down at the soil's surface, aiding fertility and humus levels, and suppress weeds if they are thick enough, but most importantly they conserve soil moisture.

For most gardeners a shortage of soil moisture is more of a problem than low fertility. With sufficient moisture, fertility can be created by the soil life; without moisture the soil cannot even use a fertiliser supplied. Every effort must be made to capture every drop of rain and store it till needed. Water butts can hold only so much, while the humus in the soil can hold much more, as it soaks water up like a sponge.

Once the winter rains have drenched the soil a mulch prevents it evaporating away again. Any mulch helps, but the looser and thicker, the better. Less than 5cm/2in is ineffective; add more after a few months as the initial applications will pack down.

When organic material for mulching is in short supply, use inorganic ones. Sharp sand and gravel make good moisture-retaining mulches and are cheap and sterile.

Grass clippings are an excellent mulch, if applied in thin layers – though if applied too thickly in wet conditions they may make a nasty, sticky mess. Clippings provide a rich source of nitrogen and encourage soil life. They soon disappear and need topping up. Continuous applications slowly make the soil less alkaline and more acid, which is often advantageous.

Despite mulching and enriching the humus content, watering is often required. It is essential for new transplants until they have been established for at least a year, particularly for evergreens which cannot drop their leaves if under stress and survive dormant. Water before it is too late; if a plant is wilting it is already suffering badly!

Soak one plant's roots each day on a rota rather than give a daily splash to each one. It is bad practice merely to wet the soil surface. This draws the roots up to form a surface mat, while much is

**Carpet mulch**

wasted by evaporation. A good soaking descends and draws the roots after it; thus they become deeper and more able to find other soil moisture on their own.

Remember that watering should be done well or not at all. If you bury a length of hosepipe with the roots of a tree, you can inject the water right where it is needed during the critical first few years. Likewise a pot or funnel pushed in nearby is a useful aid. When time is limited and cash more abundant, it is wise to invest in automatic watering equipment. Drip feeds and seeping hoses will allow a constant and even supply of water without the gardener's constant attention, and soon repay the investment.

**Green manure before composting under a plastic sheet**

**Grass-clipping mulch**

# WEED AND GRASS MANAGEMENT

**Sheep grazing an orchard in early evening**

When woody perennial plants are mature, they are less badly affected by general weed competition but still suffer, especially where the weeds are allowed to grow over them and steal light and air as well. In order to prevent weeds we can use mulches, but they do not create a very good garden ecology, so instead we tolerate ground-cover plants. These occupy the ecological niche to advantage and with less detriment than the weeds they prevent.

The most convenient ground cover is usually grass sward. Once they are well established it is traditional and often convenient to grass down underneath most tree fruits and between the more vigorous soft fruits. Grass competes vigorously, especially if kept closely mowed as a lawn. However, grass sward is simple to maintain, ornamental, hygienic and prevents worse weeds. Turf is durable, it

Weeds compete with our crops for space, water and nutrients, and they are better at it! Worse, they harbour pests and diseases. For maximum growth, all our plants require weed-free conditions, especially when they are small, not well established and only just sown or planted.

Keep all weeds from appearing within a radius of about each plant's own height as this is the area most densely filled with their root systems. For perennials, this clear circle should be kept clean of all weeds for three years before planting companion plants, ground cover or grassing down. We often start trees off in a small circle of bare soil a mere 30cm/12in or so across, cut into a neatly cropped lawn; a bare circle a couple of metres across will do some real good.

Complete elimination of all weeds from an area before planting is invariably worthwhile. It can be by several cultivations with plough, harrow, or simply spade and rake. It is less effort to use sheet mulches of plastic or carpet, or even, once off, a 'safe' weed killer if you are non-organic. Whichever of these you choose, it is much easier than trying later to weed among the plants.

Once the established weeds are all gone we have only to control new ones coming from seed. Such weeds are easily prevented from germinating in bare soil by covering it with several centimetres of mulch.

As mulches are also useful for adding humus and retaining water, they are the most sensible way of controlling weeds under most fruiting plants. However, occasionally we want bare soil. In these areas the weeds are best controlled with a sharp hoe. Use a hoe weekly when weeds are a problem and fortnightly when they are thought banished.

**Mulch around the base of an apple tree**

**Carpet and plastic mulches in the fruit garden**

resists wear well and soon repairs damaged patches. If mulches spill over grass sward, and so yellow the leaves, it soon recovers. The clippings themselves are a free source of mulching material, and can contribute much fertility to our plants.

Grass sward produces most useful clippings when the grass is cut often and not too closely. Long grass grows more quickly, is more drought-resistant and suppresses turf weeds better than if it is closely cropped. Of course, if you let it get too long, it becomes wet to walk on and is brown underneath when you cut it short again. However, cut your grass regularly and frequently with slightly greater height of cut, and you soon see a better sward resulting. The longer, more vigorous grass soon chokes out most weeds.

Traditionally orchard grass was allowed to grow long and flower in late summer and autumn when the fruit was ripening. The grass took up nitrogen, other nutrients and water and prevented the trees making late, soft growth. The low nitrogen level in the soil also helped the fruit to keep well and turned the apples redder.

When grassing down, it is sensible to include clovers in the grass seed mix as they have the advantage of fixing nitrogen from the air to aid the grasses. A clover and grass mixture also stays greener for longer in hot, dry summers and, if left to flower, the clovers attract bees and other insects that are beneficial.

Providing you are not growing ericaceous plants or fine, bowling-green grasses you should lime all your turf every fourth year, even if you have lime in the soil. Most swards slowly become acid in the topmost layer, and this encourages mosses and acid-loving weeds. If such weeds, for example daisies, are increasing, you need to add more lime: up to a couple of handfuls per square metre/ square yard per year. You probably also need to raise the height of your cut. If weeds that like wet, acid soils such as buttercups appear, lime is desperately needed and probably better drainage as well.

Although four-legged livestock may be too risky to our plants in a garden, they are fine lawnmowers in meadow orchards with well-fenced trees. For the private gardener geese are the safest option. They graze grass closely and soon eradicate favourite snacks, so are usefully borrowed to remove buttercups, dandelions and clovers rapidly – even if you do not want them full-time.

**A Muscovy duck**

**Weed control is greatly assisted by a plasic mulch**

# PEST AND DISEASE CONTROL

The aim of this is to preserve the yield or appearance of our crops, but we must ensure that the costs incurred in the process do not outweigh the gains. Commercial apples are, ironically, sprayed to prevent scabby patches on their skin, which is now peeled and discarded to avoid the very residues left by many such sprays.

For the home gardener the main causes of fruit loss in most years is the weather. If we grow crops that are, on average, successful only in good years in our area, such as grapes in central England, we must accept that in other years we will do badly. There is very little we can do to make the sun come out, the wind stop or the rain fall.

The second cause of loss is probably the gardener. We all leave action too late, skimp preparation and routine tasks, put plants in less than their optimum positions, and then often overcrowd them as well. What we must remember is

**Raspberries damaged by the raspberry beetle**

that our plants 'want' to leaf, flower and crop. They are programmed as tightly as any computer. If we give them the right input, they must produce the right output for us.

If we give our plants the right conditions, they are also healthy and vigorous enough to shrug off most pests and diseases. Healthy plants grow in a well-suited site and soil, with shelter and water when they are small, and are not overfed. Excess fertiliser makes plants flabby and prone to problems. Keep them lean and fit with well-made compost and mulches. Many pests are like wolves, eliminating the sick and weak, ignoring the healthy.

Disease is most efficiently prevented by vigilance and prompt action combined with hygienic pruning and healthy air circulation. Spraying diluted seaweed solution once a month throughout the growing season acts like a vitamin pill. It makes plants more resistant to diseases, and many pests. This is probably because seaweed contains minute amounts of almost every element and thus corrects for soil deficiencies.

However, our plants will still be attacked by some pests and diseases that do require action. Most of the time these do not take all of a crop and often we do not truly need all of it either! All we have to do is to achieve what we want with the minimum interference, and any surplus can be left for the wildlife anyway.

The most effective way to control pests is to persuade

**Scab on apple fruit (Golden Delicious)**

others to do it for you. The natural ecology always controls them in the long run. We can help it quickly reach a balance of more ladybirds, thrushes and frogs with fewer aphids, snails and slugs. Our allies require shelter, nest sites, food out of season, water and companion plants. If we provide these, they increase in number and thus the pests decrease.

With careful selection of which cultivars we grow, we can have resistant varieties that do not suffer as much from a given problem. There are varieties of most fruits that are more or less resistant to many of their common diseases, such as scab with apples and root rots with strawberries and tomatoes. Resistance to pests is rarer as they soon adapt and overcome the host's resistance. However, the white- and yellow-fruited forms of normally red fruits will escape while the birds wait for them to turn.

Timing can be of service. For example, late raspberries usually escape the depredations of their fruit maggot. Having many fruits which ripen at the same time also reduces damage. When successive plants ripen they are picked clean by small numbers of pests which are over-whelmed by a glut, as may be the gardener!

The simplest method of protection is to use a barrier to prevent pests or disease reaching the plant. For example, strong netting will generally stop birds, and plastic sheet umbrellas over peach trees during winter prevent peach leaf curl.

An impenetrable woven or plastic sheet mulch fitted tight to a tree trunk prevents pests emerging from underground reaching the open and equally prevents them crawling down to the roots. Provision of fine holes must be made in plastic sheets to allow both air and water to pass freely. Their appearance can easily be improved by adding thin mulch on top.

Traps of corrugated cardboard, carpet or old sack can be made by rolling strips around trunk or stem. These attract pests by replicating creviced bark. They hide within and we unwrap and dislodge them in winter. Non-setting sticky bands applied to aluminium foil wrapped tightly around trunk, branch or stem stop pests climbing up and down. Do remember to paint the support as well.

Sticky traps can be bought which lure flying pests to them with pheromone sex attractant 'perfumes'. Others use the smell of the fruit or leaf to entice the pest to a sticky end. Jars of water with lids of foil containing pencil sized holes trap wasps when baited with fruit juices or jams.

Putting down mulches in late winter seals in the spores of many diseases before growth starts. Raking mulches aside in early winter will reveal pupae of over-wintering pests which can be left to the birds.

Only when the preventative measures and traps have failed should we turn to direct action. The most ecological spray of all, in fact, is simply a powerful jet of water. Although many pests may clamber back they are unlikely to if shot half way across the garden. Obviously project them to an area without plants on which they can survive – the open lawn is best.

Soap sprays kills most small insect pests by suffocation and is remarkably safe for us and the environment. People used to employ ordinary household soap flakes, but some improved soft soaps are now sold specifically for pesticidal use. Ordinary household baking soda, sodium bicarbonate, contained in almost every cake and patent medicine, was similarly used as a safe fungicide. Bordeaux mixture is another old-fashioned fungicide. It is wholly chemical, being made from copper sulphate and lime, but it is allowed to organic gardeners if used in moderation.

Derris and pyrethrum are insecticides made from plant products. They are the strongest allowed to organic gardeners and degrade rapidly, but they do kill pests which are immune to soft soap. They must be used according to instructions. Please spray at night when the bees have gone home!

**Currant aphids on young currant leaves**

The commonplace pests and diseases of fruit all have their time-honoured remedies.

### Birds
Birds are the cause of most loss in many areas. Netting is the answer. If the whole plant cannot be enclosed or moved under cover, then protect each fruit or bunch with waxed paper or netting bags. These can be made from sections of nylon stockings. Lengths of stocking or hosepipe painted like snakes, fake spiders and cats of fake fur are all good bird-scarers but have to be moved often to fool them for more than the first day. Things that flash, such as pieces of foil and humming tape, all work but likewise only for a short time. Scarecrows rarely work at all! Sacrificing some fruits and leaving these on the ground, or better still on a table, is easier than keeping birds away entirely!

### Aphids
Aphids are more often an inconvenience than a real problem for established perennial plants. With some, such as redcurrant leaf blistering aphis, no harm is detectable. Indeed, they are performing the equivalent of summer pruning for us. However, heavy aphid infestations may require a soft soap spray. Usually ants are involved in these infestations as well, needing simultaneous extirpation.

**Aphid eggs overwintering on apple wood**

**Currant bushes covered with nets as bird protection**

## Ants

A minor problem on their own, ants farm aphids and scale insects, making these more of a threat. Put out some sugar, watch where they take it home, then pour boiling water down their hole.

**Garden slug on strawberry leaf**

**Adult ant on a leaf**

## Slugs and Snails

These are attracted to real beer in a saucer which entices many to drown themselves. (Ground beetles, which are useful allies, may also come. Put a few twiggy sticks in the saucer to give them a way out.) Slugs and snails can be spotted with a torch on warm, moist evenings and can be destroyed.

**Garden snail on a vegetable**

## Wasps

Wasps are valuable allies early in the summer when they control caterpillars and other pests. Later on in the year, they turn to fruit and need trapping with jars (see p. 229). Dusting them with flour enables you to follow them home. Nests can be destroyed with derris dust puffed in the entrance when wasps return in the evening.

**Tree wasp**

**Wasp feeding on a pear fruit**

## Scale Insects

Scale is most troublesome on plants under cover and on walls. Hand pick minor infestations and spray them with soft soap. There are now also some commercially available predators.

**Brown scale insects on the woody stem of a grapevine**

## Red Spider Mites

These are a serious threat under cover and on walls and even in the open. Spraying water and keeping the greenhouse air humid discourages them.

Attract them on to plants of broad beans which are then composted, spray with soft soap and derris, and introduce the commercially available predator, *Phytoseuilis persimilis.*

*Phytoseuilis persimilis* **preying on red spider mite**

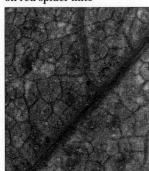

## Whitefly

Whitely are mostly a problem under cover. Thin out flying adults with a vacuum cleaner, spray plants with soft soap and introduce the commercially available predator *Encarsia formosa.*

**Whitefly infestation on tomato leaves**

## Vine Weevils

The adult weevil is dark grey, beetle-like, 1-2cm/½in long, with a very long snout. It takes rounded bits out of leaves, but most harm is done by the grubs which are up to the same size with a grey/pink body and brown head. They destroy the roots of many plants. Adults can be trapped in rolls of corrugated cardboard, in bundles of sticks or under saucers, where they hide during daytime. Chickens run underneath tall crops can ensure that no adults survive long enough to lay eggs. The grubs can be destroyed by watering on the commercially available predatory nematode/ eelworm.

**Adult vine weevil beetle on a strawberry leaf**

**Vine weevil larvae on soil**

## Rabbits

Only netting the area will keep rabbits out. In case they get in, have a plank ramped against the fence so they are not trapped inside and eat even more. If the perimeter cannot be secured, surround or wrap each plant in wire netting. If this is impossible, feed the rabbits when snow stops them finding their own food and before they bark your plants! Just the smell of a ferret or its droppings will drive them away.

# POLLINATION AND COMPANION PLANTING

Almost all our fruits require their flowers to be pollinated. Many are self-fertile and can set by pollinating themselves, but crop better if cross-pollinated. Some of these, for example figs, have varieties that will produce fruit parthenocarpically, without pollination; thus they are often seedless. A few fruits, such as **Conference** pears are partly parthenocarpic: if not pollinated by another variety, their fruits are different and oddly shaped.

Some fruits do not have male and female flowers on the same plant and so we have to grow a non-fruiting male to pollinate every half dozen or so females. Kiwis and grapevines are good examples. For convenience we have bred varieties that carry both sexes.

Some fruits and many nuts are wind-pollinated, others by bees and other insects. Under cover, neither of these natural pollinators exists and we have to assist. A rabbit's tail, a cotton ball or piece of wool lightly touched on each flower should suffice. We can lure more insects to help by growing attractant companion plants and this can add a bit of colour and life as well. Commercial tomato growers even buy cardboard nests of bumble bees to pollinate for them.

Outdoors early in the year there are few insects about and for the earliest flowerers pollination is risky. Again hand pollination is effective but tedious. It is better to ensure insect pollination by increasing the numbers. Planting companion plants as attractants helps; taking up bee-keeping makes an enormous improvement.

To pollinate each other, not only do varieties have to be compatible, but they also have to flower at the same time. All reputable catalogues have a choice of suitable cross-pollinators indicated. When in doubt, choose the wild species, which is often the best pollinator for most of its varieties. Alternatively, simply plant more varieties. This is especially true for a few fruits which are not good pollinators themselves. For example the apples **Cox's Orange Pippin** and **Bramley's Seedling** never crop together, but if you add a **James Grieve**, all three fruit.

Companion planting is of immense benefit to most fruiting plants as it brings in and supports pollinating and predatory insects, and maintains them throughout the rest of the year. We must aim at having a continuity of flowers throughout the year as it these that provide nectar and honey for the bees, hoverflies and other beneficial insects.

Of particular usefulness is *Limnanthes douglassii*, the **poached egg plant**, which is a low-growing, self-seeding, weed-suppressing, hardy annual. I find it especially beneficial under soft fruit and gooseberries. *Phacelia tanacetifolia, Convolvolus tricolor*, pot marigolds and clovers are all very good for beneficial insects.

*Limnanthes douglassii* **with gooseberries**

Other plants can be good companions to our fruiting plants by repelling pests. French marigolds are one of the strongest and their smell will keep whitefly out of a greenhouse. Planted about the fruit garden, they disorientate pests sniffing for their quarry. The aromatic herbs such as rosemary, thyme, sage, southernwood and lavender are all excellent companions as they not only camouflage the air with their perfume but they are long-flowering, also benefiting the various pollinators and predators.

Alliums are valuable companions. Their smell deters many pests, yet their flowers attract beneficial insects. They help protect the plants they grow with from fungi and are even claimed to improve the scent of roses. Garlic and chives are the easiest to grow and use in quantity at the base of most fruit trees and bushes.

**Chives flourishing under apples**

Many companion plants help access nutrients and make them available for our fruiting plants. Clovers, lupins and the other leguminous plants are especially good as they fix nitrogen from the air and the surplus will feed our crops. Alfalfa/lucerne is exceptionally deep-rooted and brings up minerals from depths other plants cannot reach. It should be included in the seed mixture for orchard and wild garden swards. Similarly a few thistles and docks can be tolerated in those areas for the same purpose. Clovers and chicory should be included whenever grass is seeded as the sward that is produced will be both richer and lusher.

In grass at the base of trees, dense shrubs and hedges, bulbous, spring-flowering plants can be fitted in with no difficulty. These areas can remain uncut till the bulbs' foliage dies down and their flowers will be a rich source of pollen and nectar for the earliest pollinators and predators. Some ivy in the hedges will provide late flowers to feed the insects in autumn before they hibernate.

Ground-cover plants provide habitats for ground beetles and many other useful creatures, but may also harbour slugs, snails and overwintering pests. On the whole it is better to have such habitats kept as far as possible from soft fruit and seed beds – after all, the beetles, frogs and hedgehogs can walk further than slugs and snails!

Some plants are specifically helpful to others and a few hinder. These are noted with the entry for that particular fruit. For example, the Romans noticed that oaks were bad for olives and cabbages were not good companions for vines, but rue benefited from the presence of figs.

**This attractive garden of herbs enjoys the semi-shade of a peach tree**

# HARVESTING AND STORING

## Picking and Ripening: Fruit Stores

Without doubt most fruits are best, and certainly are enjoyed most, when they are plucked fully ripe off the tree or vine. Only a few, such as melons, are improved by chilling first. The majority are tastiest fresh and warmed by the sun. Some, such as pears, have to be very carefully nurtured till they are fully ripe. They then need to be picked early and brought to perfection, watched daily, in a gently warm, not too dry, dim room, Medlars are similarly picked early and are then ripened, or bletted, to the point of rotting.

The best date for picking will vary with the cultivar, the soil, the site and the season which can only be determined by experience as these factors will all vary considerably. Of course, it will generally remain much the same in relation to other fruits nearby which are also subject to the same conditions, i.e. in a late year, most fruits are late, which is pretty self evident anyway.

On any tree, the sunny side ripens first. In the northern hemisphere, this is usually the south eastern corner, as the morning sun is stronger than the afternoon, because

**Mara des Bois strawberries**

the air is clearer. Fruit will also ripen earlier where any extra warmth is supplied, so that growing sites next to a wall, window, chimney or vent, or just close to the soil, are favourable places for finding early fruits. Likewise, when all the rest have gone, you may still find some hidden away in the shade.

If you want to store fruits for home use they need to be at just the right stage. Most fruits store best when picked just under-ripe. They may keep much longer if picked even younger, but this is at the cost of both flavour and sweetness.

Although we occasionally store some fruits, such as pears, for a period to improve their condition, predominantly we store fruit to extend the season so that we can enjoy them for as long as possible. On the commercial scale tremendous advances have been made with gas, humidity and temperature-regulated cool rooms. Many fruits can be stored for months, some even a year or more, in these conditions. Of course we amateurs cannot duplicate these conditions, but none the less we can keep most fruits for longer if we treat them well.

To be stored, all fruit must be perfect. Any blemish or bruise is where moulds start. It is no use trying to store anything that has any real damage. Use it up straight away or process it into juice, jelly or puree. Choose varieties that are suitable for storing - many early croppers are notoriously bad keepers! Waxing fruits is undoubtedly good for extending their life

but could help shorten yours! Some fruits will keep as well if they are wrapped in oiled paper. Another early, successful method of mould deterrence was to dip each fruit in a solution of sodium bicarbonate and then dry it before storing. This worked well, but it could leave a powdery appearance.

Common, long-keeping fruits such as apples and quinces can be stored at home for months, or even up to a year. The major problems, apart from the moulds, are shrivelling through water loss and the depredations of rodents and other bigger pests. A conventional store is too large for most of us and the house or garage is too warm, too cold or too dry. I find dead deep freezers and refrigerators make excellent compact stores. They are dark, keep the contents at the same constant temperature and will keep out night frosts easily. Most useful of all, they are rodent-proof, and they can even be locked to deter two-legged rats!

Some ventilation is needed and can be obtained by cutting holes in the rubber door or lid seal. If any condensation occurs, it usually indicates insufficient ventilation, but too much draught will dry out the fruits. The unit can stand outdoors, as it needs no power. In a shed it is out of sight and better protected against the cold, but may then get too warm. In the UK, have it outdoors in the shade or in a cool shed. Extra frost protection is simply ensured, in extreme

conditions, by putting a sealed bottle of warm water inside the unit each night and morning. To save space, providing the water table is low, a dead chest freezer can be sunk into the ground and the lid painted over.

When putting fruits in the store it is usually best to leave them to chill at night in the trays and to load them into the store in the morning when they have dried off, but before they have warmed up again. Similarly it is helpful to chill and dry off the fruits initially by leaving the store open on chill dry nights and closing it during the day for a week or two after filling.

Most types of fruit are best removed from the store some time before use, so any staleness can leave them. Care should be taken not to store early and late varieties together or any that may cross-taint. Obviously it is not a good idea to site your store in the same place as strong-smelling things, or substances such as onions, paint or creosote! Likewise, although straw is a cheap, convenient litter, it taints the fruit if it gets damp. Shredded newspaper is safer, though it also has a slight whiff. Dried stinging nettles are reckoned good but dangerous to handle.

Always inspect stored fruits regularly. They can go off very quickly. Remember, if only one in ten goes off every month, you have to start with two trays just to have one tray left after six months. So do not store any fruit long just for the sake of it, but store well what you will use.

A Moorpark apricot surrounded by typically lush foliage

**Grapevines growing in a glasshouse**

## Juicing

I find juicing to be the very best way of storing fruit, other than turning it into wine, but that's another book! Not all fruits can be juiced, but the majority can be squeezed to express the juice, or heated or frozen to break down the texture and then strained. Sugar may be added to taste as it improves the colour, flavour and

**Bob using a grape crusher for his gooseberries**

keeping qualities. When the juice remains unheated, honey may be substituted though it has a strong flavour of its own. Sweet juices such as apple can be mixed with tart ones like plum.

Fruit juices may be drunk as they are, added to cocktails, drunk as squashes diluted with water, and used in cooking. They take less space in a freezer than the fruit itself and are fine for use afterwards. I freeze mine in the wax cartons and plastic bottles milk comes in, leaving a small space for expansion.

Grapes are the easiest to press and the most rewarding, and you can ferment the pips and skins afterwards. Such wine tastes no worse than most of my regular home-made brews, though that is not difficult! Grapes are best crushed first to break the skins. Most of the currants and berries can be squeezed in the same way. Apples and pears must

**A cider press**

be crushed first and then squeezed: they will go through the same juicing equipment as grapes (see left), but more slowly than the more juicy fruits.

Pulpy firm fruits such as blackcurrants and plums are best simmered with water till they soften, then the juice

can be strained off. If you repeat the process and add sugar to the combined juices, you also have the basis for jellies. Raspberries, strawberries and fruits with similar delicate flavours are best frozen, then defrosted and strained, to obtain a pure juice which is unchanged by heating.

Suitable equipment for processing large amounts of fruit is widely available if the quantities are too large for kitchen tools. Many different presses and crushers are sold and hired for home and small-scale wine-makers.

Commercially juices are passed through microfine filters or flash-pasteurised. At home they will ferment rapidly in the warm, last longer if kept cool in the refrigerator, and keep for months or years deep frozen. I have two freezers, one for juices and one for everything else, as I want to drink at least a pint of apple, grape or strawberry juice a day.

**Redcurrants preserve well**

## Jellying and Jamming

These methods preserve the fruit in sugar gel. Jelly is made from the juice only, without the seeds and skins, while jam is made with and often also contains whole fruits or pieces thereof. A conserve is expensive jam, usually implying more fruit and less sugar or filler. (Freezer jams are conserves made with so little sugar they go mouldy quickly unless kept frozen and then used from the refrigerator.)

Almost any fruit can be jammed or jellied and many fruits are palatable only if so treated. The fruit is cooked to the point when the cells break up so that the juices run. The juice is then turned to a gel with sugar which acts as a preservative as well. Most fruits need to have up to their own weight of sugar added to them to make a setting gel.

With jellies, the juice is often augmented with the squeezings of the fruit pulp reheated with some water. This thinner part then requires proportionately more sugar to set. Jellies are made from the strained juice and these washings, so they set clear and bright and are appreciated by many as there are no seeds, etc. It is easy to pick and prepare fruits for jelly as the odd sprig, hard or under-ripe fruit or bit of leaf will be strained out.

Many prefer the texture (and don't forget the nutritional value) of jams with the seeds and skins, and so on. But these do require much more careful picking and preparation. My solution for, say, blackcurrants, is to pick the very finest berries carefully first, and then more roughly pick the bulk of the fruit to jelly. As the bulk is going to be strained there is no need to be so careful to keep out the sprigs. The bulk is simmered down to a juice, strained and then before it is set with the sugar the finest berries are added.

White sugar is usually used for jamming and jellying unless a strong flavour is required. Honey is not really successful as the flavour is strong and it goes off when heated as much as is needed for jam. Similarly concentrated juices can add too much flavour. The amount of fruit can always be increased and the sugar decreased if your technique is good and you can eat the jam quickly!

Ideally, you should simmer down the fruit with the absolute minimum amount of water. Strain if it is for jelly, add the sugar and bring to the boil. Skim off any scum and then pot in sterile conditions. Hot jars and clean lids that are put on immediately will improve results. Store, once cold, in a dark, cool place.

Some fruits are difficult to set, particularly strawberries in a wet year. Add chopped apples to the jelly fruits or their purée to the jams to supply the pectin needed to make any jam set. Extra acidity for a pleasing tartness which brings out the sharp flavour of some jams is often achieved using lemon juice. Whitecurrant juice is a good substitute and redcurrant even better, especially where the jam colour is important. Adding whitecurrant or redcurrant juice also aids the setting of difficult jams. Their flavour is so tart yet mild that their jellies make good carriers for more strongly flavoured fruits in shorter supply, especially for raspberries and cherries.

Finally, here is an important tip. It is far quicker and easier to make four 2.4kg/5lb batches of jam than one 5kg/11lb batch. The result is always better. Large batches have a low heating and evaporating surface compared to their volume and take much longer to process, so the fruit degrades more. Remember: quickly simmer down to a pulp, add the right amount of sugar, bring back to boil, skim and pot. No standing around watching some great cauldron bubble all day!

**Jam-making equipment**

**Air-drying peaches**

## Drying

Many fruits can be dried if they are sliced thinly and exposed to warm, dry air. Sealed in dark containers and kept cool and dry, they may be stored for long periods to be eaten, dried or reconstituted, when required. However, in the UK and much of maritime Europe and North America, the air is too humid and so drying process is not quick enough. Nor is it helped by the low temperatures in these regions.

Solar-powered dryers, simply wire trays under glass, with good ventilation, allow fruit to be dried to a larger extent, but in regions of the highest humidity the fruit may still go mouldy before it dries. Flies and other insects must of course be excluded!

I find that slicing the fruit thinly and hanging the pieces, separated by at least half their own diameter, on long strings over my cooking range provides the dry warmth and ventilation needed to desiccate most within a day or two, or even just overnight for the easier ones, such as apple.

Oven-drying with artificial heat is risky as it can cook the fruit, destroying the value, texture and keeping properties. However, it is possible if the temperature is kept down and the door kept partly open. It may be more convenient to finish off partly dried samples in the cooling oven after you have finished baking. The dying heat will desiccate the fruit well and contains little risk of it caramelising.

## Freezing

Most fruits freeze easily with little preparation, unlike vegetables which need blanching first. Obviously only the best are worth freezing as few fruits are improved by the process! Most fruits turn to soggy lumps in a pool of juice when defrosted, which is not quite as appetising as the fine-textured fresh product. However, they are still packed full of sweetness, flavour and vitamins, so are well worth having for culinary use, especially in tarts, pies, sauces and compotes. A mixture of frozen fruits is marvellous if they are partly thawed but not totally defrosted, so they retain their frozen texture like pieces of sorbet, served with cream.

For most fruits merely putting them in sealed freezer bags or boxes is sufficient. However, they then tend to freeze in a block, making it difficult to use them piecemeal later. If you freeze them loose on open wire drying trays or greased baking trays, they can be packed afterwards and will stay separate. Fruits that are cut or damaged need to be drained first or, if you have a sweet tooth, they can be dredged in sugar, which absorbs the juice before they are frozen.

Stone fruits are best de-stoned before freezing as

**Alpine strawberries**

otherwise the stone can give an almond taint. The tough skin of some fruits, such as tomatoes or plums, is most easily removed after freezing and before use, by carefully squeezing the frozen fruit under very hot water; the skin will then slip off easily.

Fruits lose value slowly in the freezer. The longer they are frozen, the less use they are nutritionally, but they do not deteriorate as badly as vegetables or meat and fatty products. Although a freezer is an electrical expense and a capital cost, it is wonderful to have the choice of your own fruits and their juices throughout the year – just whenever you fancy some.

**Small tomatoes such as Gardener's Delight freeze easily whole**

**Gooseberries are another fruit which preserve well**

**Cox's Orange Pippin apples store very successfully**

# THE YEARLY CALENDAR

These are reminders of the essential tasks for the majority of amateur fruit gardeners. Obviously the exact timing varies with locality, site and soil. If you grow some of the more unusual exotica, there are other requirements.

## Late Winter

- Check stores, remove and use any fruits starting to deteriorate before they go over and infect others.
- Spread a good layer of compost or well-rotted manure under and around everything possible, preferably immediately after, but not just before, a period of heavy rain.
- Spread a good layer of mulch under and around everything possible, preferably immediately after a period of heavy rain.
- Lime most grass swards one year in four, more often on acid soil, but not among ericaceous plants or lime haters!
- Once ground becomes workable, plant out hardy trees and shrubs that missed the autumn planting.
- Sow very earliest crops for growing under cover.
- Ensure good weed control, make sure no weeds are getting away, hoe fortnightly or add some extra mulch on top.
- Do major pruning work to trees and bushes missed earlier or damaged in winter (but not stone fruits or evergreens.)
- Prune autumn-fruiting raspberries to the ground.
- Spray everything growing with diluted seaweed solution at least once a month, and anything with

**Vines sprouting in spring from woody stock**

deficiency symptoms even more often.
- Spray peaches and almonds with Bordeaux mixture against peach leaf curl.
- Make a health and hygiene check and examine each plant in your care for pests, diseases and dieback.
- Apply sticky bands and inspect the sacking bands on apple trees, and others if they have suffered from many pests.
- Check straps and stakes after the gales.
- On still, cold nights protect the blossoms and young fruitlets from frost damage with net curtains, plastic sheet or newspaper.

## Early Spring

- Spread a good layer of compost or well-rotted manure under and around everything possible, preferably immediately after, but not before, heavy rain.
- Plant out evergreen and the more tender hardy plants.
- Protect them from frost and wind the first season.
- Sow plants grown under cover or for later planting out about now.
- Ensure good weed control, make sure no weeds are getting away, hoe fortnightly or add extra mulch on top.

- Cut the grass at least fortnightly, preferably weekly, returning the clippings or raking them into rings around trees and bushes.
- Spray everything growing with diluted seaweed solution at least at monthly intervals, and anything with deficiency symptoms more often.
- Spray peaches and almonds with Bordeaux mixture against peach leaf curl at this time.
- Spread wood ashes under and around plants, giving priority to gooseberries and culinary apples.
- Make a health and hygiene check and examine each plant in your care for pests, diseases and dieback.
- Prune back tender plants and evergreens and protect the new growth against frost afterwards.
- Pollinate early-flowering plants and those under cover by hand.
- On still, cold nights protect the blossoms and young fruitlets from frost damage with net curtains, plastic sheet or newspaper.

**Ladybirds on blackcurrants**

## Mid Spring

- Ensure good weed control, make sure no weeds are getting away, hoe weekly or add extra mulch on top.
- Cut the grass at least weekly, returning the clippings or raking them into rings around trees and bushes.
- Sow seed for plants grown under cover or for later planting out.
- Plant out more tender hardy plants under cover or with protection.
- Spread a good layer of mulch under and around everything possible, preferably immediately after a period of heavy rain.
- Spray everything growing with diluted seaweed solution at least at monthly intervals, and anything with deficiency symptoms more often.
- Spread wood ashes under and around fruit trees, giving priority to gooseberries and culinary apples.
- Water all new plants established within the previous twelve months whenever there has been little rain.
- Deflower or defruit new plants to give them time to establish themselves.
- Pollinate plants under cover by hand.
- Tie in new growths of vines and climbing plants.
- Make a health and hygiene check weekly and examine each plant in your care for pests, diseases and dieback.
- On still, cold nights protect the blossoms and young fruitlets from frost damage with net curtains, plastic sheet or newspaper.
- Make layers of any difficult subjects that you possess.

**Early flowers are important for beneficial insects**

### Late Spring

- Ensure good weed control, make sure no weeds are getting away, hoe at fortnightly intervals or add extra mulch on top.
- Sow plants grown under cover or outdoors.
- Plant out tender plants under cover or other suitable protection.
- Pollinate plants that are under cover by hand.
- Cut the grass at least fortnightly, preferably weekly, returning the clippings or raking them into rings around the bottoms of trees and bushes.
- Water all new plants established within the previous twelve months, especially whenever there has been little rain.
- Deflower or defruit new plants to establish them.
- Spray everything growing with diluted seaweed solution at least once a month, and anything with deficiency symptoms even more often.
- Make a health and hygiene check twice weekly and examine each plant in your care for problems such as pests, diseases and dieback.
- Tie in new growths of vine and climbing plants.
- On still, cold nights protect the blossoms and young fruitlets from frost damage with net curtains, plastic sheet or newspaper.
- Make layers of the most difficult subjects.
- Protect almost every ripening fruit from birds and other greedy creatures.

### Early Summer

- Ensure good weed control, make sure no weeds are getting away; hoe at fortnightly intervals or add extra mulch on top.
- Plant out the tender plants now, or move them out for the summer.
- Cut the grass at least fortnightly, preferably weekly, returning the clippings or raking them into rings around trees and bushes. Raise the height of cut of your mower.
- Spray everything growing with diluted seaweed solution at least once a month, and anything with deficiency symptoms even more often.
- Water all new plants established within the previous twelve months, especially whenever there has been little rain.
- Make a health and hygiene check twice weekly and examine each plant in your care for problems, such as pests, diseases and dieback.

### Summer Pruning, Part One of Three

- From one third of each plant, remove approximately half to three-quarters of each new shoot, except for leaders. This applies to all fruit such as redcurrants and whitecurrants, gooseberries and all trained apples and pears. Prune grapevines back to three or five leaves after a flower truss.
- Carefully tie in fragile, new growths of vines and other climbing plants.

**Protect your fruit from birds!**

### Fruit Thinning, Part One of Three

- Remove every diseased, decayed, damaged, misshapen, distorted and congested fruitlet. This applies to all apples, pears, peaches, apricots, quality plums, dessert grapes, gooseberries and figs, especially to trained forms.
- Compost or burn rejected fruitlets immediately. Of course usable ones, such as the larger gooseberries, may be consumed.
- Take soft cuttings if you have a propagator.
- Make layers of the most difficult subjects.
- Protect almost every ripening fruit from birds and other animals.

**Apart from being beautiful, butterflies are a useful addition to the garden**

### Midsummer

- Ensure good weed control, make sure no weeds are getting away; hoe at fortnightly intervals or add extra mulch on top.
- Cut the grass at least fortnightly, preferably weekly, returning the clippings or raking them into rings around trees and bushes. Raise the height of cut of your mower.
- Spray everything growing with diluted seaweed solution at least once a month, and anything with deficiency symptoms even more often.
- Water all new plants established within the previous twelve months, especially whenever there has been little rain.
- Make a health and hygiene check and examine each plant in your care for pests, diseases and dieback.
- Tie in new growths of vine and climbing plants.

## Summer Pruning, Part Two of Three

- From the second third of each plant remove about half to three-quarters of each new shoot, except for leaders. This applies to all redcurrants, whitecurrants, gooseberries and all trained apples and pears. Prune grapevines back to three or five leaves after a flower truss. Blackcurrants may have a third to half the old wood removed after fruiting. Stone fruits are traditionally pruned now to avoid silver leaf disease.

## Fruit Thinning, Part Two of Three

- Remove every diseased, decayed, damaged, misshapen, distorted and congested fruitlet. This applies to all apples, pears, peaches, apricots, quality plums, dessert grapes, gooseberries, figs and especially to trained forms. Compost or burn rejected fruitlets immediately. Of course, it is always nice to consume usable ones.

- Take soft cuttings if you have a propagator, root tips of the black and hybrid berries.
- Protect almost every ripening fruit from the birds.

## Late Summer

- Ensure good weed control, make sure no weeds are getting away; hoe at fortnightly intervals or add extra mulch on top.
- Plant new strawberry plants, if you can get them.
- Cut the grass at least fortnightly, preferably weekly, returning the clippings or raking them into rings around trees and bushes. Lower the height of cut of your mower.
- It is a good idea to spray everything that is growing with diluted seaweed solution at least once a month, and anything that has deficiency symptoms even more often.
- Water all new plants established within the previous twelve months, especially whenever there has been little rain.
- Sow green manures and winter ground cover on bare soil that is not mulched; grass down orchards.
- Make a health and hygiene check and examine each plant in your care for pests, diseases and dieback.
- Apply insect traps like sticky bands and sacking bands to apple trees, and other fruit trees if they suffer from many pests.

## Summer Pruning, Part Three of Three

- To last third of each plant remove approximately half to three-quarters of each new shoot, except for leaders. This applies to all redcurrants, whitecurrants, gooseberries and all trained apples and pears. As before, prune grapevines back to three or five leaves after the fruit truss.

## Fruit Thinning, Part Three of Three

- Remove every diseased, decayed, damaged, misshapen, distorted and congested fruitlet. This applies to all apples, pears, peaches, apricots, quality plums, dessert grapes, gooseberries, figs and especially to trained forms.
- Compost or burn rejected fruitlets immediately. Of course, the usable ones may be consumed.
- Protect almost every ripening fruit from birds and other hungry beasts.
- Root the tips of the black and hybrid berries.

## Early Autumn

- Ensure good weed control, make sure no weeds are getting away; hoe fortnightly or add extra mulch on top.

**Malling Jewel raspberries**

- Plant out any pot-grown specimens also, as well as those that can be dug with a decent rootball or moved with little disturbance.
- Cut the grass at least fortnightly, preferably weekly, returning the clippings and fallen leaves or raking them into rings around trees and bushes.
- Sow green manures and winter ground cover on bare soil that is not mulched; grass down orchards.
- Spray everything that is growing with diluted seaweed solution at least once a month, and anything that has deficiency symptoms more often.
- Make a health and hygiene check and examine each plant in your care for pests, diseases and dieback.
- Apply sticky bands and sacking bands to apple trees, and to others if they suffer from many pests.
- On still, cold nights protect ripening fruits from frost damage with net curtains, plastic sheet or newspaper.
- Protect first the tops then the stems and roots of more tender plants before the frosts come.
- Bring indoors tender plants in pots or protect them.
- Take cuttings of plants as soon as they start to drop their leaves.
- Prune early-fruiting raspberries and hybrids, and blackcurrants and other plants as they start to drop their leaves.
- Protect almost every ripening fruit from the usual hordes of hungry pests.
- Root the tips of the black and hybrid berries.

**Alpine strawberries and thyme on a low bank**

**Winter trap**

### Mid Autumn

- Ensure good weed control, make sure no weeds are getting away, so hoe fortnightly or add extra mulch on top.
- Plant out bare-rooted hardy trees and bushes if soil is in good condition and they are dormant.
- Cut the grass at least fortnightly, preferably weekly, collecting the clippings with the fallen leaves or raking them into rings around the bottoms of trees and bushes.
- Spray everything that is growing with diluted seaweed solution at least once a month, and anything that has deficiency symptoms more often.
- Make a health and hygiene check and examine each plant in your care for pests, diseases and dieback.
- Top up the sticky bands and inspect the sacking bands on apple trees, and on others if they suffered from many pests.
- Check straps and stakes before the gales.
- On still, cold nights protect ripening fruits from frost damage with net curtains, plastic sheet or newspaper.
- Take cuttings of hardy plants as they start to drop their leaves.
- Prune early fruiting raspberries and hybrids, and blackcurrants and other plants as they start to drop their leaves.
- Protect first the tops then the stems and roots of more tender plants before the frosts come.
- Check stores, remove and use any fruits starting to deteriorate before they go over and infect others.
- As before, protect almost every ripening fruit from the birds.

### Late Autumn

- Ensure good weed control, make sure no weeds are getting away, so hoe fortnightly or add extra mulch on top.
- Plant out bare-rooted hardy trees and bushes if soil is in good condition and they are dormant.
- Cut the grass at least fortnightly, collecting the clippings with the fallen leaves or raking them into rings around the bottoms of trees and bushes.
- Make a health and hygiene check and examine each plant in your care for pests, diseases and dieback.
- Look at the traps; top up the sticky bands and inspect the sacking bands on apple trees, and on others if they suffered from many pests.
- Check straps and stakes before the gales.
- Spread a good layer of compost or well rotted manure under and around everything possible, preferably after, but not immediately before, any heavy rain.
- On still, cold nights protect ripening fruits from frost damage with net curtains, plastic sheet or newspaper.
- Take cuttings of hardy plants as they start to drop their leaves.
- Prune late fruiting raspberries, hybrid berries, currants and vines, trees and bushes as the leaves fall.
- Protect first the tops then the stems and roots of more tender plants before the frosts come.
- Check stores, remove and use any fruits starting to deteriorate before they go over and infect others.
- Protect almost every ripening fruit particularly from the birds.

**Espalier-trained peaches on a red brick wall**

### Early Winter

- Ensure good weed control, make sure no weeds are getting away, so hoe at fortnightly intervals or add extra mulch on top.
- Plant out bare-rooted hardy trees and bushes if the soil is in good condition and they are dormant.
- Collect the fallen leaves and use for leafmould or rake them in rings around trees and bushes.
- Make a health and hygiene check and examine each plant in your care for pests, diseases and dieback.
- Top up the sticky bands and inspect the sacking bands on apple trees, and on any others if they suffered from many pests.
- Check straps and stakes before the gales.
- Spread a good layer of compost or well rotted manure under and around everything possible, preferably after, but not immediately before, a period of heavy rain.
- Prune late fruiting trees and bushes as their leaves fall and do major work to trees and bushes (but not to stone fruits or evergreens).
- Check stores, remove and use any fruits starting to deteriorate before they go over and infect others.

### Mid Winter

- Make a health and hygiene check and examine each plant in your care for pests, diseases and dieback.
- Check straps and stakes after the gales.
- Check stores, remove and use any fruits starting to deteriorate before they go over and infect others.
- Take it easy and look back over the successes and mishaps of the previous year, enjoy the fruits of your labours and plan for even more fun and endeavour in the coming seasons.

**Bedford Giant blackberry**

# FURTHER TRAVELLER'S TALE FRUITS

### *Adansonia digitata*
### Baobab/ Monkey Breadfruit
### Bombacaceae
This large African tree has a swollen trunk often hollowed by age. The leaves are eaten as a vegetable and the fruits, up to 30cm (1 ft) long, are fat, cylindrical, dark and hairy. They have a floury white pulp that reputedly tastes like gingerbread, with small black seeds that have been ground and eaten in times of famine.

### *Butyrospermum parkii*
### Shea butter tree
### Sapotaceae
A native of central Africa, this small stout African tree has white fragrant flowers followed by plum-like fruits with a thick pericap that bleeds when green. Once fully ripe, this has some pulp which is sweet and perfumed, but the fruits are gathered more for their seeds which have a high fat content and are used to make shea butter. The wood is resistent to termites.

### *Canarium edule/ Dacryoides edulis*
### Safu
### Burseraceae
The fruit is a large violet drupe that is too bitter to be eaten raw, but is fatty and nutritious once cooked. It is popular in West Africa.

### *Canarium commune*
(Chinese olive/Java almond) is a closely related, rather attractive tree from south eastern Asia which is grown for the tasty kernel.

### *Chenopodium foliosum*
### Beetberry
### Chenopodiaceae
This bizarre annual relation of the weeds Fat Hen and Good King Henry has strange, small, red, mulberry-like fruits in the leaf azils. These are very seedy and bland to taste. They are interesting, though have little nutritional value, but are worth breeding from.

### *Emblica offinicalis*
### Indian Gooseberry
### Euphorbiaceae
The fruits are small marbles of yellow or green. They are too acid to be eaten raw, but are amazingly rich in vitamin C, containing three hundred times as much as orange juice. They are often jammed and pickled and used to treat scurvy.

### *Grewia asiatica*
### Phalsa/Pharsa
### Tiliaceae
This is a shrubby reddish tree from India and the East Indies, which has many small red berries that are too acid and dry to eat many of. However, they make the most delicious sorbets and syrups, and are very popular in northern India.

### *Heteromeles arbutifolia*
### Christmas berry/Tollon
### Rosaceae
This is an easy-to-grow, attractive pot plant closely resembling a holly with white scented flowers and red, holly-like berries. It is a unique plant, found only in California, where it makes a shrubby tree 9m (30ft) in height. It may also be hardy enough to grow on a wall in southern Britain.

### *Irvingia gabonensis*
### Duika/Wild mango
### Irvingiaceae
This is a large central African tree which has an inferior mango pulp, but the seed is oily and is used for cooking and soap-making. It is also used in Gabon chocolate or *pain de dika*.

### *Parinarium curatefolium*
### Mupunda
### Chrysobalanaceae
There are a number of other closely related fruits found in Africa. This is considered the best, with reddish-brown or greyish plum-sized drupes on a shrubby bush.

### *Sicana odifera*
### Musk cucumber/ Casabanana/Curuba/Coroa
### Cucurbitaceae
This South American climbing vine resembles a lushly grown and prettier cucumber plant, but its tendrils really serve to glue themselves at the tips as well as twine. A perennial in Brazil and Ecuador, it can be grown very easily in more northern climates as an annual or conservatory subject. A very vigorous plant, it has yellow flowers and yellowish-red fruits with a sweetish flavour, but which are strongly fragrant – too strong for many. The fruits can be eaten young as vegetables and ripe as fruits, most commonly in jams.

**Christmas Berry**

# USEFUL BY-PRODUCTS

### Wood Turning, Natural Dyes, Scented Firewoods and Smoking Foods

Most fruit trees and some bushes and vines produce thick branches and trunks which may have value as timber once the productive life of the plant is over. However, most is burnt on bonfires or in the grate without considering any of the other uses.

Treen is the term used for any small object made from wood. Many different and useful implements, and especially kitchen utensils, can be fashioned out of home-produced fruit woods once they have seasoned for a year or two. Platters, bowls and jam spoons, rolling pins, egg cups, pestles and mortars, nutcrackers, lemon squeezers, cruet sets, napkin rings, moulds, bobbins and children's blocks and toys are easy to make and well within the reach of any of us. Grape stems are traditionally turned into corkscrew handles. Fruit woods have fine colour and grain which enhance such objects and also make them suitable for inlay and marquetry work.

Barks, fruits and leaves were used for dyes long before our modern bright chemical colours were invented. Many prefer the muted colours and pastel softness of such dyes which visually blend more easily than their vibrant modern counterparts. Apple, pear and cherry barks yield dyes in shades of yellow as do the roots and stems of berberis, while reddish-yellows come from pine-cones. Walnuts stain everything they touch and need no mordant to help fix their dye which can be obtained from the roots, leaves and husks. In the past walnut dye was used to give a suntan to pale gypsies, as a hair dye and a floor stain. Elder bark with an iron mordant gives a black dye, the leaves with an alum mordant give a green dye and the berries produce shades of purple, blue and lilac, often used as hair dyes. Rowan berries give a black dye, plums and sloes a blue dye and their bark yields a red-brown colourant, while Junipers give an olive brown.

Scented leaves and flowers, especially citrus ones, can be used for perfumes and pot pourri. Most are at their best collected in early morning once the dew has dried and before the heat has parched their scented oils away. The soluble perfume may be collected and concentrated into fats and oils or the plant material can be dried and used as it is. Quinces are particularly aromatic and were once very popular bases for pomanders.

Much of the wood from orchards and their hedges are useful fuels, though others are less so, as this traditional rhyme puts well:

*Logs to burn, logs to burn.*
*Here's a word to make you wise.*
*Logs to spare the coal a turn.*
*Listen to my woodsman's cries.*

*Beech wood burns bright and clear,*
*the Hornbeam blazes too*
*if the logs are kept a year,*
*seasoned through and through.*

*Oak logs they'll heat you well*
*once they're old and dry.*
*Larch logs like pine do smell*
*and their sparks do fly.*

**Fruit wood turning on a lathe**

**Smoking equipment**

*Pine itself is good as Yew
for warmth on bitter days.
Beware the Poplar, Willow too
long to dry and short to blaze.*

*Birch logs they burn too fast
Alder, Elder, scarce at all.
Chestnut logs the best to last
if they're felled in fall.*

*Holly logs will roar like wax
you can even burn it green.
But Elm like smouldering flax
will never flame be seen.*

*Pear's wood and Apple logs
they will scent your room,
Cherry logs across the dogs
smell like flowers in bloom.*

*But worth their weight in gold
are Ash logs, smooth and grey,
Burn them young or burn them
old
Buy all that come your way.*

Not only do these fruit trees
give a burnable wood, but a
sweet scent is also produced
from their burning logs
which is much esteemed
by those with open fires.
When choice wood like this
becomes available, it is often
saved for celebrations and
special occasions.

Major pruning or felling of
trees is done in autumn and
winter but the timber must
be dried before it can be
burned efficiently. Generally
the older and drier the
wood, the better for heating;
for scenting, though, it is
best one year old. Timber
should be sawn into logs
while fresh and green as it
is cut most easily then. The
logs should be stacked
horizontally so air can pass
the ends and water cannot
soak in, ideally covered over
the top to keep rain off.

All prunings from the
orchard that ared too small
for logs can be used for
kindling once dried. Smooth
clean prunings can be used
to make wildlife shelters,
and if you have a shredder
they can be processed and
then composted. However,
to prevent any build-up of
diseases and pests, all
infected and diseased
material should be burnt
straight away. It is also
usually sensible to burn
thorny material, such as
bramble stems.

Bonfires burn best if
started with a little good
tinder and then fed with
material piecemeal. Ideally
support the fire off the
ground on old bed irons or
similar so air can get
underneath. This reduces
pollution and makes the fire
roar upwards instead of
smouldering and drifting.
Once the fire is finished and
cooled, the ashes should be
collected for use as fertiliser
or for making soap.

The smoke from burning
many fruit woods can be
used for smoking foods. This
is a traditional way of
preserving foods such as fish
and meat, and/or improving
their flavour, as with cheese.
It is not unusual, either:
cheese smoked with apple-
wood is on sale in almost
every delicatessen and
supermarket so there is
obviously a demand for it.

Smoking foods is not
difficult. They are often
hot-smoked for immediate
consumption, but generally
most are smoked in cool
temperatures, as this
prevents the fats going
rancid. Most meats and
many fish are pretreated
with salt, by pickling,
marinading or part-drying
before smoking. For safety,
please refer to specialist
books for more precise
details. However, in
principle the smoking
process is very simple. The
food is hung from racks or
suspended in a container
through which the cool
smoke from sweet-burning
woods passes for several
hours. After this it is
matured for some time to
let the flavour permeate
throughout the food.

I make my own apple,
peach and pearwood-
smoked cheese in the
chimney of my house. It is
unused and cool during the
summer so I hang the
cheese down inside the
chimney and light a small,
cool, smouldering fire of
fruit-wood sawdust and
prunings in the stove
underneath. The fire is kept
smouldering overnight and
in the morning the cheese
is beautifully smoked. In
theory the cheese should
mature in a cool place for a
month before it is used, but
in my house it rarely stays
uneaten that long!

**A selection of foods suitable for smoking**

# PAST GLORIES

Victorian and Edwardian gardeners were fascinated by the wide range of tropical fruits available from the countries of the Empire. These truly magnificent pineapples were grown in England at the end of the nineteenth century. They are exampes of what could be achieved without the use of modern chemical pesticides and fertilisers. The green houses were usually south-facing to make the best use of the sun's heat. Steam and hot water pipes were used to generate internal heat and keep the greenhouses at the optimum temperature. The results, as shown below, were quite remarkable. May the growers of the past inspire your own efforts!

# SOME USEFUL NAMES AND ADDRESSES

Organisations that have facilities for visitors are marked with an asterisk.

The Henry Doubleday Research Association,
National Centre for Organic Gardening
Ryton on Dunsmore
Coventry
CV8 3LG*

The Soil Association
86 Colston Street
Bristol
Avon
BS1 5BB

*At same address:*
British Organic Farmers,
Organic Growers Association
Bookshop*

The Royal Horticultural Society
Vincent Square
London
SW1P 2PE

*and at*
Wisley*
Woking
Surrey
GU23 6QB

The Centre for Alternative Technology
The Quarry
Machynlleth
Powys*

The Northern Horticultural Society
Harlow Car Gardens
Crag Lane
Otley Road
Harrogate
W. Yorkshire*

The Biodynamic Agricultural Association,
Woodman Lane
Clent
Stourbridge
West Midlands
DY9 9PX

Elm Farm Research Centre
Hamstead Marshall
Newbury
Berkshire
RG15 0HR

WWOOF (Working Weekends On Organic Farms)
19 Bradford Road
Lewes
Sussex
BN7 1RB

**Suppliers of Useful Lines**
The Gardener's Seed and Cutting Exchange
56 Red Willow
Harlow
Essex
CM19 5PD

**For fruit seeds:**
Thompson & Morgan
Poplar Lane
Ipswich
Suffolk
IP8 3BU

Chiltern Seeds, Bortree Stile, Ulverston, Cumbria
LA12 7PB

Future Foods
20 Gastard Lane
Gastard
Corsham
Wiltshire
SN13 9QN

**For citrus and conservatory plants:**
Read's Nursery
Hale's Hall
Loddon
Norfolk.

**For good quality hardy trees and plants I recommend:**
R.V. Roger
The Nurseries
Pickering
North Yorkshire
YO18 7HG

**For a very wide range of hardy fruit try:**
Deacon's Nursery
Godshill
Isle of Wight
PO38 3HW

**For sundries:**
Chase Organics
Coombelands House
Addlestone
Surrey
KT15 1HY

# SOME INTERESTING BOOKS

These are a few of the many worth looking for. Although they are not all directly concerned with fruit, they contain useful and relevant advice. Some are now out of print and need unearthing from libraries.

L.D.Hills
**The Good Fruit Guide,**
*Henry Doubleday Research Association*

**Hillier's Manual of Trees and Shrubs**
*David & Charles*

**The Oxford Book of Food Plants**
*Peerage Books, 1969*

Oleg Polunin
**Trees and Bushes of Britain and Europe,**
*Oxford University Press, 1976*

Long Ashton Research Station
**Science and Fruit**
*University of Bristol, 1953*

Richard Mabey
**Food for Free**
*Fontana/Collins. 1972/75*

Hardy Plant Society
**The Plant Finder**
*1987*

George E. Brown
**The Pruning of Trees, Shrubs & Conifers**
*Faber & Faber, 1972*

Werner Schuphan,
**Nutritional Values in Crops and Plants**
*Museum Press, 1965*

E.A.Ormerod
**Handbook of Insects Injurious to Orchard and Bush Fruits**
*Simpkin, Marshall, Hamilton & Co., 1898*

R.B.Yepsen (ed.)
**Organic Plant Protection**
*Rodale, 3rd printing 1976*

Anthony Huxley
**Plant and Planet**
*Allen Lane, 1974*

William Cobbett
**Treatise on Gardening**
*1821*

**Plant Physiological Disorders**
*ADAS, HMSO, 1985*

**The Diagnosis of Mineral Deficiencies in Plants**
*HMSO, 1943*

Sir John Russell
**Soil Conditions and Plant Growth**
*Longmans, 8th edition 1954*

Robbins, Crafts & Raynor
**Weed Control**
*McGraw Hill, 1942*

Ed. U. P. Hendrick
**Sturtevant's Edible Plants of the World**
*Dover Publications, 1972*

# INDEX

# PHOTOGRAPHIC ACKNOWLEDGEMENTS

Page 1; S.M.
P.3; S.M.
P.6/7; N.H.P.A., background
P.8/9; C.T., background; S.M., bottom right
Pages 10-13; ET Archive
P.14/15; S.M.
Pages 16/17; H. Angel, background; S.M., bottom right
P.18; S.M.
P.19; J. Hurst, top right; S.M., top left and bottom
P.20; C.T., top; P.H., bottom
P.21; C.T., top right and bottom; S.M., top left
P.22; S.M., top; C.T., bottom left; M.G., bottom right
P.23; M.G.
P.24; S.M., top right; J. Hurst, bottom left
P.25; J. Hurst, top left and right; M.G., bottom left and right
P.26; S.M.
P.27; S.M.
P.28; A. Blake, top right; C.T., bottom left
P.29; S.M., centre; M.G., top and bottom
P.30; Holt Studios, top right; C.T., bottom
P.31; M.G., top; C.I., bottom
P.32; C.T., top right; G.P.L., bottom
P.33; H. Angel, bottom left; M.G., right
P.34; C.T., top left; P.H., right
P.35; A. Blake, top left; M.G., top right; P.L., centre; S.M., bottom right
P.36; P.I.
P.37; M.G.
P.38; S.M.
P.39; J. Hurst, top left; M.G., top right; G.P.L., bottom right
P.40; C.T.
P.41; M.G., top right; G.P.L., bottom left
P.42; S.M.
P.43; C.T., top left; G.P.L., bottom right
P.44; M.G., top right; C.T., bottom left
P.45; M.G.
P.46; P.H., top right; S.M., bottom left
P.47; G.P.L. top left; M.G., right
P.48; C.T., top; P.H., bottom
P.49; C.C.L., top right; C.T., bottom left; M.G., bottom right
P.50; S.M., centre; H. Angel, bottom left
P.51; P.H., top left; M.G., top right and bottom right
P.52; P.H., top right; S.M., bottom
P.53; C.C.L., top right; M.G., right; H. Angel, bottom left
P.54; S.M., top right and bottom right; C.T., centre right
P.55; P.H., top; M.G., centre right; J. Dixon, bottom
P.56/7; S.M.
P.58; C.T.
P.59; M.G., top right; S.M.centre left and bottom right
P.60; C.T.
P.61; H. Angel, top left; M.G., bottom right
P.62; G.P.L., top right; S.M., bottom left
P.63; M.G.
P.64; S.M., top; P.H., bottom
P.65; P.H., top left; M.G., top and bottom right
P.66; S.M.
P.67; P.H., top left and bottom left; M.G., top and bottom right
P.68; H. Angel
P.69; P.H., top left; H. Angel, bottom right; M.G., top right
P.70; C.T., left; S.M., top right; M.G., bottom right
P.71; C.T., top; S.M., left; M.G., bottom
P.72; S.M., bottom; P.H., top right
P.73; S.M., bottom; C.T., top left; M.G., top right
P.74; S.M.
P.75; P.H., top left and bottom; M.G., top right and centre
P.76; S.M., top right; C.T., bottom left
P.77; S.M., top left and right; M.G., bottom
P.78; S.M.

P.79; P.H., top left; C.T., top right; S.M., bottom right
P.80; P.H., top; C.T., left; S.M., right
P.81; C.T., top; M.G., right, bottom right and left
P.82; S.M.
P.83; P.H.
P.84; S.M.
P.85; M.G.
P.86; A. Blake, top; P.H., bottom
P.87; P.H., top and centre; M.G., bottom
P.88; S.M.
P.89; S.M., bottom left; M.G., right
P.90; S.M., top right; C.T., bottom
P.91; C.T., top; S.M., bottom left; M.G., bottom right
P.92; C.T., bottom left; S.M., top right
P.93; C.T., bottom left; M.G., top right
P.94; S.M.
P.95; C.T., top right; S.M., bottom left, right and centre
P.96; Janet Price
P.97; M.G., top right and bottom right; Janet Price, bottom left and centre
P.98/99; C.T., background
P.100; S.M.
P.101; S.M., top right; C.T., top left and bottom right; M.G., bottom left
P.102; C.T.
P.103; C.T.
P.104; G.P.L. (Michael Howes), centre; S.M., bottom
P.105; P.H., top, C.T., bottom left and right
P.106; J. Hurst
P.107; P.H., top left; C.T., bottom left; J. Hurst, right and bottom right
P.108; C.T.
P.109; C.T., top left; Peter Knab, top right; Julie Dixon, bottom
P.110; The G.P.L. (John Glover), top right; C.T., bottom right
P.111, C.T., top left; P.H., right
P.112; P.H.
P.113; P.H., top left; C.T., bottom right; Peter Knab, centre right
P.114; S.M.
P.115; C.T., top left; S.M., top right; P.H., bottom left and right
P.116; S.M.
P.117; M.G.
P.118; C.T.
P.119; C.T., top left; A. Blake Photo Library (Rosenfeld) centre right; G.P.L. (Michael Howes), bottom left; M.G., bottom right
P.120; G.W.Lennox, top; C.T., bottom
P.121; S.M., top left and centre right; Peter Knab, bottom left, M.G., bottom right
P.122; J. Hurst, top right; S.M., bottom left
P.123; H. Angel, top; S.M., bottom
P.124; J. Hurst
P. 125; J. Hurst, bottom; S.M., top
P.126/127; N.H.P.A., background
P.128; S.M.
P.129; C.T., top left and bottom left; S.M., top right; J. Hurst, bottom right
P. 130; H. Angel, top right; C.I., bottom left; S.M., bottom right
P.131; S.M., top and centre right; M.G., bottom
P.132; C.T., top right; M.G., bottom
P.133; P.H., top; M.G., bottom
P.134; S.M., top; C.T., bottom
P.135; S.M., top; C.T., bottom left; M.G., bottom right
P.136; S.M., bottom left; P.H., top and bottom right
P.137; P.H., top right; G.P.L. (J.S Sira) centre; M.G., bottom right
P.138; H. Angel, top; S.M., bottom left; M.G., right
P.139; P.H., top; M.G., bottom right
P.140; C.T., centre; M.G., bottom right
P.141; S.M., top; C.T., bottom right
P.142/143; N.H.P.A.; P.144
H. Angel, top right; S.M., bottom left
P.145; A-Z B. Col. (D.C. Clegg), top right; M.G., bottom right

P.146; S.M., top; C.T., bottom right
P.147; C.T., top left, bottom left; M.G., right; S.M., bottom right
P.148; S.M., top; A-Z B. Col. (G.A. Matthews), left; M.G., right
P.149; S.M., top; M.G., bottom.
P.150; P.H., top; C.T., right; S.M., bottom right
P.151; G.P.L., (Lamontagne), top right; P.H., bottom
P.152; S.M., top left; M.G., centre right and bottom right; G.W. Lennox, bottom left
P.153; M.G., top; C.T., bottom left; G.W. Lennox bottom right
P.154; M.G., top right and bottom right and centre; H. Angel, top left; G.P.L. (Steven Wooster), bottom left
P.155; M.G., centre right; S.M., bottom right; G.W. Lennox, bottom left
P.162; S.M.
P.163; C.T., top left and bottom; S.M., top right
P.164/165; C.T.
P.166; P.H., top right; S.M., bottom
P.167; M.G., centre right; S.M., bottom right
P.168; Bjorn Svensson, centre; G.P.L. (Aary Rogers), bottom left; M.G., bottom right
P.169; M.G., top right and bottom right; S.M., centre; C.T., bottom centre
P.170; S.M., top left; G.P.L (Brigitte Thomas), centre; M.G., bottom right
P.171; G.P.L (J S Sira), top; S.M., centre; M.G., bottom right
P.172; A-Z B. Col. (Lamontagne), top left; M.G., bottom right
P.173; H. Angel, centre; S.M., top right; M.G., bottom right
P. 174; P.H., top right; S.M., bottom
P.175; P.H., top left; M.G., centre right; S.M., bottom right
P.176; C.T., left; Botanical Collection (T.G.J. Rayner), bottom right
P.177; P.H., top left; S.M., bottom right
P.178; S.M., top left; P.H., bottom left
P.179; G.P.L (Linda Burgess), top left; M.G., centre right; S.M., bottom right
P.180; P.H., top; G.P.L (J.S. Sira), bottom
P.181; P.H., top; A-Z B. Col. (Maurice Nimmo), bottom left; S.M., bottom right
P.182; A-Z B. Col. (Andrew Brown), top; C.T., bottom left; P.H., bottom right
P. 183; P.H., top left; S.M., top right; H. Angel, bottom
P.184; P.H., top; S.M., bottom
P.185; G.P.L. (Christopher Fairweather), top left; H. Angel, top right; P.H., bottom left; M.G., bottom right
P.186; A. Blake Photo Library (H. Brown), left; H. Angel, top right and centre right; M.G., bottom right
P.187; S.M., top left; A-Z B. Col. (Maurice Nimmo), top right, (Andrew Brown), bottom left, (Leslie J. Borg), bottom right
P.188; H. Angel, top and bottom; A-Z B. Col. (Glenis Moore), centre
P.189; G.P.L. (Sunniva Harte), top, (Mayer/Le Scanff), centre; P.H., bottom
P.190/191; P.H., background
P.192; S.M., top; A-Z B. Col. (Malcolm Richards), bottom
P.193; A-Z B. Col. (Jiri Loun), top; A-Z B. Col., bottom; M.G., bottom right
P.194; S.M., top; A-Z B. Col. (Irene Windridge), bottom
P.195; S.M., top; M.G., right and bottom
P.196 ; S.M., top; A-Z B. Col. (Peter Hallett), bottom
P.197; C.T., top; P.H., centre; M.G., bottom
P.198; S.M., top and bottom
P.199 ; C.T., top left and bottom left; M.G., top right and bottom right
P.200; S.M., top; A-Z B. Col. (Elsa M. Megson), bottom
P.201; A-Z B. Col. (Geoff Kid), top right, (John Klegg), bottom right; M.G., left

P.202; S.M., top; A-Z B. Col. (Michael Ward), bottom
P.203; A-Z B. Col. (Michael Ward), top; M.G., bottom
P.204; S.M., top left; M.G., top right; A-Z B. Col. (Alan Gould), bottom
P.205; S.M., centre; M.G., bottom
P.206; S.M., top; A-Z B. Col., centre, and (John Pettigrew), bottom left; M.G., bottom right
P.207; A-Z B. Col., top; S.M., centre; M.G., bottom
P.208; S.M., top and bottom
P.209; H.S. Int. (Inge Spence), top, (Nigel Cattlin), bottom
P.210; H. Angel, top and bottom
P.211; H. Angel
P.212; H. Angel, top; H.S. Int. (Rosemary Mayer), bottom
P.213; J. Hurst, top and bottom
P.214; S.M., top right; C.T., bottom left
P.215; S.M., top left; C.T., top right and bottom left; H. Angel, bottom right
P.216; C.T., top and bottom
P. 217; H. Angel
P.218; H.S. Int. (Nigel Cattlin)
P.219; H.S. Int. (John Adams), left, (Rosemary Mayer), right
P.220; J. Hurst, top; Sue Cunningham, bottom
P.221; H.S. Int. (Nigel Cattlin)
P.222; C.T.
P.223; S.M., top left and bottom; J. Hurst, right
P.224; C.T.
P.225; C.T.
P.226; J. Hurst, top left; S.M., bottom right
P.227; C.T.
P.228; H.S. Int. (Nigel Cattlin)
P.229; S.M., bottom left; H.S. Int. (Nigel Cattlin), top and bottom right
P.230; H.S. Int. (Nigel Cattlin), top left, centre right, and bottom left and right; Ardea London (D.W. Greenslade), centre
P.231; H.S. Int. (Nigel Cattlin), top left, bottom left and right; H.S. Int. (Phil MacLean), top right; S.M., top centre
Pages 232–235; C.T.
P.236; Ardea London , top; C.T., bottom left; S.M., bottom right
P.237; C.T.
P.238; Ardea London , top left; C.T., top right and bottom left and right
P.239; S.M.
P.240; H. Angel, top; S.M., bottom
P.241; C.T.
P.242; C.T., top; S.M., bottom
P.243; P.H., top; C.T., bottom
P.244; S.M., top left; J. Hurst, top right; C.T., bottom
P.245; C.T.
P.246; S.M.
P.247; S.M.
P.248; from *The Gardener's Assistant*, by Robert Thompson, revised edition edited by Wiliam Watson, published by the Gresham Publishing Company, 1901.


KEY

| | |
|---|---|
| C.T. | Christine Topping |
| S.M. | Sally Maltby |
| M.G. | Michelle Garrett |
| A-Z B.Col. | A-Z Botanical Collections |
| C.C.L. | Christie's Colour Library |
| C.I. | Christies Images |
| G.P.L. | Garden Picture Library |
| H.S.Int. | Holt Studios International |
| N.H.P.L. | Natural History Picture Library |
| P.H. | Photos Horticultural |
| P.I. | Photos International |